The Oxford History of the Third Reich

Robert Gellately is Earl Ray Beck Professor of History at Florida State University. His publications have been translated into over twenty languages and include the widely acclaimed *Lenin, Stalin, and Hitler: The Age of Social Catastrophe* (2007), *Backing Hitler: Consent and Coercion in Nazi Germany, 1933–1945* (2001), and *Stalin's Curse: Battling for Communism in War and Cold War* (2013), the last two also published by Oxford University Press. He lives in Tallahassee, Florida.

T0347202

The historians who contributed to *The Oxford History of The Third Reich* are all distinguished authorities in their field. They are:

OMER BARTOV, Brown University
HERMANN BECK, University of Miami
DAVID F. CREW, The University of Texas at Austin
ROBERT GELLATELY, Florida State University
PETER HAYES, Northwestern University
RALPH JESSEN, University of Cologne
JONATHAN PETROPOULOS, Claremont McKenna College
DIETER POHL, Alpen-Adria-Universität Klagenfurt
HEDWIG RICHTER, Hamburg Institute for Social Research
MATTHEW STIBBE, Sheffield Hallam University
JULIA S. TORRIE, St. Thomas University

The Oxford History
of the Third Reich

Edited by

ROBERT GELLATELY

OXFORD
UNIVERSITY PRESS

OXFORD
UNIVERSITY PRESS

Great Clarendon Street, Oxford, OX2 6DP,
United Kingdom

Oxford University Press is a department of the University of Oxford.
It furthers the University's objective of excellence in research, scholarship,
and education by publishing worldwide. Oxford is a registered trade mark of
Oxford University Press in the UK and in certain other countries

© Oxford University Press 2023
Copyright in the Introduction and Chapter 10 © Robert Gellately 2018
All rights reserved

The text of this edition was published in The Oxford Illustrated History of the Third Reich in 2018

The moral rights of the author have been asserted

First Edition published in 2018
Second Edition published in 2023

Impression: 1

Published in the United States of America by Oxford University Press
198 Madison Avenue, New York, NY 10016, United States of America

British Library Cataloguing in Publication Data

Data available

Library of Congress Control Number: 2022951168

ISBN 978-0-19-288683-5

DOI: 10.1093/oso/9780192886835.001.0001

Printed and bound in the UK by
Clays Ltd, Elcograf S.p.A.

Contents

List of Maps

Praise for The Oxford History of the Third Reich

'Having assembled an impressive group of experts, the volume proceeds thematically to address almost every aspect of the Third Reich. All ten chapters are well informed by contemporary scholarship but accessible to a lay audience. Politics, culture, war, society, and economy all receive their due.'

Robert Dassanowsky, *Journal of Modern History*

'For a reader who wishes to choose one source to learn about the Third Reich this book is a good choice.'

Paul Bookbinder, *European History Quarterly*

0.1 Europe under German domination in 1942 (courtesy of Robert Gellately)

Arckangel'sk

German Reich

Powers cooperating with the Axis

Areas under German occupation

Italy and areas under its occupation

FINLAND

Helsinki

Leningrad

Magnitogorsk

Tallinn

Kazan

Pskov

Moscow

Riga

Kuybyshev

REICHSKOMMISSARIAT
OSTLAND

Volga R.

Kaunas
(Kovno)

Vitebsk

Minsk

U   S   S   R

arsaw

Don R.

Kiev

Stalingrad

GENERAL
OVERNMENT
POLAND

REICHSKOMMISSARIAT
UKRAINE

OVAKIA

Rostov

Odessa

Caspian Sea

ROMANIA

Sevastopol

Bucharest

R.

Tiflis
(Tbilisi)

Baku

Danube

grade

Sofia

Black   Sea

BULGARIA

Istanbul

Salonika

Ankara

IRAN

REECE

T U R K E Y

Athens

Smyrna

IRAQ

SYRIA

CRETE

CYPRUS

Baghdad

0.2 Western USSR and territorial acquisitions under Stalin (courtesy of Robert Gellately).

Introduction

The Third Reich

Robert Gellately

Historians today continue raising questions about the Third Reich, especially because of the unprecedented nature of its crimes, and the military aggression it unleashed across Europe. Much of the inspiration for the catastrophic regime, lasting a mere twelve years, belongs to Adolf Hitler, a virtual non-entity in political circles before 1914.

He had been born in 1889 and was not even a German citizen. Moreover, during his largely 'normal' youth in Austria-Hungary, he revealed no signs of his future, and by age 20 he was a drifter with little education and socially withdrawn. He had no passionate ambitions save to become an artist of some kind, a vocation for which he had no formal training. He dabbled in painting, vaguely aspired to become a designer of the sets for the operas he adored, yet on that score, he made no progress whatsoever, and in the autumn of 1909, he hit rock bottom when he landed in a Viennese homeless shelter. In February the next year, he left to take residence in a men's hostel, where he stayed for just over three years, when in May 1913, thanks to receiving a tidy sum of money that was due from his father's inheritance, 'the artist' Adolf Hitler left for Munich, with dreams of becoming an architect. Once more, however, he made few friends, could find no work, and again had to paint postcards to get by. He appeared doomed never to achieve much of anything, given the existing order with its rigid class and political structures that allowed relatively little social mobility. But then the coming of what would be the Great War in 1914 turned the world upside down. The prospect of fighting for Germany excited this young man's nationalism, as it did for millions of others in nearly all parts of the globe, and he soon volunteered. The war would have revolutionary consequences, driving out the old orders, and ultimately making it possible even for social outsiders such as him to entertain lofty ambitions.

However, in November 1918, on his return from the war lost by Germany, we have no evidence that Hitler dreamed of becoming some kind of revolutionary leader, and his ambition was the more modest one of staying in the army as long as he could. Like so many in Germany, he was convinced that the Home Front had betrayed the 'undefeated army', had stabbed it in the back, and, like millions of others, he would believe in this legend for the rest of his life.

At age 30, he could count practically no accomplishments and he remained a rootless loner, a corporal in the shattered army, with no money and few prospects. However, he soon attracted the attention of officers on the lookout for enlisted men they could train to address the demobilizing troops with nationalist messages. During the brief schooling that followed, Hitler did quite well. In the course of 1920, he helped found a new political entity, the National Socialist German Workers Party (NSDAP), or Nazi Party. He quickly became its leading figure, though the ragtag operation was only one among the dozens like it on the political landscape of the dispirited country.

A little more than twenty years later and astonishingly, in autumn 1941, Adolf Hitler, now 52 years old had become Germany's unrivalled and worshipped leader, standing at the head of a restored economic powerhouse. Moreover, by mid-1940, he had rebuilt, armed, and used decisively the newly named Wehrmacht to defeat Poland and more remarkably still, to capture most of western Europe. Then a year later, he had directed his dynamic armies against the Soviet Union, so that in December, the Germans were at the gates of Moscow and Leningrad.

At that moment in late 1941, Hitler appeared—however briefly— to be the most powerful ruler on the planet. He could survey a vast continental empire that included nearly all of Europe from the English Channel, then north to Norway and east to Leningrad, onward far south into the Caucasus; and in a grand arc southwestwards, to the Balkans, Greece, and parts of North Africa. By now the new Germany, in its quest for more 'living space' had shaken the foundations of western civilization to its core, and was in the midst of a mass murder campaign aimed mainly at the Jews across eastern Europe. Before its collapse, the Third Reich's deeds would turn it into the epitome of evil, and it would leave scars across Europe and beyond that remain visible to this day.

* * *

Given this dramatic turn of events, it is little wonder that since 1945 generations of historians keep trying to explain how it all happened. In this book, specialist experts will distil that work, present their own up-to-date research, and provide a balanced and accessible account of the era. Each chapter focuses on specific questions and issues, and at the end of the volume, we provide a select list of Suggested Further Readings. The authors show that our understanding of the Third Reich has evolved over the years as we unearthed new materials and documents, adopted new methods and approaches, or studied what happened from different perspectives that give new meaning to the old evidence.

Initially in 1945, Allied lawyers and prosecutors from the west in Germany began investigating the crimes of top Nazi officials as part of the post-war trials. The emphasis at that time was on a relatively small circle of perpetrators, an approach that early post-war writers followed, as did Hannah Arendt, driven from Germany before the war. She portrayed National Socialism as a system of 'total domination' whose 'monstrous machine'—manned by lowly characters such as Adolf Eichmann—was responsible for the 'administrative murder' of the Jews. This line of argumentation postulated that something like unthinking robots or 'totalitarian characters' operated a smoothly running, efficient government killing-machine. However, as the late David Cesarani pointed out, since the 1960s and 1970s, scholars have discovered that National Socialist Germany was no 'totalitarian monolith'. Instead the Third Reich was a multifaceted system of competing and overlapping agencies 'over which Hitler presided erratically and in which policy emerged as a compromise between powerful individuals and interest groups'.

Another image of the war developed in eastern Europe, where Soviet leader Joseph Stalin's adaptions of the so-called agent theory of fascism prevailed. Perhaps its most influential formulation came from Georgi Dimitrov, the head of the Communist International, who said in 1935 that since the Great Depression, certain 'imperialist circles' were 'trying to shift the whole burden of the crisis onto the shoulders of the working people. That is why they need fascism.' As for the Nazi regime, he concluded that it was 'the most reactionary variety of fascism', had nothing in common with socialism, and was more like 'fiendish chauvinism. It is a government system of political gangsterism, a system of provocation and torture practiced upon the working-class and the revolutionary elements of the peasantry, the petty bourgeoisie and the intelligentsia. It is medieval barbarity and bestiality; it is unbridled aggression in relation to other nations.'

This highly influential condemnation, unfortunately led scholars away from trying to understand that the National Socialists headed a revolutionary movement in its own right, and that it had deep roots in German society. Although 'capitalists' had contributed some money to the party on its way to power in 1933, in fact it had been largely self-funded. After 1933, the new regime crushed the working-class movement and the trade unions, though it would be a mistake to believe that workers remained immune from the many appeals of the Third Reich.

In the 1980s and outside the Soviet Union, mainly younger scholars began reshaping our understanding of the Third Reich. They started looking at how ordinary people experienced the Nazi era and some of them studied how non-officials and civilians had participated in the terror system in Germany and across Europe during the occupation years from France to Poland, and beyond. In the last several years, and belatedly, a great deal of work has been directed at the efforts of the Nazi regime to create a 'community of the people', a racially based, exclusive, and harmonious society that Hitler had promised the Germans even before he became chancellor in 1933. This approach, as with previous efforts to write pioneering history, set off stormy and continuing controversies.

In this book, we focus on four overriding and interrelated themes that link together to form a coherent account of the Third Reich.

Hitler's Role

First, we underline the significance of Adolf Hitler as a charismatic leader, an approach that Ian Kershaw artfully employed in a massive biography that still ranks as the standard work on the topic. Historian Volker Ullrich, in 2016 and the first major German biography of

Hitler since Joachim Fest's classic account from 1973, uncovers new, or little used, documents to adjust Kershaw's picture, though he also underlines the importance of Hitler's charismatic appeal. If such an approach doubtless offers important insights, we should nonetheless be cautious when using the term 'charisma'. Since the 1980s, when this word began to become popular in everyday language, its meaning has become hopelessly clouded, and it is often taken as a positive attribute or a synonym for anyone or anything possessing exceptional magnetism, great charm, or stunning appeal.

Historians borrowed the concept of charisma, that 'special gift', from the famed sociologist Max Weber, who wrote about it long before the Third Reich. Weber said that religious or political leaders in the distant past had exercised 'charismatic authority' when their followers regarded them as possessing a 'divinely conferred power or talent'. During times of distress over the centuries, whether psycho-logical, religious, economic, or political in nature, certain 'natural' leaders arose to rule through this unique form of authority. For Weber 'The mere fact of recognizing the personal mission of a charismatic master establishes his power.' Thus, when we speak about Hitler's charismatic appeal, we need pay particular attention to the content of his messages, so that the real issue is not merely about his supposed magical personality or allegedly captivating blue eyes. We also should examine how people understood his mission, what they thought he stood for, and the extent to which they accepted and identified with some or all of it.

When did Hitler discover he possessed this 'special gift'? During his youth and in the First World War he exhibited no signs of possessing any extraordinary abilities whatsoever, least of all as a public or political person. If anything, he was generally shy, reclusive, and devoid of any 'proper' connections to the governing classes. He had left Vienna for Munich in 1913, perhaps partly to dodge the draft in his native land. Yet in Munich, he thrillingly celebrated the coming of war in August 1914, cheered its announcement, and promptly volun-teered to fight for Germany. In the dragged-out struggle on the Western Front, he won well-deserved honours, and yet he remained a loner apparently possessing few if any leadership qualities or unwill-ing to assume the role of an officer. Nevertheless, in his own mind, as early as 1915, he began attaching special meaning to the slaughter he saw at first hand. That year, he began thinking of the struggle in ominous terms, to go by a February letter to a Munich acquaintance. In it, he said that when he and his comrades made it home, he hoped they would 'find it purer and cleansed of foreignness'. Surely, 'the daily sacrifices and suffering of hundreds of thousands of us' would 'smash Germany's enemies abroad but also destroy our internal internation-alism—that would be worth more than any territorial gains'.

Instead, on his return to Munich in late November 1918, and convinced the Home Front had let down the troops, he found a city riven by revolution, and a right-wing counter movement already raging against the evil of 'Jewish Bolshevism'. If it was true that a number of the revolutionary leaders, such as Kurt Eisner and some of his comrades in Munich were Jews in Munich's revolution of 7 November, two days before Berlin's, in fact the revolutions across all of Germany were the product of widespread social discontent with the sacrifices of four years of war.

Hitler wanted nothing more than to remain in an army role, which he managed when officers selected him for training to speak on nationalist matters to demobilizing troops. His superiors also assigned him to monitor political groups in Munich, like the tiny German Workers' Party (DAP), one of many marginal right-wing and anti-Semitic parties in the area. He was sufficiently impressed such that only a week after attending one of its meetings in September 1919, he joined up, soon became its star attraction, and in 1920 he helped to transform it into the National Socialist German Workers Party, the NSDAP or Nazi Party. On 31 March 1920, when Germany had been his home for over five and a half years, the 30-year-old—pushed out of the military or not—took an uncharacteristically bold leap into politics. Socially, psychologically, and politically he began creating a new identity and even a new personality. Soon he could draw 2,000 listeners for one of his speeches, and still more came to hear what he had to say as his reputation spread.

Although a confirmed anti-Semite since 1919—to go by the only reliable written evidence we have—he soon revealed a radical streak on that score, as indicated privately to Heinrich Heim, a young Munich law student, who became a life-long confidant. In one of his letters from August 1920, recently found by biographer Volker Ull-rich, Heim quotes Hitler as saying, 'As long as Jews remain with their pernicious effects, Germany cannot convalesce. When it comes to the existence or non-existence of a people, one cannot draw a line at the lives of blinkered [German] ethnic comrades and even less so at the lives of a hostile, dangerous, foreign tribe.' Thus, he gave a preview of his 'redemptive' version of anti-Semitism, by which he linked the salvation of his country to 'pushing out' the Jews, though what that meant would keep changing.

Meanwhile as the post-war runaway inflation reached catastrophic proportions in 1923, his messages found an ever more enthusiastic response, at least in Bavaria. For a time, he became the veritable 'king of Munich', so much so that in November that year at the peak of the inflation, he attempted what turned out to be a poorly organized coup. After its ignominious failure, he would make certain never again to be too far ahead of the people, a political view he developed in *Mein Kampf*, the autobiography he wrote mostly in prison, which revealed how he thought and what he planned. We now know that it is a myth that no one read his book when it appeared in the mid-1920s, and we also know that Hitler was definitely its author. It remains less certain what role the large work in two volumes had in winning people to the cause.

We should realize, however, that he did not need to convert all the followers, many of whom, like the top Nazi leaders, were already in accord with similar ideas to his, before they laid eyes on him. Perhaps above all, they shared his commitment to the mission of 'redeeming' a defeated and broken Germany, a quest that marked the careers of such key figures in the party as Heinrich Himmler, Gregor and Otto Strasser, Ernst Röhm, Hans Frank, Rudolf Hess, and the two Baltic German émigrés Alfred Rosenberg and Max Erwin von Scheubner-Richter.

In the case of Joseph Goebbels, Germany's future Propaganda Minister, we have his voluminous diary that provides almost daily clues to his own political awakening. Like the others, he was a product of the psychological and political atmosphere of post-war disenchantment and aimlessness. Long before he had even heard of Hitler, Goebbels had become pro-Greater Germany, and 'anti-international', as well as deeply anti-Semitic—a commonplace in those times. He turned away from leftist materialism, though not necessarily against some kind of German socialism.

Although Goebbels was no activist at war's end, like so many in the country he longed for the return of a 'great man', perhaps on the model of the Iron Chancellor Otto von Bismarck or Field Marshal Paul von Hindenburg, the war hero and future president. Goebbels confided to his diary in mid-1924 that Germany 'yearns for the One, the Man, as the earth longs for rain in summer'. For a short time, he thought he himself might be that man (others did as well), at least until he heard Hitler speaking for the first time on 12 July 1925. Goebbels's response was to stand outside 'and cry like a baby. Away from other people.' Later he noted of the experience, that it was like a 'resurrection. What a voice. What gestures, what passion. *Just as I wished him to be.*' The emphasis is added here, because it almost seems as if Hitler was Goebbels's psychological projection, his own dream fulfilled. On finishing the first volume of *Mein Kampf*, Goebbels still had questions, though semi-worshipful ones about its author: 'Who is this man? Half-plebian, half-god! Is this really Christ or just John the Baptist?'

After Hitler's release from prison in late 1924, he began his political work almost from scratch, and together with a handful of loyalists, soon refined the Nazi Party machine. Nevertheless, it was an uphill battle until another major social calamity visited the country in the guise of the Great Depression in 1929. More than anything it was this economic chaos and mass joblessness that made people psychologically ready to receive the Nazi message, and to see hope in Hitler's vague promises. The great breakthrough came in the national elections in 1930, the first vote since the stock market crash. Overnight, the 'marginal' Nazi Party, with an army of militant true believers, became a power with which all others had to contend. Early the next year, in a private missive, Hitler was again declaring himself a prophet—one of his favourite poses—now claiming to predict 'with near oracular certainty', that he would have power within two and a half to three years. This time he was right.

After he was appointed chancellor in January 1933, a concerted official effort was made to convey the new national leader as if God-sent to fulfil a sacred calling. Soon the great majority would embrace the mission he articulated and thus implicitly accept his right to act based on charismatic authority. Max Weber sagely noted, however, that this authority's revolutionary core begins to diminish if it becomes routine. Hitler instinctively grasped what this quandary entailed in ruling, so that from his first days in power, and to an extent even before, he worked against the grain and avoided bureaucratic tasks. Perhaps he was simply indolent, though no doubt, he recognized how even holding cabinet meetings (which soon stopped) would erode his personal appeal, and he would cease to appear as divinely ordained and above politics as usual.

Although self-taught and a voracious reader, he claimed to intimates that he liked to learn also by speaking with them privately about their views, such as on how to organize the economy and society. Already, however, he preferred those around him to hail him as the Führer (not Chancellor) to symbolize his identification with a people's movement and to reinforce his standing as not just another politician.

Yet even on the road to power, the National Socialists did not need to invent many of the sentiments on which they built. There already existed strong anti-Weimar feelings, along with the deep conviction of the injustice of the Versailles Peace, anti-Semitism, and anti-Bolshevism. At the end of March 1933, Elisabeth Gebensleben, a mother (born 1883) and a passionate female party member in Brunswick, while enthralled by Hitler and overjoyed with his recent victory at the polls, noted that only then did the communists burn their red flags and seek to join her movement. 'Of course that is impossible', she wrote to her married daughter in Holland; 'first, they will have to make it through a three-year test-period in a concentration camp. The same for the Social Democrats.'

Hitler went on to exercise enormous influence throughout the years of the Third Reich, and right to the bitter end. Felix Römer, a young German historian, has summed up the man's appeal for the German prisoners of war (POWs) in Allied captivity who he studied in an insightful book, still not available in translation. Römer concludes that 'in the eyes of these men the Führer embodied all that was positive and attractive about National Socialism', while they attributed all negativities to those in his immediate entourage, blamed other authorities, 'or conveniently explained them away'. The avowals of loyalty of the men in captivity cut across old religious, class, and political lines, and to the extent that any prisoners now claimed to reject Hitler and Nazism, they tended to belong to older oppositional clusters. The 'community of the people', at least in a psychological sense, persisted inside the Wehrmacht in captivity, even after June 1944, when it should have been obvious that defeat was inevitable.

The Dictatorship's Use of Plebiscites and Elections

The *second theme* we explore in the book is the related notion of Hitler's regime as a curious mixture of dictatorship and appeals to the public via plebiscites and elections, a system we can label one of plebiscitary dictatorship. In *Mein Kampf*, he said he wanted an authoritarian regime, backed by the people, and once in power, to demonstrate that support he could use elections or the plebiscites permitted by the Weimar constitution. Nor was he alone among dictators in wanting to put all kind of issues to the vote. However, partly because the Nazis overwhelmingly won these exercises during the first six years, many people at the time and scholars ever since, doubted the validity of the results. But were these events and the plebiscites all fixed and terror-filled? Although historians commonly insist that they were, recent investigations show otherwise, as we do in this book. In fact, the government or the Nazi Party stepped in when local Nazis took obviously illegal measures to hinder or change the vote, because Berlin did not want outside observers to cast doubt on the overwhelmingly positive results.

Members of the Social Democratic Party underground, and Nazism's sworn enemies wrote in their secret reports that 'the fascists' had already made enormous gains. In November 1933, when the Nazis took 90 per cent of the vote in a plebiscite and 87.9 per cent in simultaneous national elections, the socialists wrote that 'critical foreigners' were tempted to assume these outcomes were obtained by 'force or terror'. Alas, the socialists despairingly had to admit that such views misperceived 'the real and profound influence fascist ideology has upon all classes of German society'. The underground report concluded with grudging acknowledgement that generally the results were 'a true reflection of the mood of the population', and the turnout in favour of Nazism indicated 'an extraordinarily rapid and effective process by which society was becoming fascist'.

In 1936, to take another example, Hitler was already bathed in a popular applause too obvious to ignore, thanks to the first steps to restore the economy and 'good order'. That success was undoubtedly reflected in the positive results of the Saar plebiscite (January 1935), allowed by the Versailles Treaty of 1919. Another election to the Reichstag on 29 March 1936 took place as a plebiscite supposedly authorizing Hitler to remilitarize the Rhineland—a bold step he had already taken. That move flaunted certain stipulations in the same, much-hated Versailles Treaty, and here the regime managed an astounding 98.8 per cent of the votes. Although the underground socialists usually emphasized disagreement and discord in their accounts of people's attitudes to the Nazi regime, on 17 March 1936 their observer in Munich had to admit, after witnessing a parade there of the newly named Wehrmacht, that 'the enthusiasm was enormous. The whole of Munich was on its feet.' He added, as if in reply to comrades—and future historians—who point to Nazi terror for explaining the evident consensus behind Hitler's regime: 'People can be forced to sing, but they cannot be forced to sing with such enthusiasm.' The reporter had experienced the heady nationalist enthusiasm at the outbreak of war in 1914, and now he could only say, 'That the declaration of war [back then] did not have the same impact on me as the reception of Hitler on 17 March.' The leader had 'won popularity' and 'is loved by many'.

Why did Hitler need elections? In fact, he had no use for them as such, though he and Joseph Goebbels took them very seriously because, as the Propaganda Minister put it in an interview in 1933, the regime wanted to show the world that the entire nation stood behind the regime's legislation. Thereby, the government would demonstrate the unity of the people and their leader. If there was doubtlessly some coercion or moral suasion from the neighbourhood or the party to get out and vote, observers like the Socialist Party underground at the time did not think that terror was always involved.

How could the nation get on side so quickly? German scholars after 1945, partly for psychological reasons, shied away from the obvious fact that for a time most of the nation had supported Nazism. Indeed, so many people joined the party or one of its affiliated organizations that the membership eventually included practically everyone in the country. After the war, many scholars emphasized the repressive character of the regime and its unprecedented crimes, while at the same time these academics put aside questions as to the social support the regime had enjoyed. However, after several generations of research and writing, we have now reached quite different conclusions. As Ulrich Herbert, one of Germany's leading historians, suggested recently, during the era of the Third Reich—with the obvious exception of its last months—perhaps 95 per cent of the German population 'lived relatively securely and fairly undisturbed under the Nazi regime', and this great majority was 'never even remotely endangered by state repression'.

Nazism's Social Vision

The *third theme* that runs through this book pertains to the 'community of the people', a concept that was in the air in the 1920s and even earlier, and which the Nazis made their own. Given that Hitler's version would exclude Jews and many others deemed 'racially inferior', medically unfit, or politically suspect, how seriously did anyone take this highly touted social vision?

In 1934, several hundred members of the Nazi Party submitted essays in a famous contest sponsored by Theodore Abel, a Columbia University professor. He promised prizes based on the best autobiography, and particularly for an account of what had led them to Hitler and the party. Most underlined that they wanted a 'community of the people' in which class conflict would end and there would be a 'return' to social harmony. A significant minority said they also wanted the Jews and other foreigners pushed out. Others went over to the party primarily by their attraction to Hitler and his (surprisingly vague) promises of change. Having read many of the essays myself, now held at the Hoover Institution on the campus of Stanford University, I certainly agree with Abel's conclusions. Perhaps the writers, consciously or not, toned down their anti-Semitism, given that they were writing for an American professor, but that prejudice comes through indirectly, in numerous ways.

Today historians debate the extent to which the regime created the much-heralded 'community of the people'. Although some are convinced that such a mythical community never existed, and amounted to little more than a cheap propaganda device, simply dismissing the idea of 'community' is too easy. It was precisely this element of Nazi ideology that dictated the structure of the promised utopia. True enough, there was never a serious attempt to bring social equality to all, because only the racially pure were valued, anyone who did not fit would be excluded, and real class differences persisted. Nevertheless, the select majority enjoyed a social-psychological sense of belonging to a special racial community.

The regime sought to pave the way for the many to enjoy the luxuries and pleasures that until then had been open only to the social elite. Hence, Hitler promised a people's car, the Volkswagen, and millions deposited five Reich marks per week 'to become car owners in four years'.

Although customers had to pay well in advance and collected no interest, tens of thousands soon signed up, though none of them ever got the finished product. Nevertheless, historian Hartmut Berghoff underlines the significance of their 'virtual consumption', that is, while 'racial comrades' did not get their own car or house as promised, the publicity campaigns surrounding these and other dreams allowed them a measure of consumer satisfaction. They could envision driving down the new autobahn in their own car. In addition, for the first time in history, the German government showed real concern for ordinary people, sponsored crusades to clean up and beautify the workplace, as well as small towns and villages, and these efforts impressed many erstwhile doubters. Opportunities existed for them to enjoy opera, or to contemplate vacations to foreign lands on cruise ships, pastimes until then reserved for only the well-to-do. Visits to the cinema multiplied many times over, as did excursions to art galleries, the symphony, operas, and exhibitions. Then there were festivals like 'the day of German art', during which there were parades of floats bedecked with historical characters from the German past, which made National Socialist ideology visible in ways meant to appeal. Besides trying to win over the workers, the new regime reached out to engage all of society, including the often-ignored peasantry. A special 'Harvest Festival', introduced in September 1933, built on old traditions. It brought hundreds of thousands together at Bückeberg in Lower Saxony, and in addition localities across the country celebrated the event as well.

Of course, the underlying reason that so many turned in favour of Hitler and National Socialism was that the regime ended unemployment, though even that did not happen overnight. Nor did work creation projects help all that much, because rearmament did far more to overcome joblessness. Economic historians provide various estimates for military expenditures, though all agree on the enormous increase from the first year of Hitler's rule down to the outbreak of the war. Hans-Ulrich Wehler suggests that military spending went from 4 per cent of the national budget in 1933 up to 58 per cent in 1938. This massive infusion of capital additionally created good jobs and some communities prospered as never before. Moreover, with the reintroduction of the military draft in March 1935, ever-larger numbers of young men went into the armed forces. Whereas until that year the number serving in the military was limited to 200,000, by August 1936 a new armaments plan called for the wartime strength of the army to reach 4,620,000 by 1 October 1939. By comparison, the numbers employed in constructing the highly touted autobahn were modest, going from 4,000 in December 1933, increasing slowly and only topping 100,000 for the first time in May 1935.

If beating the Great Depression was a long struggle, Germany eventually succeeded. No doubt Hitler bolstered the effort by exuding confidence and setting a new psychological tone. Being part of this 'community of the people' came with its rewards. Even members of the working-class parties who had been the strongest opponents of Nazism prior to 1933 came, if reluctantly, to accept that the economy was improving. In fact, Volker Ullrich has shown that a majority of workers, like other social groups, changed their negative opinion of Nazism and Hitler with remarkable ease and sometimes overnight. One contemporary looking back recalled fondly, 'Suddenly everything seemed possible.'

This is not to say that terror had ceased completely after the excesses in early 1933. However, this terror was not random, for it aimed overwhelmingly at those already feared, like recidivist criminals; or the despised, as were the vagabonds, Gypsies, and 'others'. There were special campaigns to clean up the streets from prostitutes, pimps, and pornography. The greatly empowered police also enforced more rigorously the laws already on the books against homosexual acts, while new laws made it possible to sterilize anyone deemed to be racially or physically 'defective'. In addition, the notorious 'Gestapo methods' were no post-war invention, though they were used selectively, above all to crack the underground communist movement and later in 1944–5, to track down pockets of resistance and crime. Although it is difficult to generalize about how 'good citizens' reacted to these developments, there is evidence to suggest that many welcomed the crackdown in the name of 'law and order'. When asked recently about these kinds of crimes, one grandmother said simply 'We did not worry about them.' If later on her Jewish friends or acquaintances simply disappeared, she said, 'But that was just how things were, we did not ask any questions, perhaps we were scared.'

War and Empire

The *fourth and final theme* in the book pertains to war and the Nazi empire. In Hitler's view, fostering the economy and building a 'community of the people' were not ends in themselves, as much as they were prerequisites to fulfilling his expansive plans on the foreign policy front. During his first years in power, even small, bloodless diplomatic victories or his speeches pleading for peace, made him more popular, while at the same time he grew more confident and assertive. Those who had known him during the 1920s hardly recognized him by the late 1930s when they saw him again.

The broadly shared dream among the German elite was that once they created a 'harmonious' and conflict-free society at home, the country would be in a position to break out of what nearly all Germans deemed to be an unjust post-war peace settlement that the victors imposed on them in 1919. Hitler and those around him wanted much more, including the defeat of the external enemies and then the seizure of Lebensraum in the east. In these vast lands, reaching into Ukraine, perhaps to Moscow and even to the Ural Mountains, the conquerors would establish a new order, a Germanic utopia for the 'master race'. New settlers would then push out the nations already there, enslave or even murder them.

The easy first attainments, which Hitler chalked up in foreign policy, encouraged this brutal vision of Lebensraum in the east. On top of that, ceaseless propaganda infected many in the Nazi Party well down the line. Apart from the leader, others in the hierarchy dreamed of a grand empire, and their plans, along with those of the academic experts and the *Schutzstaffel* (SS), called for nothing less than the

deliberate starvation of millions. Today, these visions and others, such
as those that were part of the General Plan East, read like tales of
horror, replete with wars of conquest, plunder, and enslavement on
into the future until perhaps a showdown with the United States.
Outlandishly, the ambitions grew in scale even after Germany began
losing the war.

Moreover, it was in the context of creating a Germanic empire that
the regime set about the truly monstrous undertaking of murdering all
of Europe's Jews. Although many in the Nazi hierarchy had entertained murderous thoughts about the Jews for years, most historians
insist that the decision or decisions for the 'final solution' came only
after war began with the Soviet Union in June 1941.

Back in 1933, Jews in Germany had been well integrated and thus
slow to accept how fundamentally their lives would change when the
Nazis came to power. The Jews were a small minority in the country,
and though they made up less than 1 per cent of the population, they
stood out in the larger cities, and a strand of German public opinion
resented them even before the Nazis made anti-Semitism more popular. It did not matter that the Jews had lived in these lands for over
1,000 years, or that in the new Germany founded in 1871 they had
obtained equal rights under the law, and enjoyed more opportunities
for social advancement than almost anywhere on earth.

For Hitler and the Nazi Party, reversing those rights and forcing the
Jews out was a top priority. However, most citizens did not take anti-
Semitism nearly as seriously. Thus, in April 1933, an officially sponsored boycott of Jewish businesses and professionals was a propaganda
flop. Nevertheless, Hitler whispered to the Italian ambassador Vit-
torio Cerutti that he wanted far more than such a boycott, and he
appallingly predicted, 'That in 500 or 600 years the name Hitler will
be universally glorified as the name of the man who, once and for
all, eradicated the global pestilence that is Jewry.' Indeed, his anti-
Semitism would grow more virulent by the year.

Official and informal discrimination slowly escalated as Hitler
gained popular support and more freedom of action from international pressure, especially in September 1938 when Germany
obtained the Sudetenland at Czechoslovakia's expense. Just over a
month later in November, the Nazis unleashed one of the worst
pogroms in the nation's long history in the outrageous 'night of broken

glass', or *Reichskristallnacht*. Thereafter, the Jews had to sell off their properties at bargain basement prices in the so-called Aryanization campaign, the state-sponsored robbery that spread everywhere the Germans went in the war years.

With the conquest of Poland in September 1939, the Third Reich found itself faced with millions of Jews, and uncertain about what should happen to them. As soon as the war against the Soviet Union began in June 1941, special task forces began shooting thousands of Jews in the east and forcing millions into ghettos. On 10 July, during an evening in the Führer's bunker, one of his adjutants, Walter Hewel recorded a particularly horrific statement, when he quoted Hitler as saying: 'I feel like the Robert Koch [1843–1910] in politics. He discovered the bacillus and pointed medical science in new directions. I discovered the Jews as the bacillus and the ferment of all social decomposition.' Such thinking rationalized the murderous acts already under way, for by then the special task forces were shooting not just male Jews, but also females and children.

Hitler crossed an important line in September 1941, when he decided on the deportation of all the Jews remaining in Germany (the Altreich). Indeed, by the last week in October, to follow Christopher Browning's conclusion, 'the close circle around Hitler, and gradually others as well, knew what Hitler expected of them and in what general direction they planned to proceed'. By early November, construction began on the first death camps, whose sole purpose was to produce death, and that development, among others, suggests that shortly before he had given an order, or uttered a wish, to kill all the Jews in Europe as far as his armies could reach. On the other hand, in recent years, historians point to an important meeting of Nazi leaders on 12 December 1941, the day after Hitler—in a step not called for by the treaty with Japan—had declared war on the United States. Finally on that date a World War had arrived, a moment when Hitler first 'prophesized' (on 30 January 1939) what would happen to the Jews. The result, he had said, would not be 'the Bolshevization of the earth, and thus the victory of Jewry, but the annihilation of the Jewish race in Europe!'

Apart from continuing arguments among historians as to the date or dates of a possible Hitler order or decision for the Holocaust, recent studies underline the role of 'ordinary' Germans, that is, men (and some women) who were not in the party or the SS, who volunteered to serve in police battalions, and soon found themselves in the killing fields. Millions in the Wehrmacht not only saw the events themselves, they often cooperated with the SS and sometimes became involved in the killing. Certainly, the German occupation forces did not have to search for collaborators in the killing in eastern Europe, for in many cases locals rushed to take advantage of the situation.

During the war, the fear that haunted Hitler, and to a surprising extent those in the officer corps of the armed forces well down the chain of command, and not just among SS and party fanatics, was a recurrence of the 'stab-in-the back' of 1918. According to that myth, the Home Front let down the battlefront and brought about the defeat of the army in the First World War. In a sense, many of the steps the regime had taken during the years of peace after 1933 and especially during the war were in part efforts to ensure that history did not repeat itself. Thus, Hitler did not want to ask Germans to sacrifice too much, so that Goebbels had an uphill struggle to win his support for 'total war', and by the time he got the go-ahead, it was already far too late.

To avoid the demoralization that enemy propaganda might bring, the regime outlawed citizens listening to foreign radio, such as the BBC or Radio Moscow; the police took immediate steps to arrest offenders and all potential 'enemies within'; and the concentration camp population expanded. The war also created new social problems, above all in the form of millions of forced labourers brought in to make up for the millions of Germans in the armed forces. Most were from Poland and the western Soviet Union. They were marked with badges, treated like slaves, and told that if they dared have any sexual relations with Germans, the punishment would be death, a threat often carried out.

The empire of camps created in the occupied eastern areas began to invade the Home Front, especially when, in September 1942, Hitler gave armaments minister Albert Speer permission to establish sub-camps on the premises of existing factories. Himmler had wanted the industries brought to the camps, though in this case, Hitler favoured private enterprise, with the result that soon Germans worked side-by-side with either enslaved foreign workers or concentration camp prisoners. As Marc Buggeln indicates in a study of the camps and sub-camps in Hamburg, these institutions were not self-contained laboratories sealed off from society, for contacts were unavoidable and inevitable. Did not the prisoners in striped clothing at the workplace confirm the 'community of the people' by appearing as 'racially inferior slaves'? Many workers identified with the Nazi regime and willingly supported the oppression of all camp prisoners, or at least accepted the slavery with a shrug of the shoulders.

At war's end, as Ulrich Herbert reminds us, 'less than 5 per cent' of the prisoners in concentration camps were German. Most were foreigners, including Jews from Hungary and elsewhere brought to Germany in the full-blown emergency of 1944–5. Almost none of the companies voiced concern about using camp prisoners, nor did city administrations, and even those involved in supplying essential materials to the military did not treat prisoners any better. At war's end, they all wanted the SS to take the prisoners out of Hamburg—to use that example—in order to prevent riots and to avoid besmirching the city's image should the Allies, about to arrive, see them as a city of slaveholders.

The death camps outside Germany were another matter. Three of the very worst of them—Bełżec, Sobibór, and Treblinka—that had opened toward the end of 1941 or in early 1942 as Operation Reinhard, were completely gone by the end of 1943. Their aim had been to murder the more than two million Jews of Poland.

The last evacuation of Auschwitz, the greatest single murder site of all, began in January 1945, when many of the survivors, along with the prisoners of other camps, began what became death marches. The rumours that Germans must have heard about the mistreatment of those in the concentration camps came home to the garden gate in those last months of war, as guards drove weakened prisoners through towns and villages to destinations unknown. Local citizens or party members helped to hunt down any that escaped, as the catastrophe unfolded for all to see.

Red Army units first discovered the death camps and massive war crimes, and during the war, the Kremlin began holding trials. It also sent in the long-named Extraordinary State Commission for the Investigation of Atrocities Committed on Soviet Territory by the German Fascists and Their Accomplices, known by the Russian initials, ChGK. Their reports provided graphic and disturbing details of crimes committed by the invaders, often with the collaboration of locals. Soviet authorities used some of the material selectively at the time and then confined much of it to the archives. Only since 1991 has this evidence become more accessible. Today readers can find selected translations of this documentation in *The Black Book of Soviet Jewry*, delayed from publication by the Soviet censors, and there is often dramatic personal testimony in *The Unknown Black Book* (2008). However, it is only in the last few years that scholars have begun to integrate this material, and other documentation held in the Soviet Union, into broader studies of Hitler's regime and the Holocaust. Much work remains to be done.

1

The Weimar Republic and the Rise of National Socialism

Matthew Stibbe

Since 1945 historians have typically sought to explain the rise of the Nazis in terms of the inherent structural weaknesses of the Weimar Republic and/or the supposed peculiar authoritarian tendencies in German history going back to the nineteenth century or even earlier. Either Weimar lacked the necessary constitutional levers and responsible statesmanship to ward off the threat of extremism from both the left and right, it is alleged, or it was undermined by representatives of the pre-1918 conservative elite who continued to dominate key institutions such as the army, the judiciary, and the civil service and were determined to find anti-democratic alternatives to parliamentary rule. The national economy was also ruined by more than four years of war between 1914 and 1918, followed by the harsh peace settlement of 1919, the hyper-inflation of the early 1920s, and over-reliance on American loans in the late 1920s, rendering it particularly vulnerable to the Great Depression of the early 1930s. In short, Weimar's 'failure' led to the Nazis' success.

A case could nonetheless be made for arguing that the Nazis' rise to power, and their growing success and popularity after 1933, are historical topics that cannot be defined and explained solely with reference to national developments. At the regional level, the early Nazi movement—and its claim to represent the 'true' Germany—were very much structured by conditions prevailing in post-war Bavaria, where a variety of conservative, anti-republican, and ultra-nationalist groups vied for supremacy in the years 1919–23. At the same time, many of the NSDAP's core messages in the 1920s and 30s, for instance anti-Bolshevism and belief in anti-Jewish conspiracy theories, were part of a common response from fascist and right-wing circles across Europe to the Russian Revolution of 1917 and to the temporary military victory of left-wing uprisings in Berlin, Munich, Budapest, and elsewhere in 1919.

In terms of German domestic politics, National Socialism has often been characterized as a movement of militarist extremism, racist refusal to recognize Jews and other ethnic minorities as fellow citizens, uncompromising hostility towards the Weimar 'system', and violent rejection of the Versailles peace settlement. Certainly it was all of these things, as we shall see in more detail in the various sections of this chapter. But it was also something more: a movement which succeeded first in channelling a range of contradictory emotions and cultural anxieties thrown up by the 1914–18 war and the many challenges it posed to the existing social and gender order, and second in moulding these anxieties into a new radical nationalist vision for Germany and for Europe as whole.

The Radical Right in Post-War Bavaria and the Early Nazi Party

The Nazi Party (known at first as the German Workers' Party, DAP, and later as the National Socialist German Workers' Party, NSDAP) was founded in Munich in January 1919 by Karl Harrer, a journalist, and Anton Drexler, a railway locksmith who had been involved during the war in the short-lived right-wing Fatherland Party. Both Harrer and Drexler believed that the DAP could be a means of winning workers away from Marxism and the cause of left-wing revolution. They also fostered links with a variety of other, more shadowy racist groups on the fringes of Munich politics, including the occultist Thule Society, the *Aufbau* circle made up of Russian émigré groups opposed to the Bolsheviks, and the rabidly anti-Semitic German Order (*Germanenorden*). Adolf Hitler, an Austrian-born German war veteran and reputedly an employee of the intelligence branch of the Bavarian Reichswehr (the new name for the Imperial army), joined the party in September 1919, having been sent (according to some historians) to spy on it by his boss, Captain Karl Mayr.

Sympathetic officers in the Bavarian Reichswehr were indeed an important source of initial funding for the (NS)DAP and of training for its paramilitary wing, the storm troopers (*Sturmabteilungen,* SA).

Although they were principally a political grouping, the early Nazis also gained the backing of various independent armed militias, citizens 'defence' associations and veterans' leagues that remained committed to combating 'Marxism' in a military sense in Bavaria and across Germany after 1919. The most extreme were the followers of Franz Ritter von Epp, a highly-decorated army colonel and commander of the *Freikorps Epp*, a volunteer brigade that had spearheaded the brutal crushing of the Munich Soviet Republic in May 1919 from its base in Ohrdruf near Gotha. Some of the NSDAP's later members (and leaders) also joined the irregular military formations fighting against Poles, Bolsheviks, and other 'enemies' on Germany's eastern borders in 1919–21, especially in the Baltic states and Upper Silesia. Meanwhile, together with Drexler and the economist Gottfried Feder, Hitler was centrally involved in drawing up the party's first programme, the so-called 'Twenty-Five Points', in February 1920. By this time Harrer had already resigned from the party, and Drexler too soon found himself sidelined, leaving Hitler as sole leader by 1921.

Hatred of Jews, liberals, and socialists, belief that the Imperial army had been 'stabbed in the back' by traitors at home in November 1918, and commitment to a vaguely-formulated and supposedly non-denominational 'Positive Christianity' were the Nazis' main propaganda themes in the immediate post-war years. For instance, the Baltic German publicist Alfred Rosenberg, an early recruit both to the *Aufbau* circle and the NSDAP, was responsible for promoting the anti-Jewish Protocols of the Elders of Zion, a Tsarist forgery, in the Munich press, and clearly influenced Hitler's emerging views on the so-called 'Judeo-Bolshevik' threat. Later he became editor of the party's newspaper, the *Völkischer Beobachter,* and for a time was recognized as the NSDAP's 'chief ideologist'. The wealthy journalist and playwright Dietrich Eckart, who was one of Hitler's earliest mentors and helped the party to purchase the *Völkischer Beobachter* in December 1920, argued that Germany's national 'reawakening' would only occur in opposition to what he called the 'Jewish materialistic spirit within and about us'. According to the historian Derek Hastings,

alongside Eckart, the early Nazi Party was influenced by a variety of
other Catholic racist thinkers, and was labelled by its critics as a
'Christian-nationalist anti-Semitic sect that . . . calls for a new Crusade
against the Jews'. This changed only in September 1923, when Hitler
aligned himself with the decidedly anti-Catholic *Deutscher Kampfbund*
(German Combat League), a short-lived alliance of 'patriotic' veterans
groups, Protestant nationalists, and militarists formed at the *Deutscher
Tag* (German Day) in Nuremberg, and thereby alienated some of his
original Catholic sympathizers.

While the influence of religious forms of Catholicism on early Nazi
thinking remains a matter of controversy, there is wider agreement
that the National Socialist movement was at first very provincial and
south German in outlook, even if it managed to establish a handful of
branches beyond Bavaria's borders in 1920–1. In August 1920 Hitler
travelled to Salzburg, Austria, to attend a meeting of national socialist
parties from central and western Germany, Austria, Czechoslovakia,
and Poland, all of which promoted some form of ethnic German
nationalism and all of which would likely have subscribed to points
1 and 2 in the NSDAP's programme ('union of all Germans in a
Greater Germany' and 'abrogation of the peace treaties of Versailles
and St. Germain'*). As a young man growing up in pre-war Linz and
Vienna, Hitler had greatly admired the Austrian Pan-German thinker
Georg Ritter von Schönerer, who combined hatred of Jews, Czechs,
political Catholicism, and the multi-national Habsburg state in equal
measure. Now he sought to adapt these ideas to the changed, post-war
geopolitical context.

For at least the next two and a half years, the focus was on building
up the party's profile regionally, and eliminating competition from
rival right-wing groups such as the German-Socialist Party (*Deutscho-
zialistische Partei*, DSP). In October 1922 modest success came when
Hitler and 800 of his supporters attended the 'German Day' in
Coburg, in the very north of Bavaria, and battled with leftist opponents who had come across from neighbouring Thuringia to support

---

* The Treaty of St. Germain, signed between Austria and the victorious
western Allies in September 1919, forbade union between Austria and Germany
and confirmed the loss of the German-speaking parts of Bohemia and the Sudetenland to Czechoslovakia.

local trade union protest against the presence of militarists in the town. The day ended with Hitler enjoying a round of drinks with the former Duke of Saxe-Coburg and Gotha, Carl Eduard, and his entourage. Carl Eduard, who later became a high-profile functionary in the party and the SA, was the grandson of Prince Albert and Queen Victoria, a one-time member of the British royal family (until being divested of his titles in 1919), and an ex-soldier with contacts to a variety of anti-communist paramilitary organizations, among them the infamous Ehrhardt brigade and the *Freikorps Epp*. At around the same time, the NSDAP managed to persuade a large part of the Nuremberg chapter of the DSP, including the anti-Semitic rabble-rouser Julius Streicher, to put themselves at its disposal. According to Ian Kershaw, this brought an effective doubling of the party's membership to around 20,000, still miniscule when compared to racist groups with a 'national' presence in Germany at this time, such as the Pan-German League and the *Deutschvölkischer Schutz- und Trutzbund* (German Völkisch Defence and Defiance League), but nonetheless large enough to establish a significant influence on the political scene in Protestant-dominated Franconia as well as the more Catholic parts of Bavaria.

Crisis Year 1923

During the course of 1923, membership of the party grew again, this time substantially. By November 1923 the figure had reached 55,000, but with core support still very much centred on Munich. The year began with the Franco-Belgian occupation of the Ruhr industrial area following Germany's default on reparations payments due under the peace settlement. The invading armies intended to seize finished goods as well as raw materials in lieu of missing gold mark deposits and timber and coal shipments, but were part thwarted when the Reich government in Berlin—with the support of Germans from across the political spectrum—declared a policy of passive resistance. German workers in the Ruhr were instructed to go on strike rather than submit to delivery orders issued by the French and Belgian military authorities. More and more money was printed to pay them to stay at home. This in turn meant that hyper-inflation, which had already begun in the summer of 1922 and was itself preceded by record levels of 'ordinary' inflation in the years 1914–22, reached catastrophic proportions. By the autumn of 1923 prices for basic food items were increasing several times each day, with the cost of a kilogram of rye bread reaching 78 billion marks on 5 November and a staggering 233 billion marks on 19 November. Middle-class savings were obliterated, millions of families faced poverty and hunger, and the political future of the Weimar Republic now hung in the balance. In addition to the failed 'Beer Hall Putsch' in Munich in November 1923, of which more in this section of the chapter, the new Reich government under Gustav Stresemann faced left-wing uprisings in Thuringia, Saxony, and Hamburg in October, and was forced to use emergency powers to restore order at home and end the Ruhr crisis on terms acceptable to the Allies.

In Bavaria, the Ruhr invasion caused as much outrage as in the rest of Germany. A part of Bavaria, the Palatinate, had already experienced the stationing of French soldiers from 1920 under the Treaty of Versailles' provisions for a fifteen-year Allied military presence in German territory west of the Rhine. Bavarians had joined others at national and international levels in protesting against the French use of North and West African troops to bolster its occupation force (dubbed in contemporary German parlance as the 'black shame on the Rhine'). The invasion of the Ruhr, although involving European troops only, and not affecting Bavarian territory, was regarded as another provocation. Interestingly, though, the Hitler movement took a different approach to most other nationalist groups in Germany, refusing to endorse the policy of passive resistance and instead calling for a national uprising against the Berlin government first, placing this ahead of any military reckoning with the French. This also put the NSDAP at odds with various far-right groups in northern Germany who had formed a bizarre and temporary alliance with the Communists in order to battle against French 'imperialism' and western 'finance capitalism'. One of their number, Count Ernst zu Reventlow, even contributed to an exchange of articles on the subject of 'National Bolshevism' that appeared in the communist daily *Die Rote Fahne* at the height of the Ruhr struggle.

Encouraged in part by the success of Benito Mussolini's 'March on Rome' in October 1922, Hitler's ultra-anti-republican stance nonetheless drew some sympathy from the broader panoply of right-wing leaders and militarist groups now vying for hegemony in southern Germany. Through his involvement in the above-mentioned *Kampf-bund*, for instance, the former wartime army Quarter-Master General Erich Ludendorff made it known that he was willing to collaborate with the Nazis and other conspiratorial organizations in the sphere of training for new paramilitary units. This was in contravention of the disarmament clauses of the Treaty of Versailles, which the Stresemann government in Berlin—to their disgust—seemed determined to fulfil.

More complex was the stance adopted by the existing political and military authorities in Bavaria, and in particular the 'triumvirate' who were responsible for maintaining law and order in Munich: Gustav Ritter von Kahr, the state commissioner of Bavaria, Hans Ritter von Seisser, head of the Bavarian police, and Otto von Lossow, commander of the Bavarian Reichswehr. Their attitude would be crucial to the success of any coup attempt, but their politics—while determinedly anti-republican—also differed significantly from National Socialism. In particular Kahr, who had served as Bavarian Prime Minister from 1920 to 1921 after the removal of his Social Democrat predecessor, Johannes Hoffmann, was more of a conservative monarchist and Bavarian separatist than a Greater German nationalist. Nonetheless, he had consistently refused to hand over right-wing extremists to Berlin during his time in office, and continued to block extradition requests in his new role as regional governor of Upper Bavaria from 1921 to 1923. After being appointed state commissioner with emergency powers on 26 September 1923 as part of the Bavarian government's initial response to Berlin's decision to end the Ruhr struggle, one of his first actions was to order the expulsion of over one hundred foreign-born Jews from Bavaria, a clear concession to far-right opinion.

In the drama of 8–9 November 1923, Kahr and his monarchist associates Seisser and Lossow vacillated, at first seeming to give their blessing, albeit under duress, to the conspiracy hatched by Hitler, Ludendorff, and the *Kampfbund* to launch a 'national uprising' in Munich, but later changing their minds. Without the support of the police and Reichswehr, the putsch—which ultimately boiled down to a poorly thought-out plan to seize control of the Bavarian War Ministry building after a march through the centre of Munich and the taking of members of the city council as hostages—was doomed to fail. Crown Prince Rupprecht, heir to the vacant Bavarian throne, and Cardinal Michael von Faulhaber, the Archbishop of Munich, both declined to give the putsch their approval. Most of the Reichswehr barracks and police command posts in the Bavarian capital also refused to hand over their weapons or side with the conspirators. Hitler and Ludendorff nonetheless resolved to go ahead with their plans on the morning of 9 November. Fourteen putschists lost their lives in a dramatic shoot-out with armed police and military detachments on the Odeonsplatz in front of the Feldherrnhalle in central Munich, as did four police officials. Hitler fled the scene, thus incurring Ludendorff's disapproval, but was arrested a few days later.

In the subsequent trial, held from February to April 1924 amid significant international as well as national publicity, Hitler was convicted of high treason and sentenced to five years' imprisonment, while Ludendorff was acquitted. The trial was used by Hitler as a platform to put forward his extreme nationalist views, and—somewhat misleadingly—to claim himself as the sole political leader of the conspiracy, thereby marginalizing Ludendorff's contribution. The sentence was surprisingly lenient and reflected the conservative sympathies of the presiding judge, Georg Neithardt. The latter also refused to consider a request from Reich officials to arrange for the Nazi leader to be deported to his native Austria at the end his sentence on the grounds that the laws protecting the state against foreign-born agitators 'should not apply to a man so German in his thinking as Adolf Hitler'.

Imprisoned alongside Hitler at the Landsberg Fortress, some 40 miles west of Bavaria's capital, was Rudolf Hess, subsequently to become the party's deputy Führer in 1933. In the days after the verdict was announced, a list of candidates appearing under the name *Völkischer Block* (National-Racist Block), in reality an alias for the now banned NSDAP, won 17.1 per cent in elections to the Bavarian parliament on 6 April, and 16 per cent of the Bavarian regional vote in elections to the German national parliament, the Reichstag, on 4 May. In Munich the *Völkischer Block's* support in these two elections was even higher, at 34.9 per cent and 28.5 per cent respectively. This unexpected success, alongside the lessons learned from the failure to secure police and military support for an illegal bid to seize power in one part of Germany, now convinced Hitler that the path to future victory lay through the ballot box. This was also the conclusion of his autobiography, *Mein Kampf*, mostly written while he was in Landsberg, and eventually published in two volumes in 1925 and 1926.

Relative Stabilization

The years 1924–9 have been described by Detlev J. K. Peukert, among others, as a period of 'deceptive stability' for the Weimar Republic. In October–November 1923 a new currency, the *Rentenmark*, was introduced, which brought hyper-inflation to an abrupt end, albeit at a cost to millions of small savers and pension-holders. Reparation payments were subsequently revised under the Dawes Plan in 1924, a scheme which also made new American loans available to Germany. Although Stresemann stepped down as Reich Chancellor in November 1923, he acted as Foreign Minister through a succession of coalition governments from then until his sudden death in October 1929. Under his watch, Germany signed the Locarno treaties recognizing its borders with its western neighbours in 1925, entered the League of Nations in 1926, and negotiated a phased withdrawal of Allied troops from the Rhineland between 1927 and 1930, five years ahead of the schedule set out under the Treaty of Versailles. Relations with the west, and with France in particular, improved enormously, and in 1929–30 a further revision of reparations payments was concluded under the Young Plan.

Some of the consensus that Stresemann had built up around foreign policy also reached into the domestic sphere. Certainly there was a noticeable reduction in support for far-right parties during this period. In the December 1924 Reichstag elections, for instance, the *Völkischer Block*'s share of the vote in Bavaria fell from 16 per cent to 5.1 per cent, and in Germany as a whole it managed only 3 per cent. Ludendorff, standing as the *Block*'s candidate in the first round of the presidential elections in March 1925, won a catastrophic 1.1 per cent and withdrew from the contest, doubtless to Hitler's satisfaction. The latter, who was released after serving only nine months of his prison sentence, formally refounded the NSDAP in February 1925, but it too initially struggled to make any electoral headway. During its first national test of support, in the May 1928 Reichstag elections, it secured just 2.6 per cent of the vote, and even in its Bavarian heartland it chalked up less than 6.4 per cent. In Berlin the result was a paltry 1.6 per cent. Admittedly, membership of the party continued to grow, to around 100,000 by the end of 1928, but attempts to rebuild support in working-class areas in particular fell on stony ground. Regional bans prevented Hitler from public speaking in most of Germany until 1927, and in Prussia, the largest state, until 1928.

Even so, it would be wrong to dismiss these 'wilderness years' as a time of complete failure for the NSDAP. For one thing, as Kershaw argues, it was now that Hitler managed to obtain complete 'mastery over the movement', retaining older supporters and winning over new followers on the basis of a shared commitment to 'eradicating' Marxism and destroying the so-called 'Jew-Republic'. For another, the party's structures were overhauled, with propaganda among the masses now receiving priority over paramilitary activities (the latter nonetheless remained important, despite periodic bans on, and from time to time, open revolts within the ranks of, the SA). Gregor Strasser, formerly the NSDAP's agent in Lower Bavaria, was brought to Munich to run the party's new Political Organization (PO). His remit was to establish branches across Germany, and to ensure that only persons officially approved by the PO were able to speak on behalf of the party. However, his authority was counter-balanced by that of the regional *Gauleiter* or party bosses, appointed because of their absolute loyalty to Hitler above considerations of policy. Tensions between the PO and the *Gauleiter* were inevitable, but the common denominator holding all elements of the party together was the belief that Germany had been brought to its knees in 1918 by the machinations of 'internal enemies' and that the only realistic path to national recovery lay through a policy of unrelenting attacks—both by word and by deed—against the left and the Jews.

One particularly important recruit to the party during this period was the future Reich Propaganda Minister Joseph Goebbels, a demagogic Rhinelander, Jew-hater and lapsed Catholic who, like Strasser, initially wanted to place more emphasis on the anti-bourgeois and 'socialist' elements of National Socialism. In September 1926 Goebbels became *Gauleiter* of Berlin, where he repeatedly organized violent clashes with the Communists, and in May 1930 he took charge of the party's central propaganda office in Munich. Meanwhile, the establishment of a national presence for the NSDAP was aided less by a change of overall political emphasis—indeed, such a move was explicitly rejected by Hitler at a meeting of senior party figures in Bamberg in February 1926, where he denounced Bolshevism as 'a Jewish creation', referred to Italy and Britain as 'natural allies', and reiterated his commitment to the 'Twenty-Five Point' programme of 1920—and more by the collapse of other far-right groups into warring, leaderless factions. The above-mentioned Count Reventlow, for instance, quit a rival fringe party to join the Nazis in 1927, and although his relationship with Goebbels and other leading figures in the Berlin NSDAP remained tense, they managed to work together.

The political atmosphere in Germany by 1927 had of course shifted dramatically since 1923. Behind the frequent changes of coalition in Berlin lay a broader sense that parliamentary government could be made to work for the people, as seen, for instance, in the generous public financing of new housing programmes and the creation of a nationwide, state-backed unemployment insurance scheme for most wage-earners. Against this background, the Nazis' message seemed largely irrelevant. Nonetheless, many ordinary middle-class people had still not been won over to the republican system. One early indication of this came during the second round of the presidential elections in April 1925, when the former commander-in-chief of the armed forces during the First World War, the aristocratic Field Marshal Paul von Hindenburg, won an unexpected victory against the main republican candidate, Wilhelm Marx of the Catholic Centre Party. The result was all the more surprising given that Hindenburg had not even stood in the first round of the contest.

During the first five years of his initial term as Reich President, Hindenburg largely stayed out of political matters and seemed to accept the parliamentary system, even if he remained an authoritarian monarchist at heart. After the May 1928 Reichstag elections he even agreed to appoint a new government headed by the Social Democrat Hermann Müller. However, in one area his influence was crucial, namely his support for attempts by the army to protect itself from 'unwarranted' public criticism or democratic oversight over its activities. Occasionally these efforts led to heated domestic controversy, for instance when it came to blocking (or condemning as 'unpatriotic') attempts by left-wingers to expose the Reichswehr's use of secret funds and contacts abroad, particularly in the Soviet Union, to pursue a policy of covert rearmament in violation of the restrictions imposed at Versailles. In October 1928, the relatively small matter of whether the Müller government would proceed with the building of a pocket battleship (*Panzerkreuzer A*), in accordance with plans laid by its predecessor, again underlined the extent to which the Reichswehr, and in particular its political leadership under General Kurt von Schleicher, was determined to maintain control of defence policy.

The presidential elections in 1925 and Hindenburg's victory had also marked an important event in the contested politics of war commemoration in Weimar Germany, symbolized by the rival colours used by the 'people's candidate' Marx (the black-red-gold of the republic) and the 'candidate of the Reich' Hindenburg (the black-white-red of the old empire). Right-wing veterans groups like the *Stahlhelm* (Steel Helmet), with between 300,000 and 350,000 members in the 1920s, had long accepted the myth first put forward by Hindenburg in 1919 that the Imperial German army had been 'betrayed' by democratic politicians at home rather than being defeated in the field. Refusing to admit Jews after March 1924, the *Stahlhelm* focused on commemorating great exploits on the battlefield, involving itself, for instance, in the campaign, completed in 1927, for a huge 'Tannenberg Memorial' to be erected near the site of Hindenburg's famous victory against the Tsar's armies in East Prussia in September 1914. Ranged against them was the republican, anti-war and largely social democrat-oriented *Reichsbanner Black-Red-Gold*, formed in 1924 and with membership rising to around 900,000 in 1925–6. As Benjamin Ziemann has recently shown, the *Reichsbanner* had a very strong presence in Weimar's commemorative culture, but not quite strong enough to ensure the complete dominance of democratic narratives of the war experience over anti-republican, militaristic, and revanchist views. 'War memory' therefore remained fragmented and a terrain for competing political discourses rather than a means for constructing a sense of national unity.

'War memory' was not just an issue for war veterans and their families, however. As the historian Michael Wildt puts it, 'for adolescent German men—those too young to have been drafted and yet too old to recall the war as merely a distant childhood memory—the war also became a thorn in their sides, reminding them of a missed opportunity to prove themselves...'. In particular, a substantial portion of the fanatical Nazis who later made their way up to senior positions in the SS or *Schutzstaffel*, the elite security wing of the NSDAP, were born in the years 1900 to 1910. Among them was Heinrich Himmler who joined the party in 1923 and was appointed Reichsführer SS by Hitler at the age of just 29, in 1929; and Reinhard Heydrich, an officer in the post-war German navy who was placed in charge of the SS's intelligence division in 1931 and rose to become head of its Reich Security Main Office in 1939, when only 35 years old. These younger, more educated recruits into the NSDAP and its police and terror apparatus belonged to a particular social milieu which was bound not by a sense of joint class interest or memories of a common war experience but by an uncompromising attachment to National Socialism as an ideological world-view. Like the *Freikorps* veterans and brown-shirts in the SA, from whom many of their number were recruited, they were drawn to the militaristic values and masculinist ethos behind the NSDAP's leadership principle. However, they were attracted by something else too, namely the Nazis' ability to present the post-war world as a place in which political disorder, sexual chaos, and economic turmoil reigned permanently, and 'peace'—even in the years 1924–9—appeared as nothing more than a mirage. The only way out of this perpetual state of emergency, it seemed, was the hierarchy and discipline offered by a movement which, more than any other nationalist grouping, was able to legitimize—and mobilize—violence in the name of establishing a radically new social order.

Finally, in a more prosaic sense the 'Hitler movement' was given a fresh boost in its campaign to achieve national prominence by the sharp rightwards movement taken by the DNVP or German National People's Party, the dominant (Protestant) conservative party in Weimar Germany, following its poor performance in the May 1928 Reichstag elections. Between 1924 and 1928 the DNVP had taken part in various 'bourgeois' coalitions, but refused to serve in the Social Democrat-led government which took office in June 1928. Instead, it elected a new leader, the press magnate Alfred Hugenberg, who was determined to place his substantial media empire behind attempts to forge a realignment and consolidation of the 'national opposition' to

Weimar. As part of this process, in July 1929 Hugenberg launched a campaign, also supported by the *Stahlhelm*, the Pan-German League, the National Rural League (*Reichslandbund*), and the NSDAP, for a national referendum against the Young Plan, the revised scheme for settling Germany's reparations debts with the Allies.

The referendum eventually went ahead on 22 December 1929 and was, ostensibly, a disappointment for its backers who won only 5.8 million votes, far short of the twenty-one million or so needed to force a change in government policy. Nonetheless, the Nazis managed to gain in profile as a result of their involvement in this joint nationalist enterprise, and saw a modest improvement in their performance during local and regional elections held in the winter of 1929–30. More importantly, they were able to exploit divisions and weaknesses within the DNVP itself, for instance by repeatedly pointing to the latter's approval of the Dawes Plan in 1924, by including scurrilous attacks on Reich President Hindenburg as well as the Müller government in campaign literature, and by backing a proposal—put forward by the Pan-German League, but opposed by DNVP moderates—to include an additional statement in the referendum which would make any government minister seeking to approve the Young Plan liable to criminal prosecution for treason. In this way, the NSDAP was slowly able to outmanoeuvre and replace the DNVP as the main—and more energetic—right-wing opposition to the so-called 'Young parties' from 1930 onwards.

The Great Depression and its Consequences

Historians have long disagreed on how stable or unstable Germany's economic recovery was in the second half of the 1920s. However, there is a much greater degree of consensus around the claim that, regardless of the nationalist commitment they showed during the Young Plan referendum and their sudden emergence as a key opposition party in 1930, the Nazis were not the prime determinants of the circumstances in which they were able to come to power in 1933. More important than anything the party did or did not do was the economic calamity brought about in Germany by the Great Depression. This was triggered in the first instance by the stock exchange crash in New York in late October 1929 and reached its depth in early

1932, when six million German men were out of work and industrial production fell to 58 per cent of the level recorded in 1928.

In terms of political culture, the Depression accelerated the realignment of the right referred to above and also brought to a head a more general 'crisis of classical modernity' (Peukert) which had been simmering under the surface of 1920s 'stability'. All of the Weimar-era projects for social reform, some of which had been more successful than others in the period before 1930, came to a screeching halt, while the state-backed unemployment insurance fund soon collapsed under the sheer weight of demand. Conservative economists and businessmen now demanded a curb on trade union powers, arguing that workers' wages had been too high during the good times. In face of a continued decline in food prices since 1924, made worse as the economy deflated after 1929, agricultural experts predicted an imminent collapse of the farming sector unless radical measures were taken to increase tariff protection or government subsidies or both. Church and political leaders, and even some trade union bosses, joined forces to protest against so-called *Doppelverdiener*, married women who 'selfishly' remained in work instead of returning to the home and making way for men or single women. Eventually a bill allowing the dismissal of married women in state employment was passed through the Reichstag in May 1932. The expansion of higher education opportunities under Weimar was now accompanied by calls for new solutions to what forecasters suggested might become a 'superfluous generation' of permanently unemployed graduates. Anti-Semitic student groups soon joined the debate, seeking more direct ways of advancing their social position by agitating for restrictions on the number of Jews enrolled on university courses.

In the meantime, left-wingers stepped up their long-running campaign to abolish article 218 of the Reich Penal Code, which outlawed abortion, and in the process presented women's reproductive rights as part of the class war and the struggle to improve ordinary workers' lives. Hoping to influence government policy, a variety of 'non-political' experts also proposed radical new ways of reducing the welfare bill, for instance through a programme of 'voluntary' sterilization of the 'hereditarily ill' (later made compulsory by the Nazis in 1933), the relocation of the long-term urban unemployed to rural land settlements, and the setting up of new labour service schemes for young people out of work. With the partial exception of the campaign against the *Doppelverdiener*, very little of this was indicative of a conservative desire to turn the clock back to the period before 1914. 'Crisis' itself was seen by some as a creative force—not least by the Communists who predicted social revolution and the end of capitalism, and the National Socialists who preached national revolution and a new politics of 'purifying' violence and 'action' instead.

Democratic values were also significantly undermined by the upholders of the system itself. Even before the grand coalition government led by Hermann Müller collapsed on 27 March 1930 after failing to reach a compromise over the future level of unemployment benefits, the centre and centre-right parties in the coalition had planned to form a new minority administration backed by use of the same emergency presidential powers that Hindenburg—following advice from anti-republican elements within his close circle of military and civilian advisors—refused to offer to Müller.[†] The latter's successor as Reich Chancellor, the conservative Catholic Centre Party politician Heinrich Brüning, was determined to push through sweeping reductions in public spending with or without majority backing in the Reichstag. In so doing he allowed himself to become increasingly dependent on the favour of Hindenburg, leading to the *de facto* suspension of parliamentary rule and its replacement by a more authoritarian form of presidential government.

The new political climate played into the hands of the Nazis, who achieved their first significant national breakthrough in the elections of September 1930, called when Hindenburg ordered an early dissolution of the 1928 parliament in a doomed attempt to win some kind of popular mandate for Brüning's budget cuts. By contrast, the Social Democrats, the DNVP and the smaller centre-ground parties had all found themselves, at different times and over different issues, in the awkward position of having to lend tactical support to Brüning's

[†] Under article 48 of the Weimar constitution, the Reich President could declare a state of emergency and/or pass emergency decrees without obtaining the prior approval of the Reichstag, in circumstances where 'public security and order are seriously disturbed or endangered'. Under article 25 the President could also order a dissolution of the Reichstag, provided fresh elections were held within sixty days.

economic measures in the Reichstag, and lost credibility as a result. In fact, the only other party to increase its share of the vote in September 1930, albeit more modestly than the Nazis, was the Communists. Meanwhile, the parliamentary system was brought into further disrepute when Reichstag deputies failed to respect the anti-austerity verdict of the electorate and continued to 'tolerate' Brüning's minority government in the absence of any viable alternatives. When 'toleration' failed in particular instances, Hindenburg simply signed off legislation under article 48 of the constitution, thereby sidestepping the need for parliamentary approval.

In fact, the Reichstag came together on fewer and fewer occasions, with the number of sittings falling from ninety-four in 1930 to forty-two in 1931 and just thirteen in 1932. Political argument now moved away from parliament to the streets, with regular battles taking place between opposing uniformed groups such as the SA, the *Stahlhelm*, the *Reichsbanner*, and the Communist Red Front Fighters' League, especially during elections. Already from March 1930 to March 1931 politically-motivated fighting had claimed the lives of up to 300 people, and in the next twelve months and beyond, the toll was set to rise even higher. Hundreds more were seriously injured. Although the Nazis were sometimes exposed to negative publicity as a result of their clear-cut association with much of this violence, they also gained in equal measure by building on their reputation as the group most willing to take on the much-feared Communists. Membership of the SA stood at 100,000 in January 1931, 290,941 in January 1932 and 445,279 in August 1932, with the *Stahlhelm* now trailing behind, albeit still on around 350,000 members.

Meanwhile, further backstairs manoeuvres brought not just parliament, but the entire Weimar political system to a virtual halt by the summer of 1932. For instance, on 12 May Wilhelm Groener, a senior military general who—although far from being a convinced democrat—had worked successfully with the Social Democrats over the years and had served in both the Müller and Brüning administrations, was forced to resign as Reichswehr Minister after first supporting and then implementing a nationwide ban on the SA. Elements in the army, it seemed, in particular Kurt von Schleicher, state secretary in the Reichswehr Ministry and a key mediator between the military and the political parties, feared that Groener—and by extension

Brüning—were still too wedded to the Versailles system and its disarmament clauses. The Hitler movement was now being sized up as a possible ally in a scheme to rid Germany once and for all of the military shackles imposed in 1919, although professional soldiers were also deeply suspicious of those elements in the SA calling for an incorporation of right-wing paramilitaries into the Reichswehr, and liked to hold on to the pretence that the latter was still an institution dedicated to the 'idea of the state' rather than 'politics'.

Worse was to follow in July 1932, when Franz von Papen—Brüning's highly authoritarian and ultra-conservative successor as Reich Chancellor—ordered an illegal coup against the Social Democrat-led state government in Prussia and had its ministers and senior police chiefs, in particular those held responsible for enforcing the now overturned SA ban, summarily removed from office. This was a highly significant moment, as Prussia had remained one of the key bastions of democratic-constitutional rule in Germany up to that point. Eleven days later the Nazis emerged from the 31 July Reichstag election as the largest party, winning 37.3 per cent of the national vote and 230 seats, an impressive performance but still someway short of an absolute majority. By now the question was not so much whether the Weimar Republic would survive but what would replace it: a Hitler-led government with full presidential powers, a·coalition supported by Hitler and commanding a majority in the Reichstag, or an army-backed dictatorship. As Hindenburg still refused to consider the first option, and as Hitler rejected the second option when offered the post of Vice-Chancellor in a Papen-led administration in August 1932, the result was continued paralysis. The army for its part, responded positively to the Papen cabinet's vocal support for German rearmament, but distanced itself from plans suggested by Schleicher—who had made himself Reichswehr Minister under Papen—to recruit members of the SA into a new government-backed militia with access to unspecified levels of military-style training.

Finally, the Depression worsened an already very deep divide, going back to the period of war and revolution from 1914 to 1919, between the moderate, pro-republican Social Democrats (SPD) and the more left-wing, pro-Bolshevik and (since 1925) pro-Stalin Communists (KPD). Both parties openly proclaimed themselves to be anti-fascist, and between them continued to gain somewhere between

36 per cent and 38 per cent of the national vote in the Reichstag elections of the early 1930s. Representing those workers who still had jobs, and whose real wages actually rose slightly as food and other prices fell under Brüning's deflationary measures, the SPD just about managed to hold on to its position as the principal party of organized labour. However, as the Depression deepened, it lost an increasing number of young, unemployed, and impoverished urban voters to the more radical KPD, which was also able to profit from working-class disillusionment at the SPD's 'toleration' of Brüning.

Neither left-wing party, it seemed, was willing to collaborate with the other in joint opposition to Nazism. The KPD's strict 'class against class' policy, for instance, dated back to resolutions passed by the Communist International at its sixth world congress, held in Moscow in July–August 1928. This led it to condemn the Iron Front (*Eiserne Front*), a new republican defence organization founded by the SPD in December 1931 and backed by the free trade unions, the workers' sports associations, and the *Reichsbanner*, as 'social fascist'. In line with Stalin's thinking on international questions, Iron Front representatives were also denounced as 'henchmen of the German bourgeoisie', 'willing agents of French and Polish imperialism' and harbingers of Germany's systematic slide towards a 'moderate' form of fascism in alliance with the capitalist west. The Iron Front in turn criticized not only the KPD's heavy reliance on the Soviet Union and its crude espousal of Stalinist doctrine, but also the more violent, confrontational tactics deployed by the communist-dominated Red Front in its regular clashes with the SA in towns and cities across Germany. More generally it rejected extremism of both the left and right, and championed the Weimar constitution and the rule of law as the best guarantors of workers' rights. When later challenged to defend the more controversial policy of 'tolerating' Brüning from October 1930 to May 1932 rather than adopting a tough stance against government cuts at a meeting of the Labour and Socialist International (LSI) in Paris in August 1933, the SPD chairman Otto Wels declared: 'To a greater extent than the [social democratic] parties of any other country, we were driven by the force of circumstance ... [and] were forced to choose a policy of the lesser evil ... It was six million unemployed who created the pressure to which we finally succumbed.'

Differences between the social democrat and communist camps in Germany were most evident in early 1932, when the SPD, alongside other centrist parties, backed Hindenburg in the two-round presidential election as the person most likely to defeat Hitler, while the KPD put up its own leader, Ernst Thälmann, as the candidate of the revolutionary working class;[‡] and again in the summer of 1932 when the SA and the Red Front repeatedly attacked each other and the police in violent street battles. Towards the end of 1932 there were, admittedly, signs of greater collaboration between the rival workers' parties in some local-ities, including attempts to forge a 'common proletarian front against fascism'. The counter-factual argument that the Nazis could have been stopped had the SPD and KPD worked together at national level does not hold much water, however, given what Heinrich August Winkler calls the 'unbridgeable' political and ideological differences between them, and given the SPD's determination to hold on to its last bastion of power as head of the state government (and state police) in Prussia, which required them to maintain some kind of modus vivendi with the centre-right 'bourgeois' parties. This was the balancing act that they tried to establish at least until Papen's coup of 20 July (and in fact until sometime after this, as SPD ministers continued to present themselves as the legitimate rulers in Prussia in legal proceedings launched against the Papen government).

Who Supported the Nazis?

The Nazis, as we have seen, did not create the circumstances in which they came to power in 1933, any more than the SPD was responsible for producing the circumstances in which it was unlawfully ousted from the Prussian government in 1932. Nor was Hitler elected into office on a majority vote. However, as well as profiting from a split on the left, when it came to fighting elections in the early 1930s the Nazis were beneficiaries of the almost total collapse of electoral support for the established middle-class Protestant parties which failed to hold on to their voters in face of the catastrophe of the Depression and their own reluctance to advance economic alternatives to Brüning's

---

[‡] The result in the second round was 53.0 per cent for Hindenburg compared to 36.8 per cent for Hitler and 10.2 per cent for Thälmann.

unpopular deflationary course. This was first apparent at national level in September 1930, when both the NSDAP and a variety of right-wing and regionally-based special interest parties benefited from defections from the conservative DNVP and the centre-right DVP (German People's Party); and even more so in July 1932, when previous supporters of the splinter parties also went over in large numbers to the National Socialists.

Much of this reflected a cultural shift away from the established Weimar parties in rural Protestant areas of the north and north west of the country, where voters had long felt ignored by successive governments in Berlin and where even in 1928 support for the DNVP and DVP had slumped, while special interest parties won up to 14.1 per cent. As Richard Bessel has shown, in eastern Germany SA violence also contributed to the mobilization of new support among farmers, farmers' sons, and small businessmen after August 1929. This was particularly noticeable in small towns and rural areas where the Prussian police or left-wing opponents could not easily send in reinforcements if caught in a surprise attack, and also in areas close to the frontier with Poland, where the SA benefited from occasional unofficial cooperation with the Reichswehr's border guard (*Grenzschutz*) units. To the south, in Bavarian Franconia, the Protestant town of Coburg became the first place to elect a majority Nazi local council, in June 1929, but thereafter the most impressive break-throughs in support came at the opposite end of Germany, in Prussian provinces such as Schleswig-Holstein and Pomerania, where already in September 1930 the Nazis were winning 27 per cent and 24.3 per cent of the vote respectively (against a national average of 18.3 per cent), rising to 51.1 per cent and 48 per cent in July 1932 (Map 1.1).

Having initially cornered a reasonable chunk of the rural and provincial lower middle-class vote in the north, and, to a slightly lesser extent, in the east in 1930, by July 1932 the NSDAP had more than doubled the size of its electorate and was well on the way to becoming a *Volkspartei* or people's party, with a mass following among all social classes and in all parts of the country. Comparing the July 1932 result with that of September 1930, how much of this extra nationwide support was down to the success of Nazi propaganda, and how much (still) to the changes in the social and political culture of Weimar Germany since the 1920s identified above, is difficult to say.

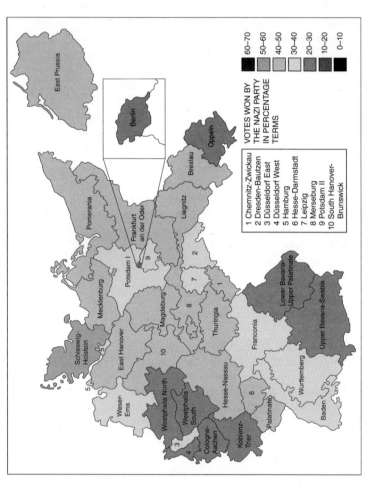

1.1 Regional variations in support for the Nazi Party in the July 1932 Reichstag election. Adapted from http://psephos.adam-carr.net/, accessed 3 March 2017. By permission of Adam Carr.

Confessional and class allegiances certainly remained important in Germany at this time, even if they had been eroded to some extent by the rise of a new class of white-collar workers and by a downwardly-mobile middle class which had lost much of its traditional financial security during the earlier hyper-inflation crisis. In Catholic areas of the south and west of Germany, where the Nazis did notably less well, support for the Centre Party or its Bavarian equivalent, the BVP (Bavarian People's Party) remained strong. Likewise voters from organized working-class communities in industrial regions and big cities tended to stick with the SPD or the KPD. However, as even Marxist historians like Tim Mason concede, the roughly thirteen million regular supporters of the left-wing parties included at best only half of the total number of adults living in proletarian households in Germany. While Catholic wage-earners often supported the Centre Party, the remainder, made up of millions of rural labourers, artisans, craftsmen, small traders, retired and semi-retired war invalids, unemployed veterans, and non-unionized members of the workforce had, similar to the Protestant lower middle classes, much looser ties to established ideologies like Marxism, political Catholicism, or old-fashioned Prussian conservatism.

Members of the (Protestant) upper middle class, the elite tier of doctors, dentists, lawyers, university professors, and so on, also tended to switch allegiance from the DNVP or DVP to the Nazis as the crisis deepened. But whether they, or any of the other new Nazi voters in 1932 were won over completely to National Socialism at this stage remains doubtful. Indeed, in much of the electoral propaganda put out by the NSDAP it was not National Socialism, but Hitler or the 'Hitler movement' that was presented as Germany's 'last hope' for national renewal. The challenge, which Goebbels, as propaganda chief, never quite mastered at this time, was how to broaden the party's electoral base beyond the just over one-third of voters who were willing to lend the National Socialists their support. In the back of his mind, too, were the six million votes which had separated Hitler from the successful candidate Hindenburg in the second round of the presidential elections in April 1932, a bitter blow even as the NSDAP rose to become the largest opposition party—and indeed the largest party—in the Reichstag and in many state parliaments.

Before 1933 radio could not be used for party-political broadcasts in Germany. Rallies and public meetings, combined with the mass distribution of posters and propaganda leaflets, were the main and most effective tools of political communication at election time, and were used extensively by the NSDAP and its opponents. Following Hitler's defeat in the second round of the presidential elections in April 1932, considerably more effort was also put into attracting female voters to the Nazi cause. As Helen Boak has shown, in Protestant regions at least, this strategy was met with some success, as women began to outnumber men among the party's supporters. On the other hand, foreign policy issues were quietly put to one side as unlikely to win the NSDAP any extra votes, particularly after reparations debts were cancelled at the Lausanne conference in June–July 1932.

The most frequent slogans used during the elections of 1932 were the simplest ones: bread and work, followed by respect for mothers and family-centred values, although such themes were also taken up by rival parties such as the SPD, the DVP, and the Centre Party. In fact, what made the Nazis stand out was not the content of their message, but the manner in which they presented it. On 10 May 1932, as historian Winkler notes, the party's organizational leader, Gregor Strasser, openly admitted in the Reichstag that he had stolen some of his ideas for work creation from proposals put forward by the Russian-born social democrat and chief statistician for the free trade unions in Germany Wladimir Woytinski. It was simply the case that his own plans *appeared* more credible than Woytinski's in view of the NSDAP's greater political distance from the Brüning government and the 'system parties'.

At the regional and local levels, the Nazis also became increasingly adept at targeting their message at particular groups of voters, including farmers, artisans, small businessmen, rural workers, factory workers, housewives, teachers, war widows, war veterans, and even lawyers and policemen. In specific milieu where previous political affiliations and loyalties were already thin, or where there was an established tradition of voting for the conservative/nationalist right, the mere presence of a handful of well-organized Nazi activists could be sufficient to ensure victory. This phenomenon was first seen at national level in July 1931, when the relatively small but extremely committed National Socialist Students' League (*Nationalsozialistischer Deutscher*

Studentenbund), which had only been in existence since 1926, succeeded in taking over the General Student Council for Germany and Austria (*Allgemeiner Studentenauschuss*) after a hard-fought election; and it was seen again in provincial towns and farming areas all over northern and eastern Germany, and even in some parts of the south and west, in March–July 1932. Furthermore, it was not just young or first time voters who felt attracted by the 'newness' and dynamism of the Nazi message. Rather, as sophisticated statistical studies conducted by Jürgen Falter in the early 1990s showed, the NSDAP took votes from all other parties, albeit disproportionately more from the right than the left. The average age for Nazi voters, although difficult to gauge with complete certainty, was also probably slightly above the norm for other parties, particularly in rural areas.

Even so, there were still significant weaknesses in Nazi support. Peter Longerich, for instance, has pointed to the NSDAP's relative lack of success in Berlin, in spite of premature boasts by Goebbels that the march towards 'victory' in the Reich capital had already begun in 1927, shortly after his arrival as *Gauleiter*. In fact, the Nazi share of the vote here was persistently lower than the national average, peaking at 28.7 per cent in July 1932. More striking still, in some of the Catholic cities in the Rhine–Ruhr region of western Germany the Nazis still languished in third or fourth place, behind the Centre Party, the Social Democrats, and/or the Communists. Thus in Cologne and Essen they scored only 24 per cent, in Gelsenkirchen only 23 per cent, and in Dortmund a mere 20 per cent. Even in Munich, the 'capital of the movement', the Nazis' share of the vote in July 1932 was 29 per cent, well below the overall national rating of 37.3 per cent and behind their performance in one-time social democratic strongholds in the north such as Bremen, where they clocked up 30 per cent, and Hamburg where they got 33 per cent. Across significant swathes of southern and western Germany, as we have seen, and even in Upper Silesia in the east, the Nazis were unable to outperform the Catholic parties. Small wonder, then, that historians such as Falter have emphasized the ongoing importance of the 'confessional cleavage' in German politics for shaping regional variations in support for the Nazis, with Protestants consistently more likely to vote for the party than Catholics.

Moreover, as both Hitler and Goebbels obviously knew, 37.3 per cent average throughout Germany was not enough to win an outright majority. Even with propaganda focused on Hitler rather than the party as a whole, nearly two-thirds of Germans did *not* vote for the NSDAP. Lack of further momentum could cause the movement to implode, particularly as more impatient putschist elements demanded an immediate seizure of power, while more moderate elements looked at ways of forming alliances with other parties—which purists like Goebbels feared would dilute the Nazis' message (even though he also briefly flirted with the idea of a 'black-brown' coalition with the Centre Party in the middle of 1932). Stuck for anything better to do, and determined to demonstrate the Nazis' radical credentials in opposition to the 'reactionary' DNVP, Goebbels formed a short-lived pact with the local Communists in Berlin in November 1932 in support of a strike directed against the Social Democrat-controlled municipal transport authority. It was not long, however, before the SA and the Red Front returned to their ongoing battles for control of the streets, with the former deliberately targeting the latter in its strong-holds in proletarian neighbourhoods such as Wedding and Neukölln.

The Path to Power

On 6 November 1932, one day before the transport strike finally collapsed in Berlin, fresh Reichstag elections were held. This time, although they remained the largest party, the Nazis lost two million votes and thirty-four seats, partly, Longerich suspects, because of Goebbels' association with the 'reds' (needless to say, the KPD's national share of the vote actually went up from 14.3 per cent to 16.9 per cent, and in Berlin it topped the poll, scoring 31 per cent compared to 23.3 per cent for the Social Democrats and 26 per cent for the Nazis). For the time being Papen was finished. He was replaced as Chancellor on 2 December by his former ally, Kurt von Schleicher, who also held onto his position as Reichswehr Minister. Schleicher had never been a member of any political party, although he had schemed, at different times, with the leaders of nearly all of them, except the Communists. His support in the Reichstag, at least on paper, was zero; if he could persuade the DNVP and a handful of smaller right-wing parties to support him, he might be able to count on the backing of, at most, sixty-five to seventy-five deputies out of a total of 584. Faced with the possibility of a no-confidence vote as soon as parliament re-opened, in reality his best chance of staying in office rested on doing some kind of deal with the National Socialists. The alternative of asking Hindenburg for yet another dissolution of the Reichstag would, even if the President were to agree, give him only sixty days before fresh elections would have to be held.

The Nazis themselves were now exhausted, having fought five major elections in the space of nine months, and several minor ones too. The party's finances were in a sorry state and there were signs that the movement could split into rival factions. In East Prussia and Lower Silesia, party 'moderates' blamed the negative publicity surrounding the SA's regional terror campaigns in the early weeks of August for the marked decline in the NSDAP's fortunes. At national level, significant differences also emerged between Hitler and Strasser over tactics and policy, leading the latter to resign from all his senior party posts in a damaging announcement on 8 December. In the past, historians have linked Strasser's departure from the NSDAP with a supposed design by Schleicher to cobble together a coalition based on support from the trade unions, the Reichswehr and some 'left-wing' Nazis. More recently, however, this idea of a 'cross-party front' (*Querfront*) has been dismissed by scholars such as Longerich and Henry Ashby Turner, Jr as a myth concocted in retrospect by Goebbels, among others. The motive was to damage the reputations of Strasser and Schleicher (who were both murdered by the SS on 30 June 1934 during the so-called 'Night of the Long Knives'), and to underline Hitler's wisdom in holding out for the position of Chancellor.

Yet if Schleicher did not, as it turns out, have any concrete plans with Strasser to split the Nazi movement, he also badly mishandled his relations with Hindenburg, Hitler, and the majority of ministers in his own cabinet. This allowed Papen, once his ally and now his foremost political rival, to negotiate behind his back to have Hitler installed as Chancellor, with himself as Vice-Chancellor. Leading business and landed interests were mobilized behind this potential constellation, or at least were lined up in favour of getting rid of Schleicher, who was now considered to be suspiciously close to the trade unions or too untrustworthy on agrarian issues. However, it would be wrong to suggest that the proposed new Hitler–Papen government was simply a tool of finance capital and the old landowning elites, as some cruder versions of Marxism would have it. Rather, the key decisions were made among Hindenburg's narrow circle of advisors who now saw a chance permanently to exclude the centre and moderate left parties from power through a realignment 'from above' of the forces of the right.

The last obstacle to be overcome was the President himself, who had long resisted the idea of appointing the 'Austrian lance-corporal' to the Chancellorship, declaring in August 1932 that he 'could not answer before God, his conscience and the fatherland if he handed the entire power of government to a single party, and one which was so intolerant towards those with different views'. Even so, Hindenburg was no democrat and if anything, his involuntary reliance on Centre Party and Social Democrat votes to win a majority in the presidential elections of March–April 1932 had strengthened his authoritarian tendencies. Ever conscious of his own public image, he wanted to distance the Presidency from what he now saw as the failed political experiments of the Brüning and Papen eras, and to achieve that, a stable government of the right and far right was deemed necessary. As soon became apparent, Schleicher, the old army intriguer, was incapable of achieving such objectives.

The international constellation at the end of 1932 also seemed to favour a shift towards a new government that would take a firmer stance on rearmament. Although it is important not to exaggerate the extent of Nazi infiltration of the Reichswehr's officer corps—indeed, Hitler was probably right to fear that the army could still be used against him and would shoot if ordered to—there was nonetheless a feeling that a Nazi-led government would be able to realise 'the vast possibilities of rearmament' (F. L. Carsten) that had been precipitated by the League of Nations' failure to deter Japanese military aggression in Manchuria in 1931 on the one hand, and the agreement between Britain, France, and Germany to cancel all outstanding reparations payments at the Lausanne conference in June–July 1932 on the other. The continual failure of the Allied powers to reduce their own armaments spending—a key theme at the World Disarmament Conference which had opened in Geneva—also played into the hands of German negotiators, whose demand for 'equality of rights' in matters of military security was conceded in principle by Britain and France on 11 December 1932. On the negative side, the Reichswehr leadership feared by late January 1933 that any of the alternatives to a Hitler-led government would undermine the advantages to be gained from this modest improvement in Germany's fragile international position, most notably by continuing to divide and demoralize those forces in domestic politics that favoured an active programme of rearmament. Even the chief of the Reichswehr command, General Kurt von Hammerstein-Equord, who had repeatedly warned Hindenburg against Hitler in the past, had come round to the pessimistic belief that another minority Papen government would be an even worse option, as it 'would lead to a general strike, if not to civil war, and thus to a totally undesirable use of the army against the National Socialists as well as against the left'.

Finally, after many secretive, behind-the-scenes negotiations, Hindenburg first dismissed Schleicher on 28 January after refusing his request for a dissolution of the Reichstag, and then appointed Hitler in his place on 30 January 1933. In the run-up to this decision, it was Papen who again took the lead in persuading the elderly president that Hitler could be controlled once in office. In fact, of the eleven cabinet members confirmed in post by Hindenburg on, or shortly after, 30 January, only three were Nazis: Hitler, Wilhelm Frick as Reich Minister of the Interior, and Hermann Göring as Minister without Portfolio and Prussian Minister of the Interior. Werner von Blomberg, a former army commander in East Prussia who was judged by Hindenburg to be 'extremely reliable' and 'completely apolitical', was recalled from his current post advising the German delegation at the World Disarmament Conference and sworn in as Reichswehr Minister several hours before Hitler was named as Chancellor. His instructions were to do 'his duty . . . and keep the Reichswehr out of politics' (Kershaw), a reference to (false) rumours circulating in Berlin that Schleicher had been planning a military coup the night before, but also, for Hindenburg, a means of protecting the Reichswehr from any unwarranted attempts at nazification or political interference by the new government. On the other hand, there was clearly no intention of reversing Papen's illegal coup of July 1932 or of allowing the Social Democrats to return as legitimate rulers in Prussia. Rather, internal policing in this state and, subsequently across the whole of Germany, was now placed in the hands of the National Socialists.

In this way, the scene was set for a domestic reign of terror, targeted in the first instance against the left, while to the outside world a false impression was created of continuity and respectability, not least when Konstantin von Neurath, Foreign Minister under Papen and Schleicher, was re-appointed to the same post. The Finance Minister, Count Lutz Schwerin von Krosigk, and the Transport Minister, Paul von Eltz-Rübenach, had also served in the previous two cabinets, as had Franz Gürtner, who was confirmed as Justice Minister after a brief period of uncertainty. It is true that not all international commentators were sanguine about the new government in Berlin and many suspected foul play when the Reichstag building was burned down in a night-time arson attack at the end of February, an event which the Nazis tried, with some success, to blame on the Communists. But a short time later, on 4 March 1933, the world was distracted by news of events in Vienna, where the Christian Social Chancellor Engelbert Dollfuss closed the Austrian parliament and assumed emergency powers in a bid to crush both the left and the extreme right. Dictatorship, it seemed, was becoming the norm in Europe, whether of the traditional conservative-authoritarian or the outright fascist kind. Democracy everywhere was on the defensive.

The Nazis, by far the most violent and ruthless of the fascist dictators, were unusual in the sense that they did not seize power or win power in an election. Despite subsequent myths depicting a triumphal 'conquest' of Germany, including heroic battles for supremacy in Munich and in famously 'red' citadels like Berlin, Hamburg, and Saxony, they were in fact appointed into office constitutionally and at a time when their popularity was fading. Nonetheless, the circumstances in which they came to power also reflected the failure of Europe's political and military elites to come up with answers to the broader challenges of economic chaos, political instability, military aggression, and insecure borders which had plagued the world since 1914. By the late 1930s, with Hitler's popularity in Germany soaring following the return to full employment, the creation of an air force, the uncontested remilitarization of the Rhineland, and the almost bloodless acquisition of Austria and the Sudetenland, solutions seemed further off than ever.

2

The Nazi 'Seizure of Power'

Hermann Beck

Adolf Hitler became Chancellor of Germany with a presidential Cabinet on Monday, 30 January 1933 at 11:30 a.m. In contrast to its predecessors, this was a coalition government between the National Socialist German Workers Party (NSDAP), and the conservative German National People's Party (DNVP). Ever since March 1930, a small circle of advisors around the aged President Paul von Hindenburg (born October 1847) had been running the Republic through men of their choice on a slim margin of parliamentary support. Hitler's coalition government, however, had well over 40 per cent of deputies behind it, based on the elections of 6 November 1932. Of its ten members, only three—Hitler as Chancellor, Wilhelm Frick as Minister of the Interior, and Hermann Göring as Minister without Portfolio and Prussian Minister of the Interior—belonged to the NSDAP. Others included the German National leader Alfred Hugenberg, the head of the veterans organization *Stahlhelm*, Franz Seldte, and conservatives without party affiliation, such as Foreign Minister Konstantin von Neurath, and Finance Minister Lutz Schwerin von Krosigk, both of whom had already served in their positions in earlier governments. This not only vouchsafed the continuity of conservative forces in the Cabinet, but also highlighted the relative weakness of its three Nazi members, further accentuated by the fact that Hitler could consult Hindenburg only in the presence of Vice Chancellor Franz von Papen, a man who enjoyed the President's full confidence.

It thus seemed to German conservatives that they had been able to engage the National Socialist mass movement for their own purposes, an assessment widely shared abroad, where no immediate sense of foreboding was felt during the first weeks of February. Curiously enough, insouciance even stretched to Hitler's domestic enemies in Germany, who already had greatly suffered at the hands of Nazi organizations in the street fights of the Weimar Republic and thus had reason to know better. Kurt Schumacher, the energetic post-war leader of German Social Democracy, then an up-and-coming 37-year-old deputy, mockingly commented upon Hitler's role in early February: 'Earlier he was a decorator, now he's a piece of decoration. The Cabinet bears his name, but the real power behind it is Alfred Hugenberg. Hitler may talk; Alfred Hugenberg acts.' In the same vein, the Social Democratic newspaper *Vorwärts* published a cartoon depicting Hitler driving a car with eager single-mindedness, unaware that Papen and Hugenberg were determining the car's course in the backseat with a second steering wheel.

All of this served to lessen the sense of imminent danger and directed some of the apprehension that should have sharpened wits against the threat of Nazism toward its conservative allies. Between Nazis and Conservatives not all was well. Even before the Cabinet was sworn in, Hitler's insistence on new elections erupted into a heated argument between him and Hugenberg, who belatedly found out about it; Papen had carefully withheld Hitler's potentially explosive demand from him, rightly fearing that the coalition deal might collapse if Hugenberg rejected new elections. The German National leader was worried that with the authority of government behind it, National Socialism would further increase its strength. The argument between the two party leaders did raise the possibility of a last minute failure of the coalition talks, especially as Hugenberg remained obdurate in spite of Hitler's assurances that the outcome of the elections would not alter the composition of the Cabinet. It was only when Hindenburg's chief of staff, Otto Meissner, burst in on the assembled Cabinet, chastising its members that it would not do to keep the Reich President waiting—it was 11:15 a.m. and the ceremony had been scheduled for 11:00 a.m.—that Hugenberg finally gave way. Hitler had scored a first important victory. Still, what happened on the morning of 30 January was merely a transfer of power. The '*Machtergreifung*', the actual seizure of power, was yet to come. It would take place in the eighteen months between 30 January 1933 and 1 August 1934, when the office of Chancellor of the Reich was fused with that of its President, both henceforth united in Hitler's person. Hindenburg, long ailing, died one day later, on 2 August 1934.

The Dictatorship Takes Shape

The calm of the first days of February 1933 was deceptive. Even though political violence initially did not exceed the level it had reached during the preceding three years, Hitler made it abundantly clear that his government stood for a radical new beginning. In the first public proclamation of his government on 1 February, he accused the administrations of the Weimar Republic of total mismanagement and the destruction of national solidarity, which as he put it, had disintegrated 'into a tangle of egotistic political opinions, economic interests, and ideological antagonisms'. He now vowed to restore the lost national unity. In the opening speech of the campaign for the upcoming elections on 10 February at the Berlin *Sportpalast*, he first alluded to a theme that would become a leitmotif of Nazi propaganda in 1933—his movement's continuity with the great heritage of the German past: 'I know that if today the graves would open, the great minds of the past, who once fought, suffered, and died for Germany, would rise from the dead and fall in line behind us.' These speeches, designed to move the whole nation, were carefully orchestrated events, transmitted by the new medium of radio (of which Weimar governments had not availed themselves), and frequently introduced by Joseph Goebbels, who succeeded in conveying an aura suffused with excitement and a powerful fresh start.

Despite the restrained pace of the first few weeks, the essential instruments to emasculate the opposition were already put in place. On 4 February, the decree on 'The Protection of the German People' permitted bans on newspapers and the disbanding of public meetings that 'abused, or treated with contempt, organs, institutions, and bureaus of leading officials of State', thus authorizing encroachments on the freedoms of press and assembly. The ordinance even made provisions for 'preventive detention' and facilitated the prohibition of newspapers that were inclined to be critical of the measures and methods of the new government. Although bans on newspapers were often lifted after court injunctions, even a temporary stoppage might spell ruin in economically uncertain times. Ironically, this decree had been prepared by Hitler's predecessors in office, who had hoped it would help control a looming civil war.

Prussia, administered by the Reich ever since Papen's *coup d'état* of 20 July 1932, and once a bastion of Weimar democracy—with the Social Democrats, Centre, and the left-liberal German Democratic Party in charge of its governments throughout the Republic—now became the state in which nazification made the greatest headway, with Hermann Göring first as its Interior Minister and then, after 11 April, Prime Minister. Prussia had been Germany's most important state since 1871. Though weakened by territorial losses in West Prussia and Upper Silesia as a result of the Versailles Treaty (1919), it still accounted for 62.5 per cent of Germany's territory and, according to the 1933 census, 61.2 per cent of its population. On 17 February, Göring instructed the Prussian police in unambiguous language to establish close relations with the national organizations *Sturmabteilung* (SA), *Schutzstaffel* (SS), and *Stahlhelm* and to turn a blind eye to their offences, while countering vigorously the actions of the left and resorting freely to the use of firearms. Five days later, Göring's integration of 50,000 storm troopers and *Stahlhelm* members into the police force as 'auxiliary police', fully equipped with pistols and rubber truncheons, became a trend-setting measure, as other German states quickly followed with similar moves of their own. Of all the practical measures adopted in the winter and spring of 1933 to further the Nazi takeover, putting SA thugs into police uniforms was among the most effective. The auxiliary police forces were later gradually disbanded when they had served their purpose—in Prussia in August 1933 and in Bavaria not until the spring of 1934.

The purging of the Prussian administration, particularly among the highest levels of provincial and district governors, had already begun during Papen's chancellorship, when victims were primarily Social Democrats. Göring now continued to oust officeholders from other democratic parties. In February 1933 alone, more than a dozen police commissioners of large Prussian cities, as well as other high officials, were forced into retirement to be replaced by experts close to the new government. This, together with the earlier purge following Papen's 1932 takeover, rendered Prussia's administrative structure unable to resist Nazi measures in March and April.

The decisive legal measure, the decree on 'The Protection of the People and the State', came in the wake of the Reichstag fire during the night of 27–28 February 1933. Regardless of who was ultimately responsible for the fire—the Dutch communist Marinus van der Lubbe, as is generally believed now, or the Nazis themselves, as was widely believed between the 1930s and 1960s—it offered Hitler's government a welcome excuse to declare a state of emergency and the means by which to establish the dictatorship. The 'Reichstag Fire Decree' provided the legal foundation for a crackdown on Communism and the SPD, the establishment of 'protective custody' and concentration camps and the suspension of basic civil rights and liberties—from now on letters could be opened, telephone conversations monitored, meetings dissolved, and suspects detained without a hearing. The decree ordered the death penalty or long-term incarceration for assassination attempts against members of the government, arson in public buildings, incitements to 'severe riot', and armed resistance against the decree. It also authorized the Reich government to take over power in those German states that failed to maintain 'public order and safety'. Unaccompanied by any guidelines that specified how the law was to be applied (the usual legal practice), this unacknowledged basic law of the Third Reich, which remained in place throughout its duration, gave the authorities all the leeway they desired in handling or fabricating suspects.

The fear of communism and an imminent coup attempt, already fanned to fever pitch by Nazis and Conservatives alike, many of whom genuinely believed in the reality of the communist spectre they constantly evoked, now knew no bounds. Göring told the Cabinet on the morning of 28 February that communists intended 'to form terror squads, set public buildings ablaze, poison public kitchens . . . and abduct the wives and children of Cabinet ministers and other exalted persons as hostages'. On 1 March, Vice Chancellor Franz von Papen told the Archbishop of Munich, Cardinal Faulhaber, that communist revolutionaries were intent on 'wearing down the people, setting fires at a hundred places at the same time, burning down farmsteads, tearing up railroad tracks, capturing the children of officials on their way to school and using them as shields during strikes, poisoning food, invading homes, and shooting down doormen and wait staff'. The Cardinal wrote it down and took it all to heart.

Coming as it did five days before the election, this seemingly effective response to what was widely considered as the very real threat of communism led to an enormous boost in public confidence in National Socialism and its ability to deal with the problems confronting the nation. The dramatic change in Germany's political climate occasioned by the Reichstag fire, coupled with the brutal harassment of democratic parties politicians, thus contributed to a significant increase in the Nazi vote.

In the 5 March 1933 elections the NSDAP received 17.277 million votes (43.9 per cent), an increase of 5.54 million votes when compared to the results of the November 1932 election. Voter turnout had risen from 80.6 per cent to 88.8 per cent, translating into an additional 3.9 million votes cast. In the Cabinet meeting of 7 March Hitler mentioned that he considered the outcome of the vote of 5 March as a 'revolution'. Given that his party had never received more than 37.3 per cent of the vote in any of the four national elections in 1932 and even declined in its percentage share from 37.3 to 33.1 per cent between 31 July and 6 November, he had indeed reason to be gratified. Still, 56 per cent of the 39.654 million votes cast were for parties other than the NSDAP and regional differences remained significant: In east Prussia, Pomerania, parts of Silesia and Schleswig-Holstein, for example, the NSDAP received well over 50 per cent, whereas in Berlin, the Catholic regions around Cologne and Aachen, and parts of Westphalia, it received barely 33 per cent. Of a total of 647 deputies elected, the Nazis had 288 (43.9 per cent), the communists eighty-one (12.3 per cent), the SPD remained virtually constant with 120 (18.3 per cent), the Catholic Centre and its more conservative Bavarian offshoot, the Bavarian Peoples Party, held fast with seventy-four (11.2 per cent) and eighteen (2.7 per cent) respectively, while the liberal parties, which had been reduced to marginality earlier on, received fewer than 800,000 votes altogether.

The elections clearly strengthened the Nazi Party vis-à-vis its conservative ally, which, with a little over three million votes and 8 per cent of the total, barely repeated its earlier performance. The DNVP had thus been reduced in comparative importance. The vibrant, dynamic, and energy-exuding NSDAP seemed fully justified in laying claim to the future. Already by the end of March, local DNVP leaders considered merging with their party's more successful coalition partner. The election brought another tangible advantage: since the Communist Party (KPD) was banned and its eighty-one elected deputies either in hiding or incarcerated, the 288 Nazi deputies alone constituted more than half of the 566 deputies left in the Reichstag; together with the fifty-two German National deputies they accounted for 60 per cent.

'Revolution' and Violence

For the next few months after the election, the German Reich found itself embroiled in the Nazis' self-proclaimed 'revolution'. The term was soon used by friend and foe alike—from the expatriate Albert Einstein to leaders of the Protestant Church and Joseph Goebbels himself. Later in the spring, the initial 'national' revolution turned into the 'National Socialist' and finally the 'German' revolution.

A key event on the road to total power was the takeover of those Länder (German states) not yet dominated by the Nazi Party, that is, Hamburg, Bremen, Lübeck, Saxony, Baden, Hesse, Württemberg, and Bavaria. The method was similar everywhere: the Nazi rank and file provoked scuffles and the resulting 'disorder' gave Berlin the opportunity to intervene and send a 'Reich Commissar' to restore order. Groups of burly SS and SA men were ready to engage anyone who stood in their way. Violence, especially widespread during the takeover of Bavaria, acted as the lubricant of the revolutionary engine.

The takeover was facilitated by the fact that the more important state governments—Bavaria, Wurttemberg, Hesse, Saxony, and Hamburg—were acting or caretaker minority governments, and thus in a weak position to defend themselves. While legality was preserved on the surface, many SA detachments went way out of bounds with no legal repercussions. The fight for control of the German states would have been the time for those parts of the opposition who were in a position to fight back to show their mettle. From what is known of some local cases, it appears that the rank and file would have been willing to resist violent intrusions, but the leadership proved loathe to shoulder responsibility for what might have been presented to Hindenburg and the German people as an illegal uprising against the legitimate exertion of state power. To the leaders of the left it seemed self-evident that not only the Reich and Länder bureaucracies, but also the small yet efficient German army and the conservative establishment including Hindenburg, would have supported the Nazi Party in the event of an uprising. Armed resistance, therefore, not only promised little success against numerically stronger and better organized Nazi organizations, it was also likely to be tainted by the odium of high treason (*Hochverrat*) against what, on the surface, was technically a legitimate national government that, to all outward appearances, pursued a legal transition. Apart from the formidable forces of state arrayed against any opposition, the mood of the public also appeared to favour the new masters, whose *élan vital* seemed to brook no resistance. Given the distribution of power, it would thus seem unfair to berate the leftist and democratic opposition for their faint-heartedness.

Another powerful factor militating against armed opposition was the proactive strike carried out by the Prussian police and Nazi organizations immediately following the Reichstag fire. KPD leaders and members were arrested, and trade union, SPD, and *Reichsbanner* (the para-military organization of the Republic) officials often met with the same fate. In the delirious excitement following the fire, amidst a widely-anticipated communist *coup d'état*, a frantic search for illegal weapons was carried out down to the smallest locality, which did much to disarm potential resisters. Throughout the second half of March, April, and May, the terror against the left gathered momentum. Members of leftist organizations formed the bulk of the detainees in 'protective custody' (27,000 on 31 July 1933), those temporarily imprisoned in the extra-judicial 'wild camps' and torture cellars of the SA (roughly 100,000) and murdered political opponents. Regional terror varied depending on the ferocity of the local SA, Nazi Party officials, and heads of police: In March and April 1933 a total of 421 people were taken into 'protective custody' in the three east Prussian governmental districts; the figure was almost ten times as high (3,818) in the Düsseldorf district in the Rhine province. The suppression of the KPD was especially thorough: In Berlin and the Ruhr large parts of the membership were arrested and in Bavarian cities there were mass arrests, whereby entire city blocks were cordoned off and systematically searched. By the summer of 1933 virtually all of Augsburg's active communists had been thrown into prisons and concentration camps. Terror against the left was made public to a far greater extent than terror against other groups, since its authors could count on broad support from the population. The suffering of victims languishing in the torture cellars and prisons of the SA was graphically described by the first head of the Gestapo, Rudolf Diels:

> I was now able to enter the torture chamber with police squads. There the floors of a few empty rooms used by the torturers were covered by straw. The victims we encountered were close to death by starvation. For days they had, in standing position, been locked into narrow closets to extort 'confession'. 'Interrogations' had begun and ended with beatings, whereby a dozen ruffians battered victims with iron bars, rubber truncheons and whips at hourly intervals. The suffering was evidenced by knocked out teeth and broken bones. As we entered, these living skeletons lay there in rows with festering, suppurating wounds on rotting straw. There was not one whose body was not covered from head to foot with blue, yellow, and green bruises that bore witness to the inhuman thrashing visited upon them.

The takeover of the Länder and the waves of violence against the left coincided and overlapped with a settling of accounts with old enemies and political opponents of Nazism. Social and political prominence provided no protection against attacks. Anyone who had fallen foul of the Nazis in the past was now in danger—there were searches in the homes of prominent politicians, such as Siegfried von Kardorff, former Vice President of parliament, and former president Friedrich Ebert's widow, while the SA ransacked Albert Einstein's house, looking for explosives. At the same time, a multitude of infringements rained down upon banks, insurance companies, and private businesses, such as extortion and blackmail of (mostly Jewish) shopkeepers, and disruptions of the economy, such as the forced closure of retail shops and harassment of their owners. The SA threatened to shut down the Berlin Stock Exchange. Mayors and upper-level local officials were forcibly removed from their posts, personally humiliated, and in some cases even physically manhandled. On 10 March, for example, Robert Lehr, the conservative Lord Mayor of Düsseldorf, was assaulted in his office by a gang of SA thugs; one of his municipal counsellors was horse-whipped in his presence.

This did not mean that the whole country descended into chaos and lawlessness. Unbridled SA terror went hand in hand with the continued smooth functioning of the rule of law in other areas of public life. As bad as things were for enemies of the regime, large sections of the middle classes perceived the late winter and spring of 1933 as a less violent period than the last years of the Republic when hundreds were killed and thousands injured. Hitler's German National allies as well as the patriotic majority of Germans endorsed the brutal suppression of the left, often to the point that Nazi terror appeared less as an instrument of suppression than an unconventional but effective means to restore order. While Nazi victims, opponents, and most of the rest of the world viewed the Nazi revolution as a violent, illegal overthrow of a constitutional system accompanied by the destruction of the rule of law, conservative and national-minded Germans defended it as an orderly legal transition of power that had saved the nation from chaos and communist rule.

The wave of anti-Semitic violence between 5 March and the summer of 1933 has largely been overlooked by historical research. Attacks were rampant throughout all of Germany, with regional focal points in Prussia—especially in Berlin and the Rhine province—the large cities in Saxony, Munich, and the Bavarian countryside. The first targets were foreign Jews within Germany, especially the so-called 'Ostjuden'—those who had emigrated from eastern Europe since the late 1870s. Most of the victims were Polish Jews, who accounted for about 60 per cent of foreign Jews living in Germany. Complaints and protest notes from the Polish embassy alone point to hundreds of violent attacks on individuals, raids on pubs, strong-armed robbery, attempts at blackmail, extortion, kidnapping for ransom, and other forms of torment.

Physical assault often combined with robbery was the most common form of attack. To give but one example: On 23 March eight SA men attacked the silk merchant Salomon Rosenstrauch in his shop in Wiesbaden, severely beat him up, destroyed his expensive furnishings, and demanded that his shop be closed immediately or else they would return and kill him. When Rosenstrauch, who had suffered severe injuries and several broken ribs, reopened his shop a few weeks later, it became clear that the attackers had been earnest about their threat. On 22 April two men forced their way in Rosenstrauch's apartment and killed him. Other forms of violent attack included armed robbery, forcible annulments of debt, destruction of property or produce, and diverse rituals of humiliation, such as attacks on synagogues by SA men in auxiliary police uniform, whereby furnishings and equipment were destroyed and worshippers had their beards cut off and were compelled to sing nationalist songs. Those unwilling to join in were beaten with truncheons.

Attacks on non-German Jews are relatively well-documented, since victims could at least file complaints with their embassies and consulates. Given the high numbers of recorded cases, it is realistic to assume that there were well over 1,000 violent attacks between early March and the summer of 1933. Few of the attacks are recorded, since the police mostly refused to log them. According to embassy reports, victims often feared reporting the crimes, anticipating that they might be beaten by storm troopers in auxiliary police uniform. Law enforcement officials, in any case, often failed to appear where alerted; victims were told 'that it was not part of police duties to protect Jews', or 'that foreigners had no right to police protection'.

The situation was different with German Jews. Here the estimated number of unknown cases was higher, since attacks, assaults, and instances of intimidation or extortion remained unknown unless victims succeeded in reporting the attacker to the police and getting protection. In the case of murder, the public prosecutor's office was compelled to launch an investigation. Yet, even when the killers were known, no sentences were passed in 1933 since offenders were released under the amnesty of 25 July 1933 for 'Crimes Committed during the National Socialist Revolution'. The spectrum of crime was even greater with German Jews. The nationwide boycott of 1 April of Jewish shops, lawyers, and doctors, though unpopular with the German population in general, was only the tip of the iceberg. In many localities they continued for weeks after 1 April 1933. During the summer of 1933 numerous local prohibitions against buying in Jewish shops for civil servants and NSDAP members were passed. Those who violated the prohibitions risked being branded—the names of buyers were reprinted in local papers or posted on town hall bulletin boards.

Another widely practised but little known category of anti-Semitic crime was the abduction of Jewish businessmen, doctors, and other professionals, coupled with severe maltreatment and threats of murder. Victims were assaulted, kidnapped, and often held for days in the torture cellars of the SA. They were then released under the condition that they leave Germany immediately or else risk being murdered. The objective was to expel them from Germany. A case in point is that of the Berlin neurologist Dr Fritz Fränkel who was arrested by a group of SA men in his surgery in the Berlin Kaiserallee on 23 March, taken to an SA torture cellar, severely maltreated, and finally released under the condition that he leave Germany immediately. With his wife and his infant child he fled to Switzerland, where he sent a detailed report of his suffering to the German embassy in Bern.

A largely forgotten form of insidious violence that was common in 1933 is the so-called *Prangermarsch* (pillory march) and 'pillorying' in its various forms. As with its medieval prototype this had the function of questioning the victim's honour while parading him or her in a humiliating way throughout town. The relentless dragging of all those things that had once been private into the public realm was the hallmark of the beginning dictatorship and a means of suppressing dissent. This very public branding served two purposes: it was a means to socially discredit those who fell foul of the regime's political codes, making them pariahs in their own communities, and it served to enforce consent to its goals. Branding of a different kind can be found in newspaper articles in which the names, addresses, and professions of citizens who had close friendships with Jews were listed for everyone to see, turning it into cause for public shaming.

Finally there were the frequent murders. There is no data as to their precise number. Estimates are unreliable since they are based solely on word of mouth, hearsay, or extrapolation. No authority or agency, German administrative body, or foreign correspondent had documentation on the total number (or even an accurate estimation) of Jews murdered in the initial phase of the *Machtergreifung*. German authorities were not interested in finding out the truth. They played down reports of anti-Semitic crimes, identifying them with 'atrocity propaganda', thus equating them with the alleged calumnies of Allied propaganda in World War I and casting aspersions on their authenticity.

Nazi attacks were not confined to Jews and members of the left. National Socialist (NS) organizations also targeted the members of their own coalition partner, the conservative DNVP. In March and April 1933 German National mayors were forcibly replaced by SA leaders, Nazi organizations frequently uttered threats of physical violence against their conservative allies, and numerous pitched battles were fought between the SA and German National paramilitary organizations, in which conservatives—usually hopelessly outnumbered—came off worse, and suffered appalling injuries such as knocked-out teeth, head wounds, and the occasional bullet wound. Even prominent conservative politicians were not spared. Paul Rüffer, leader of the German National Workers Movement, was knocked down and narrowly escaped being thrown down a flight of stairs. Psychologically, these attacks made sense, since the average storm trooper was filled with festering resentment for upper-class conservatives. During the spring of 1933 the National Socialist movement presented itself as a revolutionary, social egalitarian movement bent on abolishing privileges and levelling society, determined to reward merit over birth, break down barriers in the educational system, and blaze the trail for the deserving farm boy or young worker. Attempts were made to destroy existing hierarchies: A complaints office was set up in the Osnabrück law courts, for example, where lower and middle ranking officials, who frequently had Nazi sympathies, could lodge complaints against higher-ups, who were often close to the DNVP.

The National Socialist aversion to the conservative establishment had a distinct ideological component to it. This expressed itself in newspaper articles, speeches, and tracts directed against the established *Bürgertum* (bourgeoisie). Germany's bourgeoisie was depicted as indecisive, responsible for the great catastrophe of 1918 (since its members failed to fight the leftist revolution), and accountable for the perpetuation of a class-ridden society permeated by social conceit, thereby depriving the nation of the loyalty of millions of its best working people who, alienated, had drifted into the camp of international socialism. National Socialists, by contrast, portrayed their movement as all-inclusive. What was needed for the future, they argued, was the creation of a 'New Man' of National Socialism to make sure that the achievements of their revolution would endure. This New Man, free of class conceit and imbued with superior values—altruism, concern for the greater good, 'character', honesty, 'stature', and, supreme irony, 'readiness to lend succour to others'—would in time supersede the *Bürger*. In practice, few concrete measures were implemented, but the egalitarian tone that dominated National Socialist discourse and propaganda during the first half of 1933 could not fail to leave its mark on the popular perception of the regime. This egalitarian appeal accounted for a good deal of its newly-found popularity.

The Allure

Apart from fear-inducing violence that stifled potential opposition and brought doubters into line, the regime also had its attractions, factors generally perceived as positive by patriotic Germans of all classes that promised a distinct improvement over life in the Republic. First, there was for many the certainty that the nation had been rescued from the mortal danger of communism, a threat that seemed real enough at the time. Less than fifteen years earlier, hundreds of thousands of Russian refugees had flooded into Germany on their way across Europe with horrific tales of the cruelties and atrocities of communist rule, now permanently embodied by the unknown colossus in the east. In November 1932, nearly six million Germans had voted for the Communist Party, then the third strongest party in the Reichstag. The widespread misery of depression Germany, with its aura of despondent poverty, resigned suffering, and an unemployment rate close to 40 per cent, provided a convincing background to that fear.

Then there was the invigorating feeling of a newly-forged *Volksgemeinschaft*, a national community reminiscent of the spirit of domestic solidarity in August 1914, when ranks had closed against a sea of enemies. As Protestant bishop Otto Dibelius, no supporter of the regime, said on the occasion of his 4 April radio address to an American audience: 'Today the German Reich is united and firmly joined together as never before in our history.' Newly gained strength and self-confidence flowed from that knowledge and National Socialism was credited with bringing it about. The movement and its leader also got credit for revitalizing the nation and fortifying it with a determination to confront, if necessary, its western wartime antagonists, a determination conspicuously found wanting in the governments of the Weimar Republic. The early propaganda of the regime shrewdly emphasized the creation of an internally united and rejuvenated nation, an element that later accelerated the breakup and demise of Germany's political parties, driven by the argument that multiple political parties were but an obstacle on the road toward a united national will.

In causal connection with the drive toward single-party rule, it was widely appreciated that Germany again had a strong national government that would put an end to the perceived sellout of German national interests. Heinrich von Rendtorff, the Protestant bishop of Mecklenburg, captured this widespread feeling in a meeting of church leaders at the end of April when he spoke with relief about finally having an '*Obrigkeit*' again in Germany—a term that connotes a strong and decisive government, for which the German population should be grateful and whose occasional revolutionary 'excesses' should be overlooked.

No single event made the regime more acceptable to conservative and national-minded Germans than the so-called Day of Potsdam on 21 March 1933. At this symbolic place of Prussian military and political traditions, National Socialism succeeded through clever stage management to place itself in a line of continuity with the Prussian past. The vigorous new movement insinuated itself seamlessly into the Prussian heritage. During this day of wreath-laying (Hindenburg at the sepulchre of Frederick the Great), military parades (of Reichswehr, SA, SS, and *Stahlhelm*) and church services (filled with men in uniform), all meant to signify a turning away from the 'spirit of Weimar' toward a revitalized 'spirit of Potsdam'. The occasion was the formal opening of the Reichstag and the day itself was chosen to coincide with the meeting of Imperial Germany's first parliament on 21 March 1871.

The grandiose spectacle was attended by most of the deputies of the newly-elected Reichstag (except for communists and social democrats), the military leadership, the former Crown Prince (a stately arm chair was left empty for the Emperor), the diplomatic corps, the Nazi leadership, and Hitler, who, in a conspicuously civilian tailcoat, deferentially paid homage to the old Field Marshal. The latter embodied the qualities conjured up by the event—simplicity, sobriety, decency, and order. At Potsdam, National Socialists gave the impression of being domesticated, apparently justifying the old elites' calculation that the attempt to tame Hitler had come off successfully after all. The leadership of the Protestant Church was especially impressed: time and again it was stressed in internal memoranda that the Day of Potsdam had been the crucial event in convincing them that National Socialism would, on the whole, have a beneficial effect on Germany's future.

The widespread enthusiasm generated by the events in Potsdam blazed the trail for the introduction of the constitution-changing Enabling Act (23 March), which required a two-thirds parliamentary majority and would give Hitler's government the authority to pass legislation and conclude treaties with foreign states without consulting the Reichstag, Reichsrat (state house), or the President during its four-year duration. Nothing came of a last-minute attempt to add an amendment that would guarantee civic and political freedoms and thus lessen the powers Hitler was about to receive. The affirmative votes of the Centre, Bavarian Peoples Party, and the two liberal parties, along with those of the NSDAP and DNVP, assured the smooth passage of the bill; all ninety-four SPD deputies present (more than twenty had been arrested or fled the country) voted against it. The hundreds of threatening, jeering, and leering storm troopers in and outside Berlin's Kroll Opera House (directly across from the burned-out Reichstag building), where the deputies assembled, provided a climate suffused with threat and coercion despite the presence of foreign diplomats.

Why did some of the parties opposed to National Socialism vote for the Enabling Act? Deputies of the Centre and liberal parties later justified their affirmative votes by arguing that non-acceptance would only have led to further Nazi violence and bloodshed. A powerful factor that prompted the deputies of the Catholic Centre and liberal parties to vote for the bill was a popular mood during the second half of March that practically demanded acceptance. The Enabling Act, after all, merely gave official sanction to an already extant political reality since 'the party revolution from below' had already revolutionized power at the top. Immediately after World War II, when people still remembered the passionate fervour of the spring of 1933, a few Centre and liberal deputies owned up to the intangible pressure exerted by the *vox populi* and frankly declared that 'people had grown tired of bickering among the parties in the Reichstag'. They had never been criticized for voting for the Enabling Act, they argued; in fact had never before 'experienced such ostentatious manifestations of consent'.

Hitler's declaration during the discussion of the Enabling Act that he intended to respect the position of the Churches and that he saw in Christianity 'the unshakable foundation of the ethical and moral life of our people' reinforced the consolidation of his regime. On 28 March the Catholic bishops announced, in what amounted to a sea change in their earlier position, that their former warnings and prohibitions against the National Socialist movement were no longer necessary. The month ended with the 'Preliminary Law for the Co-Ordination of the Länder with the Reich', according to which the respective strength of political parties in state parliaments was reproportioned to correspond to the 5 March Reich election results. Now the coalition governing in Berlin was dominant everywhere. On 7 April, the law was supplemented by the *Reichsstatthaltergesetz*, stipulating the appointment of Reich governors whose task it would be to bring the policies of the Länder in line with those of the central government, thus annulling the century-old rights and prerogatives of the states with the stroke of a pen and with them the federal principle so deeply engrained in German history. Federalism was buried for good on the first anniversary of Hitler's succession to the chancellorship with the 'Law on the Re-Construction of the Reich', which did away completely with the state parliaments. Länder sovereignty was transferred to the Reich, while the Länder themselves were demoted to mere administrative units, comparable to (though larger than) French *départements*. From now to the end of the Third Reich, Germany would remain a tightly centralized state. This did not preclude, however, the development of administrative chaos and overlapping competencies of the civilian, party, and, in time, SS bureaucracies.

In many ways, March was thus the decisive month. After 5 March, National Socialism triumphed all along the line—with the takeover of the Länder, the suppression of the left, the Day of Potsdam, and finally the Enabling Act. March also saw a crucial change in the attitude of the population toward the regime. While some remained petrified by fear and believed that resistance was futile, the majority now seemed genuinely enthusiastic about the promise of a better future in a more egalitarian society, a feeling that Fritz Stern once termed 'the temptation of National Socialism'. Temptation is an apt concept since, on some occasions, especially in the display of unbridled violence against German and foreign Jews and the brutal suppression of the left, Hitler and his movement already permitted a glimpse of the dangers of that promise and a foreshadowing of what was in store for Germany and Europe.

Boycott, Censorship, and *Gleichschaltung*

Anti-Semitic attacks in Germany had triggered protests in the western press, interpellations in the British House of Lords, demonstrations in Great Britain and the United States, and protests by the Archbishop of Canterbury. The ongoing anti-Semitic outrages led to boycotts of German goods in the spring of 1933, as a result of which German exports declined sharply. In a letter of 4 May to their Chamber of Commerce, Hamburg merchants painted a grim picture of the effect of the boycott on German goods: all of Northern Africa, Syria/Palestine, South Africa, Spain, and east central Europe, from Poland to Czechoslovakia and Romania, were influenced by anti-German agitation, as were France, Belgium, Great Britain, and the United States. In many places, German travelling salesmen were no longer received and German goods were turned back. In July, German tourism statistics showed that by comparison to 1931, Germany had lost virtually half of its foreign tourists. It was clear that the country had forfeited much of the trust and reputation that Weimar governments and Gustav Stresemann's foreign policy had so painstakingly built up.

In response to foreign reactions, Hitler decided to hold German Jews responsible for the protests abroad by staging a nationwide boycott. Contrary to the assessment of contemporaries and later historians, 1 April and the days preceding it remained far from quiet. Archival files list numerous cases of abduction, victims forced to emigrate under threat to life and limb, extortions, beatings, and other forms of humiliation. At home, foreign protests met with an almost united domestic front—a closing of the ranks not unlike that in 1914. German authorities and Nazi politicians, led by Hermann Göring, vehemently denied allegations of abuse and claimed that the 'revolution' had been conducted in an exemplary fashion. Even organizations whose members could still speak freely, such as the Protestant Church with its nearly forty million adherents, supported the government, claiming that foreign criticism was just another anti-German campaign, reminiscent of the fabrications of World War I propaganda. The equation of foreign criticism with the 'horror propaganda' of World War I also dominated the reporting of the completely censored German press. In the above-mentioned radio address to an

American audience on 4 April, the eminent Protestant bishop Otto Dibelius, a non-Nazi, who later courageously defied the regime, portrayed the boycott as a purely defensive measure: Yes, he conceded, transgressions had taken place, but the regime had saved Germany from Bolshevism and, based on false reports, 'the Jewish community worldwide has now begun a campaign against Germany in several countries'. Dibelius was not the only conservative leader in whom opposition to Nazism coincided with a deeply-felt anti-Semitism.

Anti-Semitic attacks, which continued into the spring and only gradually abated during the summer, were followed by a series of anti-Semitic laws passed in April. German Jews were first excluded from the civil service through an 'Aryan clause' (that discounted anyone with one Jewish grandparent), then banned from practising law and serving as judges and public prosecutors at law courts. Jewish doctors were banned from health insurance organizations which, for those concerned, might well spell economic doom. On 25 April rigid quotas for Jewish university and *Gymnasium* students were introduced, a restriction that could make it impossible to obtain the *Abitur*, Germany's prerequisite for attending university. Due to Hindenburg's intervention, legislation was modified to grant a temporary reprieve for all those German Jews who had actively participated on Germany's side in World War I, whose sons or fathers had been killed in action, and those who already held office on 1 August 1914. Contrary to National Socialist claims that German Jews had eschewed frontline service, the fact that more than 60 per cent of Jewish lawyers remained in place testified to their active wartime service for Germany.

Reactions to anti-Jewish violence, the boycott, and the April legislation were an ominous foreboding. Those German parties that had hitherto taken up the cause of the Jewish minority of 568,000 (according to the 1925 census figures) were all fully preoccupied with their own problems—the left-liberal German Democratic Party (DDP) and the SPD, for example, had either been reduced to insignificance or undergone internal changes, as was the case with the DDP when it turned into the Staatspartei. In the spring of 1933, the SPD fought for its very physical survival. Thus, no help could be expected from them. Hitler's coalition partner, the DNVP, had more room for manoeuvre and freedom of expression than others, but with its own past tinged with anti-Semitism, little succour was likely to be forthcoming from them either. Germany's army had only a few dozen Jewish officers and men in its ranks and army leaders professed little interest in the issue. When interviewed after the war about what they did not like about National Socialism, only two of the many dozens of senior generals mentioned 'racial issues'. The army's leading political men, Minister of War Werner von Blomberg and his chief of staff Walter von Reichenau, anxiously tried to establish good relations and curry favour with the regime, since it promised to offer the army more than any of the Weimar governments. In June, Blomberg declared before senior officers that the Aryan clause could not be disregarded by the army, on 7 August members of the Reichswehr were prohibited from marrying 'non-Aryans', and in February 1934 the Aryan clause was introduced into the Reichswehr.

The Reich and state bureaucracies were all too familiar with anti-Semitic attacks since foreign embassies and consulates continually submitted complaints from foreign Jewish nationals who had been attacked by SA thugs. Officials in the Interior Ministry in Berlin and the ministries of the different states were thus well aware of what was going on. Their inter-departmental correspondence rendered it evident that when officials found themselves in a conflict between prescribed national solidarity with the perpetrators and their own sense of right and wrong, *raison d'état* prevailed. In their reports to foreign diplomatic missions, officials belittled attacks, falsified the truth, and found excuses and extenuating circumstances for the attackers—everything was done to explain, 'interpret', and rationalize the attacks. To diminish the crimes, victims were incriminated with invented 'offences'—a Wuppertal dentist and a Wiesbaden dairy merchant had been murdered because they were allegedly 'communists', an affluent Polish merchant had been beaten up because he was 'a known communist', another victim because he called out that 'all Germans are pigs', an unlikely statement by one person surrounded by half a dozen armed storm troopers. When other excuses were exhausted, reports occasionally state that the attack had taken place 'at the time of greatest national excitement'. In short, victims of anti-Semitic attacks could expect no assistance from the bureaucracy. Readers of the bureaucrats' reports are left with the impression that responsibility for the attacks lay with the victims.

On the day before the boycott, Adolf Bertram, Catholic Archbishop of Breslau and *primus inter pares* among Germany's five archbishops, asked his peers whether an interpolation with the government would be opportune. Bertram made it obvious that he himself did not think so: Such a step could be considered 'interference in a field that does not concern the Church'; it might not be successful anyway, he averred, and could actually harm the Church, since it could not be kept confidential 'and would certainly meet with the worst possible interpretation all over Germany'. And finally, had not in the past, 'the largely Jewish-dominated press consistently observed silence when Catholics in different countries were persecuted?' Faced with such manifest doubts as to the advisability of an appeal to the government, the other archbishops fell into line and the Catholic Church remained silent.

In its reaction, the Protestant Church went one step further, denying that a significant number of attacks had taken place and actually countenancing the legal measures. In a meeting of Church leaders of 26 April that dealt with the issue, it was stressed that Jews had completely monopolized certain professions, so that Church officials found themselves unable to oppose 'a legal solution to the problem'. The head of the highest executive committee of the Protestant Church, Hermann Kapler, maintained that in view of the advances of the Jews since 1918, the state was 'justified and obligated' to resort to protective measures. There was also an obvious contentment with the national government and fear of alienating the new masters, so that prudence alone mandated silence.

The leadership of political parties, the army, bureaucracy, and the Churches knew quite well what was happening. Their reactions were shaped by a mixture of indifference among Reichswehr generals, caution, fear, and blatant anti-Semitism in the case of the Churches, and willing complicity with the bureaucracy, a blend of motivations that was characteristic of large sections of German society in 1933.

In addition to censorship of the press, which began with the decree of 4 February, a stranglehold on public and semi-public utterances was imposed from early on. Two days before the March Enabling Act, Hindenburg signed the 'Perfidy Ordinance', (sometimes also called

'Malicious Gossip') according to which 'assertions grossly distorting the truth' that were likely to denigrate 'the welfare of the Reich or the standing of the government or the National Socialist Party or its organizations' could be punished with a two-year prison sentence. The open-ended wording of the decree permitted any sort of interpretation. The mentioning of simple facts, if there was even a hint of criticism of the regime, could be prosecuted. The decree was thus an effective instrument of repression since now even harmless political conversations could have fateful consequences. In 1933 alone, 3,744 violations of the decree were prosecuted before special courts, so that they could not be appealed. Since even 'non-public malicious utterances' could be punished, the perfidy ordinance brought out the very worst in people. It fostered denunciations, sowed mistrust, forced an unnatural secrecy and discretion on everyone, and thus erected barriers in interpersonal relations that survived long after the demise of the dictatorship. Life in Nazi Germany was constantly permeated by an apprehensive fear of having said one word too many.

In the highly-charged atmosphere of the spring of 1933, in which most conversations were *per se* political, the ordinance also put a damper on social intercourse and changed sociability patterns. Those privy to conversations might well feel compelled for reasons of self-protection to report 'comments potentially harmful to the state', since silence might indicate complicity. In his study of the small northern town of Northeim, William S. Allen mentions the case of a doctor, Kuno Ruhmann, who, at an evening party after one drink too many, entertained the assembled guests by imitating Hitler's way of speaking. The next morning, his hostess reported him to the Nazi headquarters of the town. As Allen writes, word of this spread quickly and social life was cut down enormously as people realized that they couldn't trust anyone anymore.

The malleable interpretation of the decree also provided authorities with the opportunity to target groups hostile to the regime, such as communists, social democrats, and Jews. It is striking to see that Jews are punished more severely than non-Jews for the same infractions. The elderly Jewish shopkeeper Minna Bloch from a village near Kehl in southern Germany was sentenced to a six-month term of imprisonment for having told her cleaning woman (in May 1933) that she could not understand why Hitler treated Jews so badly, particularly since he himself had a Jewish background. Despite Bloch's weak heart, her generally ailing condition, and the fact that her brother had died fighting for Germany in World War I, the public prosecutor rejected any pleas for leniency. In the same vein, the livestock dealer Meier Buchheim from Frankenberg in Hesse ran into trouble in April 1933. He had mentioned in a conversation with his shoemaker that 'various Jews had been hanged in the Rheinpfalz' (Rhenish Palatinate). Since there had been numerous violent anti-Semitic attacks in the area around Worms, Buchheim's assertion was consistent with the facts. That he had fought for Germany in World War I and had even been wounded was mentioned as a mitigating circumstance but did not alter the severe sentence of eight months imprisonment. In the opinion of the court, Buchheim's contention had damaged 'the welfare of the Reich' since it implied that 'there is currently a state of lawlessness in the German Reich and the authorities fail to take steps against it'.

Non-Jewish defendants fared better. When charges were pressed against the unemployed Protestant interior decorator Wilhelm Dietz, who had related stories about attacks on Jews in the Giessen area, including pillory marches and other humiliating iniquities, he was treated with leniency. Though even his wife confirmed that the substance of the charges was true, he was acquitted. And Katharina Wolff, a tailoress from Frankfurt who, in her hair salon in June 1933, recounted a story that in Munich a Jew had been killed and another greatly injured, that the Reichstag had been set ablaze by the Nazis themselves, and other remarks that were no credit to the regime, she got off with a relatively mild four-month sentence.

Göring, who had become Prime Minister of Prussia on 11 April, passed a decree against the so-called *Miesmachertum* (pessimistic mood caused by alarmists, grumblers, and gripers) on 22 June tailored specifically to officials and employees working in ministries and other branches of the bureaucracy. Declarations of dissatisfaction, defeatism, and despair about the government's measures were henceforth to be treated as 'a continuation of Marxist agitation', and complainers considered Marxist enemies of the regime and handled accordingly. Conversely, civil servants, especially those of the upper echelons, were to be educated to act in accordance with National Socialist principles, as Interior Minister Frick decreed on 15 July.

At the same time, literature and fiction were censored with similarly ruthless thoroughness as oral statements. On 10 May, surrounded by the sound of patriotic melodies and military marches, books were burned in Berlin and in other university cities. This demonstration against an 'un-German spirit' was preceded by a cleansing of public and lending libraries. In the days and weeks after the book burning, more contemporary authors were added to the list of the unwanted and banned. For fear that their books would no longer be sold in the Reich, some writers held back on their criticism of the regime— Thomas Mann waited until 1936.

The authors of the books that were consigned to the flames had allegedly offended the 'German spirit'. Under that category fell anything that might outrage standards of conventional morality, belittle Germany's great men, besmear the heroic memory of the Great War by a realistic depiction of combat in all of its squalor and misery, or betray a sceptical, searching approach to German history and politics that was deemed to jeopardize the very fibre of German strength and marshal vigour. Offending authors included socialists such as Karl Kautsky, Heinrich Mann, and Kurt Tucholsky, as well as the bestselling writer of biographies Emil Ludwig, the novelist Erich-Maria Remarque, the prominent editor-in-chief of the Berliner *Tageblattt*, Theodor Wolff, the critic Alfred Kerr, and Sigmund Freud. Many of these critical, scrutinizing, and satirical voices were Jewish.

Soon book-burning and censorship would turn into self-censorship as outlawed books, to be saved from prying eyes, would be moved to the second row of bookcases behind authors tolerated by the regime. And again for reasons of self-preservation, people quickly manufactured individualized pairs of scissors in their heads to screen and expurgate their spoken and written words for, as historians have demonstrated, unsolicited denunciations were plentiful.

The centrepiece of the NS revolution was the *Gleichschaltung*, literally coordination, the bringing into line and marching in step of all organizations of society from trade unions, professional associations, artisan guilds, and civil service organizations, down to retail merchants' associations, and sports and leisure clubs. In the end, even right-wing student fencing societies were prohibited. Following the conciliatory gesture of elevating the Day of Labour, 1 May, into a national holiday, trade unions were banned on 2 May and, together with white collar unions, eventually forced to join a newly created German Labour Front. Professional groups were absorbed into existing National Socialist organizations, such as the NS Doctors' League, and where no previous NS organizations existed, party members were always certain to constitute a majority on executive boards, taking over leadership. In the northern German town of Northeim, as everywhere else in the Reich, clubs and associations that served a similar function, such as sports activities, were combined and amalgamated. In Northeim, for example, more than a dozen sports clubs were reduced to one.

Social and hobby clubs, such as choral societies, often reflected the class structure of a town, as there existed singing societies for workers, the middle class, and the upper crust. Breaking up the multitude of these clubs and fusing them together was also an attack on Germany's class-ridden society, as bourgeois clubs were forced to jettison their exclusive nature, and served the welcome purpose of lessening social distinctions. In the new Germany social standing should be of no importance—a loudly proclaimed goal of all Nazi organizations in the spring of 1933. As a result of 'coordination', by the summer of 1933 independent social groups of all kinds, even chess clubs and philatelist societies, had ceased to exist. Whenever people now gathered in associations, societies, and organizations, party members would also be present. From the government's point of view, this did not just mean eliminating opportunities for spreading discontent, for Germans could now no longer join together in the public sphere, it also facilitated control and the monitoring of the population and provided a framework for indoctrination, as the frequent 'instruction evenings' of professional and other organizations would soon illustrate.

From there it was but a small step to force citizens into a kind of popular endorsement through their membership in what were now essentially Nazi organizations. Membership in the new Nazi groups, whether merchant guilds or professional associations, was not always mandatory, though insidious social pressure to demonstrate that one was a good 'people's comrade' made it difficult to remain aloof, especially when economic survival was at stake. Once this vast process of social restructuring that was underway between March and the late summer of 1933 had been accomplished, the potential for any kind of organized resistance was stamped out. In the propaganda of the regime, this signified the newly-won national unity and vigour of a cohesive nation that now spoke with one voice.

The End of Revolution

A mere five months after his accession to the chancellorship, Hitler declared on 6 July 1933 that revolution should not be a permanent state and would gradually shift into an 'evolution'. This announcement was made to put a stop to 'revolutionary' meddling of the SA in banks, private businesses, and administrative offices. On 14 July the 'Law against the Formation of (Political) Parties' legalized the one-party state. All other parties had been banned or dissolved themselves between 22 June and 5 July. Together with a bundle of related legislations designed to strengthen the regime, such as legalizing the loss of citizenship, confiscating the property of putative and real enemies of the regime, and making the 'Heil Hitler' greeting mandatory for Germany's more than two million civil servants, these measures brought the first successful phase of the Nazi takeover to an end.

In July, with Hitler and his government having reached a first high point in popularity, everything seemed to go the Nazis' way; even the Churches seemed likely to come to heel. On 20 July any potential resistance of the Catholic Church was neutralized by a Concordat between the Reich and the Vatican, whereby the regime promised to guarantee the integrity of Catholic cultural and charitable organizations, the free exercise of the Catholic religion, and the freedom of confession of faith. The Vatican, in return, undertook that the Church would refrain from any kind of political involvement. Three days later, Hitler's candidate for the office of head of the German Protestant Churches, Ludwig Müller, scored a victory in Church elections on that day and was elected leader of the yet to be created united Protestant Reich Church. Although uniting the Protestant Churches proved elusive—by the end of the year Hitler's plan of creating a Reich-wide united Protestant Church had palpably failed—the election signalled another astonishing success for Hitler, so that by midsummer 1933, domestic opposition seemed fully subdued.

Democratic government had been abolished and the political left, as well as other Nazi opponents, so successfully repressed that even conservatives were careful not to publicly oppose Nazi measures. All independent organizations in society had either been dissolved or 'brought into line' with the prevailing political current. The century-old federalism that characterized German-speaking central Europe since the days of the Reformation had given way to a centralized state governed from the centre in Berlin. The institutions of the past, democratic or otherwise, had been swept away, dismantled, and discarded with eagerness and enthusiasm in a high mood of national frenzy and excitement that had not been observed since the early days of August 1914. But as in 1914, so in 1933 the feeling was one of deep-seated high hopes that turned out to have no anchor in reality. By the autumn of that year national fervour and passion would give way to a widespread popular hangover. Still, the 'temptation' of National Socialism ran deep: in June 1933 even Thomas Mann speculated about the 'possibly correct core of the German movement', and the Social Democratic leader Julius Leber, later to be executed by the regime, mused about 'the great experiment' of National Socialism 'to relieve millions of Germans of their existential anxiety' (*Lebensangst*). Most intellectuals agreeable to the regime elected to stay in the country, among them actors and directors such as Gustav Gründgens, Heinrich George, and Emil Jannings, well-known names in music, such as Richard Strauss and Wilhelm Furtwängler, the playwright Gerhart Hauptmann, and the philosopher Martin Heidegger. Not all were equally enthusiastic about the new creed, in some instances the flirtation with Nazism was of short duration (for Heidegger and Carl Schmitt, for example), and all misjudged the compromises and humiliations they would have to swallow by aligning themselves with a fundamentally anti-intellectual movement. But they decided to remain, though they were prominent enough to make emigration a viable option.

Those who had to leave included the cream of Germany's scientific elite. As Hans-Ulrich Thamer once pointed out, before 1933 a dozen Nobel prize winners lived in Berlin-Dahlem on a square mile around the institutes of the Kaiser Wilhelm Gesellschaft; a year later Germany had suffered a brain drain from which the country never recovered. Almost a quarter of all émigrés came from universities and research institutes, among them Germany's famous Jewish scientists, such as Albert Einstein, Fritz Haber, James Franck, Max Born, and Otto Stern. In addition, émigrés included many of the most creative minds among German social scientists and scholars in the humanities. Though a few would return from their (mostly American) exile after World War II, with their departure the pre-eminence German universities had enjoyed since the 1830s would be lost forever. By the end of the year, the country with the highest literacy rate among industrialized nations and the greatest per capita newspaper density—in 1932 Germany published 4,703 daily and weekly newspapers, more than any other country—had lost more than one-third of its newspapers. In many ways already the very beginning of Hitler's rule spelled the end of German traditions.

Once the hyperactivity and exhilarating anticipation of the revolutionary months had passed with high hopes for decisive change unfulfilled, disillusionment set in on a large scale. This was often due to economic factors: increases in the price of foodstuffs had not been matched with corresponding wage increases; after the first wave of successes in short-term work creation programmes, often in construction, the first setback came during the winter of 1933/4 when building activity ground to a halt and lingering fears of unemployment were rekindled. In the winter and early spring of 1934 the employment situation seemed to stagnate, though through upbeat and unceasing propaganda campaigns and obligatory conscription in 'labour service' the regime did its best to assure everyone that employment remained foremost on its agenda. Owners of small artisan shops were unhappy that contrary to earlier promises, the government had failed to close down department stores; farmers smarted under constraints imposed on them by the *Reichserbhofgesetz*. Passed at the end of September 1933, this law decreed that farmsteads between 7.5 and 125 hectares had to be passed on undivided to the next heir and could not be mortgaged, severely curtailing the economic freedom and movement of farmers. Not only craftsmen, workers, and farmers had reason to be discontented—housewives complained of poor supplies of many foodstuffs, from meats to milk products. Reasons for bottlenecks in provisioning the population with necessary supplies were often seen in the conflicting, ill-advised, and disruptive interference of National Socialist organizations in the economy. Economic discontent thus had a distinctly political edge to it.

Stillborn Second Revolution and Consolidation

Disillusionment was strongest where expectations had been highest: in the ranks of the Nazi storm troopers—the SA. With the proclaimed end of the revolution in July 1933, the SA had lost its function. During the summer and fall of 1933, SA leaders were removed from positions they had commandeered in banks, insurance companies, and administrative offices, often under the guise of 'special commissars' or 'special plenipotentiaries'. At the end of the most successful year in the history of the National Socialist movement, the average SA storm trooper was thus often left empty-handed with nothing to show for the sacrifices of the 'years of struggle'.

The NSDAP had been closed to newcomers on 1 May after experiencing an unprecedented influx of about 1.7 million new members, many of whom discovered in the eventful months of March and April 1933 that in their heart of hearts they had been National Socialists all along. The SA, by contrast, remained open, pushing its numbers beyond the three million mark in the early months of 1934. In their ranks the revolutionary egalitarianism and vociferous anti-capitalism that had pervaded the whole movement in the spring of 1933 continued to live on. It was coupled with rowdy and boisterous talk of a 'second revolution' that seemed all the more aggressive and genuine because of the real frustration and betrayed hopes that lay at its root. In the spring of 1934, threats of a 'second revolution' appeared dangerous, especially when they coincided with existing popular discontent and a precarious international situation. Senior Reichswehr officers were concerned about SA leader Ernst Röhm's professed plan to create a brown militia based on the SA and to submerge 'the grey rock of the Reichswehr in the brown flood'. Hitler, who vehemently opposed Röhm's plans as he needed the professional army's expertise and technical know-how for his own foreign policy goals, made it known early on that any attempts at a second revolution would be 'drowned in blood'.

Matters finally came to a head when the simmering discontent of the SA was joined by open criticism originating from within Papen's Vice Chancellory, long known as the 'Reich Complaints Office'. The disparagement with which Papen attacked the government in a speech at Marburg University on 17 June 1934 finally propelled a hitherto reluctant Hitler into action: together with Reinhart Heydrich and Heinrich Himmler of the SS, and Röhm's old antagonists in the party leadership, Hermann Göring and Joseph Goebbels, and aided by logistical support and the general collusion of the army leadership, Hitler prepared the final crackdown. Röhm, who had been expelled by the Reich Association of German Officers on 25 June, should not have been surprised. On the morning of Saturday, 30 June, he was arrested by an irate Hitler accompanied by armed police and SS men. In the course of the next few days, Röhm and dozens of other SA leaders were fusilladed. While at it, Hitler took the opportunity to rid himself of old enemies, such as the Bavarian state commissar Gustav von Kahr, who had crossed him in November 1923 over the Beer Hall Putsch, his former second-in-command Gregor Strasser, his predecessor in the chancellor's office, Kurt von Schleicher, and Schleicher's close aide, General von Bredow (Schleicher and Strasser had allegedly joined Röhm in a conspiracy against the state). At the same time the conservative opposition around Papen was eliminated: Edgar Jung, who had written Papen's speech, Erich Klausner, who contributed to it, and Herbert von Bose, Papen's chief of staff, were all shot, while Papen himself was first placed under house arrest and then sent to Austria as special envoy and later ambassador. A law of 3 July 1934 legalized the action against Röhm as *Staatsnotwehr*—the state acting in self-defence. Close to a hundred people had been killed in what is often referred to as the 'Night of the Long Knives'. On this occasion Hitler revealed himself to fit precisely the playwright Berthold Brecht's depiction of him—the head of a gang of bandits.

The double pre-emptive strike against the threat of a second revolution coming from the SA and criticism from the conservative camp strengthened the NS regime. Hitler willingly shouldered all responsibility for the execution of Röhm and other SA leaders as 'the German people's highest arbitrator', well knowing that the action against the SA would meet with the overwhelming approval of large sections of the population who had long smarted under the lawless conduct of the storm troopers. While the killing of Jung, Klausner, and others not directly involved was condemned by the public, neither the army (which was implicated in the purge and profited from it) nor the Churches protested. On 1 August, the offices of chancellor and president were joined together, on 2 August, a long ailing Hindenburg passed away, and on the same day the army took an oath to the person of Hitler, whose authority as 'Führer and Reich Chancellor' was now fully institutionalized. On 19 August 1934 a plebiscite with an affirmative vote of close to 90 per cent endorsed the political changes. The regime had passed through its initial precarious phase and was now firmly ensconced in power.

3

Elections, Plebiscites, and Festivals

Hedwig Richter and Ralph Jessen

What a festival, what a spectacle it was, when the Nazis organized the elections of spring 1936 as a spectacular occasion. On Sunday, 29 March the whole of Germany seemed to be out and about, cheering, celebrating and yes—also voting. During the day, two Zeppelins flew over the Reich dropping leaflets: 'Vote for the Führer'. At dawn, 'coming from the East', they arrived in the Rhineland, whose militarization a few weeks earlier the nation was supposed to legitimize by means of these elections. A radio reporter on board described the flight over the 'old imperial city' of Aachen and over Cologne, where national flags attached to parachutes sailed to the ground. Down below, at the 'Deutsches Eck' monument in Koblenz, young people formed a cross in a circle symbolizing the vote for Hitler. Then came Frankfurt and on went the journey over 'a stretch of Autobahn, which cuts through the landscape like a white ribbon'. On board the airships the mood was relaxed and the crew voted: everything was done in accordance with the regulations and the law. An electoral commission was sworn in with a handshake; there was a voting booth and a ballot box to ensure secrecy: 'For the first time in the history of air travel voting has taken place between the earth and the sky.'

The towns blazed in a sea of flags in black, white, and red; on the following day, the newspapers described torchlight processions, singsongs, fireworks, and demonstrations. 'Every available band in the Reich kept Berlin and other centers in constant uproar', wrote an American journalist. In Berlin, cheering people gathered in front of the Reich Chancellery throughout the day. 'The whole of Germany is united in joy', noted Goebbels and the newspapers reported: 'The sun shone on a festive day for Germans.' Although everybody had reckoned on a 95 per cent turnout, the numbers of those who had marked a cross on the ballot paper against 'Reichstag for Freedom and Peace. National Socialist German Workers Party' still caused astonishment. With a turnout rate of 99 per cent, according to official figures 98.8 per cent had placed their cross against what was the only choice on the paper. Only half a million voters had not done so.

The Nazi bigwigs could hardly get over their good fortune: 'The nation has risen up', noted Goebbels in his diary. 'The Führer has united the nation. We didn't expect this in our wildest dreams. We are all dazed.' The leading Nazis were all undoubtedly exhausted. In the course of a frenetic election campaign they had bombarded the country with propaganda for peace and praise for the German militarization of the Rhineland. Foreign countries were also fascinated. The *New York Times* described the election festivities in numerous articles and, in particular, drew attention to the Zeppelins: 'It would have been hard for the government to have found a more fitting symbol of the pride of a sovereign and powerful people than the spectacle of those two great airships.'

Why did the Nazis hold these elections? Did not elections fundamentally contradict the dictatorial 'leadership principle' and the claim to total power? Why did they take the risk inherent in elections, even when held under dictatorial conditions? A total of four Reichstag elections and five plebiscites took place after Hitler's seizure of power in January 1933. The reason seems obvious. The Nazis used elections for propaganda purposes in a very similar way to their use of mass festivals: as pomp and spectacle for the people, in order to mobilize them, but also as a performative message to foreign observers. Like the Nazis' mass festivities they were elaborate rituals and liturgies that served to create an exalted atmosphere, lifting people out of their everyday existence.

Nevertheless, the fact that the Nazis specifically selected elections for their propaganda still requires explanation. There are some grounds for thinking that the potency of these events lay in their function of providing a comprehensive form of legitimation that would be recognized worldwide. In the age of the masses and in the age of democracy the participation and support of the 'people' represented not only an indispensable but also an unbeatable form of legitimation. How could opponents justify their opposition if—apparently—they had the overwhelming majority against them? What arguments could Great Britain, France, or the League of Nations make against Adolf Hitler if 'his people' were behind him and joining him in declaring their peaceful intentions? The Nazis really did want the vote of every voter and the success of the NSDAP cannot be understood without recognizing the effectiveness of the party's role in mobilizing voters. And it would be a mistake to attribute its victories primarily to fraud and manipulation, though they certainly happened, or to the propaganda machine. The electoral system of the Weimar Republic had remained largely intact, so that the methods for ensuring secrecy (uniform ballot papers, voting booths and ballot boxes), which worldwide had come to be regarded as prerequisites for a legitimate election, remained officially in force.

The 'Law concerning the Plebiscite' of 14 July 1933, which provided the Nazi regime with a powerful political instrument, was also not simply a new invention of the Nazi dictatorship. Article 73 of the Weimar Constitution had already envisaged an important role for plebiscites. However, the 'Leader state' had largely eliminated the mechanisms of 'checks and balances'. Whereas under Weimar the people or parliament could initiate a referendum, under the new law of July 1933 only 'the government' had this right. Moreover, in the Nazi state plebiscites could be used to suspend the constitution or parliamentary decrees much more easily than under the Weimar Republic.

The plebiscites and elections in the 'Third Reich' are often overlooked because nowadays the logic of 'democratic legitimacy' within a dictatorship no longer seems to make sense. We see the period after World War I against the background of precarious democracies that were threatened, and in some cases destroyed, by fascism. However, it was not only in Great Britain, France, or in the United States that democracy, in the sense of a wide participation by the people, was recognized as an age-old tradition. The Nazis did all they could to exploit the potential of this tradition for providing legitimacy. Also the executive of the Social Democratic Party in exile noted in 1936 about democratic traditions in Germany: 'it is a great and intelligent nation, [...] which, after all, has experienced extensive self-government for over 100 years [...] The new rulers are clever enough to recognize that they must provide some sort of substitute for it.'

The Nazi regime was not the inventor of elections controlled from above; they had existed in Italy and South America since the 1920s. The decisive factor for these 'Dictatorial Democracies'—to which from 1937 onwards the Soviet Union also belonged—was the performative support of the 'people'. Thus it is clear that elections are not only a formal procedure, but also always a symbolic act. They always serve not only to elect a person to an office, but also to define the role of the electorate and to underline the legitimacy of the social order. In every election the silent participation of the electorate in this ritual demonstrates its consent to the existing political order.

In order to explore the specifically 'democratic' and 'plebiscitary' logic of the legitimation of Nazi rule, the elections and the festivals will now be examined in more detail.

Participatory Traditions in the Dictatorship

The Nazis made no bones about the fact that they considered themselves to be the only true democrats. In their hostility to parliamentary democracy they were part of the international mainstream. This was true not only of the totalitarian states but also of countries with long-standing parliamentary traditions, where criticism of parliaments was also fashionable. Nevertheless, in the twentieth century, parliaments, just like elections, could not simply be abolished. In fact, once they had come to power, the Nazis were not aiming merely at getting rid of parliaments and elections in accordance with their strident pre-1933 demands. Rather, they eliminated democracy's liberal and competitive elements, removing from it all the 'checks and balances', the protections for minorities, the dual chamber system, and its commitment to the constitution. Their vision was a form of 'popular rule' in a kind of radicalized version of Rousseau's theory of consensus. In doing so, the Nazi regime was exploiting the dark side of democracy. For, alongside the enlightened rule of the free and the equal, democracy also always contains its obverse, namely the possibility of demagogy, populism, and a tyranny of the majority. 'I have not abolished democracy' announced Hitler in a 1936 election speech, 'but instead I have simplified it, in that I have declared that I am responsible not to 47 parties but to the German people.'

Typically, Nazism did not produce a coherent theory of the import-ance of elections and plebiscites. The assessment of voting changed not only in the course of Nazi rule but also varied depending on the individuals and agencies concerned. Thus, at least a section of the power elite assumed that the elections of March 1933 would be the last—an indication that there was no plan but that the regime impro-vised from election to election. The leading 'Third Reich' legal theorists produced philosophical justifications for the participatory legitimation of the 'leader state': Carl Schmitt, who had considered the Weimar elections 'decadent' and had advocated the total abolition of 'all remnants of the previous voting nonsense', denied that any elections after the take-over of power had the character of parliamen-tary elections. Even the Reichstag election of 5 March 1933 had been 'in reality, in jurisprudential terms', a referendum, a 'plebiscite through which the German people [had recognized] Adolf Hitler as political leader'. In 1939, the legal expert, Ernst Rudolf Huber, declared: 'Asking people to vote is intended to strengthen the Führer's position vis-à-vis the outside world and to be a clear demonstration of national unity. However, it is the Führer who continues to incorporate the true will of the nation.' Hitler was not, therefore, bound by the results of the votes. The official weekly legal journal stated: 'The appeal to the people demonstrates that the German leader state is the true form of democracy, which now contrasts with the multi-party parliamentary state which dominates the rest of the world.' A state-ment from a government source underlined the importance of elec-tions, declaring that the nation should 'not be simply providing a comment' but rather the people's decision represented a 'legal act'.

In all circumstances, however, the state had to be based on the 'will of the people'. Carl Schmitt even stated as one of the 'accepted and fundamental national socialist principles': 'The Reich government recognizes the will of the people, which it has consulted, as authori-tative.' According to Ernst Rudolf Huber, only in national socialism could the will of the people—through the Führer—be 'revealed in a pure and unadulterated form'. However, he also emphasized that the 'leader state' was not a democracy in the conventional sense: 'The German state [...] is an ethnic nationalist [*völkisch*] Führer state in which political unity is embodied in the people, while the will of the nation is formulated by the Führer.'

The Nazis kept speaking of 'true democracy', 'improved democracy' (Goebbels), 'better' and 'simpler democracy' (Hitler), or of 'genuine democracy'. During the 1934 plebiscite, the Interior Minister, Wilhelm Frick, asked: 'Where in the world is there a country that is ruled so democratically as Germany?' Hitler liked boasting, above all in the presence of foreigners, of the '40 million Germans', who stood 'united behind him'; he was not prepared 'to take any action without having reassured himself of the people's trust'. In August 1934 he told foreign correspondents: 'Every year I take the opportunity to submit my authority to the approval of the German people. [. . .] We barbaric Germans are better democrats than other nations.' The official justification for the 'Plebiscite Law' of 14 July 1933, which was designed to facilitate the 'consultation of the people', stated that this was simply a procedure based 'on old Teutonic legal forms'.

The fact that this was all about demonstrating the masses' consent to the Nazi leadership was further shown by the changes to the elections that occurred during the years of Nazi rule and not least the extensive manipulation of the voting procedure. All the parties were permitted to take part in the Reichstag election of 5 March 1933. Although the opposition parties and in particular the Communist Party and the SPD were subjected to brutal pressure, with many of their candidates having already been arrested and suffered torture, the Nazis still only secured 43 per cent of the vote. The following Reichstag election of 12 November 1933 was designed to be an acclamation. Since the other parties had been banned, the only alternative open to voters was either to vote for the NSDAP or to spoil their ballot paper. The nation was expected to show the whole world that it was saying 'yes' to the Führer's policies. In 1934 the Germans gave their retrospective approval to the Führer's take-over of the office of president. The Saar plebiscite of 13 January 1935, ordained by the Versailles treaty, was a plebiscite for the Saar population to choose whether they wished to join France or Germany or to retain the status quo. On 7 March 1936, the vote for the second one-party parliament was linked to a plebiscite on the remilitarization of the Rhineland, for only one cross was allowed on the ballot paper to cover both issues. The result was that the Reichstag election effectively became a plebiscite. Thus, according to the writer, Werner Beumelburg, 'our trip to the ballot box [. . .] is not an election or a ballot, but rather a serious, solemn, and indissoluble commitment to the destiny that we serve and to the man to whom this destiny has been entrusted'. The Nazis regarded the election of 10 April 1938 in the same light, with the voters having to vote on the 'reintegration of Austria with the German Reich' and also for the 'list of our Führer, Adolf Hitler', although on this occasion there was the option of 'no' on the ballot paper.

Reichstag elections, then, were not abolished but transformed into acclamations and, by the same token, parliament was retained. Evidently Hitler recognized how useful the legitimation provided by this institution could be. When, at the end of February 1933, the Reichstag building was set on fire and destroyed, probably by a single individual, Hitler insisted not only that the building should be retained (against the advice of his star architect, Albert Speer), but that it should even be extended. For a number of reasons the renovation work only began in 1938; the war, however, soon put an end to it. In an interview before the November 1933 election Goebbels noted two factors that explain the Reichstag's 'continuing importance': first, the government needed an authoritative body representing the whole nation, which could support it in issuing legislation; and second, the 'Führer' needed an institution with which to demonstrate 'to the world the unity of people and state'. Significantly, the traditions of the Reichstag were utilized in order to increase this propaganda effect. The symbolic importance of its continuing existence, should, therefore, not be underestimated, even if effectively it functioned primarily as a stage for Hitler's appearances or for the unanimous approval of particularly symbolic laws. After the passing of the 'Enabling Law' of 24 March 1933 the Reichstag met only nineteen times and passed only seven laws prior to its final session on 24 April 1942.

Parliament played a central role when, on 'Potsdam Day', 21 March 1933, the Nazis staked a claim to all the Reich's sources of legitimacy. For this occasion involved more than a solemn handshake between the 'Third Reich' and the Kaiser's Reich, embodied by Hindenburg wearing the uniform of a field-marshal of the old Reich, or the symbolic gesture of holding the ceremony in the town of Potsdam; there was also the ceremonial opening of the Reichstag elected on 5 March. For 21 March was the date in 1871 on which the first ever Reichstag had opened. It had been elected under one of the most modern electoral laws of its time, including universal male suffrage for those aged over 24, and, despite all their criticism of parliaments and parties, had acquired a traditional status that Germans held dear. Not surprisingly, therefore, Nazis also appreciated the prestige attached to a seat in parliament. The most important officials in the party, the SA or the SS, acquired a seat more or less automatically; other Nazi bigwigs such as Albert Speer or Fritz Todt tried in vain to get one.

The Nazi regime exploited the participatory tradition in other areas as well. In 1939, for example, the anniversary of the 'seizure of power' was celebrated with a speech by Hitler to the Reichstag. According to Goebbels the 'main theme' was 'that Germany would forever remain a Führer republic. No more monarchies!' In his speech Hitler spoke a great deal about famous figures of the past, praised Germany's peaceful intentions, and attacked the Jewish population. He considered the most important source of legitimacy to be the 'German people'. He repeatedly talked about the 'national community' and he reminded his audience of President Wilson's fourteen-point programme with its 'fundamental sentence about national self-determination'. The other states, Hitler stated, had denied this right to 'the highly cultivated German people', a right which he, Hitler, had now won back. The 'Führer' reminded the deputies of their 'sacred and eternal duty': 'You are not the representatives of a specific area or of a particular regional group; you are not the representatives of particular interests; first and foremost, you are the elected representatives of the whole German nation.'

At the same time, in his speech to the Reichstag Hitler made clear his rejection of 'alien democracy' such as had existed in Germany before 1933. The 'so-called great democracies' (elsewhere in his speech he called them 'capitalist democracies') ought to ask themselves the question: 'In the final analysis is a regime that has 99 per cent of its population behind it not a completely different democracy from those states which can often only maintain themselves in power by using the most dubious methods of electoral fraud?' 'How do they have the nerve to try and force something on us, which, as far as popular rule is concerned, we already possess in a far more transparent and superior form?' What that form of 'popular rule' by the Reichstag actually meant could be seen in the responses of the deputies whose parliamentary activity was limited to greeting every sarcastic remark of the Führer's with 'hilarity' and every threatening gesture with 'a storm of applause'.

Electoral Techniques

A mere act of acclamation was insufficient to sustain the fiction of democracy. This was shown among other things by the electoral system that the Nazis adopted. They wanted a form of legitimacy that was internationally recognized and for that they needed an electoral system that appeared to meet international standards.

Thus, according to the law, Nazi elections were 'universal'; in 1933 and 1934 even Jewish citizens were allowed to vote. In 1933 Interior Minister Frick reprimanded a local party leader to the effect that the exclusion of Jews from the electoral lists was 'against the law' and strictly forbidden. However, the fact that the Central Association for Jews recommended to its members that they vote 'yes' in the November 1933 election indicates the degree of pressure that was already being applied. It was not until the Reich Citizenship Law of 1935, one of the Nuremberg laws, that Jews were deprived of the vote, although 'Jewish Mischlinge' ['half' and 'quarter' Jews] were allowed to retain it. Significantly, the rights of 'Reich citizens' were defined above all in terms of their right to vote: 'The right to exercise the vote in political matters is restricted to Reich citizens as the possessors of full "political rights"' and 'a Jew cannot be a Reich citizen. He does not have the right to vote in political matters.'

Concentration camp prisoners were allowed to vote, at least in the first elections, and, thanks to the secrecy imposed, were able to express their opposition. After the election of November 1933 a concentration camp commandant complained: 'The result shows that around a third of all prisoners in protective custody have not understood or will not understand what it's now all about. Unfortunately, we can't find out the names of the incorrigible ones.' In Heuberg concentration camp in the Swabian Alps around half the prisoners who voted in November 1933 refused to support the Nazi regime.

To the great annoyance of the Nazi rank and file and, despite all their demands that the 'traitors to the fatherland' should be publicly stigmatized, the government stuck to electoral secrecy and in 1933 declared that 'the harassment' of voters should be prevented by 'all means', a statement that was widely circulated through the press. In another statement Interior Minister Frick ordered that 'electoral freedom and voting secrecy [were to be] maintained at all costs'. There was one case in which the electoral commission actually declared that the results in a polling centre were invalid because secrecy had not been maintained.

Nevertheless, there were repeated cases of manipulation and fraud and non- and no-voters were repeatedly subjected to political terror by the Nazis. There were individual reports that, inside the polling stations, which were covered in swastikas and portraits of Hitler, party members marked the ballots of those considered 'unreliable', or more or less blatantly kept the voting booths under observation. The demonstrative avoidance of the use of the polling booths by fanatical Hitler supporters also contributed towards undermining electoral secrecy. And, when counting the votes, many election committees ignored 'no' votes so that they could report the result expected by the regime. However, there is much to be said for the view that, if one excludes the 1936 election, fraud and manipulation were not so prevalent as to fundamentally distort the results. This has been repeatedly confirmed by regional studies of the procedure of actual elections and by the records of private individuals. 'Voting itself was undoubtedly secret', reported the British ambassador of the autumn 1933 elections, and the *New York Times* reported after the elections in April 1938: 'As noted by neutral observers watching the ballots being taken out of the envelopes, the vote did in truth run better than 97 per cent or 98 per cent for Hitler and the Anschluss.' The, for the Nazis, relatively disappointing, results of the plebiscite on the presidency of August 1934 also point to the relative freedom of the election: Despite their total domination of the election and the political pressure they imposed, the Nazis 'only' received 90 per cent of the votes. That means that substantially more than seven million of those entitled to vote did not choose to do so or voted 'no'. On the day after the plebiscite, the political leadership was in a sombre mood as they joined Hitler and tried to work out 'what had gone wrong'. For the next election in 1936 the regime had learned its lesson, ordering that all ballot papers that were not marked with a cross against the only choice of 'yes' should, nevertheless, be counted as 'yes' votes. This was probably the most glaring example of the Nazis' electoral fraud—if one ignores the fact that none of these elections offered people a choice.

The reason for the Nazis' inhibitions about indulging in electoral fraud was the fear that this would delegitimize the elections. They had no illusions about that. The transformation of the 'no' votes into 'yes' votes during the 1936 election was in fact severely criticized by the foreign press, as was the fact that it was impossible to give a 'no' vote. The Nazis corrected this in 1938: the ballot papers once more offered the option of a 'no' vote and ballot papers that were blank or marked incorrectly were no longer counted as 'yes' votes.

Thus, all in all, elections could make a remarkable impact. The Jewish Romance scholar, Viktor Klemperer, for example, considered the plebiscite of November 1933 a definite triumph for Hitler: 'I too', he wrote, 'am beginning to believe in Hitler's power and that he's here to stay.' Following these elections the Social Democrats too had 'to overcome a deep depression', according to their committee in exile. The Nazis regarded it as crucial that the election results should have the desired effect abroad. After the election of March 1933, for example, in its election analysis *The Times* in London joined in the jubilation: 'There has never been any public feeling in England against the union of Austria and Germany, nor is it in itself the slightest bar to an understanding between Grossbritannien and Grossdeutschland.' After the Reichstag election of 1938 the *New York Times* commented: 'Adolf Hitler's Germanic empire received its baptism of ballots yesterday when nearly 50,000,000 voters in the new Reich gave silent affirmation to the annexation of Austria.' Even after the vote on the presidency in 1934, in which the Nazis had been disappointed by the numerous 'no' votes and abstentions, the *New York Times* spelled out the reality of the situation: 'Adolf Hitler is the Führer of the Reich with absolute power by the vote of almost 90 per cent of the Germans in it.' And even when, in 1936, there was criticism from abroad about the invalid ballots being counted as 'yes' votes, a correspondent from the *New York Times* played it down: 'That Hitler won an overwhelming election victory despite this confusion is beyond doubt.' In the case of the plebiscite on the Anschluss in 1938 the reporter of the *New York Times* was unimpressed by doubts and criticism. Whatever was being said by foreigners about an allegedly pointless plebiscite on an issue that had already been decided (the Anschluss with Austria) the vote was 'a tribute to Hitler no less than a fervid profession of national and racial solidarity'. With the exception of the March 1933 elections the foreign correspondents barely mentioned the terror used against the opposition.

Mobilization and Modernity

The propaganda machine was relentless in its ruthless drive to dominate the public mind. Members of the Hitler Youth, students, ordinary party members—all were mobilized. The preparations for elections went on for weeks beforehand and in the final hours before the vote feverish attempts were made to engage the population: flags were hung out on public buildings and churches; meetings of the Nazi factory cell organization were held at people's places of work; final arrangements were made to enable German expatriates to vote on ships; there were torchlight processions by male voters, mass choirs, and church bells were rung on the evening before the vote. The regime used every technical means to demonstrate its modernity and euphoric belief in progress, from Zeppelins in the sky to loudspeakers in underground stations broadcasting Hitler's speeches. In Berlin, on election day itself, masses of people surged around, shouting themselves hoarse, calling for Hitler; and, throughout the country, Germans got together to hear the election results being broadcast on the radio, booing news of 'no' votes. In Vienna in 1938 thousands of euphoric citizens marched along the Ring singing patriotic songs such as: the Horst-Wessel Song and the Deutschland Song, and shouting: 'We want to see our Führer!' In rural areas brass bands serenaded the countryside. During the 1933 elections, people flocked to church services. In some rural areas SA men were considered especially pious and their brown uniforms stood out among the churchgoers. When the election results were declared, all over the country the announcement read: 'Record victory: the number of votes as follows.'

The Nazis' anti-elitist, anti-patriarchal, and modern propaganda, their rhetorical appeal to the workers, and their tough behaviour appealed to sections of the population who had felt marginalized under the Weimar Republic and were happy to participate in this mood of protest. Above all, youth was attracted—the SA was a young man's scene. Through their comprehensive social mobilization the Nazis enabled many people to rise in the world, humiliating old notables in the process. They had Socialist ministers and Jewish millionaires hounded through the streets or subjected to mockery in their socks and underwear. The Germans profited from the regime's lust for plunder, enriching themselves at the expense of fellow citizens who had been murdered. In some respects the much trumpeted unity of people and regime proved to be true and found remarkable symbolic expression in the elections. On the 1933 ballot paper the state used the familiar you (*du*) form and, with echoes of the marriage vow, the question on the paper asked: 'Do you German man and you German woman approve the policies of your Reich government, and are you willing to declare that they express your own views and your own wishes and to solemnly commit yourself to them?'

Despite the Nazis' penchant for male forms of spectacle and male bonding activities and rituals, there is much evidence to show that they specifically intended to appeal to both genders: 'German women and men!' The Nazis definitely did not want women to be confined to the kitchen. On the contrary, in the course of the 1920s the NSDAP had come to recognize how important it was for a mass party to win the support of women and to keep it. Many electoral appeals were, therefore, specifically directed at women. During the elections of November 1933, 'in order to avoid misconceptions' the Nazis even felt obliged to issue a clarification 'that, in the Reichstag election and plebiscite of 12 November, as with all previous elections, women have the same right to vote as men'.

In order to demonstrate the unity of people and leader the mobilization had to be total. In the early hours of election day, often when it was still dark, boys from the Hitler Youth and BDM girls marched noisily through the streets, blowing trumpets and banging drums to remind Germans of their 'duty'. In Berlin's working-class districts long queues built up even before the polling stations had opened. During the 1934 election, almost every second person qualified to vote had already voted by 11 o'clock. Since the aim was to make a bigger and bigger impression, this Sunday morning electoral sport became ever more elaborate. During the elections for the Anschluss in 1938, SA men, Nazi motor and air units, fire brigades, and whoever else could be organized and was capable of making a loud noise went around waking people up. In some places, 80 per cent had already voted by midday. Party members used cars to ferry the old and the frail to the polling stations; special polling stations were set up in hospitals. Those citizens who had failed to vote were subjected to repeated visits and reminded of their 'duty'.

The function of elections to mobilize support was aimed particularly at the party members. They were kept on the go for weeks before election day, cycling through the countryside to propaganda events, riding around on motorcycles or in fleets of cars getting the message across and, on election day itself, tirelessly ferrying their fellow citizens to the polling stations. Just like Stalin, Hitler used elections to control his agents and to spot flaws in the organization.

There was no law requiring people to vote, but everywhere people were reminded by party members, newspapers, radio, and keen fellow citizens of the absolute necessity of voting and of their 'duty of loyalty and gratitude towards the Führer'. On the day before the 1934 plebiscite, Göring told Germans: 'Nobody can be permitted to stay away, thereby proving that they are unworthy of their Führer's trust.' We must 'confront the whole world with a powerful demonstration that will sweep away all the lies and distortions about the new Germany. We must show that in all their thoughts, actions and sentiments Adolf Hitler and the German people have become one.'

As the Weimar electoral law, including secret voting, remained in force, there were no cases of people being taken to court for not voting at all or for not voting in the right way. However, there were cases of civil servants, who had not voted, being subjected to disciplinary action, although the Interior Minister did not allow the matter to be pursued with much energy. Since the Interior Minister had expressly forbidden the harassment of non-voters, in order to apply more pressure the Nazis had the idea of marking people who had already voted. Thus, throughout the Reich canvassers distributed badges to show who had voted. The newspapers reported: 'Everybody wore the "yes" badge" with pride.' In some places the canvassers distributed 'certificates for fulfilment of election duty'.

Disciplinary Action, Complicity, Resistance

According to an American correspondent who analysed the plebiscite of 1938, the quite violent annexation of Austria had not been seen as enough of a victory in itself. 'The National Socialist code prescribes a plebiscite', he explained, 'so that the eligible voter may be impressed with his share of responsibility in determining the destiny of the nation.' That was a shrewd observation. A few days before the elections in November 1933 the venerable liberal newspaper, the *Vossische Zeitung*, printed an interview with Goebbels in which the editor kept asking what was the point of parliamentary elections if there was only one party and no longer any opposition. Finally, the journalist hit the nail on the head by summing up: 'In that case the Reichstag election must be a test of the right thinking and the inner discipline of the German voter.' Whereupon the propaganda minister replied: 'That's right.'

By voting, every citizen was giving the regime his or her approval. The trip to the polling station became a public performance of subordination, indeed of complicity. The free vote had to remain in order to increase the significance of the ritual of subordination. This involved not only the absence of a legal requirement to vote but also an early vote on election day, which in every dictatorship counts as proof of particular loyalty. The celebratory mood also made a decisive contribution towards giving the election the character of a demonstration of loyalty. The *Nationalzeitung*, a Nazi Party newspaper, wrote about the elections of March 1936: 'It was not an election, it was a solemn act of celebration in which every man and every woman was glad through their vote to thank the Führer for all his wonderful deeds and achievements.'

How difficult was it to resist this propaganda and not to vote, to vote 'no' or to spoil the ballot paper? Even if, in principle, voting was secret, people had to reckon with disapproval. The milder form of pressure was exercised by the canvassers: After midday, members of the Hitler Youth and numerous party members would ring the door-bells of voters who had not yet voted in order to get them to vote. In more extreme cases SA men would hound non-voters through the streets shouting at them, accompanied by a mob crying: 'String them up!'

The pressure at election time could be even more brutal: on 29 March 1936, in a village in the Saarland, a curate and his housekeeper had used the polling booth. As a result, a Nazi had become suspicious and had unobtrusively marked the two ballot papers with an ink spot. When the votes were being counted, and it was revealed that both ballot papers contained 'no' votes, the inhabitants of the village gathered in front of the vicarage, dragged the two Catholics outside, hounded them through the streets and mocked them. The same thing happened to a factory owner from Lower Saxony, who was forced to vote and was then locked up, mistreated and only released the following day. Moreover, there were cases of people who were hounded through the streets with a sign around their necks saying: 'I didn't vote because I'm not interested in Germany's honour and peace.' Although these were probably isolated cases, they do throw light on the general atmosphere of repression and fear that was sufficient to persuade the majority of voters to conform.

The relatively large number of people who, before the elections, received permission to vote outside their home districts suggests that some voters tried to escape this pressure. Presumably, many opted for this in order not to be harassed on election day and then, either not to vote at all, or to vote 'no' in a more anonymous environment. The government responded to this development by instructing that the polling stations should remain open until 6 o'clock so that every voter had the chance to vote.

The fact that hundreds of thousands of people either refused to vote or voted 'no' shows that elections and plebiscites under Nazism were not simply rituals of approval and subordination, but simultaneously perhaps the most important opportunity for people to distance themselves from, or to oppose, the regime. That does not apply only to the March 1933 elections, in which, despite massive pressure by the Nazis, over 56 per cent of the electorate voted against Hitler becoming a dictator. Even more significant were the results in the following elections of November 1933, by which time the dictatorship had become fully established. In the elections of November 1933 there were 2.1 million 'no' votes and in the 1934 plebiscite as many as 4.3 million. Against that, however, one could argue that the large number of opposition votes shows that terror used against opponents during the elections was the exception and that it was quite possible to express opposition.

Political Festivals in the 'Third Reich'

Looked at from today's perspective, it is easy to underestimate the great significance of political festivals for Nazi rule during the peacetime years of 1933 to 1939. Our view of Nazi Germany is powerfully shaped by its destruction of democracy and the ruthless force which the regime used against all those it deemed 'enemies' of the nation and of the 'Aryan race', culminating in the 'Holocaust'. The image of jolly festivals and enthusiastic people cheering Hitler does not square with this history of oppression, violence, and terror. Nevertheless, festivals and terror, inclusion in the self-celebratory 'national community' and the violent exclusion of 'community aliens' were not contradictory but rather were closely related. The fact that a number of particularly vicious repressive measures were closely linked to spectacular celebrations is evidence for this. Following the brilliant staging of the alleged continuity between Prussian history and the 'Third Reich' on the 21 March 1933, which came to be known as Potsdam Day, two days later democracy was destroyed by the passage of the 'Enabling Act'. Only a day after more than a million people in Berlin had celebrated 1 May as National Labour Day, the regime destroyed the free trade unions. In 1935 the notorious 'Nuremberg Laws', designed to remove Jewish rights, were drafted in back rooms during the NSDAP's Reich Party Congress, the most elaborate event in the party's list of 'annual political ceremonies'. And the wave of terror, which caused the death of hundreds of Jews on 9 November 1938, was launched by Hitler and Goebbels during the annual commemoration of the failed Munich putsch by the Nazi Party in 1923. Sometimes violence and oppression were even dressed up in the form of a solemn ritual, as with the 'book burnings' of May 1933.

Nevertheless, it would be wrong to see the numerous festivals that took place in the 'Third Reich' simply as platforms for the preparation of violence or as a tactic to divert attention from oppressive measures. Political festivals also served the regime's image management vis-à-vis its own population and foreign countries. Participants in the great mass meetings could feel that they were part of an emotional community and were apparently experiencing the vision of the classless 'national community' as a lived reality. Political festivals with their heightened emotion and elaborate scenarios provided a venue where the aestheticization of politics, so typical of Nazism and Fascism, could have a direct and effective impact. At the same time, the rituals and symbols of the festivals contributed towards the political sphere acquiring a sacred aura. If Nazism is to be described as a form of political religion then public ceremonies represented a central part of its liturgy. The direct encounter between the 'Führer' and 'the people' at political festivals was both an instrument and an expression of charismatic rule and represented an important basis for the 'Hitler myth' (Ian Kershaw, 1987) on which the loyalty of a large number of Germans depended. It was not only at election time that mass events served both to demonstrate the 'new Germany's' power and modernity and to intimidate domestic and foreign opponents. March-pasts, demonstrations, and military parades, organized with exceptional logistical and technical sophistication, presented the German Reich as a modern, efficient state, one that was looking towards the future and, not least, was capable of offering its citizens a good show: bands and good-looking young men in uniform, torchlight processions, fireworks and 'cathedrals of light', the experience of travelling to events together in special trains, the overnight stays under canvas, and the binge drinking sessions after the event—all of that provided great entertainment.

Like elections and plebiscites, political festivals were a means of integrating the German population into the Nazi regime without giving it the opportunity to influence policy. Such festivals involve elaborate scenarios, presupposing the presence of all participants in one place, and can last for hours or days at a time. As in the case of elections, their ritualistic, liturgical programmes set them apart from the everyday world. Although the speakers, the politicians who are present, the participants in a march-past, and the 'public' that is watching have different roles, they all, as members of the festival community, form a unity in which the 'public' itself becomes an actor. The simultaneous presence of all the participants, their interaction, and their inclusion in symbolic acts are capable of producing powerful emotional resonances, which in turn can influence political attitudes and behaviour. Political festivals are loci of feelings, of moods, and of the amalgamation of real and symbolic worlds. The Nazis exploited all this in a variety of ways in order to integrate the population in their regime.

The Nazis' 'Festival Calendar'

Right from the start, political festivals played a key role in the self-projection of Nazi rule and for the representation of the unity of 'people' and Führer. This can be shown by a brief account of the first year of the 'Third Reich'. When, after 30 January 1933, Hitler and the NSDAP began to demolish Weimar democracy, to persecute their political opponents, to ban the other parties, and to 'coordinate' all independent organizations, the path to dictatorship was accompanied by a veritable 'firework of festivals'. A series of public events on a large scale, and elaborately choreographed, were accompanied by numerous smaller-scale parades, meetings, and ceremonies taking place in the Reich's towns and villages, in which traditional elements of the local culture were married with the symbols and rituals of the Nazi movement. These numerous smaller-scale festive occasions taking place during 1933 provide a particularly illuminating insight into the redemptive expectations which, through a mixture of opportunism, hope, and enthusiasm, many Germans projected onto Hitler. They also show the determination with which the party, SA, and Hitler Youth functionaries set about conquering the public sphere and occupying it with their signs and rituals. The main festivals and their multifaceted echo in the provinces not only served to project an attractive image and, as external decoration, to cover up the brutal conquest of the state. They were also a kind of 'social rite of passage' and as such an important step in the process of establishing the dictatorship.

The first big event was Potsdam Day on 21 March 1933. As already mentioned, the parliament, which had been elected on 5 March, was opened not in Berlin but in neighbouring Potsdam, the town which, with its barracks, its palaces and the tomb of 'Frederick the Great', was the most important memorial site of the Prussian state myth.

Although much had to be improvised at short notice, the organizers, led by Goebbels, succeeded in creating an impressive show. It was intended to demonstrate the reconciliation between the 'revolutionary' Nazi movement and 'Prussian traditions'. The regime hoped that the magic of the place would bestow upon it the legitimacy of history. However, it was in fact only later that the photograph of the handshake between Hitler and the aged Reich President von

Hindenburg became the most famous symbol of this transfer of authority from the representative of one historical epoch to the next. The immediate emotional effect derived rather from the 'Prussian' atmosphere of the Potsdam ceremony and from the inclusion of the whole nation in the great transfer ritual. It was not only in Potsdam that thousands lined the streets. Germans throughout the land were called upon to put up on their houses either the black, white, and red flag of the old Reich or the Nazi swastika and, that evening, the 'rebirth of the nation' was celebrated with numerous torchlight processions and 'freedom ceremonies'.

Only a few weeks later, the nomination of 1 May 1933 as 'National Labour Day' served symbolically to integrate the working class into the 'national community'. For the first time in German history the labour movement's traditional day of protest was made a public holiday. This was a clever move, a symbolic recognition of the workers, who, even before the world economic crisis with its mass unemployment, considered themselves the losers from modern capitalism. However, this symbolic recognition came at a high price. On 'National Labour Day' in 1933 there were no mass meetings and marches in which members of trade unions and left-wing parties could demonstrate in support of the interests of the working class. Instead, at the heart of the May Day celebrations, was a mass meeting, organized by the state, of over a million people on the 'Tempelhofer Feld' in Berlin. Here the young Albert Speer won his spurs as the man responsible for creating a stage on which the Hitler cult could flourish. Speer's staging of the event contained many of the elements typical of later mass occasions: Huge swastika flags provided the backdrop for the rostrum from which Hitler spoke to the crowd; modern loudspeakers carried the speech to the million people gathered in front of him; a radio reporter broadcast live from an airship that floated over the city. Torchlight processions and fireworks provided an impressive end to the day. The festivities were followed by brute force. On 2 May, the free trade unions were banned and their property was confiscated. The 1 May of the working class and class struggle had been transformed into the 1 May of the 'national community'. In certain respects, like Potsdam Day, this mass festival was a transitional ritual from the free public sphere of the Weimar Republic to the performative public space of the dictatorship, in which every participant was allocated a fixed role. During the following years, the Nazi 1 May departed further and further from its roots in the labour movement. From the middle of the 1930s onwards, the day was celebrated as an unpolitical spring festival with new traditions such as the 'May tree' and with entertainment provided in the 'workplace community', i.e. the factory or office. 'Enjoy life' was the unpolitical motto given out by Dr Robert Ley, the head of the German Labour Front, for the May celebrations in 1936.

The next event in the ceremonial year of 1933 was the 'Reich Party Congress of the NSDAP'. This took place in Nuremberg and lasted from 30 August until 3 September.

In fact, it was a party congress in name only. Above all it was a ritual demonstration of the charismatic relationship between Hitler, the 'movement', and 'the German people'. Every year, several hundred thousand functionaries, members and supporters of the Nazi Party and its numerous ancillary organizations gathered in Nuremberg to participate in a variety of events lasting several days. Its impact depended less on the content of the political speeches and more on the experience of being part of a community. The NSDAP had started the Nuremberg rallies in the 1920s, but it was only from 1933 onwards that they were planned as major occasions, becoming increasingly elaborate as the years went by. Commissioned by Hitler himself, the film of the 1934 party congress, directed by Leni Riefenstahl and titled 'Triumph of the Will', has become famous. The very fact that this film is not a documentary but rather extremely suggestive propaganda clearly indicates the message the party congress was intended to convey. It shows masses of enthusiastic people cheering Hitler in a variety of different contexts. Uniformed columns marching in formation across huge parade grounds against a pompous backdrop and according to a strict choreography were another leitmotif of the film, coming to be seen as a model of perfect discipline. Even if there is no doubt that it was Hitler who was playing the central role in this spectacle, the focus in what was effectively a self-portrayal of the 'movement' was continually on the loyal and disciplined supporters and the faithful 'people'. For this great Nuremberg party festival and its concentrated representation on film were celebrating above all the unity of 'people' and 'Führer'. In addition, these ritual performances were very important in demonstrating to the participants the special and 'sacred' character of the Nazi movement and its 'Führer'. Hitler's arrival by plane was an example of this, as were the torchlight processions through Nuremberg at night, and also the 'dedication' of new party flags. This took the form of Hitler touching them with the so-called 'blood flag', which had allegedly been soaked with the blood of party members shot by the police during the failed 1923 Munich putsch. This gloomy ritual is a particularly good example of the way in which the party congress's liturgy borrowed from the tradition of Christian martyrs. And, finally, Nuremberg was where the Nazis concentrated their architectural efforts with the aim of providing an appropriate location for party festivals. While the march-pasts through the medieval old town were intended to show the party's link with German history, the vast new buildings on the Reich Party Congress site, which were, in fact never completed, with their grand-stands and stadia, streets, halls and parade grounds, were to provide the backdrop against which the close relationship between the 'national community' and its Führer was to be acted out. It was an architecture of power within which people were never allowed to perceive themselves as individuals but could only act in a disciplined collective and see themselves as part of this 'mass'.

On 2 October 1933, a month after the end of the party congress, the 'Reich Harvest Festival' had its premiere on the Bückeberg near the north German town of Hamelin. While the 1 May festival aimed at the demonstrative inclusion of workers in the 'national community', the bringing together of 500,000 people in provincial Lower Saxony was intended to celebrate rural Germany's link with the 'new Germany'.

Even if the title of the festival was reminiscent of Church traditions and peasant culture, it was an entirely invented occasion. In many respects the mass meeting on the Bückeberg was similar to the Berlin event of 1 May, even if, by inviting groups dressed in traditional costume and using rough wooden platforms, an attempt was made to create a rustic ambience. Moreover, the venue where the 'Reich Harvest Festival' was celebrated from 1933 to 1937 had only a very superficial connection with nature and rural life. The flat elevation of the Bückeberg was transformed at great expense into a parade ground for a million people, who were bussed in from far and wide. It was constructed so that the participants could feel part of this mass meeting and at the same time look down on the military march-pasts and manoeuvres that were taking place in the valley below as if they were on a platform. In the final analysis, however, here too both the festival programme and the spatial arrangements were geared above all to staging an encounter between the 'Führer' and his 'people'. In the middle of the festival arena was the so-called 'Führer Way' leading up the mountain. This was used by Hitler and his entourage who, with the applause of a crowd of hundreds of thousands ringing in their ears, 'walked through' the people. In 1933 this walk 'through the people' is estimated to have taken a full forty-five minutes and this charismatic moment of proximity between Hitler and the 'people' was repeatedly reproduced in photographs of the 'Harvest Festival'. The political 'Harvest Festival', which was held annually and ever more elaborately until 1937, was not, however, limited to the major event held on the Bückeberg. Just as '1 May' was celebrated as a day to reaffirm the 'national community' not simply in Berlin but in numerous other places and factories, the 'Reich Harvest Festival' was marked in villages and small towns up and down the country. There the focus was not the charismatic encounter with the Führer; instead, these local celebrations were a combination of traditional elements of rural festival culture and expressions of local identity with new political symbols, and aggressive assertions of their presence by the local Nazi organizations and functionaries. Whether these small-scale events were able to establish themselves and win the affection of local communities or degenerated into political routine depended very much on whether or not they succeeded in integrating the ideological messages into local popular festival culture.

Finally, the last great celebration of 1933 took place on 9 November in Munich. Since 1925 the NSDAP had marked this day in commemoration of the failed Hitler putsch of 1923. This amateurish attempt at a coup, which was crushed without much difficulty by loyal Bavarian policemen, was transformed by the party into a core foundation myth of the Nazi movement. In particular, after 1933, there was an increasing emphasis on the cult of martyrdom associated with those putschists who had been shot. Here, even more than with the 'Reich Party Congress', it was the Nazi Party that was the main focus of attention. The NSDAP used Hitler's annual memorial address in the 'Bürgerbräukeller', the re-enactment of the putschists' march through the city, and an increasingly pompous death cult, to create a myth of heroism and sacrifice, thereby helping to form the party's identity. Thus, the 9 November celebration was not primarily about the link between the charismatic 'Führer' and the 'national community'. What was being celebrated and given a legendary status was rather the purported 'community of struggle' associated with the party's early so-called 'years of struggle'. In Munich every year on 9 November an invented tradition was being staged in which the movement's 'old fighters' were continually confirming in their own minds that they were a sworn community of the Führer and represented the elite of the 'Third Reich'. Not least for this reason, of all the regime's rituals this festival contained the most elements of a political-religious liturgy: Year after year, the 1923 'blood flag' that had been turned into a party relic, was carried ceremonially through the city. The sixteen dead of 1923 acquired the status of political martyrs and, in 1935, in a grandiose ceremony were buried in two newly constructed 'temples of honour' in the Königsplatz. Every year their names were read out in the emotionally potent form of a 'roll call' in which, after each name, the huge crowd shouted in chorus: 'here', thereby invoking the mystical unity of the 'fallen heroes' and the living supporters of the movement.

While Potsdam remained a unique event, up until 1939 the other festivals established themselves as fixed points in the Nazi calendar, following the same annual rhythm. In 1934 other less spectacular occasions were added to it. The 'National Day of Mourning', during which the dead of the First World War were remembered, was transformed into a 'Heroes' Memorial Day' integrating remembrance of the war into an aggressively heroic narrative. Also, the hitherto purely commercial 'Mothers' Day' was given an enhanced status as the 'Day for Remembering and Honouring German Mothers'. In addition to these annual festivals, which remained part of the political liturgy of Nazism until the outbreak of the Second World War, there were also large-scale ceremonies to mark particular events. They included 'Potsdam Day', but also the ritual book burning in 1933, the Olympic Games in 1936, German Art Day, which was held irregularly in Munich, and the celebrations to mark Hitler's birthday on 20 April 1939.

During the 1930s, Nazi festival practice developed four different trends: first, there was a move towards developing a canon. Thus, although the programmes, symbols and rituals were continually being changed, in general there was a move towards standardization. While, for example, in 1933 the local festive processions organized on 1 May and on the occasion of the Harvest Festivals contained many elements deriving from regional traditions, later on the tendency was to imitate the events being organized centrally. Second, there was a tendency to make the big political celebrations ever more elaborate and grandiose: the number of participants continued to increase, the programmes became more ambitious, and the sites and buildings that were constructed for the party congresses and Harvest Festivals acquired gigantic proportions. Third, rearmament and the preparations for war meant that military aspects became increasingly important. At the Nuremberg party congresses, military parades and the display of modern weapons became part of the programme and during the 'Reich Harvest Festival' in 1937 a million participants watched an hour-long mock battle involving 10,000 soldiers as well as tanks and bombers. When Hitler celebrated his fiftieth birthday in 1939 he took a parade lasting four and a half hours in which more than 40,000 soldiers, 5,000 motor vehicles, and 600 tanks participated. Fourth, the modern mass media acquired increasing importance. To succeed and make an impact, festivals depend on the physical presence of all participants and on the interaction and communication between them. This limits their impact to those who attend and participate. Thus, early on, Goebbels tried to communicate the atmosphere of the political festivals by using the most modern forms of media technology in order to reach as much of the population as possible. From the very beginning, radio broadcasts formed part of the propaganda repertoire as well as the use of original and innovative techniques of live reporting. By providing short film reports, cinema newsreels could give at least a superficial impression of the 'total work of art' (Gesamtkunstwerk) to which the festivals aspired. However, Leni Riefenstahl's extremely elaborate and technically revolutionary films of the party congress of 1934 and the 1936 Olympic Games in Berlin were far more impressive. From 1936 onwards, there were also experiments with television broadcasts, although because of the primitive technology they reached only a few viewers.

Führer Myth and 'National Community': the Function of Political Festivals

The Nazis maintained and developed their festival programme right up until the outbreak of the Second World War. This involved a vast amount of effort and resources. Millions of people were mobilized; many thousands of party functionaries and civil servants were engaged in the organization; large amounts of money were spent in performing the ceremonies and on the gigantic buildings in Berlin, Nuremberg, and on the Bückeberg. Why was there so much pomp and spectacle? What functions did these political festivals perform for the Nazi dictatorship? What do they tell us about the nature of this regime and about the reasons for its popularity among the German people? In a famous essay published in 1936 the philosopher, Walter Benjamin, referred to the 'aestheticization of political life' under fascism. The transformation of politics into a brilliant show served, he said, to organize and fascinate the people, in order to bind it to the regime, while at the same time disregarding their real interests. This analysis is undoubtedly plausible, but it stops short of explaining the importance of Nazi festival culture, for the festivals were not simply a method of diversion and manipulation. Above all, the major ceremonies—1 May, the Nuremberg party congress, the 'Reich Harvest Festival', and the Munich death cult of 9 November—acted as a stage on which 'people' and 'Führer' could encounter one another face to face. The physical presence of Hitler, the possibility of this face-to-face communication, the proximity of the idol to his worshippers, as well as the strict regulation and ritualization of this encounter within the ceremony were important preconditions for the creation and maintenance of the charismatic constellation and the 'Führer' myth.

Furthermore, both the big festivals of state and party and the small-scale events in the provinces, with their processions, mass meetings, and demonstrations, were occasions at which the participants could see themselves as members of a homogenous 'national community'. Festivals, as exceptional social situations, are by their very nature designed to generate feelings and moods. Nazi festivals sought to overwhelm the participants visually, acoustically, and performatively. The standardized symbols and the political rhetoric that was geared towards the inclusion of the participants and the exclusion of alleged 'enemies of the people' formed the basis for the creation of an emotionally charged community. Participation in the festival simultaneously implied participation in important political events. This collective sense of being part of a consensus and the feeling of participating were much more important than the actual political propaganda being put out by the speakers.

Finally, the Nazi festivals between 1933 and 1939 were an important instrument by which, through rituals, show, and symbols, the regime could bring under control and neutralize the dynamic that had developed in the course of the party's 'struggle' for power under Weimar. During the crisis years of German democracy, the SA and NSDAP had acquired and maintained their momentum by developing a style of permanent action and mobilization. Street demonstrations, electoral battles, and fights in beer halls were routine. Many Nazi activists had anticipated that this revolutionary dynamic would continue after the take-over of power. With the establishment of the dictatorship, the 'coordination' of the bureaucracy, and a new emphasis on the military, the party leadership moved towards exercising power through agencies of the state and the organized terror of the SS and Gestapo rather than by mobilizing the SA or through pressure from below.

Political festivals also served to strengthen the charismatic relationship between 'people' and 'Führer', to ensure that the 'national community' could be experienced on an emotional level, and to maintain the sense that this was a dynamic regime. Its success depended on efficient image management, which could satisfy the needs of the Germans for a sense of identity and orientation. To achieve it, on the one hand, it fell back on familiar motifs, on the other, it came up with innovative ideas derived from modern mass culture and the entertainment industry.

One mechanism used to ensure credibility and to focus collective expectations was the invention of traditions (E. J. Hobsbawm), through which the NSDAP provided itself and its festivals with historical legitimacy. These invented traditions can be clearly seen in the choice of justifications for the particular festivals. The 1 May referred back to the traditions of the labour movement, the Harvest Festival was borrowed from Christian tradition, 'Mothers' Day' was also already established, and in the case of the martyrs cult associated with the 9 November, the Nazi movement was in effect creating its own tradition. This strategy of creating traditions was demonstrated by the way in which the festivals were made to follow an elaborate rhythm. Year after year, the festivals' programme followed the same order of events, just like the Christian calendar. The reference to history, the rhythm and the repetition all gave the festival programme an aura of continuity and authenticity.

Second, for the major events the directors of the Nazi festivals selected venues of symbolic and historic significance. The specific aura attached to them provided backing for the invention of the traditions and was intended to give them greater credibility. With its picturesque old town and important medieval history, the party congress city of Nuremberg illustrated the Nazis' claim to embody 'true' German history. A similar invention of tradition was associated with the Bückeberg in Lower Saxony, which was sold as symbolic of the German peasantry.

Third, Goebbels and the other Nazi festival managers had no compunction about utilizing an assortment of completely disparate festival traditions. Christian customs and rituals, such as processions and the cult of martyrs and relics, were exploited in exactly the same way as festival traditions of the nineteenth century with their penchant for parades and patriotic decoration. The youth movement with its romanticization of nature and cult of authenticity made a contribution, as did the Socialist labour movement, viz. 1 May. This eclectic appropriation of different forms and practices enabled the Nazis to appeal to many people from conflicting milieus while removing from these practices the original meanings attaching to them. This mobilization or invention of traditions was combined with elements that were blatantly modern. These include—the fourth point—the design of the public spaces in which the festivals took place. It is true that at the local level they used many elements of traditional culture: for example, processions through festively decorated towns or richly decorated farm wagons for the Harvest Festival. On the other hand, however, the festival buildings in Nuremberg or on the Bückeberg were quite new, as was the design of the Tempelhofer Feld in Berlin. The gigantic architecture in the grounds of the Reich party congress and the transformation of the slope of the Bückeberg to accommodate a million people facilitated a qualitatively new form of mass choreography and of collective experience. It aimed, above all, at identifying the individual with the imagined community. The architecture of domination associated with these new spaces provided the big festivals with an appropriate stage; without the context of totalitarian mass choreography it was completely pointless.

Fifth, the Nazi festivals were examples of modern event management in which all the possibilities provided by up-to-date technology were brilliantly utilized. To be able to bring hundreds of thousands or even a million people to a remote spot in Lower Saxony or to the provincial city of Nuremberg and provide for them for a short time was in itself a remarkable logistical achievement. The use of the most modern loud speakers, highly effective lighting arrangements, the deployment of airships and aircraft, military parades with thousands of soldiers and the most up-to-date weapons—all these combined to make the political festivals between 1933 and 1939 popular demonstrations of technical and military modernity.

Sixth, the mass media: Nazi festivals were intended to integrate the participants as 'totally' as possible into the events and to make 'politics' as comprehensive an emotional experience as possible. Rational arguments and political debates were irrelevant. In order to ensure that this experience did not remain confined to the participants, the transmission of the ceremony to a broad national public was intended right from the start. Newspaper reports and photographs, radio and cinema were designed to turn a big local event into an experience of the whole nation. Although the attempt was made to use radio reporting to facilitate a synchronized national experience, and although the Riefenstahl film of the party congress of 1934 was seen by many Germans, the success of this media strategy is doubtful. For the special character of a festival community lay and lies precisely in the fact that all participants are present. The more it was a matter of emotions, experiences, and community, the more difficult it was, given the state of technology at the time, to communicate this quality of the experience through the media. This undoubtedly limited the effectiveness of Nazi festival culture.

The continuing need for the relationship between 'the Führer' and 'the movement' to be actively experienced was of decisive importance for the legitimation of this charismatic regime. Like the elections, the ceremonies served to demonstrate the apparently 'democratic' nature of the regime. Elections and festivals maintained the fiction of a mass movement, even if this had become frozen in rigid rituals. At the same time, they contained the movement's latent dynamic. Hitler's and Goebbels's success in launching an unprecedented wave of terror against German Jews with such ease on 9 November 1938 had, among other things, to do with the fact that it took place on the day the party had devoted to the memory of the 'time of struggle' and 'the fallen heroes'. And the growing self-confidence of the regime vis-à-vis foreign countries and its own population during the 1930s was, not least, a consequence of the elections and plebiscites, those demonstrative rituals of assent and exclusion that appeared to clarify the views of the masses—and the powerlessness of the opposition.

4

Architecture and the Arts

Jonathan Petropoulos

In March 1945, Adolf Hitler sat in the model room of his Berlin Bunker. In front of him was an elaborate miniature of the cultural complex being planned for his adopted home town of Linz, with the Führer Museum as the centrepiece. Hitler turned to Ernst Kaltenbrunner, the head of the Reich Security Main Office, and observed, 'My dear Kaltenbrunner, if both of us were not convinced that after the victorious conclusion of the war we would build this new Linz together, I would shoot myself today.' These comments, which intertwined the war and the construction of a cultural complex, represented delusions of grandeur and a faulty understanding of the military situation, but they also show how Hitler focused attention on artworks and other cultural matters, even in the most dire of situations. The dictator spent hours with his models and the albums documenting the paintings collected on his behalf. He even personally selected some of the artworks that adorned the bunker, including a portrait of Frederick the Great (meant to invoke the miraculous survival of Prussia and its king at the end of the Seven Years' War). Other Nazi leaders shared an interest in the arts and would have understood Hitler's symbol-laden communication. The Berlin Bunker invariably calls to mind the end of the story, but the fact is architecture and the arts played an essential role in the evolution of National Socialist Germany right from the start.

The arts proved central to the National Socialist ideology from the inception of the movement in 1920. According to founding ideologues Anton Drexler, Gottfried Feder, Dietrich Eckart, and of course, Adolf Hitler, 'Aryans' were bearers of culture who fostered sublime art. Jews subverted and exploited culture, churning out meretricious work that they swindled others into buying. Additionally, because Hitler conceived himself as an artist, and due to the 'Führer Principle' (*Führerprinzip*), the expectation grew that Nazi subleaders would follow Hitler and evince an interest in culture. This sometimes proved forced: architect turned Reich Armaments Minister Albert Speer recalled beer-laden *Gauleiter* falling asleep during performances of Wagner's operas in Nuremberg. But the fact that the leaders made an effort to attend cultural events and pose as patrons in itself proved significant. The Nazi ideological principle of '*Gleichschaltung*' (a vaguely untranslatable term appropriated by the Nazis that denoted coordination) and the concerted efforts to create mass organizations like the Reich Chambers of Culture also made the arts important to the broader history of Nazi Germany. More generally, the arts also served as a means to rationalize murderous policies. Many believed the superiority of German culture justified the ideological war that ensued, arguing, 'We are cultured and not barbarians, and hence are fighting a noble fight.' In short, the arts were central to the propagation of the Nazi *Weltanschauung*.

After the Nazi seizure of power in January 1933, the arts played a significant role in the government's economic programmes. The public works projects meant to stimulate the economy included increased expenditures on the arts. One of the first structures commissioned by Hitler was the House of German Art in Munich. The Nazis subsequently passed a law on 22 May 1934 requiring that at least 2 per cent of a building's budget go to art and decorative projects. The Nazi leaders spent record sums on culture, and many artists received their income from the Nazi state and its officials. This induced many artists to view the leaders as patrons or customers. Later on, the Nazis' ambitious arts programme was in part financed by plunder and other rapacious actions, especially in the occupied lands during the war. The proceeds from plunder enriched the Nazi state and helped fund artistic projects. The Führer Museum planned for Linz would house the paintings looted from across Europe, and architects Albert Speer and Hermann Giesler, who led the team for *Sonderauftrag Linz* (Special Project Linz), received this commission for a colossal project from state-sponsored larceny.

The arts also became a central component of the Nazis' propaganda campaign—'the war that Hitler won', to quote historian

Robert Edwin Herzstein. After quickly establishing domination over nearly all media, the new leaders convinced most of the German population that the regime was advancing the country's interests, and won them over to many Nazi ideological positions: notably regarding Jews and other ethnic groups, with respect to nationalism and a sense of duty, and, of course, an increased reverence for Hitler. Five years of Nazi domination of the media preceded the watershed event of *Kristallnacht* in November 1938, and the use of culture to indoctrinate a large segment of the German population provided a crucial precondition for the Holocaust. Fewer Germans would have killed or accommodated themselves to the killing in 1933—that is, prior to the Nazis' propaganda initiatives. There was a process of gradual radicalization that unfolded, and the arts were part of that process.

Running contrary to the theme of the arts as a tool of social control, cultural activity also proved important to the history of the Third Reich because it offered certain artists and intellectuals a means of criticizing the regime, even if these efforts remained confined to the private sphere. The ostracized Otto Dix, for example, painted his allegorical work *Seven Deadly Sins* from his 'inner emigration' on Lake Constance, even if he added the iconic Hitler moustache to the central figure right after the war. Max Beckmann's symbol-laden master-pieces from German-occupied Amsterdam allowed him to explore themes relating to culture and barbarism. Victims of National Social-ism often persisted with their work. German-Jewish painter Felix Nussbaum executed a series of remarkable self-portraits that chron-icled his life before his tragic death in Auschwitz in 1944, and the inmates of the Theresienstadt concentration camp continued to create art and music, oftentimes, right up until being deported to Auschwitz.

From the very beginning, however, the Nazi seizure of power precipitated the greatest flight of talent in history. This emigration, first from Germany and then from other European countries, has spawned a vast scholarly literature. These émigrés helped mobilize world opinion against Nazi Germany, and did so in a timely manner. Émigrés often styled themselves as representatives of the 'other' Ger-many—one that stood in contrast to the Reich dominated by Nazi barbarism. In the United States, they helped create organizations like the American Guild for German Cultural Freedom and the

Hollywood Anti-Nazi League, and contributed to works that attacked Hitler and his regime. Their efforts ranged from films (think Conrad Veidt as Major Strasser in *Casablanca*, or Fritz Lang and Bertolt Brecht's *Hangmen Also Die!*, the latter based on the killing of Reinhard Heydrich), to novels by Thomas Mann, Erich Maria Remarque, and Anna Seghers. The efforts of the émigrés to expose the evils of Hitler's regime arguably helped President Roosevelt convince the US Congress to declare war in December 1941, as well as adopt a 'Germany first' policy. Hitler depleted the ranks of academics by some 43 per cent and the flight of talent represented a 'brain drain' that clearly hurt the Axis powers during and after the war. The departure of Jewish scientists like Albert Einstein, Hans Bethe, and Lise Meitner, as well as the general disdain for 'Jewish' science (including quantum physics), insured that the Germans did not obtain the atomic bomb.

The themes above can be seen in the distinctive arts themselves. To take an array of the most prominent arts, it is helpful here to focus on individual artistic spheres: architecture; the visual and plastic arts; music; and literature. Because of David Crew's contribution to this volume on photography and cinema, these fields will not be discussed in this article. Regardless of the sphere, one can speak of 'official' and 'non-official' culture, although the lines were often blurred. In an effort to achieve a more integrated cultural history of the Third Reich, the arts-specific discussions that follow move from the official sphere to the unofficial. Regarding the latter, it is important to recognize that even after gradual radicalization—the expulsion of the Jews from the Reich Chambers of Culture in 1935, the prohibition on art criticism in 1936, and the ban on pursuing one's profession ('*Berufsverbot*'), which became more common from 1937 onward—more independent and less coercive spaces remained in Nazi Germany.

Architecture

Although Hitler professed a love of opera stretching back to his youth in Linz, he came to favour architecture above all other art forms. If he had received the technical training he probably would have pursued a career as an architect; but he never passed the requisite engineering and mathematics courses. Instead, he moved in another direction and became a painter of both oils and watercolours, for which he showed decent, if unremarkable facility. Hitler himself knew this, but thought that his skills with brush and pen would make him an excellent architect. The dictator possessed a formidable command of architectural practices and could manage details the same way he did with certain libretti and the tonnage of ships (among other military details). It showed what interested him: music and art on the one hand, and war on the other. Although Hitler was limited in innumerable ways, he also possessed abilities that made him an effective patron of architecture.

With regard to 'official' or state-sponsored projects in the Third Reich, certain themes and ideas emerged, even if there was no uniform style. Buildings have always been highly communicative; or to use the book title of Robert Taylor, they represented 'The Word in Stone'. Taylor acknowledged that there was no consistent architectural idiom, but rather, Hitler was driven by the idea of 'community', as exemplified by the Nuremberg rally grounds, the Berlin Olympic stadium, and the cultural complex intended for Linz, among other public spaces that drew the dictator's close attention. Historian Jochen Thies went a step further and argued that Hitler's architectural programme reflected his plans for global domination. The monumentality of the structures conveyed the power and ambitions of the new regime: they exerted a visceral effect on viewers, who were dwarfed by these creations. Even if many of the buildings that Hitler and his architects planned were never constructed, the elaborately scaled models communicated the intent. The Great Hall (*Grosse Halle*) planned for Berlin would hold 180,000 people and feature its own microclimate, such that it would periodically rain inside the dome.

The Nuremberg Zeppelin Tribunal, which was actually built, held over 200,000 (90,000 parading and 124,000 seated). The party rallies were conceived as Wagnerian '*Gesamtkunstwerke*'—or 'total works of art'—that combined theatre, music, and choreography, among other elements. Yet it was the architectural design that established the foundation, the framework, for these spectacles.

Hitler and the other leaders turned to a neo-classical idiom for most of the major buildings commissioned in Germany. The style conveyed order and, by sheer repetition and scale, allowed for monumentality. Stone was the preferred material for representational buildings.

The granite, limestone, and marble favoured by the Nazis were often mined by concentration camp labour, with Himmler's SS serving as a major provider. In a sense, the stone structures embodied the linkage of culture and barbarism. But Hitler and his associates also believed that stone conveyed a sense of power and permanence, even if Albert Speer's notion of 'ruin value' (the idea that structures would be built without rebar and other modern features that would undermine their beauty as ruins many years hence) was actually a post-World War II idea. With monumentality, neo-classicism, and stone as key features, the Nazis, like their fascist counterparts in Italy, developed a distinctive, if not homogeneous style (although the latter was far more tolerant of modern architecture and art). Still, Nazi buildings often proved immediately recognizable—then, and now. Whether it is the Tempelhof Airfield in Berlin (now used as a convention centre) or the Paul Ludwig Troost buildings near the Königsplatz in Munich, the structures stand out, and some would say, have an aura about them. During the Third Reich, these buildings would have been adorned with swastikas and other decorations of an ideological nature, making them still more illustrative of the regime.

Even among the official, state-sponsored projects, there were exceptions. In order to realize their geopolitical ambitions, the Nazis needed industrial infrastructure, and many of the factories were constructed in a modern, or more functional idiom. The Hermann Göring Works in Linz offer one example of practical buildings that utilized modernist designs. Scholars have long recognized that many Bauhaus architects found work in the Third Reich. While such modernists usually did not work on the representational buildings, there were exceptions, such as Albert Speer engaging Peter Behrens to design for the remodelled Berlin, or Paul Bonatz creating sleek autobahn bridges and receiving a commission for the new railway station intended for Munich.

Among the key practitioners in the architectural sphere in Nazi Germany, Albert Speer stands out. Intelligent (his IQ as tested at Nuremberg in 1945 was 128), talented, and hard-working, Speer emerged after the war as the 'good Nazi'. The young architect had impressed Professor Heinrich Tessenow at the University of Berlin, who was an acerbic critic, but nevertheless became a mentor to Speer. Tessenow had designed the garden housing settlement at Hellerau near Dresden, and helped remodel the *Neue Wache* memorial in central Berlin, and he generally worked in a modernist idiom. Tessenow had a profound influence on Speer, who borrowed accordingly, favouring straight lines and sparse, or at least selective decoration. Speer was ambitious and opportunistic and when Hitler's first court architect, Paul Ludwig Troost, died in 1934, an opportunity arose. Speer took on an array of high profile projects, including the remodelling of the German Embassy in London and the German Pavilion for the Paris World Exposition of 1937. The latter, a towering, even soaring, building with a Reich Eagle atop it, won a gold medal and sealed his position as the dictator's favoured architect. Speer proceeded to increase his influence, being named a professor, and then General Building Inspector for the Reich Capital, which gave him considerable power. At the same time, he served on an array juries, editorial boards, and government committees, making Speer a formidable power in the cultural bureaucracy; this, before being appointed Reich Armaments Minister in early 1942.

Speer continued to design and see his architectural projects realized well into the war—to around the time he became a Reich Armaments Minister and wartime rationing limited building, especially those structures not essential to the war efforts The Congress Hall in Nuremberg was very near completion and would have been finished had the Nazis revived the annual party rally. Yet much of Speer's work consists of models. The exceptions included his efforts at Nuremberg and the New Reich Chancellery in Berlin, which was completed in 1939. He claimed to finish the latter in one year, when, in fact the demolition work had begun in 1937 (and the planning process stretched back further). The architect liked to propagate myths about himself, particularly that he worked independently of Hitler, and that he completed projects faster than others. Speer also liked to denigrate rivals, including Hermann Giesler, whose name Speer misspelled throughout his memoir, *Inside the Third Reich*. But Speer was a survivor, escaping a possible death sentence at Nuremberg, hiding much of his art collection with a friend in Mexico (and later recovering it), and then becoming a bestselling author. He knew at some level that he was complicit in something malevolent. As he noted in his memoirs about the gigantic projects, 'these monuments were an assertion of his [Hitler's] claim to world dominion long before he dared to voice any such intention even to his closest associates'. Speer made his 'Faustian bargain' in order to build for a once dominant dictator and in the process assumed considerable power himself.

The non-official architectural sector was characterized by a greater diversity of styles. On the one hand, there were the historicist styles favoured by most Nazi leaders, among other patrons. Their private homes, including Hitler's Berghof, Hermann Göring's Carinhall estate, Goebbels's Schwanenwerder enclosure on Lake Wannsee, the Ribbentrops' villa in Berlin-Dahlem, and Robert Ley's luxurious spread, Leyhof, near Cologne represent but a few of the *grandes maisons* of the elite. They and others also commissioned a dizzying array of objects. For the Nazis, less was rarely more when it came to their own homes. Nearly all the leaders had custom-made cutlery, china, crystalware, wine openers, and the like. Their tastes have helped support an entire industry in Nazi memorabilia that flourishes today. The authorities launched periodic campaigns against 'kitsch' and were not always successful, but there continued to be high quality arts and crafts, as well as capable design work during the Third Reich. The Nazi state and party impinged on the applied arts in innumerable ways—architects had to be members of the Reich Chamber for the Visuals Arts and meet building codes—but there was some measure of freedom.

Among the key practitioners who worked in the non-official sphere, at least for a time, were Ludwig Mies van der Rohe and Walter Gropius. The last director of the Bauhaus, which had moved from Dessau to Berlin in 1932, Mies had tried to save the institution, and negotiated with Alfred Rosenberg and Gestapo leader Rudolf Diels before the famed school was closed in April 1933. Mies still enjoyed a stellar reputation and was not Jewish. He was among the architects invited to submit a proposal for the Reichsbank competition in 1933, as was the founder of the Bauhaus, Walter Gropius. Both, designed monumental yet sleek structures, offering syntheses between the modern and the fascist. Although each believed that his work merited selection, a member of the jury, Heinrich Wolff, turned out to be the winner of the competition (and a massive if unremarkable structure went up between 1934 and 1938). Yet Mies, like Gropius, continued to believe that his work should be accepted. Both joined the Reich Chamber for the Visual Arts and filled out all the paperwork required to work as an architect in the Third Reich, and both participated in the 1934 exhibition, *German People, German Work* (*Deutsches Volk, Deutsche Arbeit*). This propagandistic spectacle about the superiority of the (non-Jewish) German worker featured modernist design, including a poster created by former *Bauhäusler* Herbert Bayer. Mies, like Gropius, submitted entries for other architectural competitions in 1933 and 1934: Mies for the German Pavilion at the Brussels World Exposition planned for 1935 and Gropius for another complex undertaken by the regime's mass leisure-time organization. Both architects included swastika flags as part of their models and designs. The inclusion of these symbols signified their wish to find accommodation with the Nazi regime.

Gropius soon recognized that there was no place for him in Nazi Germany, especially with the gradually more radical and oppressive (not to mention anti-modern) policies of the regime. Gropius had been friends with Professor Egon Hönig, the first President of the Reich Chamber for the Visual Arts, and he kept well-informed of current events. Hönig himself was replaced with the more radical painter Adolf Ziegler in 1936, but by that time, Gropius had relocated to England. The architect made every effort to keep his affairs in order in Germany, and to avoid antagonizing the regime. He even requested permission to accept the chair for architecture at Harvard University, writing to Goebbels that he would be replacing a Frenchman and that this appointment reflected well on Germany. Mies persisted longer, but gradually followed his friend and rival (both were under consideration for the Harvard post) to America, where in 1938 he took a professorship at the Armour Institute of Technology in Chicago. Both Mies and Gropius became associated with the anti-Nazi German emigration, and as symbols of American freedom, their careers flourished in the post-war era. 'Mr. Bauhaus' (Gropius) helped design the US embassy in Athens between 1959 and 1961 and was invited to the presidential inauguration of John F. Kennedy in 1961. Mies's Seagram's building on Park Avenue became a landmark early on. But their efforts to work with the Nazis rarely entered into the narrative. Recent scholarship has allowed for a more nuanced portrayal.

The architects who sought to work with the Nazis generally exhibited tremendous self-confidence and believed that they could build in any system. But Mies, like Gropius, was too well-established, and was identified with modern architecture, which raised the hackles of the anti-modernist elements in the Nazi Party. Hitler and others would not allow Mies or Gropius to reinvent themselves. The younger and less accomplished Albert Speer had far less baggage—only a mentor, Heinrich Tessenow, who was a tad too modern and critical of the official building projects. But Speer could be forgiven for that.

The Visual and Plastic Arts

An apt image that conveys the essence of Nazi art involved a visitor to the studio of Nazi sculptor Josef Thorak; when asked where he could find the artist, an aide explained that Thorak was 60 feet above them, working in the ear of his creation. Even the Nazis realized that finding an official style that yielded good art was a daunting challenge. Hitler had applied his slogan of 'Give Me Four Years' Time' (to transform Germany) to the visual arts, and with the opening of the House of German Art in Munich in July 1937, he met his deadline. The dictator had formed a selection committee and charged its members with identifying the works to be exhibited. They did so, but he was so dismayed by their selection that he took over the judging himself (with the help of photographer Heinrich Hoffmann). Hitler remained dissatisfied with the result, especially with regard to painting, and this view was shared by other Nazi leaders, including Goebbels, who frequently lamented the state of contemporary art in his diary entries. That said, Hitler, Goebbels, and other leaders purchased numerous works from the annual *Great German Art Exhibitions* (*Grosse Deutsche Kunstausstellungen* or *GDK*), helping make the works in these shows the most representative of the Nazi regime.

In the state sponsored realm, there was a distinctive ideology underpinning this art. Painting and sculpture were especially important for this racist regime because they were among the few art forms to render the human body. Nazi sculpture featured *Übermenschen*, literally supermen, with their muscles and monumentality. Depicting 'racially healthy' types remained a constant in official art, although the sculptures tended to be aggressive, while the paintings often appeared saccharine or bland. Many landscapes featured in the *GDK* were kept in Bavarian government offices after the war. The portrayal of 'racially pure types' and the relative absence of 'others' characterized Nazi art. Stylistically, the official works tended to feature a kind of realism—or at least, a lack of abstraction—although some artists who created 'combat art' during the war cut against the grain in this respect. The notion of 'degenerate art' gradually gained traction during the 1930s. With intellectual roots extending back into the nineteenth century, especially in Jewish cultural critic Max Nordau's 1892 book, *Entartung (Degeneration)*, the idea that 'degeneration' found expression in the visual arts emerged as a key tenet in the National Socialist ideology. Even before Hitler's seizure of power, the exploitation of cultural politics proved an effective instrument in the Nazis' toolbox. For many Nazis, those who made modern art were biologically inferior and could not see colours as they really were or shapes as they truly existed. Alternatively (or additionally), these artists were part of an international movement, one promoting rootless styles, and were hence 'cultural Bolsheviks'. Racially inferior or politically subversive, that was the message, and it was also propagated in books, such as Wolfgang Willrich's *Cleansing of the Art Temple* of 1937.

Although National Socialist art was far from monolithic, two typical figures were Adolf Ziegler and Arno Breker, with the former serving as President of the Reich Chamber for the Visual Arts from 1936 to 1943. His appointment signalled a turn against modern art and an expansion of state authority, even though he had once worked in a more progressive style (art historian Franz Roh had regarded him as one of the most promising proponents of magical realism in a 1925 study). Ziegler became known for his stiff nudes in classical settings. Certain contemporaries quietly mocked him as 'the Master of the German Pubic Hair', sensing the odd qualities in his work. Ziegler's paintings, however, became strangely iconic—among the most oft-depicted works of the Third Reich. His racialized subjects, idealized landscapes, and accentuated realism are such that they are frequently included in exhibitions involving Nazi culture. The Bavarian State Painting Collections owns Ziegler's *Four Elements* and frequently loans it (such as to the Guggenheim Museum in New York for an exhibition titled *Chaos & Classicism*). Ziegler had considerable technical facility: he had been a professor at the Academy in Munich beginning in 1933, and taught a generation of students. Although he produced relatively few works, they attracted a great deal of attention: a tapestry version of *The Four Elements* adorned the central hall of the German Pavilion at the Paris World Exposition in 1937 (and won a gold medal), with the original painting located outside Hitler's office in the *Führerbau* in Munich.

His prominence as an artist aside, Ziegler attained infamy for leading the initiative to purge state collections of 'degenerate' art. The three-man committee he headed purged some 21,000 artworks from museums. He himself delivered a vitriolic speech to open the *Degenerate Art Exhibition* in Munich in 1937 (Hitler had officiated at the inauguration of the House of German Art the day before). Ziegler's notorious address brought together his *idée fixe* about 'cultural bolshevism', the linkage between 'blood and soil', and the pernicious threat posed by Jews. In the years that followed, he worked against the modernist artists who remained in Nazi Germany, and it is somewhat ironic that this illiberal zealot should be brought down when arrested by the Gestapo in early 1943 for expressing defeatist views. Ziegler was sent to the Dachau concentration camp, but Hitler personally ordered his release after six weeks and allowed him to retire quietly. His post-war career was also uneventful. Adolf Ziegler lived in a village outside Baden-Baden until his death at age 67 in 1959.

Few artworks capture the spirit and style of National Socialism as Arno Breker's sculptures. Towering like the racially superior *Übermenschen* they were meant to represent, and often rendered in threatening or militaristic poses, Breker's massive figures stood prominently in state museums and adorned official Nazi buildings. He was rewarded with a professorship, an elaborate factory in Wriezen on the Oder River where he oversaw the mass production of his work, and a castle that was once owned by the Frederick the Great. In producing monumental, heroic sculptures for the regime, he strayed far from his roots as a modern artist—a young sculptor who had been taken in by French modern masters like Aristide Maillol. Breker once had been widely regarded as the best hope to emerge as a new German master, and even Alfred Flechtheim, the famed Jewish dealer of modern art, took him on as an artist in the late 1920s. But Breker witnessed the potential of monumental sculpture while on a fellowship to Fascist Italy in 1932 (this, at the time when Mussolini's regime was moving toward the more grandiose 'Empire Style'). Goebbels visited Breker and the other artists at the Villa Massimo in Rome in the spring of 1933 and made a plea for the sculptor to return to the new Germany. Breker complied and soon found a key patron in Albert Speer. The two men would become remarkably powerful in the cultural sphere (and beyond). Speer controlled massive budgets and he made sure to direct a good sum of it to Breker: bills in the millions of Reichsmarks remain part of the archival record. Both men enriched themselves as they created for the Reich.

In the non-official sector, support for Expressionism and other kinds of modernist art continued up until 1945. Indeed, the push for Expressionism had also occurred in the state-sponsored realm. Pro-modernist students who became cultural bureaucrats, such as Otto Andreas Schreiber, Hans Weidemann, and Fritz Hippler, worked under Goebbels's aegis and promoted modernism through journals like *Kunst der Nation* and exhibitions in factories. Because factories were secure sites, other Nazi agents could not enter the premises. This gave the young pro-modernists the opportunity to organize exhibitions of modern art, and they included works by Karl Schmidt-Rottluff, Gerhard Marcks, and Max Pechstein in their shows. Pro-modernist forces always existed within the Nazi Party. Indeed, some experts maintain that modernism might well have become the official style of National Socialism, except for Hitler. Former Hitler Youth leader turned Reich Governor for Vienna Baldur von Schirach even sponsored an exhibition featuring modern art in 1943. The show, *Youthful Art in the German Reich (Junge Kunst im Deutschen Reich)*, proved too radical for Hitler, especially with the total war measures coming into effect, and was quickly closed down.

Modern art nonetheless persisted in Nazi Germany, if in more private spaces. Oftentimes, artists worked in the countryside, such as Ernst Barlach in his atelier in Güstrow in Pomerania, who continued to be productive until his death in October 1938. Max Pechstein also worked in Pomerania, while Otto Dix painted in Hemmenhofen on Lake Constance. Even if they felt constrained by the government— Dix favoured landscapes and allegories out of fear of an investigation—many experienced productive years during the Third Reich. Desperate times sometimes foster great art. Accordingly, dealers of modern art remained in business up until 1945. Bombs were falling on German cities in the spring of 1945, and most dealers had taken refuge in the countryside, but they kept selling, using the Reichspost to ship paintings by Karl Schmidt-Rottluff and Erich Heckel, among other modernist artists.

Emil Nolde stands out as a modern artist who continued to work during the Third Reich. Hailing from the borderlands between

Germany and Denmark, he nonetheless believed that his art was truly German. Nolde himself identified as an ethnic German and this in part motivated him to join the Danish branch of the Nazi Party in 1920. A path-breaking painter who had been affiliated before World War I with the New Secession in Berlin and then *Die Brücke* in Dresden and Berlin, Nolde enjoyed great success through the 1920s. The fact that Nolde had 1,052 pictures confiscated from German museums in 1937 and 1938—the most of any artist—stands as a testament to his previous commercial and critical success. With his home in Seebüll near Flensburg and a flat in Berlin, he had both good working conditions but also a place to interact with other creative types; his friends included dancers Gret Palucca and Mary Wigman, both of whom he painted. He also attempted to cultivate relations with Nazi leaders, and accepted an invitation in November 1933 to be a guest of Heinrich Himmler's at lunch at an event to commemorate those who died in the Beer Hall Putsch. Nolde recorded his experiences, writing letters about meeting Himmler and feeling somewhat ill at ease among the party leaders. But he craved official acceptance. He had supporters in the Nazi leadership—Goebbels and Speer expressed admiration for his work, and utilized it to decorate the former's home early in the Third Reich, and Reich Education Minister Bernhard Rust made positive statements about him. Nolde was much like Ernst Ludwig Kirchner, who considered himself and his art to be German, even in the latter's case, while residing in nearby Switzerland.

Nolde suffered public stricture, but he continued to work. When he received a '*Berufsverbot*' (ban on practising his profession) in 1941, he challenged the sanctions, writing to Goebbels. In fact, he retreated to Seebüll and continued his work. The story that the Gestapo would inspect his brushes is mostly myth. This did not mean he did not fear an inspection: it well may have motivated him to create the small-format watercolours, which are odourless and easier to conceal. He did create some 1,300 'unpainted pictures'; but he also painted twelve oil paintings during the war. His art was bought and sold, although he himself took great care because selling his recent works would consti-tute a violation of his 'ban on profession'. He survived the war, wrote a very brief account on his experiences during the Third Reich (that in no way represented a 'mastering' of this past), but he lived undis-turbed in Seebüll. As long as his health permitted, he continued with watercolours until shortly before his death in 1956, and his pictures now sell for millions.

On the spectrum of official acceptance during the Third Reich, painter Charlotte Salomon occupied a place toward the extreme of exclusion. A Berlin Jew, an Expressionist, and a woman working in a misogynist society, she is best known for her autobiographical series of pictures, *Life? or Theater? A Song-Play* (*Leben? Oder Theater? Ein Singspiel*). At the age of 19 in 1936, Salomon managed to matriculate at the United State Schools for Pure and Applied Arts, where she spent the following two years. But the rising anti-Semitism undermined her education and career. Salomon's father was arrested after *Kristallnacht* and interned in Sachsenhausen (she imagined his experiences and painted them). Charlotte (or Lotte) was sent off to stay with her grandparents in the south of France. After spending time in a cottage on the grounds of a luxurious estate belonging to Ottilie Moore, an American ex-patriot, they moved to an apartment in Nice. She and her grandfather tried to escape France by heading over the Pyrenees in 1940, but they were captured and sent to the internment camp at Gurs. Released because of her grandfather's infirmity, they returned to Nice, where Salomon focused on her magnum opus.

In creating *Life? or Theater? A Song-Play* Charlotte Salomon executed 769 gouaches, plus sketches and transparencies amounting to 1,325 pages, and then assembled and labelled them. She documented the experiences of her family, capturing the tragedy in what art historian Griselda Pollock called 'one of the twentieth century's most challenging art works: radical in its modernist hybridities, intertextualities, formal daring, and diversity'. The images capture Jewish life in Europe, the rise of the Nazis, and efforts to emigrate from Europe, but mostly, her own private world, where the quiet girl spent her time creating pictures. Many of the later images treat sickness, suffering, and death, and scholars have discerned that she seemed to sense her impending fate. She gave the works to Dr Georges Moridis in 1943, a trusted friend, with the words, 'Keep this safe. It's my whole life.' Salomon had married another German-Jewish émigré, Alexander Nagle, and together, they were dragged from their home in Nice, sent to Drancy, and then deported to Auschwitz. Salomon, then 26, and her unborn baby were gassed on arrival there on 10 October 1943. She was not alone among Jewish artists killed by the

Nazis: other victims included painter Felix Nussbaum, sculptor Otto Freundlich, and painter Elfriede Lohse-Wächtler, the latter murdered on 31 July 1940 in the gas chamber at the sanitarium Pirna-Sonnenstein as part of the 'T-4' programme to kill the mentally and physically handicapped.

Because the visual arts are created in a relatively private sphere, it was often possible to continue to produce work that ran contrary to official aesthetic dictates. The Reich Chamber for the Visual Arts appeared fairly generous in distributing supplies (even well-known modern artists like Otto Andreas Schreiber received permission to buy paints late in the war). There was no such thing as the oft-touted '*Malverbot*' (ban on painting). Yes, painters suffered intimidation and persecution, and often in the case of Jewish artists, worse fates, but many modernist artists persisted throughout the Third Reich, often with startling results.

Music

The homeland of Bach and Beethoven continued to feature a wealth of talent, despite the massive emigration in this realm. When one considers the musical talent that remained in Nazi Germany, it is indeed impressive and included Richard Strauss, Wilhelm Furtwängler, Herbert von Karajan, Elisabeth Schwarzkopf, Carl Orff, and until 1940, Paul Hindemith—and this just for a start. There was a tradition of *Hausmusik* (literally music in the house), and a vast array of choirs and local ensembles that the Nazis strived to 'coordinate'. Berlin had three major opera houses and great symphonies flourished not only in the capital, but also in Dresden, Munich, and Vienna, among other cities. Bayreuth continued to be mecca for Wagner aficionados and actually increased in stature during the 1930s. Hitler's close personal relationship with Winifred Wagner, and the considerable financial support he provided, tied the regime to the festival.

The Nazi leaders, of course, attempted to shape music according to ideological principles. The Third Reich saw a profusion of marching music, martial in character, while SS choirs banged out patriotic anthems. There was an elaborate array of agencies of musical administration, beginning with the Reich Music Chamber, which effectively licensed all musicians. In instances where 'credentials looked dubious', the musician had to pass a competency test administered by a local committee. This could result in the individual being demoted to the lesser category of occasional player. The *Degenerate Music Exhibition* opened in Düsseldorf in 1938, following its counterpart in the visual arts, and featured the usual racist propaganda, but this time with greater emphasis on people of African descent (the monkey-like figure with a saxophone and a Star of David serving as an iconic image). Besides jazz, the other style of great derision among many Nazis was atonal music, which they saw as Jewish (and hence meretricious). Yet music presented many challenges in terms of regulation (one could play most anything in small groups). This did not eliminate the dangers of music that Nazi ideologues viewed as subversive, but the most pronounced intervention of the authorities generally concerned the purging of Jewish practitioners from the nation's musical life.

Among the key musicians in Germany, Richard Strauss stands out. The most prestigious musical figure in 1933, he had been composing at a prodigious rate since the 1880s, with *Thus Spoke Zarathustra* (1896), *Elektra* (1906–8), *Der Rosenkavalier* (1910–11), and *An Alpine Symphony* (1915), among many other works, contributing to a stellar reputation. A transitional figure between the Romantic and modern eras, Strauss composed sweeping melodies, while also exploring chromaticism and dissonance, especially in earlier works, such as *Elektra*. Although he had held prominent administrative posts during his career—he headed the Permanent Council for International Cooperation among Composers—it was a big step for him to become the first President of the Reich Chamber of Music in the autumn of 1933. It tied him to the regime, and put his fame in service of the Nazis. He later said he tried to mitigate the harm done by the new rulers, and this rings true in certain respects. With good reason, he believed that his cooperation with the regime would improve the musical life of Germany, and also help those close to him, especially his Jewish daughter-in law and grandchildren. He used his influence to intervene on their behalf after they had been arrested by the Gestapo in Vienna and had them remanded to house arrest at his villa in Garmisch. But he was also induced to serve as President of the Reich Music Chamber by his sizeable ego. As historian Frederic Spotts observed, 'If Furtwängler longed to be the *Führer* of musical performance, Strauss wished to be *Führer* of what was performed.'

Strauss's behaviour proved a mixture of courage and collaboration. On the one hand, he tried to continue his partnership with Jewish librettist Stefan Zweig, and his letters to the recent émigré that were intercepted by the authorities, and which led to his resignation as President of the Reich Music Chamber in 1935, revealed a critical stance toward Hitler and the regime. Yet, as indicated above, he continued to compose and conduct in a manner that benefited the Nazis. Back in 1934, he had penned, '*Das Bächlein*', which he dedicated to Goebbels. The piece concluded by repeating the word 'Führer' three times—rendering it unambiguously propagandistic. Strauss conducted at a festival in Antwerp in March 1936 at the height of the Rhineland crisis when anti-German sentiment in Belgium was on the rise. Later, in 1943, he wrote the '*Festmusik*' for the fifth anniversary of the *Anschluss* and completed a commission for Baldur von Schirach, the Nazi Governor of Vienna. Michael H. Kater has noted that Strauss 'had a deep distrust of "Negroes", constituting one seed for his unmitigated dislike of jazz...'. Strauss also detested light entertainment music. This posed a problem because Hitler liked this genre, and Goebbels thought it useful as a kind of opiate for the masses. At several points, the composer found himself in serious trouble for having mocked Franz Lehár, one of the Führer's favourites. Fellow conductor Arturo Toscanini captured the man's contradictions, famously quipping, 'To Strauss the composer I take off my hat; to Strauss the man I put it back on again.' Arrested by American troops at his Garmisch home in April 1945, he was treated with utmost respect by commanding officer, Lieutenant Milton Weiss, who himself was a musician. Strauss reportedly descended the stairs of his grand home and announced, 'I am Richard Strauss, the composer of *Der Rosenkavalier* and *Salome*.' Lieutenant Weiss nodded with recognition, then placed an 'off limits' sign in front of the home, so as to protect the owner. Strauss expressed no remorse about his actions during the Third Reich and passed away in 1949 at age 85.

Another key figure in the musical sphere who defies easy categorization is Carl Orff (1895–1982). Like Strauss, Orff's experiences during this era raise the question of whether great artistic accomplishment was possible under Nazi rule. His cantata *Carmina Burana* offers one of the strongest arguments in the affirmative. Based on twenty-four thirteenth-century poems, with largely simple harmonies, the piece became hugely popular in Nazi Germany after its premiere in Frankfurt in 1937. George Steiner argued that it is 'terrifying when the singers spit out their Latin fricatives like jack-booted automatons'. Yet the work has stood the test of time and the song, *O Fortuna* has become a recognizable classic. Orff's accomplishments certainly pose a challenge to the claim of musicologist Rudolf Stephan that National Socialism 'played no role in those masterpieces that did arise' between 1933 and 1945 (he added, 'it created nothing positive, it only destroyed').

In 1939, two years after *Carmina Burana*, Orff submitted music for *A Midsummer's Night Dream* when the Nazi authorities called for music to replace that of Felix Mendelssohn, which had been banned due to the composer's Jewish origins. In this instance, Orff received a commission of RM 5,000 from the city of Frankfurt. While Orff and his defenders later maintained that he had begun composing music for Shakespeare's play before the Nazi seizure of power, the fact remains that the premiere of this work in Frankfurt in October 1939 constituted a propagandistic celebration, one officiated by the Mayor of the city, Friedrich Krebs, who also headed the local Fighting League for German Culture. Despite these instances of ostensible collaboration, Orff was friends with Professor Kurt Huber, a leading figure in the White Rose resistance group. After Huber's arrest in 1942, Huber's wife asked Orff to intervene, but the composer refused, saying he would be 'ruined' if he did so. Carl Orff suffered acute guilt for his refusal to act, even writing a letter to the dead professor in January 1946 asking for forgiveness. Yet he survived denazification and enjoyed a productive career in the post-war period. He turned to the ancient world, a safer subject, as a setting for many of his later works, but he also tried to influence the real one in which he lived, developing a reform programme for children's musical education called '*Orff Schulwerk*'. His was a holistic approach that combined movement, singing, and improvisation. Carl Orff, like Strauss, had company in maintaining musical life during the Third Reich: Wilhelm Furtwängler, Herbert van Karajan, Elisabeth Schwarzkopf, and Karl Böhm were among the towering figures who continued their careers with a considerable degree of accommodation with the regime.

As noted above, the non-official musical sector also flourished. Music historian Pamela Potter has noted, 'Music censorship was perhaps the least rigid, rendered impractical, if not impossible, by the variety and abundance of musical outlets lying beyond government or police controls.' Certain composers, such as Paul von Klenau and Winfried Zillig experimented with serialism, while 'salon dance music', played by musicians who had often been classically trained, could be found in most urban centres, and even occasionally on state-controlled radio. A variation of this music, but with a strong violin presence (often giving the music a more 'saccharine timbre') was also common. *Unterhaltungs-musik*' therefore enjoyed a measure of toleration, as Goebbels and other Nazi authorities sometimes enjoyed it. Jazz had come to Germany after World War I—some believe that German POWs heard it in camps in France and helped make it popular, while others focus on the Allied occupation forces in the Rhineland, where the soldiers brought this fare with them. The proliferation of theatres and cabarets in Berlin and other big cities in Germany had helped the new music take hold during the Weimar Republic.

In 1933, however, jazz was officially banned, or placed on the index of proscribed music. Viewed by many Nazis as the product of blacks and Jews, jazz came under attack from Nazi ideologues, such as Professor Peter Raabe, who took over from Richard Strauss in 1935 as President of the Reich Music Chamber. Raabe had attacked jazz in the first convention of the Reich Music Chamber in early 1934; at the same time he 'berated the influence of Jews, especially in the distribution of inferior music'. But the German public's interest in this kind of music would create a continuing challenge. During the war, the British proved especially adept at inducing the Germans to listen, and they intermixed jazz and popular music—George and Ira Gershwin, Glenn Miller, and Benny Goodman, among others—with news reports. Even though Goebbels issued an order in September 1939 prohibiting listening to foreign radio broadcasts, the transgressive behaviour continued (especially because updates on the military situation were eagerly sought). The Wehrmacht leadership informed Goebbels that the soldiers were increasingly listening to English broadcasts, and the Reich Minister, despite his personal antipathy to 'distorted rhythms' and 'atonal melodies' permitted more 'rhythmic dance music' on the airwaves, especially later in the evening. Even the music of black musicians like Louis Armstrong and Duke Ellington was played on German radio, although their names were concealed. This liberalization, however, drew to an end in 1943, with the implementation of the stricter total war measures.

The Swing Youth and Edelweiss Pirates constituted more specific subcultures, but were linked to jazz and daring American swing music. After a quasi-public dance in February 1940 involving some 500 Swings who utilized a hidden hall located near the main building of the Kaiserhof Hotel in Hamburg-Altona, a Gestapo agent reported, 'The Swing dance was being executed in a completely hideous fashion. English music was played along with English vocals, while our soldiers are engaged in battle against Britain.' Music was just one aspect of the identity of the Edelweiss Pirates. Consisting mostly of young men, ages 14 to 18 who avoided the Hitler Youth by leaving school, but who were too young for the armed forces, these 'pirates' opposed the Nazi regime in most respects. Even though they were loosely organized, they treated the Hitler Youth as a rival street gang, ambushing patrols and taking great pride in beating them up. The Pirates engaged in other kinds of oppositional behaviour, such as assisting deserters, although they mostly sought freedom, whether in a music club or on a hiking trip. Their use of jazz and popular music as part of a subculture of resistance has made them the stuff of Hollywood movies (*Edelweis Pirates* from 2004). These youths cannot be said to have succeeded in altering the course of the regime, but they showed great courage in behaving in a transgressive manner.

Literature

Although there is a rich historiography on literature during the Third Reich, the discipline has sometimes seemed to exist in the shadows of other art forms during the period. This may be because Hitler and the regime did not promote writers in the same way as they did certain architects, artists, and musicians. Yet we now know that Hitler was in fact an avid reader and that he amassed a library of over 16,000 books. He often read late into the night and marked up his copies with marginalia that scholars have begun to analyse. The Reich Chamber for Literature also stood out as a large and significant corporatist body: at the start of the war, it regulated 3,000 authors, 2,500 publishing houses, 23,000 bookshops and fifty national literary prizes.

An average of 20,000 new books appeared annually during the Third Reich, making Germany the largest producer of books in Europe. Because of a nearly 100 per cent literacy rate, literature was considered a vital form of propaganda. Hitler's *Mein Kampf* was the best-selling book during the Third Reich, with over six million copies sold, although many owners of the tome never read it. However, the regime fostered other works that promoted the desired themes, including Führer-worship, a belief in a racial hierarchy (with the concomitant anti-Semitism), a spiritual connection between the people and the land ('Blood and Soil' or '*Blut und Boden*'), and a kind of hyper-nationalism.

The burning of books on 10 May 1933 by Nazi students stands out as one of the most symbolic acts of the twelve-year regime. The events in university towns and at the Humboldt University in Berlin—the destruction of books deemed 'against the German spirit'—probably surprised even Goebbels in terms of the expressive force. It also generated negative publicity abroad. The Reich Propaganda Minister never again ordered another public burning of books,although he permitted some modern art purged from German state collections—1,004 paintings and some 3,000 graphic works—to be immolated out of public view at Berlin's Main Fire Station in March 1939. Officials at the Reich Literature Chamber routinely proceeded by bureaucratic means, censoring Jewish, modernist, and left-wing authors, especially if they were more than one of these things. Goebbels also issued orders in 1936 prohibiting literary criticism, although, in fact, the guidelines were meant mostly to intimidate those penning reviews that might offend Nazi officials. Nonetheless, these rules stated that reviews were to follow a pattern: as historian Richard Grunberger noted, 'a synopsis of content studded with quotations, marginal comments on style, a calculation of the degree of concurrence with Nazi doctrine and a conclusion indicating approval or otherwise'.

Representative of writers in the official sphere is Hans Johst (1890–1978), the author of the 1933 play *Schlageter*, which glorified a Nazi martyr who had defied the French and Belgian occupation of the Ruhr in 1923 and had been executed by the French. The play included the famous line, 'when I hear the word culture, I release the safety catch on my Browning'. Meant to implore the protagonist to fight rather than to study, Johst's words alluded to the link between culture and barbarism in Nazi Germany.

Premiering in 1933, *Schlageter* counted as an example of the 'heroic theatre' favoured by the Nazis. Johst was considered by many to be the 'Nazi Poet Laureate', and served as President of the Reich Literature Chamber from 1935 to 1945. In this capacity, he interacted with Goebbels and many other top Nazi leaders. He was also a colonel in the SS and counted among Himmler's favourites (he addressed letters '*Mein Reichsführer, lieber Heini Himmler!*'). Johst had once shown Expressionist tendencies in his writing and occasionally helped modernist colleagues, such as Gottfried Benn, but he became a proponent of the more ideological, 'blood and soil' themed literature of the time. His output tapered off as he devoted himself more to administrative work, but he continued to publish poems, as well as essays and speeches, including *My Earth is Called Germany* (*Meine Erde heisst Deutschland*) from 1938, and the 1940 volume, *Call of the Reich, Echo of the People* (*Ruf des Reiches, Echo des Volkes*). In September 1944, Johst was placed on the list of 'artists protected by God' (*Gottbegnadeten Künstlern*). Yet after the war, he was put on trial and sentenced to a three-and-a-half year term, which was lengthy for the standards of the time. A ten-year writing ban also ensued. He published poems under a pseudonym in *The Clever Housewife* (*Die Kluge Hausfrau*), a magazine produced for the German supermarket chain Edeka, but Johst was treated as a serious threat by authorities in the Federal Republic and effectively marginalized.

Gottfried Benn (1886–1956), a physician with a specialty in venereal diseases, was in many ways unlikely to become a great poet, especially of the Expressionist persuasion. But emerge he did, with pre-World War I collections like *Morgue and Other Poems* (1912), and works appearing in the Expressionist periodical *Die Aktion*. Benn evinced a strong interest in the irrational forces in life—the passions, emotions, and instincts that drove human beings. His was a dark vision of humanity and of life. After serving as a front-line physician during World War I, he returned to Berlin, where he continued his medical practice and also participated in avant-garde artists' groups.

He became a friend of George Grosz's, with the artist inspiring Benn's collection titled *Fleisch* (*Meat*). Benn made such a mark on contemporaries that he was elected to the prestigious Prussian Academy for the Arts in 1932. But for all his associations with avant-garde figures in Weimar Berlin, Benn also evinced support for National Socialism, and in February 1933, he was appointed the provisional head of the poetry section of the Academy. As such, he helped the Nazis carry through their *Gleichschaltung*: at the Academy, this forced the resignations of Heinrich Mann, Käthe Kollwitz, and other modernist figures, and the elevation of pro-Nazi writers such as Hanns Johst, Hans Grimm, and Erwin Guido Kolbenheyer. A crucial moment for Benn and his relationship to the regime came on 24 April 1933, when he delivered a radio address titled, 'The New State and the Intellectuals'. Literary scholar Egbert Krispyn summarized his remarks: 'He derided all liberalism and proclaimed that intellectual freedom had to be subordinated and sacrificed to the totalitarian state. At the same time he hailed the National Socialists as representing the new heroic biological type to whom the future belonged.' Benn engaged in a public exchange with émigré Klaus Mann about the role of intellectuals in the 'new' Reich, and also articulated a highly racialistic worldview. At times, he combined the two themes, writing, for example, 'Will you not finally realize, on your Latin shore, that the events in Germany are not political tricks, to be twisted and talked to death in the well-known dialectical manner, but are the emergence of a new biological type, a mutation of history and a people's wish to breed itself?' He also remarked,

> Will you amateurs of civilization, you troubadours of Western progress not realize, at last, that what is here at stake is not forms of government but a new vision of the birth of man—perhaps an old, perhaps the last grand concept of the white race, probably one of the grandest realizations of the cosmic spirit itself, preluded in Goethe's hymn *To Nature*?

Benn's racism also found expression in a September 1933 piece he wrote for the periodical *Die Woche*, where he called for the 'removal or segregation' [*ausscheidung*] of the 'less valuable part of the *Volk* . . . not only for reasons to do with racial fitness, but also for macro-economic [*volkswirtschaftlichen*] reasons'. In short, Benn openly and forcefully articulated a racist, eugenic programme. His high-brow, culture-based arguments can be seen as buttressing what would evolve into a genocidal programme, although again, he himself made no call for killing, let alone persecution. In addition to the biological component to his thinking, Benn's views dovetailed with National Socialism in other ways, including the glorification of the state and a call for the subordination of the individual to this state.

His vision of Third Reich proved illusory, for he hoped that the new rulers would embrace modernism, including Expressionism, and that they would revive the dismal country. He grew distressed by the increasingly violent and radical government, and already in June 1933, he gave up his position as Head of the Poetry Section of the Prussian Academy. However, it was the murderous Night of the Long Knives in June 1934 that precipitated Benn's break with the regime. Hitler, Göring, and Himmler led the assault on the SA leadership, but also other sundry political opponents. To this day, there is no precise number for the deaths, but some believe it to be upwards of 200. Benn surveyed his options: as a writer tied to the German language, emigration appeared particularly daunting. The son of a minister from Pomerania, he felt he knew his *Heimat* and could not leave it. He therefore, and now famously took the 'aristocratic form of emigration' and joined the army. Benn re-enlisted in 1936, which in his case involved practising medicine, so at least he was not taking the lives of others. He continued to write, albeit privately, and as his vision grew still darker, he conveyed a degree of remorse for his earlier enthusiasm for National Socialism. He penned the novella *Das Weinhaus Wolf* (*Wolf's Tavern*) before the war in which he quoted a Chinese proverb, 'he who rides a tiger cannot dismount', and concluded, 'no one can now see history as anything but the justification of mass murder: rapine and glorification—there's the mechanism of power'. Benn by and large retreated from public life, and in this way he was like Ernst Jünger (1895–1998): a figure who had inspired many Nazis with his tales of heroism and sacrifice during World War I—in particular, his best-selling, *Storm of Steel* (1920). Jünger refused to join the Nazi Party and exhibited a marked ambivalence about Hitler. In his own writing, he took care not to cross the line into subversion, but allegorical works like *On the Marble Cliffs* (1939) left little doubt that he had concerns about the direction of the regime. Like Benn, Jünger navigated an inner-emigration. He reduced his public profile, published less, and yet continued to write. Also like Benn, Jünger eventually re-entered the army. Stationed in Paris during the German occupation, the writer took advantage of the cultural life of the French capital, meeting with Picasso and other contemporaries. Both men revived their careers in the post-war period: Benn receiving the Cross of Merit in 1952 from President of the Federal Republic Theodor Heuss, and Jünger earning the distinction as Chancellor Helmut Kohl's favourite author.

Because writing stands out as the most private of the arts—one does not even need painting supplies—it offered the best opportunity for opponents and victims of the regime to capture their experiences and articulate their views. Among the writers who were persecuted by the Nazis, one counts Walter Benjamin (1892–1940), Gertrud Kolmar (1894–1943), and Else Lasker-Schüler (1869–1945). Poet Paul Celan (1920–70), who wrote while in a Romanian ghetto and translated Shakespeare's sonnets, penned 'Death Fugue' (*Todesfuge*), arguably the most famous poem about the Holocaust, while incarcerated in a work camp in 1944–5. Born Paul Antschel, to a German-speaking Jewish family from northern Bukovina (Romania, but earlier, a part of the Habsburg Empire), the precocious poet tried to weather the storm of World War II by returning to his home in Cernăuti. Instead, he found himself subjected to forced labour, including clearing debris from the steadily destroyed ghetto and then being imprisoned in a work camp. Celan was liberated by the Soviet Red Army in February 1944, whereupon he went to work as a caretaker in a mental hospital. He soon relocated to Bucharest, where he became active in the Jewish literary community. It was at this time that he published 'Death Fugue'—in both German and Romanian. Each stanza begins with 'Black milk of daybreak, we drink . . . ', a repetitive phrase that evokes an industrial process, which Celan then combines with the image of smoke from the crematoria. The haunting phrase from the poem, 'Death is a master from Germany', has also become iconic. Celan moved to Vienna in 1947 and subsequently to Paris, which served as his primary residence. He suffered from loneliness and alienation and committed suicide in 1970 by drowning himself in the River Seine. He was among a number of Holocaust survivor-authors who took their own lives, including Jean Améry (born Hanns Chaim Mayer) (1912–78), Primo Levi (1919–87), Tadeusz Borowski (1922–51), and Sarah Kofman (1934–94).

Paul Celan stands among a cohort of remarkable authors whose work drew on their experiences during the Third Reich and the Holocaust, including Waldyslaw Szpilman (1911–2000), Elie Wiesel

(1928–2016), Imre Kertész (1929–2016), Ruth Klüger (b. 1931), and the aforementioned Primo Levi, among the Jewish authors (of varying nationalities), and Charlotte Delbo (1913–85), Heinrich Böll (1917–85), Günter Grass (1927–2015), Christa Wolf (1929–2011), and Borowski among the Christians. Because the Nazis subjugated such a vast geographical expanse, these (and other) authors covered a wide range of European experiences. An array of memoirs also chronicle the era, including the now famous efforts of Victor Klemperer (1881–1960), Emanuel Ringelblum (1900–44), and Anne Frank (1929–45) among others. Clearly, the crucible of life in these dark times yielded profound insights into the human condition.

Conclusions

Some fifty years ago, David Schoenbaum, who authored a social history of Nazi Germany up until 1939, posited a distinction between 'objective social reality' and 'subjective social reality': the former represented the statistically measurable consequences of National Socialism, while the latter applied to people's perceptions—what they thought was transpiring. Many Germans perceived shifts in society—class divisions, income distribution, and gender roles, among others—that did not correspond to actual events. The state-directed culture and propaganda convinced many of the illusory transformations. With their Manichean worldview, the Nazi leaders effected a subjective social reality where one side emerged as a positive imaginary, what historian Peter Reichel termed 'the beautiful veneer of the Third Reich' ('*Das Schöne Schein des Dritten Reiches*'). The obverse side, of course, inculcated racism and hate, foremost being what Jeffrey Herf called in his study of Nazi propaganda 'the Jewish enemy'. At times, the two sides came together, such as in the film about Theresienstadt, *The Führer Gives the Jews a City* (*Der Führer schenkt den Juden eine Stadt*), set in the camp after it was temporarily beautified in September 1944. Shortly after the completion of this film, Kurt Gerron, a Jew who served as its director, was 'evacuated' to Auschwitz and gassed upon arrival.

Because the Nazi leaders understood the importance of culture, they competed vigorously (and at time ferociously) for authority in this sphere. Most viewed themselves as artistically inclined: Hitler as a painter/architect, Heydrich and Ribbentrop as violinists; Streicher and Rosenberg as painters; and von Schirach as a poet, to take a few examples. Their belief that they represented a cultured nation helped them rationalize the ideological war and genocide. Culture and persecution were linked in very direct ways. Stealing a people's art and cultural property constituted a step along the twisted road to Auschwitz. The expropriation of this property helped dehumanize the victims, and when the latter were forced into abject poverty, malnourished, and often became sick, as was common in the ghettos, the journey advanced still further. Back in the early 1970s George Steiner observed:

> Art, intellectual pursuits, the development of the natural sciences, many branches of scholarship flourished in close spatial, temporal proximity to massacre and the death camps.... Why did humanistic traditions and models of conduct prove so fragile a barrier against political bestiality? In fact, were they a barrier, or is it more realistic to perceive in humanistic culture express solicitations of authoritarian rule and cruelty. (p. 30)

Germany, one of the most culturally advanced countries in Europe, descended into savagery and this with a regime whose leaders cared deeply about architecture and the arts. We are left with lasting images: Hans Krása's children's opera *Brunidbár* being performed in Theresienstadt, with the composer and most of the cast being transported to Auschwitz and killed after a September 1944 production; or an orchestra playing Bach and Beethoven at the gates of Auschwitz.

In *The Third Man*, an early post-war film set in Vienna, Orson Welles's character observes, 'In Switzerland, they had brotherly love, they had five hundred years of democracy and peace, and what did that produce? The cuckoo clock.' This was certainly not the case for Nazi Germany. And that is a key point: while the Nazis restricted and limited culture, and tried to stifle creativity, their efforts ultimately did not diminish the importance of culture during the Third Reich. In fact, the opposite was true. The cultural history of Nazi Germany features a multitude of stories, involving important and talented individuals (to be expected after the Weimar renaissance), and the issues at play cut to the core of human existence. This is one of the reasons that a number of talented post-war German artists have explored the nexus of culture and barbarism, including Hannah Höch, Joseph Beuys, Georg Baselitz, Anselm Kiefer, and Gerhard Richter. As Peter Watson observed at the conclusion of his nearly-1,000-page tome, *The German Genius*, 'The German predicament is not easy...'.

5

Photography and Cinema

David F. Crew

Examining the production and consumption of photographic and filmic images in the Third Reich is important for two reasons. First: one of the Nazis' main priorities after 1933 was to transform the ways that Germans saw the world and themselves. Although this project of reshaping popular perceptions and subjectivities employed written and spoken language, as well as music, it depended heavily upon images, particularly photographic and filmic images. Second: the Nazi rise to power coincided with the breakthrough of photography and film as mass cultural and social practices in Germany. Between 1933 and 1945, millions of Germans took photographs and millions more consumed photographic images in illustrated magazines and went to the movies. What role did this unprecedented and pervasive visualization of popular culture play in constructing new views of the world that were consonant (or perhaps also in tension) with Nazi values?

I have cast this chapter as an exploration of the encounters with photographs and filmic images that an ordinary German could experience as he/she pursued the activities that constituted his/her everyday life. My aim is to look at photography and film not only in terms of the images themselves but more importantly as mass social and cultural practices that became normal, ubiquitous constituents of everyday life in the Third Reich. To make this discussion manageable, I focus upon Berlin (the media capital of Germany at that time) and upon a series of important 'sample' years in the Nazi Third Reich: 1933, when Hitler came to power; 1938, the year of *Kristallnacht* ('Crystal Night'), the nationwide pogrom against German Jews, as well as the annexation of Austria and the Sudetenland; 1939, the opening of the Second World War with the invasion and subsequent brutal occupation of Poland; 1941, the year of the German invasion of the Soviet Union and the progressive implementation of the Holocaust; 1945, the year in which the war finally came home to Germany, producing massive destruction of German cities from the air as well as the highest casualty rates sustained by German military forces in the entire course of the war. Although I will try to give readers a clear sense of all the different sites where Germans might have engaged with photography and film during the Third Reich, I will concentrate on three of the most important mass practices—reading illustrated magazines, going to the movies, and taking private photographs.

Using 'Address Books' (*Adreßbücher*) published in the 1930s and 1940s, I have selected the names of real Germans who lived in Berlin. I then construct an imagined but altogether possible visual journey that these individuals could have taken during a typical day or week after they left their apartments for the streets of Berlin on their way to work or to some leisure activity. In 1933, the year that Hitler came to power, the Berlin *Adreßbuch* listed seventeen individuals as 'household heads' in the apartment building at No. 4 Chausseestraße in the Mitte district of Berlin. This street was an extension northwards of the Friedrichstraße which ran past a main train station and then south across Berlin's main boulevard, Unter den Linden. A few blocks north of the train station, Friedrichstraße intersected with Oranienburgerstraße, the location of one of the more imposing of the city's synagogues. The neighbourhood around the synagogue was heavily Jewish. Further to the east could be found the *Scheunenviertel*, a neighbourhood populated with many recent Jewish immigrants from eastern Europe and the former Russian Empire. However, No. 4 Chausseestraße was removed from this Jewish world not far to the east. In the nineteenth century, the social profile of this part of Berlin had been shaped by the Borsig Locomotive Works, one of the prime movers of the industrialization of the city. At the end of the nineteenth century, the firm moved further north to Tegel. By 1930, Borsig was on the verge of liquidation; the locomotive business was only saved by a merger with the German General Electric Company (*AEG.*)

Only two of the seventeen household heads living at No. 4 Chaussestraße in 1933 could still be found there in 1941, G. Große, a bank clerk and K. Klatt, a postman. All the others, who were employed in jobs ranging from mechanic and bookkeeper to lorry driver and a woman tailor, had all either moved elsewhere, died, or been sent to fight on one of the many fronts of the Second World War. Let us imagine that we follow the bank clerk and the postman as they leave their apartments at No. 4 on their way to work on 12 March 1933, less than two months after Adolf Hitler has been named Chancellor of Germany. Their first encounter with photographic images would probably have been at one of the many local neighbourhood newspaper kiosks selling dozens of different types of daily and weekly publications, including the most important illustrated newspapers. In the 1920s, more Germans probably read illustrated newspapers and magazines than went to the movies. Karl Christian Führer shows, for example, that the *Berliner Illustrierte Zeitung* (*Berlin Illustrated Newspaper*, hereafter *BIZ*) had a circulation of 945,472 in 1934 and we can assume that many hundreds of thousands more Germans read this and other magazines than had actually bought them because reading circles (*Lesezirkeln*) offered these publications for rental. Führer has found that by 1938 about one million Germans subscribed to such reading circles. The 1933 Berlin *Adressbuch* listed nine *Lesezirkeln*, including the *Lesezirkel* Fahrenholz, founded in 1880 with two different locations in the metropolis.

Although the selection of publications was still impressive in 1933, including even foreign newspapers, our two residents of No. 4 Chausseestraße would probably have been aware that certain illustrated newspapers and magazines on offer before Hitler came to power were now banned—above all the Communist *Arbeiter Illustrierte Zeitung* (*Workers' Illustrated Magazine*). They would also no longer find photographs taken by or stories written by Jewish or left-wing photographers and authors. To work in the media under the Nazis required membership in the appropriate section of the Reich Chamber of Culture (*Reichskulturkammer*)—Jews, leftists, and other 'undesirables' were *de facto* excluded. What then, might Große or Klatt see in the illustrateds that they could buy? Illustrated magazines did not display a thematic coherence but rather sought to offer something for everyone in the attempt to boost sales. How they tried to do that under Hitler displayed remarkable continuities with the Weimar past but also significant changes.

Compared to the major Nazi Party illustrated magazine, the *Illustrierter Beobachter* (*Illustrated Observer*), which specialized in the visual portrayal of the Führer and the Nazi movement, the *BIZ* may have seemed politically more restrained. Nevertheless, the *BIZ* did display Hitler's picture prominently. The cover of the 23 April 1933 issue presented a striking and by now well-known photograph of Hitler in uniform surrounded and supported by strong, determined young men in SA (*Sturmabteilung* = Storm Detachment) uniforms. We cannot see the heads of the young Storm Troopers in the last row, suggesting perhaps that their ranks stretch off endlessly beyond the frame of the picture itself—the message is that there are so many young men dedicated to Hitler that it would be impossible to give any true sense of their immense numbers in one photograph. This particular front page picture might appear to be pure propaganda for the Nazi cause; yet, it also displays important continuities with the pre-Nazi past. Hitler is a new celebrity. Like actors and actresses, or Weimar statesmen, Hitler now has become a hot story.

Cover photos tried to grab potential readers' attention and help them to decide to buy one particular illustrated magazine, rather than the others on offer, but readers might detect no consistent visual strategy in the front-page pictures they saw each week. Visually, the cover of the 12 March 1933 issue of the *BIZ* was not particularly compelling, even though it pointed to what promised to be a thrilling tale of German aviation—the photo showed three important fliers at an engineering school in Weimar, but all appeared in very staid suits and ties. The next week, 19 March, the image shown on the front page was quite different. Entitled 'The Sun in Springtime (*Frühlingssonne*)', it presented a cute, blonde young girl. A Special Issue published on 21 March put politics on display with a photograph taken at night of columns of hundreds of SA men carrying lit torches as they marched through the Brandenburg Gate. The lead photo on the 9 April issue showed a young (presumably native American woman) on a horse in jeans and wearing a headdress to stimulate readers' interest in a story about 'A Visit to the Hopi-Indians in the Desert Cliffs of Arizona'. This was followed on 16 April by a cover image drawing attention to a report about the dedication of a monument in Mannheim to Carl Benz, founder of the well-known German automobile firm. The picture showed a smiling woman dressed in nineteenth-century costume at the wheel of a three-horsepower, one-cylinder Benz automobile from that period. A week later, the *BIZ* presented the picture that we have already discussed of Adolf Hitler surrounded by young SA men on the occasion of his 44th birthday. At the end of April, another Nazi leader, Herman Göring, appeared with Vice Chancellor von Papen and Vatican officials on the occasion of a state visit to the Pope. Another Special Issue commemorated the first Nazi Day of National Labor on 1 May with a photo taken from below of a Zeppelin with a large Nazi flag fluttering on the left hand side of the image. Two weeks later, 14 May, the cover of the *BIZ* bearing the title 'The Soldier as Sportsman' showed disciplined ranks of soldiers stripped to the waist performing their daily morning calisthenics. Hitler was featured again on the front page of the 11 June issue on the occasion of his visit to the navy (*Reichsmarine*). Unlike the earlier Hitler picture, however, this photograph showed only Hitler accompanied by one high-ranking naval officer. On 25 June, the *BIZ* front-page image entitled simply 'Mother's Hands' displayed a small child this time sitting on the ground and stretching up to hold two fingers of an adult whose hands and lower arms alone appeared in the frame of the image. Readers would see no consistent pattern—other than variety—in the cover photographs that announced each week's new issue of the *BIZ*. That was in fact the main point—the editors probably understood that they might not retain readers if too many covers showed Hitler, for example, yet they also understood that lead photos could not simply retreat from politics into everyday life. Instead, the pictures presented on the front page needed to alternate between the two creating an appealing balance. Similar principles governed the internal layout of the magazine which juxtaposed a series of seemingly incongruous topics and photo stories.

One example is the issue published on 12 January 1939. The cover showed four young women in what appeared to be a boudoir, all dressed in some type of lingerie. The caption explains that the photograph is a scene from the nine-hour general rehearsal of a new Berlin musical review in which the young women sing a new pop song (*Schlagermelodie*); 'I love dark hair but you are blond. I love tall and you are small. I myself don't know how we got here—it must be your sweet smile!' The women have rehearsed the song over and over until the performance is perfect. The same issue carried a story celebrating Himmler's tenth anniversary as *Reichsführer* SS with a picture of Himmler and Hitler walking together at the Obersalzberg.

Underneath this image, another showed the Prime Minister of France, Edouard Daladier in Tunis and a parade of native troops with, on the left side of the same page, a photograph of the Queen of Egypt, Farida, with her baby daughter, Ferial. This same issue also celebrated the opening of Hitler's new gigantic Chancellery Building in Berlin designed by Albert Speer. On the right-hand side, one picture showed Hitler talking with the cleaning women who worked in the building. Another showed Hitler with Speer in the Führer's enormous new 'work room'. In a third image, a worker ceremoniously gave Hitler the key to the new building and yet another picture showed workers listening to Hitler's speech telling them that they should be proud of the job they had done. At the bottom left side of the page, readers could find an incongruous photograph of an English engineer who had tried but failed to get his Russian wife out of the Soviet Union by plane. His second attempt worked. The picture shows the couple re-united during a short stopover in Berlin. Further on in this issue, three 'dramatic' images taken with an automatic camera mounted in a plane showed scenes from the air war in Spain. But in the bottom half of the page, the theme shifted to 'Scandals and Problems' in America with a photograph of Costa-Musica, an ex-convict who had managed to become General Director of a large American pharmaceutical concern. He was guilty of swindling millions of dollars which he used to furnish his villa like a Chinese palace.

It has been suggested that illustrated magazines such as the *BIZ* presented their readers with only a sanitized version of the reality of the Third Reich, diverting their attention from the brutality of the regime. Yet the *BIZ* certainly did not shrink from displaying to its readers the abhorrent anti-semitism that was the lodestar of the Nazi movement and of the Nazi regime after 1933. Although it may not have sunk to the same depths as party publications such as the *Illustrierter Beobachter* or the notorious *Der Stürmer* (*The Stormtrooper*), the *BIZ* did not simply ignore these key components of the new Nazi reality. Between 9–10 November 1938, a wave of violence, subsequently known as *Kristallnacht*, tore through Germany, Austria, and the newly occupied Sudetenland. According to Saul Friedländer, 7,500 Jewish businesses were vandalized, 267 synagogues were destroyed and ninety-one Jews were killed all over Germany. Thirty-five thousand Jews were arrested and sent to concentration camps. On Goebbels' instructions, German newspapers engaged in crude anti-Semitic hate propaganda. Pictorial magazines, such as the *BIZ* were allowed to be more muted in their approach. On 17 November 1938, just two weeks after *Kristallnacht*, the cover of the *BIZ* showed an elegant couple dancing together which it identified as the British amateurs, John Wells and Renee Sissons, 'The Best Dance Couple in the World', who for some years now had been international champions and who had enjoyed yet another triumph at a recent international contest in Berlin. The *BIZ* did not, however, completely ignore the recent violence against Jews. That same issue included a two-page spread on the annual Nazi commemoration of their attempt in Munich to overthrow the Weimar government on 8–9 November 1923. Although this putsch failed, the Nazis presented it as the beginning of their implacable rise to power in 1933. A large photo on the left-hand side of the page showed readers 'Where the [Nazi] Victims Fell'. A smaller picture to the right showed the Sudeten Nazi leader, Konrad Henlein, attending the ceremonies in Munich for the first time. The story continued on the right-hand page but then at the bottom under the title 'After the Murder in Paris' included photographs about the shooting of the German embassy official, Ernst vom Rath, by the 17-year-old Polish Jewish boy, Herschel Grynszpan which Goebbels used as the pretext to unleash the wave of anti-Jewish violence. Later in this same issue, the *BIZ* included a two-page story with the title 'The Global Problem: The Jews'. This first instalment of a multipart series focused upon the Jews of Lodz (Łódź), the Polish Manchester, where, it claimed, almost every second inhabitant was Jewish. The caption for a large picture at the top of the left-hand page claimed that in the textile industry that dominated the economy of Lodz, 'large-scale dealers, small traders and [the owners of] transport firms were all Jews'. From Lodz 'streams of Jewish emigrants' were flooding into western Europe. One photograph showed young Jewish couples strolling on Lodz's main boulevard, the Piotrkowska, the corso of those who had 'made it'. Here, one displayed worldly elegance, one had a bank account in England or America, relatives in every great commercial metropolis, recognized no real connection to the city in which one had been born, and was waiting only for a big opportunity in another country.

The issue of the *BIZ* published on 5 January 1939 carried the second instalment of this anti-Jewish series. This story focused on Romania. It began on the upper side of the right-hand page with a large photograph of a heavy man in evening dress. A woman in an evening gown sat to his left smoking a cigarette. The caption identified the man as 'one of the richest Jews in Romania, the metal king Ausschnitt'. The story claimed that sixty years earlier, his father had emigrated from Galicia and become a luggage porter and dealer in scrap metal. A few years later he got a contract to supply the military. When he died he left his son a million *Lei* (Romanian currency-DFC) in gold. Through stock market manipulations, the son gained control of the entire metal industry of the country. He was one example that stood for many others. In Romania 'it is going splendidly for the Jews'. Underneath this photograph, the story included a drawing from a Romanian newspaper with grotesque caricatures of Jewish men on the Romanian side of the border beckoning to other similarly carica-tured Jews on the Galician side. The Romanian Jews told the Galician Jews that they should come over to Romania because 'here we live as if in Abraham's lap'. On the upper right-hand side of the page a map claimed to show the distribution of Jews across Romania. In several regions of the north east, Jews made up as much as 25 per cent of the population. Even though the Romanian people and the state had repeatedly attempted to limit the influence of these 'aliens' through residence restrictions, limiting Jewish acquisition of property, expul-sion, and numerous pogroms, the Romanians had lost this defensive battle. In Bucharest, Jews were now one-quarter of the population, they allegedly exerted control over the entire money market, foreign trade, the free professions, and industry. Altogether, the number of Jews had been estimated at 1.9 million of the inhabitants of Romania, or one-ninth of the entire population.

The next instalment of the series that had already shown Jews in Lodz and Romania told readers that 'The Rothschilds Control the World'. This story claimed to show pictures that were not supposed to reach Germany and that the *BIZ* had only been able to obtain 'under particularly difficult conditions'. The photos claimed to document an extravagant Gala Evening hosted by the Rothschilds in Paris which offered guests expensive culinary delicacies, fine wines, and the opu-lent surroundings of the Rothschilds' town villa.

We can speculate about the effects of these kinds of anti-Semitic photo stories. At the very least they would have shown readers that this kind of racial hatred was now considered to be a normal component of the everyday visual economy of the Third Reich. The world visually constructed in the *BIZ* in the 1930s promised Aryan Germans who qualified as members of the racial community that elegance, enjoyment, adventure, and consumer wellbeing were or in the relatively near future would be the new realities of everyday experience in the Third Reich. These three anti-Semitic picture essays identified 'World Jewry' as the enemy of that promise. Perhaps they also meant to remind readers that in Germany, unlike in Poland, Romania, or France, the Nazi state had already implemented aggressive anti Jewish policies which excluded Jews from all influence over German public life. Germany's Aryan citizens could hope to enjoy the 'good life' that elsewhere in Europe was being taken over by the Jews.

Going to the Movies in the Third Reich

At the end of their working day, the two residents of No. 4 Chausseestraße, G. Grosse and K. Klatt, might have decided to buy tickets to see a film playing at one of the splendid 'Movie Palaces' located on one of the main Berlin thoroughfares or in one of the more modest neighbourhood cinemas. The 1933 Berlin *Adressbuch* lists no fewer than 185 movie houses in the city. At least nine of these were within walking distance of No. 4 Chaussesstraße. According to Eric Rentschler, there were 5,071 cinemas in Germany as a whole in 1933. By 1941, this number had increased to 7,043. Germans were avid moviegoers. In 1933, they went to the cinema a total of 245 million times. By 1944, this number had increased to 1.1 billion. But the film culture of the Third Reich was heavily concentrated in the larger German cities with populations over 100,000. Germans who lived in small towns and rural areas did not have the same access to cinemas and films.

Most of the feature films that the postman and the bank clerk from No. 4 Chausseestraße could see in Berlin cinemas after 1933 did not differ in obvious ways from the movies on offer before the Nazis came to power. The new Ministry of Popular Enlightenment and Propaganda directed by Joseph Goebbels exercised far-reaching control over film-making in Nazi Germany but the top priority of both the Nazi government and German film-makers was to draw audiences into cinemas. This meant producing movies that would entertain, amuse, and enthrall. The film culture of the Third Reich certainly included substantial numbers of political propaganda films such as *Hitler Youth Quex* (1933), Leni Riefenstahl's *Triumph of the Will* (1935), and *Olympia* (1938), as well as the anti-Semitic historical melodrama *Jud Süss* (1940) which had been seen by some twenty million Germans by 1945. But the great majority of movies made during the Third Reich were entertainment films. Rentschler observes that of the 1,094 German feature films produced between 1933 and 1945, 295 were melodramas and biopics, 123 were detective films and adventure epics and 523 were comedies and musicals. One of the most successful of the films made in the 1930s, *Lucky Kids* (*Glückskinder*, 1936), was an adaptation of the 1934 Frank Capra Hollywood blockbuster *It Happened One Night* starring Clark Gable and Claudette Colbert. *Lucky Kids* was set in New York and featured characters with American names.

German audiences, film-makers and even Nazi leaders were fascinated by movies made in Hollywood. In 1937, Goebbels wrote in his diary that his Christmas gift to Hitler consisted of thirty-two Hollywood 'classics' and twelve Mickey Mouse films: 'He is very pleased about it, delighted with this treasure.' Until Goebbels banned all American films from the German market in 1940, Germans could see numerous movies from Hollywood. Corey Ross observes that four of the ten most popular films screened in German cinemas in each of the years between 1935 and 1937 were made in the USA. German film-makers and Nazi officials admired the Hollywood techniques that allowed American blockbuster films to reach such diverse audiences. The Nazis wanted to use these film techniques not, as Hollywood did, to make profits (although this, too, was certainly important to Goebbels) but to create a sense of 'People's Community' (*Volksgemeinschaft*) amongst ethnically acceptable Germans. Ironically, it was sound, not just the images on the screen that helped to make the experience of moviegoing more similar for the millions of Germans who went to the movies in the 1930s. In the silent film era, cinemas tailored their screenings to the tastes of local audiences by, for example, using different types of music to accompany the film images. The transition to sound film which began in Germany in 1929 created greater uniformity in the conditions of viewing film. And because making films with soundtracks was more expensive than silent movies, fewer sound films were produced so that more Germans now saw the same films.

Feature films were, however, not all that our two residents of No. 4 Chaussesstraße would have seen in a typical outing to a movie theatre. As Eric Rentschler has shown, by the late 1930s, at least in the larger metropolitan cinemas, German audiences could expect a lengthy programme which began with advertisements, followed by a newsreel, a documentary short subject (*Kulturfilm*), then finally the main feature film. Throughout the 1930s, the top priority of film-makers and Nazi politicians was to entertain German moviegoers. Yet this commitment to entertainment did not mean that the Nazis had abandoned their political goals. To begin with, it was the promise of an entertaining feature film that drew German audiences into cinemas where they could be exposed to the more overtly political messages of the newsreels or the *Kulturfilme*. Nor were entertainment films innocent of all political meaning and purpose. Entertainment films showed audiences that the regime was responsive to popular needs and desires. Going to the movies in the Third Reich did not mean, as some Germans may have feared in 1933, being constantly bombarded with heavy-handed ideological messages. One could still enjoy the pleasures and fantasies that entertainment films had allowed before 1933. Yet, many of the entertainment films produced in peacetime Nazi Germany did convey subtle but important messages about the compatibility of individual happiness with social harmony, which may have helped the Nazis to manage popular emotions and to generate an affective alignment between viewers' perceptions of the world and Nazi priorities.

Germans taking Photographs

Readers of the *BIZ* were encouraged not only to consume photographic images but also 'to take snapshots and let yourself be photographed' as one advertisement in the magazine put it. Sponsored by both a swimsuit maker and the Agfa camera and photo company, the full page ad, which showed a smiling, attractive young woman in a bathing suit and bathing cap, announced a contest which would be 'the event' of the 1933 bathing season. The contest offered 15,000 marks worth of prizes, consisting of photographic equipment, swim-suits, and cash for the 'best pictures in a Benger's Ribana swimsuit'.

In the 1920s, Germany had pioneered in the production of small, hand-held and progressively more affordable cameras that were rela-tively easy to use and allowed millions of Germans to create their own photographic records of their lives. Maiken Umbach points to the famous Leica camera which was patented in 1925, and Zeiss Ikon's Contax which was introduced in 1933. In the 1930s and 40s, numer-ous cheaper versions of these same basic models came onto the market. In its 30 March 1939 issue, the *BIZ* carried an advertisement for both Agfa Isopan film and the Agfa Isolette (bellows) camera. The ad showed a photograph of a contemporary Nazi theme that had been taken with this camera and film—six young men drafted into the Reich Labour Service (*RAD*) who were naked from the waist up marched in a straight line while shouldering their shovels like rifles. As the Nazi re-armament drive created more jobs, Germans were able to buy more cameras. Leica alone had sold a quarter of a million cameras by 1939. If in 1933, neither of our two residents of No. 4 Chausseestraße, the bank clerk G. Große or the postman K. Klatt, already possessed a camera, they would have needed to go no further than to the Bowatz store at No. 4 Chausseestraße to buy one.

Maiken Umbach reminds us that even Germans who did not own a camera might participate in photography as the person to whom the camera was handed when a group of family members, workmates, or friends wanted a photographic memory of some occasion or activity, for example, and as the subjects of these photographs who often worked together with the person behind the camera to 'stage' a particular scene. Many seemingly candid family photos were carefully crafted co-productions of the photographer working with the photo-graphed, who decided what clothes to wear, what backgrounds to include or exclude, what poses to adopt, and expressions to display. Both the photographed and the photographer might also decide which of these private photographs would be preserved and which ones might be rejected. Taking family or other private photographs was often only the first step in a longer process of putting together a family, workplace or other group photo album which displayed indi-vidual photographs in a certain order and relationship to one another, usually accompanied by hand-written captions, all of which was meant to construct a meaningful narrative. By the 1930s, taking photographs, being photographed, and collecting photographs had become a normal component of everyday life and experience. Photography had become a new means of mass communication with its own language.

What can the millions of 'private' photographs taken during the Third Reich tell us about how ordinary Germans saw their lives under the Nazi dictatorship? The primary function of private photographs was to create visual commemorations of important events in the lives of families and individuals—christenings, school graduations, weddings, family reunions, family excursions, or gatherings of friends. This meant that many of the private photographs taken during the Third Reich might not appear to be very different than the private photographs Germans took before 1933 or would take after 1945, or even than the family photographs taken in other European countries or the USA during these same years. But the context within which these private photographs were produced was different and this difference inevitably left its mark on the practice and the meaning of private photography during the Third Reich. To begin with, public space in Nazi Germany was often quite literally plastered with Nazi signs and symbols—huge Swastika flags, for example, or anti-Semitic banners. Not all private photographs were taken within the confines of individual households where such aggressive Nazi propaganda was not on display. A German taking a 'private' snapshot of friends or family out of doors would have to decide whether or not to include Nazi signs or symbols in the frame of the shot. Linda Conze, Ulrich Prehn, and Michael Wildt have analysed two private snapshots taken in a smaller German town in the 1930s which demonstrate this problem. One shows an older woman sitting alone on a park bench. In the distant background we can see an anti-Semitic banner ('The Jews are our misfortune') stretched between two houses. The person who took this photograph obviously did not feel it was important to frame the shot so as to exclude this banner. A second picture taken in the same park, this time of a young smiling couple on a park bench, does not show the banner in the background. But it is impossible to know whether the person who took this second photo made a conscious decision to frame the shot so as to exclude the banner or whether he/she simply thought that this was a more interesting angle. What is clear, however, is that the presence in the frame of the first picture of an anti-Semitic slogan did not prevent the photographer from taking the photograph, or, presumably from preserving it as a memory of a small, pleasant moment in the everyday life of the person photographed as well, perhaps, as of the photographer. In this private picture, the blatant racism of the Nazi regime had become a 'normal' component of the photographic depiction of everyday life in the Third Reich.

The millions of private photographs taken during the Third Reich helped to construct a new image of 'normality'. This new normality was by no means dominated by crude expressions of Nazi racism. But it did, in a variety of subtle ways, connect private life to the promises made by the Nazi regime of a bright future to be shared and enjoyed by all racially acceptable Germans. This of course meant that racial others and outsiders would be excluded from the benefits of the Third Reich and frequently exploited to provide those benefits. But the practice of private photography generally ignored the fate of everyone—Jews, 'genetically deficient' Germans, non-German Europeans—whom the Nazis excluded from the *Volksgemeinschaft*. Moreover, under the Nazis, the practice of private photography itself was to be a privilege of Aryan Germans. During the war, the cameras owned by Jews and Poles were confiscated and in Occupied France only Germans in the occupying army or in the German civilian authorities were allowed to take photographs out of doors.

The main purposes of the new mass photographic practices were visual pleasure in the production and consumption of images and the creation of visual memories for the future. The very fact that private photographs fostered the belief—even though this was actually an illusion—that a 'normal' private life was possible under Hitler benefited the Nazi regime, especially if Germans credited Hitler, as many did, with creating the conditions, economic and otherwise, which made the small pleasures of everyday, private life possible after the deprivations of the Depression and the political convolutions of the Weimar Republic's final agonies (1930–3). The Nazis promised a new beginning. Germans who were not victims of the Nazi regime remembered the late 1930s and the first two years of the war as 'good times' when full employment made it possible to marry, start families, and begin to enjoy the small pleasures of life again. Private photographs documented these 'good times'.

The German War in the BIZ

In the 1930s, illustrated magazines had not been subjected to the same strict guidelines about the stories they published that applied to daily newspapers. With the outbreak of war in 1939 this changed. Military censorship and a new system of instructions from the Propaganda Ministry similar to those issued to newspapers introduced greater control over the content of illustrated magazines. When our two residents of No. 4 Chausseestraße went to the neighbourhood news-paper kiosk in September 1939 to buy the *BIZ*, they would have noticed the effects immediately. Like other illustrated weeklies, the *BIZ* celebrated German victories, glorified the exploits of the German armed forces, and gave its readers photographs that demonstrated that Hitler's new way of waging war—*Blitzkrieg*—was unstoppable. This emphasis on the relentless march forward of German forces continued to structure the *BIZ* reporting during the first two years of the war and indeed carried over into the first stages of the invasion of the Soviet Union which began on 22 June 1941. The photo stories in the 1941 *BIZ* emphasized the devastating effects of German fire-power. Two pictures in the 10 July issue, for example, showed a line of destroyed enemy tanks and trucks. The caption told the reader that between 22 and 27 June 1941, German forces had destroyed or captured '2,233 combat vehicles, including 46 of the heaviest tanks weighing 52 tons each'. Photos of Soviet POWs showed them as disoriented, often lacking helmets, their uniforms in disarray, their expressions dismayed. In contrast, the German soldiers were well-equipped, determined and moving ever forward into the Soviet Union. In the 17 July, 1941 issue, four large headshots with the title 'These are Churchill's confederates' showed unshaved, unkempt Soviet soldiers captured by the Germans. These images contrasted quite clearly with the headshots in the next story of four handsome, smiling German soldiers who had destroyed six Soviet tanks in just twenty-five minutes. Pictures of vibrant German masculinity provided a clear contrast not only to the dejected, dirty, and weak male Soviet POWs but particularly to the women who fought in the Red Army. A photograph in Issue Nr. 30, 1941, presented one of these 'unnatural' Comrade Gunwomen (*Genossin Flintenweib*). The caption explained that '[i]n the campaign against Bolshevism, German soldiers repeatedly capture women prisoners, some in women's clothing, others in uniform; [they function as] underhanded snipers, members of tank crews, or lorry drivers.'

As they leafed through the *BIZ* in 1941, our two residents of No. 4 Chausseestraße would also have encountered a series of photos depicting what the *BIZ* claimed were 'Atrocities committed by Jewish Soviet Commissars'. In Lithuania, so one story reported, the 'Bolshevist Commissars' had indiscriminately butchered men, women, and children. Gruesome photographs displayed their mutilated bodies. The report claimed that one young child had been murdered 'just because his mother was German'.

It is no coincidence that at the same time it was flooding readers with photographs of the unstoppable German advance into the Soviet Union, and of the atrocities allegedly committed by Jewish Political Commissars and Soviet secret police, the *BIZ* also carried a lengthy photo story about the Warsaw Ghetto. The scenes from the Warsaw Ghetto that the *BIZ* published in its 17 July 1941 issue tried to show how the Jews, 'the people from whom the murderers of Bromberg, Lemberg, Dubno, Białystok came [Polish towns where ethnic Germans had been killed at the beginning of the war-DFC]' lived when left to their own devices (while neglecting completely to mention that Polish Jews had been forced into the inhuman conditions of the Warsaw Ghetto by the German occupiers). The photographs contrasted the miserable conditions suffered by most of the Jews in the ghetto with the privileges that a minority of richer Jews could afford, including attendance at cabaret performances and drinks in a 'ghetto bar'. The pictures seemed to show that some Jews callously ignored, perhaps even exploited the misery of others. The German occupiers were nowhere in sight.

The War at the Movies

At the beginning of the First World War, the governments of all the countries involved had shut down popular entertainments because they seemed too 'frivolous' for such serious times. In the Second

World War, however, continuing with the normal operation of cinema, radio, and other forms of mass entertainment in order to maintain civilian morale was a high priority. More Germans actually went to the movies during the war than in peacetime, and some of the most successful German films were produced when Germany was at war. In the first two years of the conflict, the boost in film-going owed as much if not more to Germans' need for information as for diversion. With hundreds of thousands of German men sent to the front, their relatives and friends wanted to keep up to date on the fighting. For these movie-goers, the newsreel could be more important than the feature film. Corey Ross reports that several new movie houses in Berlin responded to the popular hunger for information about the war by showing only newsreels for up to ten hours each day.

In the first two years of the war, the newsreels enjoyed the advantage of being able to report—more or less truthfully—on a string of undeniable German victories. The image of the war presented to German audiences did not have to be doctored in significant ways. Yet, even before the invasion of the Soviet Union newsreel audiences began to express some scepticism about the authenticity of the scenes they were being shown. Corey Ross reports, for example, that in February 1940, German soldiers in Dresden mocked an obviously staged film of a German reconnaissance team moving across the French border in Lorraine. Nevertheless, the newsreels were quite successful in uniting the provision of information with entertainment—at least until audiences began to question the official news sources because they downplayed or simply ignored the mounting casualties in the war against the Soviet Union which began in 1941. Loss of faith in the newsreels did not, however, produce a decline in cinema attendance. In fact, more and more Germans were drawn into theatres to see the high quality, big-budget feature films the regime had decided were important to produce. According to Corey Ross, the average German went to the cinema around 40 per cent more in 1943–4 than in 1939 and three times more than in 1933. As the Allied bombing campaign destroyed many Berlin cinemas, and as the German film industry produced fewer films, our two residents of No. 4 Chausseestraße would in fact have found that it was increasingly difficult to get a seat in a first-run theatre. Ross shows that fights broke out in waiting lines and tickets could often be obtained only from scalpers.

During the war, our two residents of No. 4 Chausseestraße could see a variety of different types of films. Historical dramas depicted the genius of Germany's past leaders (*Bismarck*, 1940; *Friedrich Schiller*, 1940; *The Great King*, 1942). Other film dramas attacked Germany's current enemies, the plutocratic British Empire (*Carl Peters* and *Ohm Krüger*, both 1941) and the Soviet Union (*GPU*, 1942). Two films completed in 1940—*Jud Süß* and *The Rothschilds*—unmasked the treachery of the enemy the Nazis considered to be the greatest threat to Germany—the Jews. *Jud Süss* was one of the most successful films of the Third Reich. By 1945, over twenty million viewers or about a third of the adult population had seen the film.

The Nazis held out the promise that defeating Germany's enemies would allow the Third Reich to establish a huge new empire from which all racially acceptable Germans would profit. The Nazis hoped that big-budget feature films would not only entertain German audiences but also mobilize popular support for the war by showing Germans that their individual happiness depended upon the 'fate of the nation'. Yet individual happiness had at least for now to be subordinated to duty and commitment to victory. It is not surprising that two of Nazi Germany's most popular wartime films—*Wunschkonzert* (*Request Concert*, 1940) and *Die Große Liebe* (*The Great Love*, 1942)— told the stories of ordinary German men and women during the Second World War. Both films attracted huge audiences. Corey Ross reports that by the end of the war 26.5 million tickets had been sold for *Wunschkonzert* and twenty-eight million for *Die große Liebe*. *Wunschkonzert* was a multi-media phenomenon. The film was inspired by an immensely popular radio programme which asked listeners to send in requests for a piece of music to be played on the air and dedicated to someone important to them. During the war, this radio programme became a way of creating an audible bond between the Fighting Front and the Home Front, a 'People's Community on the airwaves' as the Nazis saw it. The renamed *Wunschkonzert für die Wehrmacht* (*Request Concert for the German Armed Forces*) asked soldiers to send in their musical requests and dedications. In December 1942, a special Christmas *Ringsendung* (multiple radio hookup) connected the listeners at home with German soldiers stationed in the distant corners of the now enormous Nazi Empire—from the Arctic Circle to North Africa, from the Atlantic coast to the Soviet Union.

The *Wunschkonzert* film told the story of a young couple, Inge Wagner (played by Ilse Werner) and Herbert Koch (Carl Raddatz), who had fallen in love at the Berlin Olympics in 1936 but then lost contact because Herbert was sent to Spain during the civil war as a pilot in the Condor Legion. After the 1939 attack on Poland, Herbert, still in love with Inge, sends a request to the radio programme *Wunschkonzert für die Wehrmacht.* The two lovers eventually find each other again. Corey Ross argues that the *Wunschkonzert* film was so successful because it wove references to recent events into a dramatic plot, because it used some original documentary footage, but above all because it told German audiences that devotion to the nation was not at odds with, but would eventually lead to, personal happiness and the fulfilment of individual desires.

German Soldiers Photograph the War

By the time Germany went to war in 1939, about seven million Germans or about 10 per cent of the population owned cameras. *Voigtländer Optik* tried to sell its cameras to soldiers with an advertisement that showed a drawing of a soldier whose life had allegedly been saved by the camera in the leather case hanging from his neck. The ad claimed that a grenade splinter had lodged in the camera rather than in the soldier's body. While still recuperating in hospital, he had ordered another of the company's Klein-Bessa cameras that had saved his life. This equipment was so tough that it could withstand most of the damage war might inflict—although, the ad joked, it was probably not a good idea to take direct aim at the camera with a cannon!

Encouraged by the images they saw in illustrated magazines and in the newsreels, many German soldiers took their cameras to war. A smaller number also packed hand-held cine cameras in their rucksacks. What types of photographs of the war did ordinary German soldiers take? Did these private pictures conform to or differ from the official photographic representation of the war created by the almost 15,000 Propaganda Company (PK) photographers who were embedded in military units by 1943? During the Second World War, these PK photographers took at least three and a half million pictures of every front on which the Germans were fighting. Hundreds of these photographs were published in mass circulation illustrated magazines and newspapers and seen by millions of readers. The illustrated magazine *Signal*, which appeared in more than twenty languages and was distributed in all of the countries occupied by the Germans, achieved a circulation of 2.5 million at its highpoint. These images helped in significant ways to shape the way that Germans and Europeans saw the war.

Pamela Swett, Corey Ross, and Fabrice d'Almeida have argued that if we are to understand why millions of Germans were attracted to, even fascinated by the Nazi regime, we need to acknowledge the pleasures it provided to those who were racially acceptable. One of the most important pleasures that the war offered millions of German men and a smaller number of women was the opportunity to travel to almost every part of the new Nazi empire. German soldiers with cameras behaved like tourists. In Occupied France, they took pictures of famous landmarks; in Paris of themselves standing on the Trocadero with the Eiffel Tower in the background (much as Hitler did on his whirlwind tour of the French capital) or of themselves on the steps of the Sacré-Coeur church, of the Moulin Rouge in Montmartre, of Versailles, the Vosges mountains, the Normandy coast. In Greece, soldier-photographers took pictures of the Parthenon. Landscapes were important subjects but Maiken Umbach suggests that the depiction of western European landscapes differed significantly from photographs taken in the east. In the west, landscapes were presented as cultivated, 'civilized', and benign. Western Europe clearly belonged to a familiar 'cultural space' (*Kulturraum*). Not so, the endless steppes of Russia which, especially when the roads became mired in mud from autumn rains, appeared uninviting, uncanny, perhaps even threatening. German soldiers did not feel at home in the vast eerie expanses of the east.

As in the First World War, German soldiers also took photographs to display the effects of the German military power that had produced the *Blitzkrieg* victory in the west; pictures of destroyed buildings, raillines, and bridges in enemy territory, destroyed or captured enemy artillery, tanks, and other weapons. Pictures of POWs also appeared in soldiers' photo albums. Black and colonial soldiers drew the photographers' particular interest. Civilians might also appear in the pictures soldiers took in France. In Russia, soldiers' interest in civilians could be more ethnographic. Soviet civilians appeared as exotic, strange, primitive others.

Many German soldiers and civilians witnessed and some photographed the widespread atrocities that defined the German war in the east. But the most common subjects of German soldiers' private photographs and photo albums were quite banal, at times comical scenes of the soldiers' everyday lives on the eastern Front—chasing geese or goats, cooking, washing clothes. What is so unsettling about some of these German soldiers' scrapbooks is the juxtaposition of the banal and the predictable with photographic horrors. Pictures of 'partisans' hanging from lamp posts in the occupied Soviet Union could sometimes be found in the same album, sometimes on the very same page with snapshots of a group of front-line comrades, damaged buildings, landscapes, orthodox churches, or other examples of local 'colour'. After the war some of the owners of these picture collections—or their relatives—clearly did appear to feel that atrocity photographs did not belong in their albums and removed them, while leaving the glue and the original captions as traces of the now absent picture.

Atrocity photographs constituted one of the important differences between official and private war photography—as we have seen, illustrated magazines did publish pictures of atrocities but only those allegedly committed by the Soviets. Yet, in other respects the visual worlds of private and official war photographs were nearer to each other than we might perhaps imagine. Ordinary soldier-photographers reproduced the motifs and perspectives they saw in illustrated magazines. Ordinary soldiers also bought some of the photographs they pasted into their scrapbooks from the professional war photographers responsible for the pictures published in illustrated magazines. While private and official war photography did not simply mirror one another they often overlapped within a shared imaginative framework that defined how the war should look.

Other Encounters with Photography and Film

There were many other ways in which Germans could encounter and use photographs and filmic images in the Third Reich. Reasons of space make it impossible to consider all of them in detail. But it is important to provide at least a brief survey of the possibilities. If one of

our two residents of No. 4 Chausseestraße were a smoker, one of the
stops in his day or week might well be the local tobacconist, Clara
Ameslower, at No. 33 Chausseestraße, a ten minute walk north from
No. 4. Here he could buy a pack of cigarettes that included collectible
photo-cards or coupons for these pictures. During the Third Reich,
circulation of these photographic images rivalled that of illustrated
newspapers and magazines. So, for example, the *Cigaretten-Bilderdienst*
(Cigarette Picture Service) created by the Reemtsma cigarette company sold at its highpoint some 2.4 million copies of the photo albums
in which customers could paste the photographs of Hitler, of the new
German armed forces, or of the 1936 Olympic Games that the
company offered with each pack of its cigarettes.

Our two residents of No. 4 Chausseestraße could also encounter
photographs in the form of mass produced postcards which, as before
1933, depicted touristic and historical sites, but also now included
images of Hitler. Some of the postcards produced by Hitler's personal
photographer, Heinrich Hoffmann, presented the Führer 'As No One
Knows Him' (the title of Hoffmann's best selling photo book, a visual
genre which was another important 'platform' for photography in the
Third Reich)—in other words, Hitler in the quiet moments of his
private life. Maiken Umbach points out that in their style and subjects,
these photographs by Hoffmann resemble the private family photos
that millions of Germans were taking during the 1930s. They were
meant to show a 'more human' side of the Nazi dictator than did the
numerous official photographs and paintings of Hitler as a great
statesman.

Photographs were also used in some of the more important Nazi
propaganda exhibitions. In 1937 and then again in 1942, our two
residents of No. 4 Chausseestraße could have visited the 'Great Anti-
Bolshevist Exhibition' or 'Bolshevism Unmasked'. In 1942, this exhibition was set up in the *Lustgarten*, not far from the building where our
two residents of No. 4 lived. The exhibition combined photographs
with lurid drawings, some in colour. On 18 May 1942, a resistance
organization named the Baum-Gruppe, led by the German-Jewish
communist, Herbert Baum tried to set fire to the exhibition. Within
days, many members of this group were arrested. Twenty were
sentenced to death. Herbert Baum was tortured to death in Moabit
prison. His wife, Marianne, was executed in Plötzensee Prison on

18 August 1942. This arson attack rattled Joseph Goebbels and other Nazi leaders. Hitler was so outraged that he told Goebbels to ensure that all the remaining Jews in Berlin be deported as soon as possible.

During the Third Reich, photography became an essential practice for a wide range of Nazi organizations and agencies. If our two residents of No. 4 Chausseestraße, or any of the other Germans living there between 1933 and 1945, were members of the Hitler Youth, the Nazi organizations for girls and women, the Reich Labour Service, the SS, the German police, or any number of other Third Reich institutions, they would also have seen (and perhaps even helped to produce) photographs of that institution's activities. Many of these organizations felt that creating their own photographic record was important enough to warrant setting up their own 'in-house' photo lab. Some organizations and agencies also published illustrated magazines which displayed these photographs for internal consumption but also to represent the organization to a wider German public. Miriam Arani has discovered that in Occupied Poland, for example, a huge number of photographs were taken by the German police and the SS. Some of these were used as instruments to identify and brutally persecute Poles, Jews, and any other categories of non-Germans whom the SS or police considered to be dangerous enemies of the Third Reich. Other photographs were published in magazines such as *Die Polizei* (*The Police*) for circulation within the agency. These photographs celebrated the 'achievements' of the German police in Poland and attempted to foster a strong self-image and sense of collective solidarity within the occupying police forces. Individual members of the German police also took their own private pictures in Poland. One Gestapo agent compiled an extensive photo album consisting mainly of pictures of people he considered to be Germany's enemies—again, primarily Jews and Poles—whom he was tasked with eliminating.

The Camera as Weapon

The Nazis understood how to use the camera as a weapon. Photographs showing the humiliation and even the murder of Jews were integral components of the visual economy of the Third Reich. In 1933, the SA took photographs of the nationwide boycott of Jewish stores and posted signs that any German who dared cross the boycott line would themselves be photographed. The SA also humiliated so-called 'mixed race' couples by parading them openly in the streets and forcing them to wear large signs around their necks confessing that 'I despoiled a Christian maiden' or 'I am a German girl and let myself be defiled by Jews'. These public humiliations were frequently photographed. Conze, Prehn, and Wildt show that in one small East Frisian town, a pharmacist commissioned by the local Nazi Party branch to take photographs of such a procession later put them on display in his shop window. In 1939, when the German army invaded Poland, Wehrmacht soldiers humiliated orthodox Jews in the streets of Warsaw by shearing their beards and locks of hair around their ears in front of the camera, or by forcing them to perform humiliating gymnastics while their pictures were being taken. According to Nicholas Stargardt, photographs of the deportation to the east from Bad Neustadt in 1941 of the last remaining Jews in this small German town were enlarged to poster size and put on display in the centre of the city. Even some of the shootings of Jews in the occupied eastern territories after the invasion of the Soviet Union were clearly staged to be photographed. Unlike the subjects of the private photographs discussed above, these Jewish victims had no say in how or whether they would appear in any of these photographs. Clearly, the actual act of forcing the victim to be photographed was important to the perpetrators. The photographs themselves would serve as souvenirs of the day when the Germans settled scores with their racial or other enemies. In this context, then, photography was the exercise of power.

Certainly the victims of the Nazis also took photographs even though for them photography was a much more difficult and even dangerous practice. Why? One reason was simply to push back, to demonstrate at least to themselves, and perhaps also for the future, that the perspectives presented in the great majority of photographs and films produced in the Third Reich were not the only ways of looking at the world. This photographic *Eigensinn* or self-assertion can be seen, for example, in pictures of Jewish weddings in occupied Europe.

The fact that Jewish wedding photographs exist at all is quite remarkable. We would probably not expect Jews to be getting married despite Nazi occupation, and the threat of deportation and annihilation. Marriage presupposes an expectation of some kind of future, even in the darkest times. We know that many of the people in these pictures would not survive. Did they have no idea what might soon happen to them? Were they deluding themselves that they would survive? The caption to the picture of a wedding party in Salonika, Greece, taken in 1942–3, tells us that the couple's 'marriage was hastily arranged two months before their deportation so that they might be able to stay together. The couple perished in Auschwitz.'

Yet, knowing what happened after photographs such as these were taken makes it difficult for us to understand what the pictures originally showed. We may know that most of the Jews in these photographs would not survive. The Jews in these photographs did not. Recognition of the distance between our 'now' and their 'then' can allow us to understand why these Jewish couples and their relatives are smiling and why they devoted so much effort and ingenuity to finding the wedding gowns and all the other accoutrements of a 'proper' wedding under the extreme conditions of wartime scarcity and Nazi persecution. These Jewish wedding photographs can be seen not as attempts to deny the horrible reality of the Holocaust but as conscious efforts to defy its grotesque abnormality by claiming a small scrap of normality, a tiny hope for the future. Pictures of Jewish weddings might also suggest that Jews could sometimes use photography to challenge the vicious anti-Semitic images produced by Nazi propaganda. In these private photographs, Jews showed themselves as they wanted to be seen, not as the Nazis portrayed them.

1945

By the beginning of 1945, the visual world of Germans was shrinking rapidly. Our two residents of No. 4 Chausseestraße, if indeed they were still alive and at this same address, would have found it extremely difficult to buy an illustrated magazine or find a cinema that was still operating. Soldiers and civilians might not have been able to obtain film for their cameras unless they went to the black market. As the boundaries of the Nazi Empire were pushed back in the east by the Red Army and in the west and south by Allied forces, the images of the war that Germans could see in newspapers and magazines came closer and closer to the Reich itself. The one visual domain that appeared unaffected was film. In the final year of the war Goebbels pumped huge amounts of money and other resources into production of the fantastic special effects of a film such as *Münchhausen* (1942/3) or the historical drama of national redemption portrayed in the Veit Harlan film *Kolberg*, that premiered on 30 January 1945. The film depicted the heroic defence in 1807 by Prussian forces of the Pomeranian fortress town of Kolberg against Napoleon's army. According to Corey Ross, this movie was the single most expensive production in the Third Reich. Even as the Red Army was already crossing into East Prussia, Goebbels ordered that 5,000 real German soldiers and 3,000 horses be sent from the front for the battle scenes while one hundred railway cars brought in salt to simulate snow. Goebbels may have hoped that this film would inspire German viewers to continue fighting on to the 'Final Victory' which Nazi leaders still insisted was possible. Corey Ross argues, however, that in the last two years of the war, the intimate connection between entertainment and politics that we can see in *Wunschkonzert* and *Die Große Liebe* had unravelled. For many Germans, films had now become simply a way of escaping the ever more depressing news from the front after Stalingrad (1943) and the devastating effects of the Allied bombing at home—at least for a couple of hours. If the films Germans saw in 1944 and 1945 were, as one contemporary described them, 'films to help us carry on' (*Durchhaltefilme*), then more and more Germans were intent on carrying on not so that Germany could win the war, but so that they and their families might survive it. Promises of the bright future that Germans could expect if only they committed themselves completely to victory had become increasingly hollow.

Germans also believed less and less in what they could see in illustrated magazines or the weekly newsreels. While both of these visual media had eagerly bombarded their readers/viewers with images of German victories, pictures of or even references to the devastating German defeat at Stalingrad in 1943 were seldom to be seen. Germans came now to rely less on what they could see than on what they could hear—rumours that circulated amongst friends and family or the German language broadcasts of the BBC.

The Afterlife of Third Reich Photography and Film

Some of the photographs taken during the Third Reich came back to haunt Germans after 1945. Atrocity pictures, seen at the time perhaps as documents of 'great times' when Germans settled scores with their mortal enemies—the Jews—surfaced after the war as what they really were—visual evidence of horrendous crimes. Yet there are many other photographs and films from the Third Reich whose relationship to Nazi terror is by no means this obvious. Private photographs of small everyday pleasures or of vacation trips but also some of the major films produced under the Nazis have been seen by some post-war Germans as evidence that there were many parts of life in the Third Reich that remained untouched by Nazi ideology and racism. Blockbuster feature films from the Third Reich still find their place in the programme lists of German TV broadcasts and before the Fall of the Wall in 1989 were aired on east as well as on west German television. These, so the argument runs, are simply very good German entertainment films with no real political content or meaning. It is likewise possible for Germans today to be convinced by the private photos they can find in thousands of family albums that these pictures show that 'normal' everyday life could be conducted without significant reference to the ideological priorities and racial demands of the Nazi system. The Third Reich appears always to lie somewhere outside the frame of these personal pictures. In this chapter, I have argued that these claims should not be accepted uncritically. We need to resituate all of the photographic and filmic images produced in the Third Reich within the actual historical contexts that gave them their meaning before we can properly understand the uses and functions of photography and film in Nazi Germany.

6

The Economy

Peter Hayes

At the centre of the history of the Nazi economy lies a paradox: the regime's productive feats seemed impressive at the time but look like jury-rigged fiascos in retrospect. The Third Reich generated the most rapid recovery from the Depression in the industrialized world and then achieved immense conquests, yet did so through a succession of desperate improvisations in economic policy that just barely and briefly worked. The fundamental problem was a continuous gap between the enormous requirements of Hitler's expansionism and the country's narrow resource base. This chasm proved sufficiently bridgeable in the short term to yield the sweeping military victories of 1939–41, but yawned ever wider with the onset of total war on multiple fronts. From 1942 on, the Reich's material deficiencies led inexorably to crushing defeat.

Adolf Hitler anticipated the problem; indeed, his chief political goal was to solve it through acquisition of the 'living space' that he saw as a prerequisite for great power status in the twentieth century. Only through the conquest of a vast, contiguous, and economically self-sufficient empire could Germany prosper and compete on the world stage, he believed. Yet, given the limitations of the nation's population and resources compared to those of potential opponents, Hitler knew that his Reich had to proceed stealthily. In his published and unpublished writings during the 1920s, he foresaw a sequential, divide-and-conquer strategy for achieving his territorial objectives, one that imitated Bismarck's unification of Germany some sixty years earlier through successive victories over Denmark, Austria, and France. Hitler planned a zigzag course of aggression, first in concert with Italy against France's allies in eastern Europe and then France itself, and then with British support or acquiescence against the Soviet Union. The defeat of the communist state there would lead to Germany's annexation of the grain and coal producing regions of Ukraine and the oil fields of the Caucasus and thus lay the basis for success in the ultimate war of the continents against the United States, which Hitler regarded as the last fortress of threatening Jewish power in the world.

The goal of Nazi economic policy was thus to offset Germany's economic weaknesses in the short run so that a land grab could eliminate them in the long run. Or, as Hitler wrote in 1927, the task of the economy was 'to secure the inner strength of [the] people so it can assert itself in the sphere of foreign policy'. Although diplomacy would play a part in that assertion, the Nazi Führer always saw expansion as ultimately a matter of military strength and economics as merely a means of generating it. On 9 February 1933, only ten days after becoming Chancellor of the German Reich, Hitler laid down the principal practical implication of this chain of thought. He told a cabinet committee, 'in future in case of conflict between the demands of the Wehrmacht and demands for other purposes, the interests of the Wehrmacht must in every case have priority'.

The primacy of military considerations is thus the red thread that runs through the history of the Nazi economy, and that primacy was ultimately self-defeating. It did play an important part in the recovery from the Depression that secured Hitler's grip on power during the first phase of Nazi rule from January 1933 until August 1936. But, in the second phase from September 1936 until September 1939, when the Nazi regime laid the economic foundations for aggression, its escalating requirements competed with each other and provoked foreign responses in ways that prompted Hitler to modify his zigzag course by fighting Britain and France simultaneously over Poland. Economic overstretch became still more characteristic of the third phase, the heady period of victory from September 1939 until late 1942, which encompassed the addition of the Soviet Union and the United States to Germany's enemies in a desperate attempt to overcome the imbalance of power between the Reich and its opponents through quick victories in the European east. Finally, during the struggle to survive from late 1942 until the end of the war in May 1945, Germany massively exploited occupied Europe in a doomed effort to stave off inevitable defeat, but could not keep up with the overwhelming productive capacities of the Reich's adversaries.

Recovery

Germany faced a daunting economic impasse when Adolf Hitler came to power. Industrial production had fallen by one-third since 1928. More than six million people were registered as unemployed. Moreover, the nation appeared unable to pay for an eventual upturn. Devaluations of foreign currencies had undercut German exports to the point that by the summer of 1933, the country possessed only enough gold and foreign currency to finance one month of imports at a minimal level. Even if demand and confidence revived, inability to purchase necessary raw materials was likely to snuff out a recovery. Yet, by the summer of 1936, this situation seemed only a distant memory. Full employment had returned, industrial output exceeded the pre-Depression high, and gross domestic product, both in toto and per capita, topped the level of 1929. Neither real wages nor popular living standards had quite recovered, but the restoration of a sense of economic security more than made up for that in most Germans' eyes.

How did Nazi Germany succeed so strikingly and swiftly in economic terms? Part of the answer is that Hitler came to power at a fortuitous moment. Because the Depression had reduced industry's fixed and factor costs to a level that favoured profitability once more, employment and the stock market already had begun to rise in late 1932. Moreover, the last two cabinets of the Weimar Republic had appropriated about 1 billion Reichsmarks for job creation programmes that began in 1933. These helped propel resurgence in the construction and vehicles industries that spread in 1934 to the consumer sector. Road building projects, also inherited from Hitler's predecessors, also added to the improving situation, though less than sometimes claimed, since they took time to gather strength. As late as mid-1934, only 34,000 people were at work on the vaunted *Autobahnen*.

More important than timing to the Nazi regime's success was the policy mix implemented by Hitler's principal economic agents, the Reichsbank President and later Economics Minister Hjalmar Schacht and Wilhelm Keppler, a veteran Nazi who became commissioner for raw materials creation in 1934. That mix had two predominant, mutually reinforcing features: extensive governmental intervention in markets and entrepreneurial decisions, and an enormous surge in military spending.

The chief driver of the interference was Germany's problematic balance of trade. It forced the regime into elaborate efforts to cut down on non-essential imports, ration essential ones, encourage exports and direct them toward countries that could sell the commodities the Reich most needed, and develop and purchase domestically produced or sourced substitutes for foreign goods (e.g., synthetic fibres for cotton and wool, gasoline from coal for crude oil, soap and greases from coal for animal or petroleum-based fats). These efforts set off a regulatory spiral that continued throughout the Third Reich, as each attempt by the state to control in- and outputs created bottlenecks and pressures that elicited redoubled efforts to channel resources in the directions the Nazi state desired.

Along the way, the regime became adept at using carrots and sticks, incentives and prohibitions, to manipulate enterprises into serving its purposes. To induce firms to enter into or expand production of import substitutes that cost too much to compete on international markets, the Reich usually promised to buy the output at prices that covered manufacturing expenses, depreciated plant within a decade, and paid a 5 per cent annual return on investments. Prototypical of the practice was the famous *Benzin-Vertrag* of December 1933 between the Reich and IG Farben, the giant chemicals conglomerate, that was intended to limit Germany dependence on imported oil. When commercial inducements did not suffice to persuade executives to produce as the regime required, it did not hesitate to resort to compulsion. This could take the form of outright conscription, as happened in 1935 when the Economics Ministry ordered brown coal manufacturers in the Ruhr region to buy shares in the *Braunkohle Benzin AG* (Brown Coal Gasoline corporation, known as BRABAG) to make motor fuels from that raw material. Conversely, when the regime wished to restrain output in spheres not vital to military power, the Economics Ministry simply forbade investments in new machinery or withheld permits to acquire increasingly rationed building supplies. Finally, to supplement import substitution, the Reich embarked on a programme of export promotion that entailed taxing corporations' domestic sales in order

Growth of German armaments production halted in May 1943.

to create a fund to partially compensate firms for selling their products on the international market for less than they could earn at home. By means such as these, Germany's ability to meet its minimal needs from abroad grew more secure by the mid-1930s and so did its ability to pour expenditures into Hitler's highest priority: German rearmament.

Already in June 1933, the Nazi regime expected to spend 35 billion Reichsmarks on armaments during the next eight years, which is to say 4.4 billion marks per year or 5–10 per cent of projected annual gross domestic product (GDP). By December, the Luftwaffe envisioned a force of 2,000 front-line aircraft and the army a force of 300,000 men by 1937. In order to meet these goals, military spending rose from 1.6 per cent of total national income and 4 per cent of all German governmental expenditures in 1933 to 6.3 per cent and 18 per cent respectively in 1934. By 1936, these figures reached 13.7 per cent and 39 per cent. The Reich's purchases of military equipment and related goods went from consuming 1 per cent of national output in 1933 to 11 per cent in 1936. As a result, the armaments budget accounted for 47 per cent of GDP growth in 1934 and almost 42 per cent in 1935. Even though private investment gradually picked up, these vast outlays dwarfed spending on civilian job creation or other forms of economic stimulus and produced, in conjunction with the expansion of the number of soldiers, the bulk of the decline in unemployment during the first three years of Nazi rule.

Spending on this scale raised financing issues, which Schacht solved by creating a parallel currency in the form of negotiable bills backed by a nominally private company, the *Metallurgische-Forschungsgesellschaft* (Metallurgical Research Corporation)—hence the name Mefo-Bills— that could be used like money for payments and cashed at the Reichsbank, but meanwhile did not show up in the national budget. He also began restricting firms' access to public capital markets, such as the stock exchange, thus funnelling investment demand toward treasury bonds, and capping corporations' dividend payments, thus prompting enterprises to build up large cash reserves that would help fund construction projects that served the Reich's economic priorities.

The overall result by 1936 was what one astute scholar has called a 'lopsided' and another a 'strongly deformed' economic recovery. Though propelled by government spending, the Nazi economic revival was not Keynesian in the sense that it put money into the pockets of consumers, who then spent it and unleashed a multiplier effect that drove growth across the economic board. Instead, Germany's resurgence took the form of a state-driven direction of national wealth into the production of arms and the infrastructure essential to them. Beginning in mid-1934, the regime moved to restrict civilian consumption—expansion of clothing produced from natural fibres was banned, and the purchase and sale of food became entirely state controlled—and to funnel resources toward output in chemicals and machinery.

Although household incomes rose, that was because more people had more work, not because real wages gained appreciably. Nonetheless, people's intake of such staples as bread, sugar, fish, and even meat rose enough for most Germans to believe they were becoming better off than before the Depression.

In order to bolster that impression the regime offered Germans the showpiece benefits of the 'people's community' under the aegis of the organization that replaced and absorbed the trade unions, the German Labour Front (DAF). These included low-priced vacations through the Strength through Joy (*Kraft durch Freude* or KdF) programme, most of them short and to destinations within Germany, as well as voyages on new ocean liners such as the *Wilhelm Gustloff* to the fjords of Norway or the island of Madeira. Some two million Germans took advantage of the programme in 1934, and three million the following year. The organizers emphasized the egalitarian aspects of people's tourism, making sure, for example, that the vessels offered only one class of cabin and that assignments occurred by lot.

The regime also gave people the opportunity to save for the People's Car (the *Volkswagen*, originally called the *KdF-Wagen*) at a price within reach of 'every German without distinction of class, profession, or property', and to buy affordable versions of other hitherto luxury products, such as the People's Radio (*Volksempfänger*).

One other aspect of the Nazi recovery was distinctly characteristic: the Reich's success in bridling and spurring German capitalism. In 1936, the economics editor of the Nazi Party's newspaper, the *Völkischer Beobachter*, boasted, 'where capitalism considers itself still untouched, it is, in fact, already harnessed to politics.... National Socialist economic policy corresponds to the technical age. It lets capitalism run as the motor, uses its dynamic energies, but shifts the gears.' He might have added, 'and does the steering'. A *monopsony* was taking shape, an economy in which one predominant buyer, namely the German state, was acquiring disproportionate influence over markets. Without interfering directly with private property rights, aside from making examples of a few recalcitrant executives by removing them, the Nazi regime was acquiring the power to subordinate most domestic economic and commercial development to political wishes. The importance of the large joint stock banks, the Deutsche, the Dresdner, and the Commerz, had been conversely reduced. So had the freedom of manoeuvre of corporate executives and with it the ability of firms to pursue business strategies different from those the Nazi regime desired.

Self-sufficiency

In the late summer of 1936, fresh from the Third Reich's successful remilitarization of the Rhineland, the German High Command drafted its first large-scale offensive plans, and Hitler resolved to make the German economy keep pace. He prepared a secret memorandum for Werner Blomberg and Hermann Göring, his deputies for military and economic mobilization, directing that the German army be made 'operational' and the German economy 'capable of war' within four years. Less than two weeks later, the Nazi Führer announced the inauguration of a Four Year Plan to the Nuremberg party congress, ostensibly in order to achieve economic security for the German Reich by reducing its need for foreign raw materials, but really in order to fulfil on time the goals he had assigned to Blomberg and Göring.

The expenditures this objective seemed to require proved huge and ever expanding. Investments under the headings of armaments and autarky (economic self-sufficiency) accounted for 67 per cent of the increase in German national production in the late 1930s. By the end of 1937, the Four Year Plan envisioned investing 10 billion Reichsmarks, primarily in producing fuel and rubber from coal, mining domestic iron ore, and manufacturing textiles from cellulose, in order to cut the nation's annual import bill in half. A year later, air force planners sought a fivefold increase in the number of German planes, the navy advanced, and Hitler sanctioned the Z-Plan for a large surface fleet, and the army was still adding divisions as well as erecting the *Westwall* fortifications along the French frontier. The deformation of German economic life became even more pronounced as the share of industrial investment that went to consumer products dropped to 17 per cent in 1938 (from 41 per cent in 1933) and the share of industrial wages earned from making consumer goods fell to ⎡ ⎤ ⎦. By 1939, real net national product had risen by 48 per cent since 1929, but per capita consumption by only 4 per cent, and military purchases were devouring 20 per cent of German gross domestic product, an unprecedented level for a country in peacetime.

Schacht's reservations about the affordability of these undertakings and the wisdom of the resulting deformation caused him to lose Hitler's favour, and influence over economic policy passed increasingly to Hermann Göring as head of the Four Year Plan. Even so, many German industrial leaders expressed doubts about sinking capital into projects that could not stand the normal tests of commercial viability, as well as concern that the financial demands of breakneck expansion would overwhelm their balance sheets. Göring squelched such qualms with both word and deed. In December 1936, he told a group of executives flatly, 'whether in every case new plants will be amortized is a matter of indifference.... We stand already in mobilization and war, only the shooting has not yet started.' In August 1937, he stifled the opposition of German steel makers to investing in the extraction of low grade German iron ore by threatening to charge them with economic sabotage, and then dragooned them into helping to fund a new, primarily state-owned and directed firm to undertake the project, which he modestly allowed to be dubbed the *Reichswerke Hermann Göring*. In February 1938, as acting economics minister following Schacht's resignation the preceding November, Göring replaced most of the Ministry's senior officials with convinced supporters of the regime's economic programme. And the following October, he so intimidated a group of leading coal and steel executives that one of them wrote, 'if we give the state cause to call our performance unsatisfactory, an expropriation will not be avoidable.... Business, especially the mining industry, never has been in such danger as today.'

The accumulated reserves of German firms proved sufficient to sustain the industrial boom of 1936–9 in conjunction with the usual government incentives and subsidies, and the state managed to fund those by imposing annual 5 per cent increases in corporate tax rates, requiring savings institutions to put deposits into government bonds, and paying other expenses with credits against future taxes. Plunder also helped keep the Reich budget afloat. In the fiscal year 1938–9, accelerated dispossession of German Jews through forced 'Aryanization' and various assessments and fees brought in 5 per cent of the national government's revenue from taxes and customs. Nonetheless, by early 1939, the Reich's financial situation was becoming acute: projected military expenditures through 1942 came to 30 billion Reichsmarks per year, an annual sum equal to 30 per cent of Germany's total national income at the outset; the Reich's short-term, revolving debt was on its way to rising by 80 per cent during the first eight months of the year; and the volume of money in circulation reached double the level of 1937, creating inflationary pressures that threatened to spin out of control.

Moreover, managing the swollen appetite for construction materials, many of which had to be imported, turned out to be as difficult a problem as paying for the many and massive new factories. As in the preceding three years, but now on a much greater scale, the Reich faced difficult trade-offs among its numerous needs and resorted to ever tighter rationing and regulation. Allocations of iron, steel, and other metals became more strictly controlled, and huge backlogs of orders accumulated. In mid-1938, the government assumed the right to conscript and distribute labour. For a time, plunder came to the Reich's rescue in this respect, too: the occupation of Austria in March 1938 doubled Germany's foreign exchange supply, and the acquisition of the Czech gold reserves a year later eased paying for imports almost as much as the Czech armaments industry and weapons stockpiles boosted the strength of the Wehrmacht. Nonetheless, early in 1939, a desperate shortage of purchasing power abroad forced the Reich abruptly to throw resources into goods for export and away from munitions. This impasse exposed the circularity of Hitlerian economics. By aiming for blockade-proof self-sufficiency and massive armaments as means to conquest, the Four Year Plan made conquest all the more necessary.

Grasping the situation, the Nazi Führer interpreted it as an indication that he had nothing to gain and much to lose by waiting until the completion of the Four Year Plan in 1940 to launch a war for living space. At a conference in late 1937, he had estimated the optimal time for fighting—the moment when his rearmament drive would have won him the largest advantage over the richer rival powers that had begun trying to catch up—as 1942/3. Now he concluded that he had built a formidable military machine, established enough capacity to produce vital domestic substitutes for essential raw materials, and turned German business into an instrument of national goals, but that his country was operating at the outer limits of its economic capacity. Only by increasing that capacity could his Reich contend with its probable enemies. That realization, coupled with Stalin's openness in August 1939 to a non-aggression pact and a deal to exchange grain and ores for machinery, led Hitler to modify his zigzag plan. By invading Poland, he accepted the risk that Britain would side with his Polish and French opponents, which he still intended to dispatch sequentially before turning again to the east.

Conquest

Despite all the expenses and exertions of the pre-war years, and despite Hitler's analysis that 1939 was a relatively favourable time for Germany to fight, the Third Reich entered World War II with considerable disadvantages. Only a portion of the army was mechanized; the British and French had more and sometimes better tanks and aircraft; stockpiles of ammunition, oil, and rubber were adequate to only a few months of combat; and the nation's population and gross national product were much smaller than those of the empires it was fighting. Moreover, Germany already was so fully mobilized that getting more military output out of its economy seemed a daunting task. The labour force was particularly inelastic because a larger percentage of German women were already at work than was ever achieved in Britain and the US during the whole of World War II (more than half of all German women between the ages of 15 and 60 were employed in 1939, and women already made up more than one-third of the German workforce). Increasing military production at a time when thousands of workers were being called to arms thus depended heavily on shifting labourers from low priority industries to high priority ones, a process that already had been going on for years.

Along with the inflow of food and minerals from the USSR, the dazzling military victories of 1939–40 masked these deficiencies and then partially alleviated them. Large numbers of Polish and French prisoners of war became available as labourers, especially in agriculture. Thousands of tons of fuel and other raw material in the Netherlands, Belgium, and France fell into German hands. Among these, the metal stocks, including nickel, copper, and steel, proved indispensable to the doubling of German arms production between January and July 1940. The territories that Germany annexed from Poland had a bumper harvest that autumn. Occupied Denmark's dairy farms became essential providers of butter, milk, and cheese to the Home Front. And the massive occupation charges levied on western Europe and later Serbia and Greece not only swelled the Reich Treasury but also enabled the Wehrmacht to pay the soldiers stationed there in local currencies. The troops used the money to pick shops clean of goods in short supply at home, which then went there via military post and softened the effects of rationing.

But the German occupied and allied states were also liabilities that exacerbated the Reich's continuing problem of needing to spread resources in too many directions. A stagnant level of coal production now had to heat homes and power factories in western Europe, as well as Germany. A certain amount of output for export had to continue in order to sustain trading ties to Finland, Italy, Croatia, Romania, and especially the Soviet Union, which demanded machinery, some of it vital to the Wehrmacht, and technological know-how in return for commodities. The army needed more men, but so did the coalmines, arms factories, and farms. Military actions depended heavily on horses, but so did agricultural output. Fertilizers and explosives required the same chemical inputs. U-Boats, artillery, airplanes, and tanks competed for common metal and mechanical components. Already in 1940, the Reich's leaders recognized the central problem that continued to bedevil German industry throughout the conflict, even as it squeezed ever more equipment out of the nation's factories: given the limits of the nation's resources, adequately increased production of any vital military tool—e.g. ammunition, shipping, armour, aircraft—generally had to come at the expense of some other one. This produced a stop-and-go pattern of military production during 1940–1 in which priorities rapidly and abruptly shifted from one emphasis to another, according to evolving strategic considerations.

Germany's economic limitations meant that increased military production required even tighter rationing of food and goods as well as further reductions in the availability of consumer goods. Real consumption per head fell by almost 20 per cent during the first two years of World War II and so did the calorie content of food rations for workers' families. The proportion of the industrial workforce employed making material for the armed forces shot up from 22 per cent in 1939 to 50 per cent a year later. Meanwhile, the fact that people had little to buy meant that savings deposits piled up—they totalled 40 billion Reichsmarks by the middle of the war—and provided the government with a reservoir of compulsory loans.

In 1940 as in 1939, recognition of continuing economic constraints prompted Hitler to try to break out of them by force. Even before the *Luftwaffe* failed to win the Battle of Britain, the Führer came to believe that seizing the grain and resources of the Soviet Union was preferable to paying for them and might have the fringe benefit of persuading the British to make peace. By December, planning for an invasion was well advanced. The centre of gravity of military production shifted from ammunition in 1940 to artillery, guns, planes, vehicles, and submarines in 1941, all intended to produce rapid victory in the east. Even assuming a quick triumph there, Nazi planners did not expect the war necessarily to end, but rather to expand, given the likelihood of American intervention on Britain's side. Thus, 1941 became the start date for even more massive investments, not only in weaponry and munitions, but also in fuel and rubber from coal sufficient to meet the Reich's needs. Emblematic of the latter effort was the founding of a triangle of huge installations at Monowitz, Heydebreck, and Blechhammer in Upper Silesia, out of reach of Allied bombers. These sites ultimately swallowed up more than 1 billion marks in construction costs.

Despite having 85 per cent of fit men aged 20–30 in uniform, Germany achieved remarkable gains in military output during the first two years of the war. Annual production of planes rose from 8,295 in 1939 to 11,776 in 1941, of submarines from fifteen to 196, and of tanks from approximately 1,300 to 5,200. Nonetheless, Britain was outproducing the Reich in the first two categories, and the Soviet Union in all three, by the time the German advance into the USSR slowed in the fall of 1941 and, in the words of Adam Tooze, 'the German war economy began to come apart at the seams'. Shortages of coal undercut both the usefulness of the western European factories to the Reich and the production of coke for steel-making that was indispensable to armaments production. Constrained fuel supplies caused military planners to conclude that Germany could not fight effectively on land and sea and in the air simultaneously. The equipment demands of the air force and the army appeared mutually exclusive. Several well-informed officials, including Ernst Udet of the *Luftwaffe*, concluded that the war was unwinnable and committed suicide. Fritz Todt, the leader of armaments production, shared their view and told Hitler so in late 1941, several months before dying in a plane crash.

Struggling to Survive

As one German industrialist later observed, during World War II the Reich's arms manufacturers were perpetually in the position 'of people who had to cover themselves with too short a blanket: the more one succeeds in his attempts to be well covered, the more the other must suffer'. After 1942, thanks to massive applications of forced and slave labour, Germany achieved Herculean surges in production: four times as many tanks manufactured in 1944 as in 1941, and three and one-half times as many planes. But the Reich's resources were so overstretched that spurts in output could be achieved only at the expense of quality or reductions elsewhere. The price of getting more planes out of the factories each month was concentration on a few standard models, such as the Heinkel 111 and the Messerschmitt 109, that the Allies already had outclassed. The quantity of ammunition produced rose for a few months at the expense of tanks, then armour at the expense of U-Boats, then rockets at the expense of cannon, and so on. It was a hopeless, losing struggle, since the productive capacities of the US, the UK, and the USSR were so much greater, allowing them to turn out six times as many aircraft as Germany in 1941–3 and four times as many in 1944, when they already held nearly total air superiority; in tanks the ratio in 1941–4 was more than 3:1. Even allowing for the fact that America and Britain also were fighting Japan, the Allies' economic advantage was overpowering, all the more so as they were not impeded by the bombs that rained down upon German industry after 1943 and diverted so much artillery and ammunition from the front lines to anti-aircraft units.

The sensible thing to have done, as Fritz Todt had urged, was to seek an end to the war on at least one front, if not both. That this did not happen was not only the product of Hitler's all-or-nothing ideology of racial conflict, but also the result of one man's infectious conviction that Germany still could win, coupled with another official's ruthlessness in scouring the European continent for labour. The stubborn believer in victory was Todt's successor as Armaments Minister, Albert Speer, and the his right hand man as General Plenipotentiary for Labour was the Nazi *Gauleiter* of Thuringia, Fritz Sauckel, who took office in February and March of 1942 respectively. Nearly as much as Hitler, these men bore responsibility for prolonging the war and thus not only for the criminal production methods the Reich increasingly employed, but also for the great majority of the death and destruction visited upon Germany during the conflict.

During Speer's first fifteen months in office, German armament production increased astoundingly, on an average of 5.5 per cent per month. To some degree, the gains resulted from measures and investments that antedated his appointment, as many new production sites came on line. But he brought tighter overall direction to Germany's economic war in the form of a new Central Planning Office headed by Hans Kehrl, a veteran Nazi and manufacturer. Speer also presided over the creation of an elaborate system of Rings and Committees, each headed by experienced industrialists and assigned to coordinate the flows of industrial inputs and outputs, respectively. Along with further standardization of models and pricing, these initiatives achieved modest gains in efficiency and productivity, but the real force behind the surge in German output came from Sauckel's ruthless efforts to recruit, round up, and bring to Germany millions of foreign labourers, most of them working increasingly under duress. In 1942, the total number of workers in tank production rose by 60 per cent and in locomotive manufacturing by 90 per cent.

Most of the new hands were foreigners, who soon constituted one-third of armaments workers and more than 40 per cent of those producing airplanes. By 1944, almost eight million of them were labouring in Germany, and they made up 46 per cent of the agricultural labour force, 34 per cent of the miners, 30 per cent of the workers in the metals industry, 28 per cent of those in chemicals firms, and altogether more than 26 per cent of the total workforce.

This foreign labour force was a form of plunder, and many of the people in it were treated as such. Italian soldiers, some 600,000 of them interned by the Germans after Italy surrendered in September 1943 and then shipped north, were subjected to particular contempt and harshness. Poles had to wear identifying P's on their clothing, and workers from further east in Nazi occupied Europe the label '*Ost*'; both groups (3.8 million people in 1944) got the hardest labour assignments, the least nourishment, and the lowest take-home pay. Contact between these labourers and the surrounding German population was severely restricted, with sexual relations being punishable by death. Western and northern European workers fared better, but absconded in large numbers nonetheless, especially as air raids multiplied.

In May 1943, stepped-up Allied air attacks put an end to the rising trajectory of German arms production, and it essentially flatlined for the next nine months. Meanwhile, Germany's defeat by the Soviets in the Battle of Kursk during the summer marked the apparent end of the Reich's capacity to mount major offensive operations. Faced with the certainty of defeat, Speer and Sauckel not only doubled down on forced labour, but entered into increasing cooperation with Heinrich Himmler and the SS to exploit concentration camp inmates as slave labourers—workers who were not paid at all, but were paid for, i.e. leased on a daily basis. Use of Jews and other prisoners by private industry had begun in the construction forces at the IG Farben factory near Auschwitz and the nearby Blechhammer and Heydebreck sites and in road-building projects involving the Philip Holzmann construction company in the German-annexed part of pre-war Poland and in Upper Silesia during 1941, but the practice had been relatively rare. Most labour by inmates prior to 1943 occurred in SS-owned factories in concentration camps or SS-directed infrastructure projects, mostly in eastern Europe. But in November 1942, Speer had

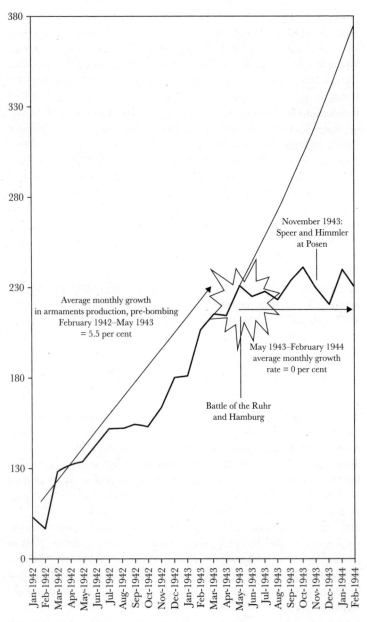

The Lopsided Recovery: Textiles Stagnate, Heavy Industry Booms.

persuaded Hitler to authorize the use of camp labour on site in factories within the Reich. Now that practice exploded in conjunction with what was perhaps the most fantastical economic initiative of the Third Reich's death throes: the Fighter Staff Programme (*Jägerstabprogram*) to bury or transfer underground most of the nation's vital factories, especially those producing for the *Luftwaffe*. These included installations for making the 'wonder weapons' on which Nazi dreams of victory increasingly relied, especially the V-1 and V-2 rockets, and which therefore consumed increasing quantities of scarce resources. The Reich poured 2 billion Reichsmarks into the V-2 programme alone, much of it to construct an assembly line through a mountain in central Germany, where thousands of camp inmates worked under horrendous conditions. In the end, almost twice as many people perished from making the rockets as from being hit by them.

The toll taken by the slave labour system, especially in the final two years of the war, was horrific. At Farben's Auschwitz plant, 25,000–30,000 inmates died in the course of construction. Altogether, probably two-thirds of the more than 700,000 camp inmates recorded as working for the German state or private industry at the beginning of 1945 were dead by the following summer. Forced labourers did not expire at anything like this rate, but the raw number of casualties was still large. At least 300,000 Soviet and Polish civilian workers perished while deployed in Germany; so did one million Soviet prisoners of war. Contrary to widespread popular misconceptions, neither the forced nor the slave labour system arose from the profit motive. They emerged out of the conjunction of Hitler's racial solipsism—his insistence that only the welfare of Germans deserved consideration—and the mathematics of the German labour supply. As the army's needs cut into the size (and quality) of the German workforce, the Reich's labour deficit ran into the millions. Germany resorted to compulsory workers because they were available and for a time seemed infinitely replaceable, not because they were cheap. In fact, they often were not, especially when used on construction, because their productivity was frequently too low to offset the charges of leasing them from the SS, and then maintaining and guarding them. But this fact created a perverse incentive for employers to economize in feeding and caring for such workers, at least as long as they remained plentiful.

Table 6.1. The economics of slave labour.

	SS rental fee for appropriately skilled inmate labour, RM	Normal German pay rates, RM	Productivity at which concentration camp labour is cost neutral, as % of German productivity norm assuming unadjusted contract prices	Actual productivity of concentration camp labour, as % of German productivity norm	Concentration camp labour more profitable than normal German labour assuming unadjusted contract prices?
Metalworking Industry:					
Skilled	0.545	1.21	45	40–60	Y
Semi-skilled	0.364	1.011	36	40–60	Y
Labourer	0.364	0.795	46	30–50	?
Female worker	0.364	0.582	63	60 +	Y
Electrical engineering:					
Female worker	0.364	0.629	58	60 +	Y
Construction:					
Carpenter, concrete specialist	0.545	0.969	56	28–38	N
Bricklayer	0.545	0.929	59	28–38	N
Road worker	0.364	0.684	53	28–38	N

Sauckel and Speer's labour system epitomized the profligate and callous futility of the German bid for continental domination. The application of foreign labour certainly helped contain the decline in German agricultural output during the war. It dropped by only 15 per cent between 1939 and 1944, and deliveries from occupied countries more than made up for the dip. Nonetheless, civilian Germans' diets changed for the worse from early 1942 on, as increased consumption of potatoes and cabbage offset steep declines in that of fats and animal protein, and the quality of the flour used to make bread deteriorated considerably. Bringing western European workers to Germany after 1941 and concentrating production there actually made strictly economic sense in the context of limited supplies of key inputs such as coal and steel. But the forced and slave labour programmes were staggeringly inefficient and politically counterproductive. They alienated occupied populations and thus contributed to the growth of the European resistance in 1943–4. They depressed productivity in occupied areas by driving many people into hiding. And they deluded Germans, including Albert Speer, into thinking that the war might still be won.

Virtually every other dimension of German plundering had the same pyrrhic quality, producing short-term gains, but never enough to compensate for the Reich's deficiencies vis-à-vis its enemies and always involving debilitating trade offs. Estimates vary, but the most reliable figures suggest that occupied Europe paid for about 35 per cent of Germany's war costs and supplied 30–35 per cent of its food requirements. Food from Belgium sustained Germans but reduced production of desperately needed coal by hungry and angry Belgian miners. Requisitioning grain and animals on a massive scale in the occupied east kept the bellies of German soldiers there full, but depressed future yields. Retaining collective farms in Ukraine so as to avoid disrupting production alienated the peasantry and thus had the opposite effect. Taking in fantastic sums in occupation charges—e.g. perhaps as much as 35 billion Reichsmarks or 30 per cent of total national income from France in 1940–4, along with more than 21 billion from Belgium and the Netherlands—came at the expense of runaway inflation, especially in the smaller occupied countries, which disrupted their productivity. The huge 'credit' of 100 billion Reichsmarks that Germany ran up in 'clearing accounts' with occupied and allied countries represented the total value of imports for which the Reich did not pay. This amounted to rapidly strip-mining Europe's resources.

Perhaps the only instance of Nazi spoliation that did not have a significant economic downside was, rather shockingly, the dispossession of the European Jews that culminated in their murder. The process proved almost entirely self-financing and, indeed, profitable to the German treasury. But although the Reich contrived to reserve much of the loot for itself, even shipping the furniture taken from the homes of Dutch Jews to Hamburg for distribution to bombed-out citizens and trainloads of personal effects collected at the death camps for the use of displaced or repatriated Germans, most of the real and fungible property taken from the Jews remained in the countries of origin. Though some of the gold object and teeth collected from Jews at the death camps did find their way to the Reichsbank, that organization failed to make use of almost half the total collected, which remained unprocessed and stored in a mineshaft at the end of the war, where American troops discovered the haul.

Most of the rest of the gold plundered from Jews disappeared into German industrial production during the war and most of the silver into the manufacture of silver nitrate, an indispensable component reconnaissance film for the Luftwaffe. The loss of ghetto labourers did not prove noticeably damaging to the German war effort, and the Nazi regime kept alive the most valuable Jewish slave labourers in Poland, the ones around Radom producing in early 1944 one-third of German infantry ammunition, until the Russians appeared on the horizon. But the massacre seriously undermined the Reich in another way: along with the general viciousness of German occupation policies, it cemented the Allies' determination to accept nothing less than unconditional surrender.

As a result of burying, dispersing, and otherwise camouflaging many production sites, German arms production achieved a final surge in the first half of 1944, after which the Allies succeeded in using air power to strangle German industry by smashing its fuel supplies and breaking its transportation and power links. Output came to a standstill as the American, British, and Soviet armies closed in at the beginning of 1945, and the completed versions of one 'wonder weapon' that might have made a difference, the Me262, the first jet aircraft, also manufactured largely by slave labour, literally could not get off the ground.

Germany's overall mobilization during World War II was extraordinarily extensive. In 1943, war production accounted for 70 per cent of nominal gross national product. Among all the belligerents, only the USSR succeeded in putting as large a share of its national income to the service of the war effort as Nazi Germany did. The volume of industrial infrastructure that the Reich created in the process was so extensive that despite enormous damage from the air, the surviving capital stock in 1945 in the area that became west Germany several years later was one-fifth higher than it had been in 1939. Many major corporations emerged similarly richer in equipment and manufacturing capacity. If, as some scholars contend, such enormous expansion laid the basis for west Germany's post-war economic resurgence, it also rested on equally enormous expenditures of life and wealth in the service of an impossible dream of a German continental empire.

7

The Holocaust

Omer Bartov

Historiography

The current perception of the Holocaust as an historical event of crucial importance in the heart of the twentieth century is relatively recent. For several decades after the survivors of the Nazi genocide were liberated, the 'final solution of the Jewish question' was not considered a central theme even in the history of the Third Reich and World War II, as any glance at historical monographs published during those years demonstrates. Subsequently, as awareness of the event's historical significance grew, interpretations of its meanings and ramifications also multiplied. Indeed, while all events of the past are constantly reconsidered depending on the place and time from which they are observed, the Holocaust has been increasingly used as a model, a warning, a foil, or a myth in order to prove often starkly contradictory assertions. Ironically, then, an event that had initially been marginalized, not least because of its almost incomprehensible extremity, has now, once again thanks to its radical nature, taken centre stage in the historiography and representation of the previous century, engaging scholars and many others seeking to draw lessons from the past for the sake of the present. At the same time, the multiple uses to which the Holocaust has been subjected indicate not only present concerns but also the complexity of its origins and the profound effects of its implementation.

In the wake of World War II numerous monuments were erected throughout Europe proclaiming 'never again'. Yet people's understanding of what precisely should never be allowed to happen once more differed substantially from place to place and person to person, depending on such factors as national affiliation, ideological conviction, and religious denomination. Moreover, such meanings changed significantly over time. Initially, before the term Holocaust came into popular use, the notion of Nazi crimes against humanity implied just that, namely crimes both against all members of the human race and against the very concept of a shared humanity. The Third Reich victimized its domestic and foreign foes, its political and perceived racial enemies, the nations it occupied and enslaved, and those that fought against it. Since Nazism was universally destructive, there appeared to be no need to distinguish between its victims, whether they died in the Blitz against Britain, were deported from France as resistance fighters, were shot in acts of collective punishment and starved to death in Belarus and Leningrad, or were murdered as Jews. Alain Resnais's influential film *Night and Fog* (1955) reflected this trend of lumping all victims together, as did the Soviet regime, which insisted that all nations of the USSR had suffered and sacrificed equally in the Great Patriotic War. The removal of monuments commemorating the genocide of the Jews, and the silencing of references to local collaboration in the Holocaust, became the staple of post-war Soviet politics of memory.

There was by that time, however, also a very different understanding of the Holocaust, as expressed, for instance, in Léon Poliakov's 1951 study, *Harvest of Hate*, which presented the genocide of the Jews as the culmination of a long history of anti-Semitism and Judeophobia, marking it thereby as essentially distinct from all other crimes of racism, war, and occupation perpetrated by the Nazis. This view was widespread among Jewish survivors of the Holocaust, especially those who came from eastern Europe, and was also dominant in the State of Israel, eventually constituting the underlying premise of Adolf Eichmann's trial in Jerusalem in 1961–62. It was during the 1960s, not least following the Six Day War of 1967, that the term Holocaust increasingly became the common designation in English of the 'final solution', whereas in Israel (and later on also in France) the term Shoah (catastrophe) was adopted. Thus, two different narratives of the Holocaust emerged: one which perceived it as a consequence of Nazi ideology, and applied it by and large to all groups persecuted and murdered by the Nazis, and another that saw it as rooted in European, Christian, and even pre-Christian anti-Judaism, with the

Nazis as only the most extreme expression of centuries-old sentiments and a timeless urge to root the Jews out of European society.

Among scholars, especially historians, two other related but also quite different schools of interpretation developed. The first, which was obviously linked to the Judeophobia narrative but also focused more clearly on Nazi ideology and especially on Adolf Hitler, came to be known as 'intentionalism'. According to this school, Hitler had mobilized deep-seated sentiments in Germany specifically and Christian Europe more generally in order to implement his world-view, which was transformed into German policy once he took over power in 1933. As Hitler saw it, human history was an endless struggle between superior and inferior races. In order to dominate the world, the Aryans had to destroy or subjugate all other inferior races and to conquer an extensive 'living space' in eastern Europe and Russia, where they would find sufficient resources to flourish and multiply. The Jews, in this worldview, were an anti-race, which both competed for dominance in the world and was entirely parasitical on other races, polluting them with its own blood even as it miraculously preserved its racial purity—a symbol of strength in Hitler's racial universe. As 'intentionalists' saw it, Hitler pursued the policy implications of this worldview throughout his twelve-year rule, seeking to build an empire in the east, subjugate the Slavs, and, especially, most consistently and relentlessly, murder the Jews. In other words, Hitler transformed the 'age-old hatred' of the Jews into an ideology and, once he came into power, into state policy.

A very different interpretation of the dynamics that led to the genocide of the Jews, which came to be known as 'functionalism' or 'structuralism', conceded Hitler's expansionist, racist, and genocidal predilections, but presented him as an essentially weak dictator whose strength emanated from the competition between different state and Nazi Party institutions for his favour. Since he was ideologically always the most extreme even within the ranks of the party, and because power in the Third Reich was associated with proximity to the Führer, those individuals and institutions (such as the NSDAP, the SS, or the Wehrmacht) who offered the most radical policies and solutions to real and perceived obstacles on the way to accomplishing Germany's goals were likely to gain more in influence and tilt policy in their favour. In this process of what 'functionalist' historian Hans

Mommsen called 'cumulative radicalization', Jewish policies increasingly came to dominate as Germany's goals of conquering and colonizing 'living space' in the east were thwarted by the resistance of the Red Army. Hence, rather than being a policy planned in advance and ruthlessly pursued by Hitler, the 'final solution' was understood as the result of the chaotic structure of the Third Reich and the tendency of its power brokers, in the words of Ian Kershaw, to 'work toward the Führer' as they ruthlessly competed with each other for influence.

More recent interpretations of the Holocaust have made use of both much greater documentation—partly made accessible after the fall of communism and partly thanks to the archival diligence of younger scholars—and of new trends in historical scholarship more generally. Three directions stand out in particular. First, as demonstrated by Timothy Snyder, there has been a growing recognition that the Holocaust took place largely in eastern Europe, where the majority of the Jews lived and were murdered. Hence it has appeared increasingly important to understand the links between Jews and their communities in those countries and to evaluate the effect of centuries-long interethnic relations on the implementation of genocide by the invading Germans in World War II. Research by such historians such as Jan Grabowski has indeed revealed the widespread collaboration of local populations in the mass murder of the Jews.

Second, as historians have increasingly researched the phenomenon of European imperialism and colonialism, scholars such as Wendy Lower have examined the links between Germany's colonial aspirations in eastern Europe and western Russia and the mass murder of the Jews. Indeed, unlike earlier historiography, the Holocaust has been interpreted—perhaps most influentially by Götz Aly—as the most extreme, and the only 'successful' component of a demographic restructuring and settlement plan of vast regions referred to by the Nazis as the *Generalplan Ost* (General Plan East). Finally, the growing prominence of genocide studies has had an impact on the understanding of the Holocaust as part of a larger context of modern state-directed mass murder. It has been argued that the Holocaust is comparable in certain respects to other cases ranging from the genocide of the Herero in German Southwest Africa at the beginning of the twentieth century, through the Armenian genocide of World War I, all the way to the post-1945 genocides in Cambodia and Rwanda, to name only the most prominent. But it has also been shown that the Holocaust was distinct from these cases in other respects, not least because of the extensive use of extermination camps as well as the Nazi regime's urge to kill every single Jew it could lay its hands on. Among the most prominent scholars working in this field are Donald Bloxham, Dirk Moses, and Jürgen Zimmerer.

While these larger interpretive frameworks have integrated the Holocaust into the context of modern history as a whole, they have also been criticized as depriving it of its historical and symbolic singularity. Another approach to integrating different perspectives of the event in reconstructing the history of the Holocaust, but also of other cases of mass violence, has put greater emphasis on the experiences, perceptions, and accounts of those subjected to it. The other approaches discussed above largely concern the perpetrators of genocide, be they the ideologues, leaders, or actual killers. From the point of view of historians writing such accounts, what needs to be explained are such questions as decision-making, motivation, and the mechanics of implementing a continent-wide undertaking of mass murder. In this kind of historiography the victims become merely the end product of decisions and actions over which they have no control. But the Holocaust, like all other genocides, was also, indeed primarily, an event in which millions of human beings were murdered, often in the most horrendous manner, and after being subjected to extreme physical and mental torment. Hence some historians, including Saul Friedländer, Alexandra Garbarini, and the present author, have increasingly turned to the diaries and testimonies of the victims in order to recreate their personal human experience, as well as to shed light on aspects of the Holocaust that were of no interest to the perpetrators and therefore cannot be found in the documents they left behind. This approach, rather than providing overarching explanations to the manner in which the Holocaust was organized, or comparing it as a whole to other genocides, seeks both to humanize the experience of the victims by giving them back the voices of which their murderers had deprived them, and to examine such relatively neglected aspects of the event as the social dynamics within Jewish communities exposed to genocide, the relationship between Jews and their Christian neighbours, and the contacts, often erroneously assumed to have been inexistent, between the killers and their victims.

In this sense, this approach is concerned with the intimate aspects of communal massacres and one-on-one violence starkly different from the impersonal character of the extermination camps.

Origins

With these changing perspectives and interpretations in mind, let us now try to examine more closely the roots, implementation, and aftermath of the 'final solution'. The deeper origins of the Holocaust can be traced back to two main sources. The first is the transformation of anti-Jewish religious theology, popular mythology, and socioeconomic resentment, into modern anti-Semitism in the last third of the nineteenth century. Modern anti-Semitism stemmed from the combined effects of Jewish emancipation and the rapid industrialization especially of central Europe, resulting in massive urbanization and displacement of rural populations, the weakening of traditional elites, and the erosion of the old middle class of small artisans and manufacturers. These were increasingly replaced by heavy industry, chain stores, a growing white collar and service sector, and mass media, all linked together as never before by a dense network of railroads. This 'great transformation', as the renowned economic historian Karl Polanyi called the industrial revolution, had particularly unsettling effects on those who could not adapt to it, even as the expanding urban spaces and communication networks facilitated the emergence of a new type of mass politics. The Jews, who swiftly entered the new economy following their emancipation in the wake of German unification in 1871, came to be identified by those socioeconomic sectors left behind as the cause of their misfortune. In that sense, the combination of economic modernization, the expansion of equal rights, and the aggressive nationalism of the new nation-state, constituted a fertile soil for the rise of political anti-Semitism as the vehicle of populist nationalist parties.

The second root of what eventually evolved into Nazi ideology was the emergence of scientific racism throughout Europe. Some of this discourse can be dated back to linguistics and the growing tendency to identify different families of languages with specific ethnic or racial origins, as in the distinction between Indo-European and Semitic languages. Another element was a reading of Charles Darwin's ideas about evolution and the origins of species as providing scientific proof for the inherent and immutable differences between human species or races, which in turn enabled the ranking of some (such as Aryans) as higher than others (such as Africans) on the evolutionary tree. Such notions combined with the concept of racial hygiene, according to which it was possible to breed ever purer, and hence superior races, whose opposite were mixed and therefore inferior or degenerate races. Since such conceptualizations of humanity stemmed from Europe and North America, it is hardly surprising that Indo-European white Aryans came to be viewed as both physically and morally superior to all other races—at least as long as they preserved their racial purity both in their own lands and even more importantly in their growing colonial empires.

Indeed, it was the conquest of colonial empires that encouraged Europeans to perceive themselves as superior, not only militarily and technologically but also culturally and morally, and for some also biologically. But it was also the rule by small European elites over masses of non-European populations that aroused the fear of going native, not only by adapting to other ways of life but also through intermarriage and hence racial mixing, thereby diluting precisely those essential superior qualities: hence the growing obsession with preserving racial purity through categorization and segregation.

Scientific racism and racial hygiene, which asserted a science of human evolution and breeding, therefore became not only part of a legitimate discourse in Europe but also signalled their practitioners' modernity and sophistication. When applied to the Jews, who came to be seen by the anti-Semitic movement as an alien, non-European race, this discourse lent scientific sanction to the politics of resentment, exclusion, and hate. It was the marriage of old prejudices and beliefs, new socioeconomic rage and fear, and the assertion of irrefutable scientific evidence for immutable racial difference that made modern anti-Semitism into such a powerful, albeit never entirely pervasive, political movement. What was still missing from this potentially explosive mix were two elements: a moment of general crisis that would allow the fear- and hatemongers to appeal to the masses, and the notion that all the seemingly insoluble problems facing society could be solved by removing the Jews.

It was this 'redemptive anti-Semitism', as Saul Friedländer had called it, that became the core of Hitler's worldview and Nazi ideology, and whose early echoes can be found in such statements as that of the late nineteenth-century German historian Heinrich von Treitschke, who popularized and legitimized the slogan 'the Jews are our misfortune', words that became the motto of the yellow Nazi rag, *Der Stürmer*. In the wake of Germany's disastrous defeat in World War I, the terrible inflation that followed and destroyed the savings of the middle class, and finally the Great Depression of the late 1920s and early 1930s, German society found itself swept from one crisis to another. The old imperial regime was gone, the sense of economic security and slow but certain progress had been eroded, national pride had been humiliated, millions of Germans had sacrificed their lives and their health for naught, and a new republican regime had been created which many perceived with suspicion as a foreign imposition controlled by social outsiders. This was a moment in which many angry and fearful Germans sought both assurances of a better future and identification and removal of those who had brought about this unexpected calamity. The 'stab-in-the-back legend', according to which Imperial Germany had not been defeated on the battlefield but rather was betrayed from within by Jews and socialists (who were seen as largely synonymous), became more than just a myth about the shocking collapse of 1918 and provided an explanatory framework for all the miseries of the Weimar Republic. It was this idea that Hitler and his new National Socialist Party latched on to: Germany could be great again, but only by liquidating the enemies from within, first and foremost the Jews. Redemption required ruthless social surgery, which Hitler promised to carry out.

Judenpolitik

To be sure, anti-Semitism was hardly unique to Germany; but it was only there that a leader dedicated to such a radically redemptive variety of it came to power and immediately set about implementing his ideology. It is also the case that the racist worldview of the Führer and his party dictated policies against other perceived biological threats and 'social outsiders', not least the handicapped and the Sinti (German Roma), as well as homosexuals, the 'work-shy', 'habitual criminals', and other so-called 'asocials'. But in Hitler's own imaginary and consequently for the Nazi state as a whole—as convincingly argued by Peter Longerich—*Judenpolitik* (Jewish policy and policies) played a central role in the consolidation of a *Volksgemeinschaft* (racial community) by distinguishing it from its ultimate internal Other, 'the Jew'. The obsession of the regime with 'solving the Jewish question', despite the presence of merely half a million Jewish German citizens, and the links made by the regime between Germany's redemption as nation and race and bringing misfortune upon the Jews, became an integral part of re-educating the German public and preparing it for the struggle to come. In 1933 Germany might have been just as, or even less anti-Semitic than some other European countries, not least in eastern Europe. But by the outbreak of the war, especially the younger cohorts of Germans had been exposed to intensive anti-Semitic indoctrination, and had repeatedly observed public displays of humiliation and marginalizing of fellow Jewish citizens. This process arguably disciplined them into viewing Jews as a dispensable and malicious presence that needed to be and indeed was thankfully being removed from their midst. Yet when these same young men and not a few women marched into eastern Europe they discovered to their horror that millions of other Jews resided there, many of them resembling the anti-Semitic stereotype of the traditional orthodox Jew much more than any they had known before in Germany.

Pre-war Nazi Germany engaged in an ongoing assault on its Jewish citizens, leading to their pauperization, marginalization, and immigration. The Nuremberg Laws of 1935 made Jews into second-class citizens and limited contact between Jews and Aryans (who were defined as non-Jews, since the Nazis could never find a way of 'scientifically' determining who was a Jew and who was an Aryan). A process of Aryanization of Jewish property brought about a vast transfer of wealth from Jews to Germans, and pressures on Jews to leave the country, despite the scarcity of countries willing to take them in, increased greatly after the *Kristallnacht* pogrom of November 1938. In the course of two days, hundreds of synagogues were burned down, thousands of Jewish-owned businesses were looted and destroyed, close to a hundred Jews were murdered, and tens of thousands of men were incarcerated in concentration camps. By September 1939 half of German Jewry had left, and those who stayed behind were disproportionally elderly and female. But many of the German Jews who left were later captured by the advancing German army and ended up like so many others as Hitler's victims.

Germany's *Judenpolitik* in the 1930s suggests that at this point Hitler had not yet conceived any plans of actually perpetrating genocide, but was rather keen on creating a *judenfrei* (Jew-free) Reich. But his ideological goal of establishing a German colonial empire in the vast 'living space' east of the Reich necessitated an encounter with populations deemed either inferior or dangerous: Slavs and Jews. In this sense, while German policy in the 1930s cannot be deemed genocidal, its inherent dynamic was murderous from the very beginning, since its goals could be accomplished only by ruthless and violent displacement of populations on an unprecedented scale. The outbreak of war soon confronted Germany with a self-imposed dilemma for which it did not have an immediate answer.

The invasion of Poland was premised on a concept that came to be articulated more clearly two years later as '*Vernichtungskrieg*', or war of annihilation. At a closed meeting with his military chiefs on the eve of the attack of 1 September 1939, Hitler reportedly urged them to behave with utter ruthlessness toward the Poles, adding 'Who speaks today of the annihilation of the Armenians?' This reference to the genocide of the Armenians by the Ottoman Empire in World War I, likely meant to allay any fears of punishment for the crimes that would ensue, is telling in several ways. While there was in fact talk of prosecuting those responsible in the wake of the Ottoman Empire's collapse, neither the new Turkish authorities nor the international organs expected to deal with such cases ended up punishing anyone. To Hitler and his ilk this obviously indicated that the perpetrators of crimes on a national scale could expect impunity, all the more so if they were victorious, which was the only alternative Hitler entertained. At the same time, the Armenian genocide was also the first instance in which an awareness of the need to mobilize the international community against state-sponsored mass murder was awakened and a new discourse on crimes against humanity was initiated, however unsuccessfully. Indeed, Raphael Lemkin, the Polish-Jewish jurist who eventually coined the word genocide and successfully led the effort to pass the 1948 United Nations resolution against this 'crime of crimes', had begun to articulate his thinking regarding this 'crime without a name' upon learning about the Armenian genocide. In fact, this systematic destruction by an empire of one of its own ethnic and religious minorities—closely observed by German military advisers—was not the first genocide of the twentieth century. That dubious credit was reserved to the genocide of the Herero and Nama peoples in German Southwest Africa in 1904, where a German general, sent to quell a rebellion by Africans whose lands had been colonized by German settlers, issued his infamous 'extermination order', leading to the killing, lethal expulsion into the desert, or enslavement, of the indigenous population by regular German military forces. Hence Hitler's assertion that no one spoke any longer of such cases did not mean he had forgotten them; quite on the contrary, he had learned that states can get away with mass murder, a lesson he applied with unprecedented determination during the next six years. That Imperial Germany had perpetrated one of these earlier genocides and had been party to the other could only further encourage the Führer to destroy his real and perceived enemies without any compunction or fear of retribution.

The rapid destruction of Poland, facilitated by Germany's alliance with the Soviet Union as agreed upon in the Molotov–Ribbentrop Pact, which divided the country between the two powers, created the occasion for the Nazi leadership to implement its ideological goals of creating an eastern 'living space' and of 'solving the Jewish question'. But as it turned out, the scale of this undertaking was much greater than expected and the two ideological goals could not easily be pursued at the same time. In their effort to expel Poles from parts of Poland annexed by the Reich and to settle there ethnic Germans coming from the Soviet Union, the Germans had to decide what they should meanwhile do with the over two million Jews living in their newly-conquered territories. The SS *Einsatzgruppen* (task forces) formed before the invasion to deal with Germany's political and 'biological' enemies engaged in a great deal of violence, which entailed both decapitating the political and intellectual leadership of the Polish state, and massacring and terrorizing Jews so brutally that even some Wehrmacht generals issued complaints. Yet the bulk of the Jewish population was eventually incarcerated in sealed ghettos, the largest of which were in Warsaw and Lodz (Łódź). It does not appear that at this point there was any consensus within the German leadership as to what should be done with these vast numbers of Jews, who were living in increasingly lethal conditions, deprived of sufficient food, shelter, and sanitation. The general goal was clear: they had to be 'removed' or 'resettled'. But the meanings of these terms changed over time. Initially, there were plans to deport the Jews of Poland to the southeastern corner of that country and let them starve to death there, but that proved impracticable, not least because the German governor of what came to be called the General Government—the parts of German-occupied Poland not directly annexed to the Reich—strongly resisted an influx of Jews into 'his' territory. Following the victorious western campaign of May June 1940 and the armistice with France, the Germans revived an old Polish idea of deporting the Jews to the French colony of Madagascar, where it was presumed that they would die in great numbers thanks to the local conditions. But not unlike the Polish leaders who had dreamed of ridding their nation of the Jews in the 1930s, the Germans in fact had no means of transporting millions of Jews across the world to an island off the coast of Africa, certainly not as long as the British navy still ruled the waves.

Mass Murder

The result was that for the next two years about half a million Jews died mostly of 'natural causes' in the ghettos, and most others were increasingly put to work for the German war effort as well as for the private enrichment of the corrupt German administrators of their ghettos. But the impatient wait for a truly 'final solution' of the Jewish question was soon to end. On 22 June 1941, Germany launched operation 'Barbarossa', invading the Soviet Union with over three millions soldiers, accompanied by Slovak, Hungarian, Romanian, and Italian allies. German commanders were issued with a series of orders that instructed them to sort out and kill political commissars in the Red Army down to the lowest level, to ruthlessly treat all suspicious elements in Soviet territories such as partisans, members of the Communist Party, and Jews, and to 'live off the land' by taking whatever they needed to sustain themselves from the often poor population they would occupy. Military jurisdiction was curtailed as far as actions against occupied Soviet citizens were concerned. Very few preparations were made to accommodate the expected mass of Red Army POWs that would result from the encirclement tactics of the Wehrmacht. Most ominously, the army high command signed an agreement with the chief of the SS and the police, Heinrich Himmler, to support the actions of the four *Einsatzgruppen* operating behind the fighting troops, made up of some 3,000 men and soon assisted by numerous police battalions, SS formations, and local collaborators. Hitler's self-declared *Vernichtungskrieg* in the east eventually caused the death of close to thirty million Soviet citizens, most of them civilians, including well over three million Red Army POWs, about two-thirds of the Soviet troops captured by the German armed forces. The war in the Soviet Union also very quickly developed into a series of mass murder actions of Jews by the *Einsatzgruppen* and their auxiliaries.

As the Red Army retreated before the invading Wehrmacht, especially the Jewish residents of those parts of eastern Poland that had come under Soviet occupation in 1939 were subjected to a series of murderous pogroms by their Christian neighbours, Poles and more prominently Ukrainians. These eruptions of local violence were often led by Ukrainian nationalist activists and units trained by the Germans, and encouraged by the *Einsatzgruppen* under command of Himmler's deputy and chief of the Reich Security Main Office (RSHA), Reinhard Heydrich. In the capital of eastern Galicia, Lemberg (Lwów, L'viv), some 4,000 Jews were massacred between 30 June and 2 July, with many thousands more butchered in other towns of the region. This initial wave of brutalities and massacres was followed by the imposition of more orderly German Security Police presence in areas occupied by the Germans as the Wehrmacht's spearheads, followed by the mobile murder squads, moved further east into the Soviet Union. Several mass shootings on an unprecedented scale took place during those early months, including the massacre in Kamieniec Podolski of over 23,000 Jews in late August, the mass shooting of up to 12,000 Jews in Stanisławów in mid-October, and the massacre of over 33,000 Jews in Babi Yar near Kiev in late September. Similarly, by late November *Einsatzgruppe* A, operating in the Baltic states, had murdered close to 140,000 people, mostly Jews, in mass shootings (Map 7.1).

7.1 The division of Poland and sites of major death camps (courtesy of Robert Gellately).

All those killings were carried out by a combination of German policemen of different units and types along with local militias and the German military. They were public affairs viewed by many bystanders and were accompanied by numerous brutalities as well as organized looting and popular plunder of property and valuables. Jews were mostly murdered and buried close to where they lived and their property was largely transferred to the occupiers and to their neighbours.

In the course of this first wave of killing, in which hundreds of thousands were murdered in one-on-one shootings and buried in mass graves throughout eastern Europe and the western parts of the Soviet Union, new ideas about how a 'final solution to the Jewish question' could be implemented were entertained by the leadership of the Reich. Scholars do not agree on when the plan for such a solution, requested in a letter sent in July 1941 by Hermann Göring, Hitler's deputy, to Heydrich, was decided upon. Christopher Browning has argued that Hitler made the decision in the 'euphoria of victory' over the USSR, some time in the fall of 1941. Christian Gerlach proposes that the decision was made only after the Soviet counteroffensive at the gates of Moscow and the entry of the United States into the war in early December, making it into a world war of the kind that Hitler had warned as early as 1939 would bring about the extermination of the Jews. This decision, he suggests, was announced shortly thereafter by Heydrich to senior Reich officials at the Wannsee Conference of 29 January 1942. For his part, Peter Longerich perceives this policy as evolving incrementally, alongside the development of ever more efficient killing methods and organization, until it ultimately congealed into a continent-wide genocide in spring 1942, at which time mass deportations to newly built extermination camps began, first from the Warsaw Ghetto and later that summer from other parts of Poland and from western Europe.

Whichever interpretation we accept, what we do know is that the construction of murder facilities began by late 1941, with the goal of killing Jews not by mass shooting where they lived but by gas in special camps to which they would be transported by train. Eventually, the Germans built four extermination camps—Chełmno, Bełżec, Sobibór, and Treblinka—dedicated only to mass murder, mostly of Jews, and two camps—Majdanek and Auschwitz-Birkenau—which combined murder facilities with incarceration and forced labour. About half of the estimated 5.5 to six million Jews murdered in the Holocaust were gassed in these camps, over a million of them in Auschwitz and almost as many in Treblinka.

While the killing of many east European Jews, as well as most Jews deported from southeastern, southern, and western Europe, occurred in the extermination camps, vast numbers of Jews continued to be murdered in their sites of habitation in the east. This kind of killing was very different from the industrial, relatively insulated, and impersonal mass murder in gas chambers, which distinguished the Holocaust from other genocides. Instead, it was intimate, face-to-face mass murder in towns where the victims, perpetrators, and bystanders often knew each other beforehand and where no one was entirely passive or could claim not to have seen, heard, or known about the killing. Performed by rather sparsely staffed stationary outposts of the Security Police scattered throughout eastern Europe, the killing was facilitated by larger formations of local auxiliary policemen, mostly reconstituted from nationalist militias that emerged following the withdrawal of the Soviets. These militias maintained their own political-ideological agendas, geared toward the creation of independent states cleansed of such undesirable elements as the Jews and other ethno-national minorities (such as most prominently the Poles in Volhynia and Galicia—former eastern Poland). Hence the genocide of the Jews in eastern Europe was also part of a major undertaking of ethnic cleansing and nation state formation in which the Germans themselves came to play an auxiliary role. This was most evident in the case of the Organization of Ukrainian Nationalists (OUN) and its military arm, the Ukrainian Insurgent Army (UPA), which devastated the lands of eastern Poland and facilitated the extraordinarily high percentage of Jewish victims in regions where German police presence was minimal. For instance, in the area of Czortków-Buczacz in eastern Galicia, an outpost of up to thirty German police personnel, assisted by several hundred Ukrainian auxiliaries, murdered about 60,000 Jews, some 95 per cent of the total Jewish population there, mostly in the brief period between fall 1942 and summer 1943.

Communal genocide was not limited to what later became the lands of western Ukraine. As the historian Jan T. Gross showed in his influential study, *Neighbours*, in July 1941 the ethnic Polish population of the town of Jedwabne murdered up to 1,600 of their Jewish neighbours without any assistance from the Germans. Further research has shown many more such cases in that region of Poland. Lithuanians, Latvians, and Estonians also participated in the killing of their Jewish neighbours. To be sure, this popular violence should not detract any responsibility from Nazi Germany, which both initiated a continent-wide genocide, and gave licence to a wide array of local organizations and individuals to attack, loot, and kill their Jewish neighbours. But for the Jews living in these east European villages, towns, and cities, who had coexisted with their Christian neighbours for centuries, the fact that their acquaintances, colleagues, classmates, and friends had turned against them, hunted them down, or delivered them to the Nazi murderers, meant that they experienced the Holocaust not just as a murderous invasion by a foreign enemy but also as a series of communal massacres in a once familiar but now lethally hostile environment.

Grey Zones

There is no doubt that the few Jews who survived were in many cases sheltered by Christian neighbours or strangers; it was almost impossible to survive without such help. Moreover, those offering help could expect that the Germans would kill them and their families if they discovered they were hiding Jews, although that did not always happen. At the same time, the motivation for rescue was clearly complex, often ambiguous, and inconsistent, and tended to change over time, ranging from exceptional cases of pure altruism to expectations of substantial monetary or material profit. Most Jews saved by Christians also reported being betrayed, at times by the very same people who were hiding them. Jews who ran out of money or valuables could expect to be denounced or killed. Conversely, some local collaborators in the killing of Jews chose to help some Jews, while not a few of those who resisted the Germans for nationalist reasons also hunted down Jews as part of their nationalist agenda. This complexity partly explains the ambivalence of survivors, and why they often took decades before acknowledging their debt to their rescuers, since they also had bitter memories of their own family members being killed or handed over by people they had considered to be friends before the war.

Germany's allies were both instrumental in the murder of hundreds of thousands of Jews and in protecting many of their own Jewish citizens, often, although not exclusively, for reasons of their own perceived national interests. Bulgaria handed over Jews living in territories it had annexed thanks to its alliance with Germany, but refused to allow its own 50,000 Jewish Bulgarian citizens to be transported to Auschwitz. Hungary, though ruled by an anti-Semitic

dictatorship, and often treating its Jewish citizens harshly, also protected them from deportations until the Germans invaded and
deported about 400,000 Jews in the spring and summer of 1944 to
Auschwitz, where most of them were gassed, in the last mass murder
operation of the Holocaust personally orchestrated by Adolf Eichmann. The Romanians killed more Jews on their own than any other
German ally, close to a quarter of a million people, but then protected
the Jews in the Regat, the heartland of Romania, from deportations,
so that more Jews survived there than in any other east European
country. The French, whose collaborationist regime retained police
control over its citizens until late 1942, assisted in the deportation of
75,000 Jews, most non-citizens, to Auschwitz, where the vast majority
of them were murdered, but then refused to collaborate in the deportation of Jewish French citizens, so that two-thirds of Jews in France
survived. Conversely, although the Netherlands had no significant
anti-Semitic tradition and its Jewish community was well integrated,
during the German occupation the country's administration and
police ably assisted the Germans in deporting to their death about
three-quarters of the estimated 150,000 Jews living there at the time,
even as two-thirds of the up to 30,000 Jews who went into hiding
survived.

Considered from the perspective of the Nazi authorities, the mass
murder of the Jews was both a major war goal and an impediment to
victory. Ideologically, 'removing' the Jews was imperative. But the
'final solution' also diverted significant manpower, organizational
know-how, and facilities from the war effort and deprived Germany
of a vast, often highly skilled, and desperately willing labour force,
fully aware that only work might spare it from murder. As Germany's
fortunes turned and its military losses multiplied, increasing numbers
of German workers had to be sent to the front and ever larger
quantities of war-materiel had to be produced. It was for this reason
that Germany now tried to keep Soviet POWs alive and exploit their
labour. Similarly, the Reich now resorted to ever greater recruitment
of initially voluntary and subsequently forced labour in occupied
territories both in the east and in the west, a policy whose side-effect
was to increase local armed resistance by men and women who feared
being bombed in German factories by Allied aircraft. Especially in
eastern Europe, where the Jews had traditionally worked as artisans,

German industrialists and military agencies were reluctant to allow them to be murdered. The argument between the ideologues, such as Hitler and Himmler, who insisted that the Jews had to be murdered in order for the war to be won, and the realists who argued that the Jews could first help win the war and then be dealt with, ended with the victory of the former. But this goal was also accomplished by making rhetorical use of the Nazi policy of '*Vernichtung durch Arbeit*', or annihilation through work. According to this logic, able-bodied Jews would be employed in essential war production, while other 'useless mouths to feed', such as children, the ill, the handicapped, and the elderly, considered a burden on the economy and depriving German citizens of scarce resources, would be killed. This rhetoric redefined genocide as an economically rational policy rather than ideological insanity at a time of total war. To be sure, once the able-bodied had been worked to the bone, they too became useless eaters and could be murdered in turn.

The ghetto in Lodz (Łódź), renamed Litzmannstadt by the Germans, was a particularly gruesome example of this logic, into which Jewish communities and their leaders were also drawn in a frantic attempt to survive. The head of the ghetto, Chaim Rumkowski, was determined to save as many of its Jewish inhabitants as possible by mobilizing them to efficiently produce war-materiel for the Germans. In return he delivered to the Germans all those deemed unable to work. In September 1942 Rumkowski demanded from the remaining population of the ghetto, which had numbered over 160,000 people when it was created in April 1940, to 'give me your children', insisting that their sacrifice would allow others to survive. Indeed, the Lodz (Łódź) Ghetto was the last remaining large concentration of Jews under German control; but in August 1944, shortly before the arrival of the Red Army, the Germans sent all its remaining Jews, including Rumkowski, to the gas chambers in Auschwitz.

Rumkowski serves as one of the examples of Jewish collaboration with the Germans, whose goal was to save 'what could be saved' but whose practice often made it easier for the Germans to murder the Jews. The numerous Jewish councils created by the Germans throughout eastern Europe were supposed to mediate between Jewish communities and the occupiers; they were normally helped by detachments of Jewish police that provided internal control of the ghettos or

Jewish residential districts. But these Jewish police forces, armed with clubs and dressed in uniforms, also helped the German police and its local auxiliaries round up the Jews and deport them. Many policemen acted as they did both in an attempt to save themselves and to protect their families. Eventually, most of them were also murdered, as were members of the Jewish councils. These policemen also became the targets of Jewish resistance groups that formed in many ghettos and camps, since they were seen as traitors and symbolized collaboration with the Germans. At the same time, not a few Jewish policemen ended up joining the resistance once their own families and communities had been murdered.

The motto, 'let us not go like sheep to the slaughter', penned in a pamphlet issued by Abba Kovner, the commander of the Jewish resistance in the Wilno Ghetto at the end of 1941, became the slogan of Jewish resistance everywhere. While small groups of Jewish partisans operated in the forests and at times worked together with Soviet partisans—even as they were often attacked by nationalist underground fighters—the single largest resistance to the Germans erupted in April 1943 in the Warsaw Ghetto, after two-thirds of its population of 300,000 had already been gassed in Treblinka. Although the battle with the Germans, which lasted several weeks, was no more than a minor and hardly costly diversion for the Germans, it had immense symbolic value for the Jews at the time and subsequently; it was also the single largest civil uprising in occupied Europe until that time, to be followed in August 1944 by the Polish uprising in Warsaw, in which many surviving Jews also fought and were killed.

Three other uprisings symbolized the horrible dilemma in which Jews found themselves during the Holocaust. In August 1943 in Treblinka, and in October that year in Auschwitz-Birkenau and Sobibór, the largely Jewish members of the *Sonderkommando* teams, charged with undressing the victims, leading them into the gas chambers, and then disposing of their bodies in crematoria or pyres, rose up against their guards and tried to escape. Most of the rebels in all three uprising were either killed in the ensuing fighting or caught and murdered later on. At least in the case of Birkenau, where the rebels also blew up one of the crematoria facilities, the goal was not only to escape but also to hamper the ongoing mass murder. Yet the moral conundrum of these uprisings was that up to that point these hundreds of young, strong men had greatly facilitated the operation of industrial murder for the Germans in the vain hope of surviving as long as possible. Since they were also charged with sorting out the victims' belonging and could easily loot them, the *Sonderkommando* personnel were also far better fed and dressed than other prisoners, leading an eerily privileged life in the very 'heart of darkness'. To be sure, all members of the *Sonderkommando* knew that sooner or later they too would be murdered; the very fact that they had seen the innermost workings of the extermination system meant that they would never be allowed to live to tell the tale. But their choice to serve in this capacity, at times even seeing the murder of their own family members and communities, made them symbolic of what Primo Levi has called 'the gray zone', to which possibly also such men as Rumkowski and many other members of the Jewish councils and Jewish police can be said to have belonged.

Motivations

In 1996 the American political scientist Daniel Jonah Goldhagen published a study called *Hitler's Willing Executioners*. The book created a stir by arguing that in the Holocaust Germans had been motivated by a unique 'eliminationist' anti-Semitism, which he traced back well into the nineteenth century, and that consequently not only was there never any difficulty finding Germans willing to kill Jews but that many of them actually enjoyed doing so. The book was attacked because it presented anti-Semitism as the sole motivator of the Holocaust and Germany as singularly infected with that disease. As we saw, there were many other reasons for the genocide of the Jews; anti-Semitism in Germany increased dramatically only after Hitler's 'seizure of power', and several other nations were at least as deeply infected. Moreover, many of the perpetrators were not at all German but belonged to local auxiliaries or to allied nations. Another attempt to examine perpetrator motivation was made by the historian Christopher Browning in his 1992 book *Ordinary Men*. Browning argued that the reserve policemen he investigated had pulled the trigger mostly because of peer pressure and obedience to authority, acting therefore in accordance with the findings of social psychologists Stanley Milgram and Philip Zimbardo. But while some individuals may have had initial qualms about killing innocent women and children, the fact of the matter is that the German police, SS, and even regular military rarely reported difficulties in recruiting men to kill other human beings even when punishment for refusing or evading orders was at most transfer to another unit or to the front. In numerous post-war German judicial investigations and trials one finds that whether the defendants had any inner objections to such actions or not—and their statement many years after the event about such responses cannot be taken at face value—German perpetrators engaged in constant, efficient, and relentless mass murder.

Such actions were normally carried out by Gestapo officials and other police and SS personnel as members of the Security Police; but many other Germans on the ground in towns and cities occupied by the Germans, such as regular soldiers, fire brigade members, administrative staff, technical experts such as engineers, railroad men, and so forth, as well as these men's families, including their wives, girlfriends, and mistresses, their children, and at times even their parents, witnessed the killings and occasionally participated in them. Almost half of the victims of the Holocaust were not killed in isolated extermination camps but in mass shootings enacted as public events viewed or heard by all the inhabitants of the towns in which they were carried out, thereby making it impossible for anyone not to engage in one way or another and often enough to profit from what the victims left behind. In other words, we cannot understand the Holocaust merely as a sophisticated, mechanical, and impersonal industrial murder, but also very much as a social phenomenon that for several years, especially in eastern Europe, created a genocidal routine in which everyone played one role or another. The comforting notion of a bystander majority that was either indifferent or concerned but played no part in the event and (as we would like to think) internally objected to it is largely a post-war fabrication, and is certainly not confirmed by the victims' accounts, which depict them as being hunted down and murdered by all and sundry.

Those leaders of Germany committed to ordering and organizing the genocide, certainly recognized no 'gray zones', no moral ambiguity, and no going back. In his infamous speech in Posen (Poznań) in October 1943, Heinrich Himmler pointed out to an audience of SS officials that what they were carrying out, namely the 'final solution of the Jewish question', was a hard but necessary undertaking. He recognized that some lesser Germans, who did not belong to his 'black order', might find it difficult to understand the need to kill each and every Jew, and might certainly relent from implementing this policy. But as he saw it and drummed into his men, what they were doing was both a 'glorious page' in the annals of history and one that would never be written, not least because the rest of humanity had not yet reached this understanding. The SS was in that sense operating outside of conventional morality, according to which the killing of innocent women and children was a crime and an atrocity, and transforming such acts into a magnificent, courageous act of self-preservation. The ability to carry out the massacre of thousands, said Himmler, and yet to remain unsullied by such acts, was what 'made us strong'.

Toward the end of the war Himmler reconsidered. Thinking about his own personal fate rather than the 'world-historical' events his organization had unleashed, he looked for ways to negotiate with the Allies and was willing to release some concentration camp inmates in return for his personal safety. When it was all over he tried to escape, armed with false papers, was arrested, and before he could be identified committed suicide. It was a wretched end for someone who had claimed to be the creator of a new race of fearless, ruthless warriors. Hitler found his chief executioner's final betrayal despicable; even more than Himmler, the Führer was convinced that victory in war and the murder of the Jews were synonymous. Because Germany had failed, the Aryan race (rather than its indomitable leader) had proven itself unequal to other races, especially the Slavs. This was ideological consistency, according to which might was right. And even after having ordered and orchestrated the single largest genocide in modern history, Hitler was certain that the Reich's defeat was a Jewish victory. As he wrote in his final testament on 29 April 1945, shortly before he committed suicide in his Berlin bunker, the war that destroyed Germany 'was desired and instigated exclusively by those international statesmen who were either of Jewish descent or worked for Jewish interests'. Yet he remained convinced that 'out of the ruins of our towns and monuments the hatred against those finally responsible whom we have to thank for everything, international Jewry and its helpers, will grow'. The very last sentence of his testament urged 'the leaders of the nation and those under them to scrupulous observance of the laws of race and to merciless opposition to the universal poisoner of all peoples, international Jewry'.

Many other officials charged with the genocide of the Jews never relented from their belief in the necessity of eradicating that 'race'; even decades after the event, those still alive showed no signs of remorse and a great deal of pride in their accomplishment. Rudolf Höss, commandant of Auschwitz, wrote in this vein shortly before his execution in 1947; Franz Stangl, commandant of Sobibór and Treblinka, could not bring himself to any statement of remorse while being interviewed by the journalist Gitta Sereny during his trial in the late 1960s. And Adolf Eichmann, the Reich's expert on deportations, whose career spanned the entire period from forcing Austrian Jews into penniless exile in 1938 to deporting hundreds of thousands of Hungarian Jews to Auschwitz in 1944, expressed pride in his deeds during his years in Argentina and told the court in Jerusalem in 1962 that 'remorse is for little children'. Rather than a bureaucratic cog in the extermination machine, as shown in great and devastating detail by the philosopher Bettina Stangneth in her study *Eichmann Before Jerusalem*, he was a dedicated ideologue who kept trying to kill Jews even after being ordered to stop by his superior Himmler. Indeed, Eichmann built his reputation in the German exile community in post-war Argentina on actually exaggerating his importance in carrying out the genocide of the Jews. What Hannah Arendt had called 'the banality of evil' in her 1963 study of the trial, *Eichmann in Jerusalem*, did not apply to Eichmann, or to many other perpetrators, in the sense that she meant, namely that they were 'desk-killers', paper pushers, and careerists who had neither a conscience nor any particularly anti-Jewish bias, but merely wanted to further their own careers. If there was any banality here, it was the manner in which they considered the vast crimes they had orchestrated as a perfectly reasonable way to resolve an issue that needed resolution, 'the Jewish question'. That this also helped them advance in the ranks and enhanced their power and influence was naturally pleasing; but what filled them with pride and a sense of accomplishment was that they had succeeded in carrying out the unthinkable and in the process made it routine.

Willi Dressen, the German Federal Republic's former director of the Central Office of the State Justice Administration for the

Investigation of National Socialist Crimes in Ludwigsburg, calculated that by 2005 altogether 106,000 people had been investigated for National Socialist crimes, of whom only 6,500 were sentenced, with a mere 166 receiving life sentences; this meant, he noted, that 'purely statistically each murder cost ten minutes in prison'. Hence while the organizers of the Holocaust felt pride in their accomplishment, the perpetrators who pulled the trigger were rarely punished and went back to their normal lives after the war; very few of them seem to have felt, and rarely expressed, any personal sense of guilt.

Aftermath

Conversely, the survivors of the genocide experienced liberation as a much more unsettling and ambivalent event than is often assumed. For one thing, liberation from German occupation meant different things to different people and in different geographical locations, and these differences projected onto the memories of those who experienced the event. As the Red Army swept into eastern and central Europe in 1944–5, it liberated the few remaining Jews still in hiding, in small partisan groups and forest camps. The Soviets also reached the extermination camps, some of which had been completely destroyed by the Germans, while Auschwitz and Majdanek had been partially evacuated. The Russian-Jewish author Vasily Grossman wrote a harrowing account at the time of his first encounter with what remained of Treblinka and the realization that it was a facility dedicated exclusively to the mass production of corpses. The Polish-Jewish filmmaker Aleksander Ford made the first documentary on the liberation of an extermination camp in Majdanek.

But while for the Jews the arrival of the Red Army meant liberation, for many of their Christian neighbours it spelled reoccupation. In western Ukraine the fighters of the OUN-UPA continued resisting the Soviets into the early 1950s, and killings of Jews by these freedom fighters also went on even after the arrival of the Red Army. The nationalists often identified the Soviets as Jews or as serving Jewish interests, whereas for Jewish survivors the realization that some of the frontline Soviet units were officered by Jews appeared almost miraculous. In Poland the Soviet imposition of a communist regime was perceived by many as Jewish revenge, and the return of Jews who had fled to the Soviet Union evoked fears that they might reclaim their property. Such sentiments, combined with the internalized anti-Semitism of the prewar era and the perception of Jews as prey during German rule, triggered off violent pogroms, the most notorious of which occurred in Kielce in 1946, in which more than forty Jews were murdered. Such responses to the return of the Jews, and the revival of the myth of 'Jewish Communism' (*Żydokomuna*), led to the mass migration to the west and to Palestine-Israel of the close to a quarter of a million Jews who had returned to Poland in the wake of the Holocaust.

In the west the arriving Allied units liberated numerous concentration camps that had been used for most of the regime's existence to incarcerate real and perceived political and ideologically-defined social enemies of Nazism but not Jews. These camps, such as Bergen-Belsen, Buchenwald, and Dachau, filled with Jews only at the end of the war when the inmates of labour camps in the east were sent on horrific death marches to the west as the Red Army drove ever deeper into German occupied territories. The survivors of these death marches arrived famished, diseased, and exhausted at the German concentration camps just as the administration of these institutions began to disintegrate, and many died there. For the western Allies, what they encountered there formed their perception of the Holocaust, or rather their understanding of the nature of Nazi crimes against political resisters and innocent civilians. Just as in the west it was not realized—and has remained quite unknown—that the back of the Wehrmacht was broken in the east by the Red Army, where the vast majority of German troops fought and were killed, so too this encounter with the concentration camps created a false understanding of what the crimes of the Nazis were really about.

This skewed perception was also reflected in the Nuremberg Tribunal of 1945, where the major surviving war criminals of the Nazi regime were tried but the genocide of the Jews played a minor role, and the voices of the survivors were hardly heard. It was only during the Eichmann trial almost two decades later that for the first time over one hundred survivors of the Holocaust testified about their experiences in an internationally reported judicial setting concerned exclusively with the genocide of the Jews. Many of those testimonies had little to do with Eichmann's specific crimes or could not be directly linked to him, which is what aroused the ire of several observers, not least Hannah Arendt. After all, there was little doubt about Eichmann's guilt and responsibility, although arguments about his motivation persist to this day. But as a didactic judicial event, the trial played a major role in bringing the Holocaust into people's consciousness as an event that was both intimately linked to and a crucial component of Nazism and World War II.

When writing *Eichmann in Jerusalem*, Arendt relied a great deal on the then recently published study by Raul Hilberg, *The Destruction of the European Jews* (even though she had opposed its publication as a reader for Princeton University Press). Hilberg had used the German documents collected for the Nuremberg Tribunal, and like that tribunal believed that using survivor testimonies added a subjective element that was neither historically reliable nor useful in persuading the public that what appeared simply unimaginable had actually taken place. But his book, based on a dissertation he was warned by his advisor would finish off his academic career, became the first of a growing list of scholarly studies in the 1970s and 1980s that finally established the centrality of the Holocaust to the history of the twentieth century and liberated it from the perception that it was 'merely' part of Jewish history. The ongoing reinterpretations and rewritings of the Holocaust today are all based on a premise that did not exist a few decades ago, namely that we cannot understand the history of our time without integrating into it the history of the Holocaust. If there is a warning here, it is that by the same token we cannot insulate ourselves from the massive crimes against humanity that have already become the mark of the twenty-first century.

8

War and Empire

Dieter Pohl

There is no doubt that the territory ruled over by Germany in the Second World War was an empire. By the end of 1942 it extended over fourteen European countries that were wholly or partially occupied and five further states that as allies were dependent on Germany. No fewer than 200 million people came under German occupation. The creation of an empire was central to the history of the 'Third Reich'. It was a means of achieving strategic status as a world power, of exploiting Europe to boost the German war economy, and of reconfiguring the continent demographically, or, to use National Socialist jargon, along 'racial' lines. Together with the Japanese and Italian war empires and including also the colonial territories of Vichy France and Belgium, though these were only indirectly a part of it, the German empire was ultimately to determine the destiny of the world.

War

The source of all these megalomaniacal plans and political manoeuvres was Germany's reaction to the defeat of 1918. Whereas representatives of the conservative elites in Germany were striving above all for a revision of the Treaty of Versailles and to some extent for hegemony in central Europe, Adolf Hitler, a politician in provincial Bavaria, had since 1925 been promoting the idea of acquiring 'Lebensraum' (living space) in the Soviet Union. The concept of 'Lebensraum' was not precisely defined and denoted not so much an area where Germans could settle as a region that could be exploited.

On 3 February 1933, just days after his seizure of power, Hitler announced to a confidential meeting of the military leadership that he intended to fight a war 'for soil'. Rearmament began immediately. The new regime could build on the work done by governments during the Weimar Republic for they had already developed secret plans for comprehensive rearmament. After 1933 military expansion rapidly exceeded the restrictions laid down by the Treaty of Versailles. It first became evident to the public when military service was introduced in 1935. From 1936 onwards rearmament was in high gear. By the time war broke out in 1939 4.5 million men could be mobilized for the new army and 2,600 tanks and 3,600 fighter planes were ready for use.

In a confidential meeting in autumn 1937 Hitler established his war strategy: first of all Czechoslovakia was to be attacked, on the pretext of protecting the German minority there. That would lead to war with France, Czechoslovakia's ally. In fact, however, the Italian leader Mussolini and the western powers intervened to prevent a war. In the Munich Agreement of September 1938 they forced Czechoslovakia to cede the Sudetenland to Germany. Hitler was robbed of his war. Even so, the annexation of Austria in March 1938 and the *de facto* annexation of the Czech territories in March 1939 amounted to a considerable enlargement of Germany's economic resources and armaments base.

Hitler now turned his attention to Poland, which he had selected to be his junior partner in the war against the Soviet Union and which was also to cede territory to the German Reich. The Polish government, however, which was trying to maintain a careful balance in its relations with Germany and the Soviet Union, was not amenable to blackmail, putting its trust in support from the west. Thus from May 1939 onwards Hitler prepared for a war against Poland. He pulled off a decisive coup in August 1939, when the Molotov–Ribbentrop pact neutralized the Soviet Union as a war enemy. In return Hitler offered to carve up eastern central Europe between himself and Stalin.

The Polish army could put up little resistance to the German invasion, in which Slovakia also took part, on 1 September 1939. Within four weeks western Poland had capitulated; on 17 September 1939 Stalin also invaded and the country was divided into two zones of occupation. Though his military victory over Poland had brought Hitler closer to his ultimate goal of a war against the Soviet Union, he had in the process caused a world war, for on 3 September 1939 France and Britain honoured the terms of their alliance with Poland

and declared war on Germany. The British dominions of Canada, Australia, and South Africa gradually joined the war against Germany and as a result powers external to Europe were engaged in the conflict from the outset.

Hitler had long hoped to wage his war together with Britain, which was hostile to Bolshevism. Now, however, Britain was turning out to be his long-term opponent. Although neither Britain nor France seized the military initiative in 1939, in the spring of 1940, when the British government made an attempt to land in Norway in order to cut off the supply of iron ore from Sweden to Germany, the Germans forestalled this intervention, occupying Denmark without resistance and Norway too after a lengthy campaign.

The invasion of France, which had long been part of the plan, was set for the end of 1939 but then repeatedly postponed. The defeat of the French army, which for many years had been the strongest military force in Europe, was then accomplished with astonishing speed in May/June 1940. France's military leaders had not expected that, rather than swinging southwards, the Wehrmacht would advance through Belgium's dense forests towards the River Meuse and then on to the Atlantic coast. The French and British troops were based in Belgium and northern France and thus were encircled. Nevertheless, a sizeable number were successfully evacuated from the Dunkirk area to England. The German army was now occupying northern France and the Atlantic coast. In spite of this, the British Isles could not be invaded, primarily because the German air force was unable to gain control of the air.

Shortly before the defeat of France Mussolini came into the war on Hitler's side and occupied the area around Nice. It was then Mussolini who in 1940 extended the war to south east Europe and Africa, in order to realize his expansionist plans for a 'mare nostrum', an eastern Mediterranean under Italian control. In March 1939, before the outbreak of war, Italy already had occupied Albania. In September and October 1940 Mussolini ordered attacks on Greece, Egypt, and the British and French colonies in the Horn of Africa. The Italian forces failed, however, which prompted Hitler to send detachments to Libya in February 1941 and thus create a new theatre of war. At the same time he was getting ready for an invasion of Greece. When as a result of a coup Yugoslavia, which had at first been a member of the

German alliance, seemed in danger of drifting away from the 'Axis', Hitler ordered both Greece and Yugoslavia to be invaded. Both countries capitulated within weeks. In fighting this war the German leaders intended not only to come to Mussolini's aid but at the same time to ward off any British influence in south east Europe.

Plans for an invasion of the Soviet Union had begun in June 1940 and in November/December 1940 Hitler decided to launch it the spring of 1941. This was the war that was actually central to Hitler's ambitions. It was prompted by his concept of 'living space', a strategic agrarian project central to his plans to feed Germany and establish its dominance. Hitler shared a rabid anti-Bolshevism with large sections of the German elites. In the concrete circumstances prevailing at the turn of 1940/1 it was a decisive factor that Germany's war against Britain had ground to a halt and Hitler wished to eliminate the Soviet Union as a potential British ally. Although a war against the Soviet Union was regarded as risky by the Wehrmacht high command, there was in the final analysis no criticism of the preparations for the attack, such as had been put forward at the end of 1939 / beginning of 1940.

In fact there was a strong belief that the Germans had the right strategy for conquering this massive country. The war against the Soviet Union was the only planned 'Blitzkrieg': rapid tank units were to penetrate deep into Soviet territory and encircle most of the Red Army west of Moscow. Infantry following behind would then eliminate the forces trapped in the 'pocket'. Optimistic German estimates assumed that the Soviet Union would collapse after eight to twelve weeks. A similar short period would be all that was needed to redirect efforts to fighting the sea and air war against Britain and eventually the USA.

A war of extermination, no less, was part of the German strategy: Germany's leaders believed that the Soviet Union would collapse faster if the basis of Bolshevism were destroyed. This basis, according to the beliefs of the German leadership, consisted not only of state functionaries but also large sections of the Jewish minority. Even before the invasion, therefore, the protection accorded by international law to the civilian population and to prisoners of war was removed and wide-ranging orders to murder were issued to the army and to SS and police units. In addition, German planners developed vast plans to starve the population. The army was to provision itself completely from Soviet agriculture and other farming produce was to be transported to the Reich. The planners envisaged mass starvation, primarily in the towns and cities and in the ethnic Russian territories. Thirty million inhabitants were to be starved to death or forced to flee.

On 22 June 1941 the German army, along with Finnish and Romanian units, embarked in the Soviet Union on the biggest war in history. Within a few weeks they had conquered extensive parts of the Baltic region, Byelorussia, and the Ukraine. Yet as early as mid-July 1941 at the Battle of Smolensk the German advance ground to a halt for weeks, thus already rendering the plan for 'Blitzkrieg' essentially obsolete. Although by October the army occupied the Leningrad area and almost the whole of the Ukraine, two assaults on Moscow in October and November 1941 failed. When the Soviets mounted a counteroffensive in December 1941 the German plan of attack finally collapsed and an end to the war was nowhere in sight. In fact, Hitler now went for broke and, in the wake of the Japanese attack in December 1941 on the US navy in Pearl Harbour, declared war on the USA.

In June 1942 the second German army offensive began in southern Russia, stretching to Stalingrad and the Caucasus. The central German objective of this offensive, namely the capture of working oil fields and refineries in the Caucasus, could not, however, be achieved. The army could not even completely capture the city of Stalingrad, but rather in November 1942 Soviet units encircled German troops and their allies and by the end of January 1943 had inflicted on them the first devastating German defeat. Hitler was forced to make his army retreat from the northern Caucasus and in June 1943 he failed in his attempt to launch a new offensive in the Kursk area. Gradually the Red Army was now liberating Soviet territory from German occupation, starting above all with the Ukraine in the autumn of 1943.

During the Battle of Stalingrad the German-Italian army suffered a defeat in Egypt near to the village of El Alamein and was forced to retreat westwards. Also in November 1942 US troops intervened in the European-African war and landed in Morocco. By May 1943 the western Allies finally achieved victory over the German-Italian army in North Africa at Tunis and thereby were in a position to move from Africa to Sicily in July 1943. As a result the fascist government in Italy deposed Mussolini the same month, whereupon the German army occupied the Italian mainland in September 1943 and took the Italian army prisoner. Allied troops also crossed at this time to the mainland, though their offensive became bogged down in southern Italy.

After lengthy preparations the Allies opened a third front in June 1944 by landing in northern France. The German leadership had long expected this development and presented it as being the decisive struggle. Though the Allies, who also landed in August 1944 on the Côte d'Azur, managed to liberate France and Belgium relatively quickly, by the end of 1944 the offensive was no longer breaking new ground.

The German army's biggest defeat was, however, in the east, where also in June 1944 the Red Army launched a large-scale offensive, shattered the entire 'Centre' group of German armies, and thus could advance to Warsaw. The German army had marched into Hungary in March 1944 and now also moved into Slovakia in order to halt the Red Army. Soviet troops swept through Romania and Bulgaria without opposition, for their existing governments were toppled and their successors declared war on Germany. By January 1945, after first setting foot on German soil in October 1944, the Red Army occupied all German territory east of the Oder and Neisse rivers. The western Allies' final offensive on Third Reich territory, and the most costly one in terms of casualties, did not begin until February/March 1945. Only then could Hungary, Czechoslovakia, northern Holland, and northern Italy be liberated from German domination. On 7 May 1945 the German army high command signed the capitulation in Rheims. It came into force the following day and shortly after midnight on 9 May the same ceremony was repeated in Berlin in the presence of the Red Army.

The German war was above all a war to achieve hegemony in Europe, supplemented by the 'flank' in North Africa and the naval war in the Atlantic, the struggle occasioned by the USA's sending of supplies to Britain. Underlying the German strategy was, however, the desire for world domination. Through cooperation with her ally, Japan, Germany's aim was to dominate the Eurasian continent, which in Hitler's view was the centre of gravity, the 'heartland', of the geostrategic world. In addition, Italy's empire and the colonies of Vichy France were to secure hegemony in Africa. Hitler never ceased to dream that one day a government well-disposed to Germany would come to power in Britain and make peace with Germany. This power base would ensure that the strongest and final opponent of the 'Axis', the United States, could be kept at a distance from Eurasia.

Such a war, however, far exceeded Germany's economic capacity and human resources. The German leadership was therefore forced to rely on two central spheres of action: on the one hand a weakening of the international system, in which the powers were to be skilfully outmanoeuvred, and on the other hand wide-ranging policies on economic development and human resources that were increasingly pursued at the expense of the occupied countries. From 1935 onwards Hitler systematically destroyed the post-war settlement established at Versailles. The western powers did little to oppose him, and nor did they oppose the annexation of Austria and the occupation of the Czech territories. The German-Soviet anti-aggression pact of 1939 was a decisive and astonishing coup for Hitler, which gave the dictators eastern central Europe on a plate. Apart from Poland it was above all Romania that found itself in the firing line and whose oil supplies were of crucial importance for Germany's war. The country now became in large measure dependent on Germany.

Hitler's policies were less successful, however, as far as forming alliances was concerned. Mussolini overestimated what his country could do and suffered one defeat after another. The alliance with Japan, on the other hand, brought about little genuine cooperation. There was too much suspicion on either side; the Japanese government was alarmed by the Molotov–Ribbentrop pact and then not forewarned about the German attack on the Soviet Union. Hitler's declaration of war on the USA in December 1941 was intended to split American resources between two conflicts, a Japanese and a German one. Although Germany's other allies in eastern Europe, with the exception of Bulgaria, took part in the war against the Soviet Union, in 1943 they began one after the other to break away from the 'Axis'. Thus the alliance politics failed.

The war could be waged and sustained only by means of the systematic exploitation of foreign resources. Even the annexation of Austria in 1938 was less to do with nationalistic sentiments of 'Back home to the Reich' and more to do with the Austrian exchequer, its raw materials and reserves of labour. The central motive behind the march into Bohemia in March 1939 was its armaments industry. The occupied territories of eastern Europe were supposed above all to provide food as well as coal, the latter from the Silesian coalfield and the Ukrainian Donets Basin. The gradual adaptation of western European industry to serve the needs of German armaments was, however, economically much more valuable. Around 70 per cent of production for Germany from the occupied territories came from western Europe. The most important booty gained from plundering eastern Europe, in particular from 1942 onwards, was forced labour.

Even though up to the summer of 1944 German occupied territories were continually shrinking, their exploitation and productivity for armaments production could be stepped up, not least by means of the ruthless exploitation of approximately 700,000 concentration camp prisoners. When, in the middle of 1944, the German economy lost access to Romanian oil and western European industry, and the chemical industry was being increasingly targeted by Allied bombing, German resources finally ran out.

All of this shows why National Socialist Germany, in spite of limited resources, was able to exercise total hegemony on the continent of Europe for almost five years. From a structural point of view the balance of economic advantage was already tipping in favour of the Allies in 1942. In spite of having lost its industrial west, as early as 1942 the Soviet economy was able to chalk up an immense armaments output and by the end of that year US armaments production was also at its peak.

Even so, it was not only relative economic strength that was decisive, but also politics and the conduct of the war. As the western Allies made only very limited interventions in the war in 1939/40, Hitler was able to conquer one country after another up to the spring of 1941. The successful war on two fronts of 1941/2 was also possible only because the Soviet leadership was guilty of serious military failures, the last being the Battle of Kharkov in May 1942. It was not until the autumn of 1942, after three years of war, that the tide began to turn. The German military leaders lost the initiative and it was only a matter of time before the economic power of the USA and the military reserves of the Soviet Union would win through. In addition, the German navy lost the war in the North Atlantic, not least because Allied military intelligence was able to decode German radio messages. Admittedly, it took another two and a half years from Stalingrad to the end of the war for Hitler's defeat, with its immense human and economic toll, to be complete.

Hitler's war in Europe cost between thirty-five and forty million lives and a further twenty to thirty million died in the Asian-Pacific conflict. To this day there are no precise statistics for the number of victims in the Soviet Union and Poland. Between fourteen and eighteen million soldiers died in the European and North African theatres of war (depending on the numbers put on the Soviet losses); eleven to twelve million people died as a result of German crimes, of whom at least 2.5 million were prisoners of war from the Red Army. Of the victims of mass murder some 600,000 were citizens of the German Reich and thus the overwhelming majority were from the occupied territories.

The shocking scale of destruction can be explained only by looking more closely at the structure of the German wartime empire, for this domain, unlike classical empires, aimed less at integrating a variety of national groups and more at 'racial reorganization' and radical exploitation. And the existence of this empire was bound up with perpetual warfare; political stability was never achieved. Hitler wished neither to make peace nor to reach any settlement with the countries he had conquered.

The German Empire

Hitler created the largest continental empire in Europe since Napoleon's day without ever pursuing a detailed plan. It was clear from an early stage that he intended to annex Austria, to subjugate Czechoslovakia and France and ultimately to set up a radical regime in the Soviet Union. The actual development of the German sphere of influence in the Second World War depended, however, above all on the—in many respects unexpected—course of the war and after that also on the political attitudes of the German elites. During the First World War plans had already been developed to create German hegemony in Europe and for a brief period the whole of southern Russia had been occupied.

At the time of the world economic crisis indirect forms of German hegemony were discussed within the context of an 'greater economic space' (*Großraumwirtschaft*), with an eye, for example, to south eastern Europe. Specialists in international law such as Carl Schmitt were working on theories of a 'greater German area', a sphere in which powers 'alien' to this area such as the USA were not allowed to intervene. While schemes for a 'Greater Germania', including the territories of Flanders and stretching as far as Norway and into the Baltic States, circulated in the SS, German 'ethnicity experts' developed blueprints for the ethnic reordering of eastern central Europe. And Germany was to 'Germanize' not only territory that had German minorities, but also regions considered to have come under German cultural influences. The head of the SS, Heinrich Himmler, from 1939 the Reich Commissar for the Strengthening of Germandom, increasingly absorbed these schemes into his portfolio. They culminated by the end of 1941 in the 'General Plan for the East', a vast resettlement project affecting large areas of Poland, the Baltic States, northern Russia, and the Ukraine. No fewer than thirty-one million Slavs were supposed to be resettled to create space in the longer term for German settlement.

The framework for this plan of occupation arose not only out of theoretical schemes conceived far from actual practicalities but also from a prevailing and widespread cultural racism. This racism was not specific to National Socialism but went back to older discourses. While most Germans regarded western Europeans as decadent but also highly civilized, the Slav population was seen as culturally inferior. Letters from soldiers and occupying forces are full of bourgeois stereotypes of cleanliness and order, which they claimed were absent 'in the East', where the proverbial 'Polish business' (*polnische Wirtschaft*), a synonym for lack of productivity, was the norm. During the occupation colonial discourses concerning the inferiority of the indigenous people were dominant. Occasionally these were referred to as 'sub-humans', although in fact this designation was supposed to be reserved for 'Jewish Muskovites'. Whereas German Catholics felt a certain connection with Polish Catholic culture, there was no such feeling as far as the Soviet Union was concerned, whose city dwellers and young people were regarded above all as Bolsheviks, while the ethnic Russians, labelled 'Greater Russians', were seen as primitive, if also docile. An implicit ethnic hierarchy developed: at the top of the tree were the Estonians, and marriage between Germans and Estonian women was not forbidden. After that came natives of the Courland, Livonia, Latgalia, Lithuania, and the Ukraine, beneath them Byelorussians, and at the bottom were ethnic Russians. Overall, however, German anti-Slavism was flexible and alliances with Slovaks or Croats posed no problem. On the other hand, the ideological doctrine of the 'Jewification' of particular cities and regions, which was applied to territories in Poland, the Baltic States, and the west of the Soviet Union with a large Jewish minority, had particularly dire consequences.

The classic stereotypes regarding the Balkans were also current in the occupation administrations, namely an alleged tendency of the population to be devious and cruel. The image of Serbia was still strongly influenced by slogans from the First World War. These discourses were widespread in Germany and among the occupying forces and formed the basis for a consensus that in large parts of eastern Europe the population was inferior and to some extent dangerous.

A specific discourse concerning international law was also one of the determining factors in this process and it removed the last constraints on exploitation and the use of violence. After its conquest, Poland was regarded as a dissolved state ('debellatio') without status in international law or the entitlement to protection from the wider international community. The same applied to occupied Yugoslavia. In the occupied Soviet territories the authority of international law was in any case completely annulled. In these territories the German occupiers regarded violence as a legitimate means, for example as a reprisal for crimes committed in August/September 1939 against the German minority in Poland or later for the activities of partisans. In western and northern Europe the occupiers were more conscious of international law, for example in the treatment of POWs, though this quickly ceased in the case of the Jewish members of the population. Whereas Jewish soldiers in the Red Army were all murdered, Jewish officers in the Polish army in German captivity, though admittedly few in number, were given the protection of international law and survived the war.

Economic exploitation was of crucial importance to the conception and realization of occupation policies. As the war went on, it assumed an increasingly vital role. At the outset looting, both on an organized and on an individual level, was a feature of every German war. There was also a clear distinction between east and west in how peoples were treated: in most regions of Poland and the occupied Soviet Union the structures supporting industry were to be destroyed, for, as in the case of Yugoslavia and Greece, the economic activity of these countries was to be reduced to that of an agrarian hinterland to the Reich. Only Bohemia was still regarded as an industrial country.

A significant part of the industrial infrastructure in Poland and the Soviet Union was indeed destroyed, cannibalized, or mothballed. Only in western Poland, earmarked for the process of 'Germanization', was industry substantially preserved, though it was completely expropriated. When, contrary to German expectations, the war began to go badly for them, they changed course. Even Poland and the occupied Soviet territories were now to use their industries to support the German army. In the end even German firms moved production from 1942 onwards to Poland in order to be beyond the range of Allied bombing.

In the occupied western and northern areas of Europe industrial production largely continued, though increasingly to supply the needs of the German armaments industry. Businesses owned by Jews were, however, expropriated. If manufacturers in occupied countries had not committed their firms to particular products and markets some time before the German invasion, they found themselves cooperating to a greater or lesser extent with the German economic administration. The Renault factories in France were an example. Economic considerations were paramount in such circumstances rather than those of national identity. The national economies of occupied countries struggled with the loss of markets for exports and raw materials, the collapse of the consumer goods industry, and the devaluation of the currency. Even so, the effects were very varied. In eastern Europe they were at times catastrophic, while in the Netherlands they were almost negligible.

As time went on, whereas the occupied countries became increasingly important economically to Germany, during the period up to 1942 in particular it was the racial ideology underlying German dominance over Europe that determined policy. At first the National Socialist leaders and their planners were working towards an extension of the Third Reich, or more precisely a 'Germanization' of many regions on Germany's borders. These expansionist ideas were not confined to those territories that had been lost in the peace treaties of 1919/20, but went beyond them. Since 1939 the key locations in this policy had been western Poland including the city of Łódź, which had never been part of the German Reich, then in 1940 also Alsace-Lorraine and from April 1941 the northern part of Slovenia also. 'Germanization' consisted of three elements: first of all, the expulsion and expropriation of 'undesirable' sections of the population; then the settlement of ethnic Germans from other eastern European regions; finally, racial selection as determined by the 'German Ethnic List'. Massive deportation plans were developed (for example, some three million inhabitants of western Poland were to be expelled to central Poland) and were already being carried out. While they often came to grief because their implementation was inadequate, in most cases they failed as a result of protests from the receiving territories. The inhabitants of Alsace and Lorraine were supposed to be deported to the Vichy region and Slovenians to Greater Croatia. These expulsions often came to nothing and were replaced by resettlement within the original territory. In a number of cases a start was made to 'Germanize' beyond the annexed territories and to begin implementation of the 'General Plan East'. Thus from the autumn of 1942 to the spring of 1943 110,000 Poles from the Zamość region south of Lublin were expelled or deported and a sizeable number murdered. They were supposed to make room for ethnic German settlers, who in fact moved to the region in only limited numbers. In total in the Second World War some two million people fell victim to such Nazi resettlement projects. The settlement of those ethnic Germans who had been forced to leave their homeland as a result of Stalin's expansion in 1939/41 was, however, to a great extent completed.

The process of sifting the entire population on the basis of German ethnicity, as was carried out in the incorporated territories, had very diverse effects in the individual regions. Thus in Danzig (Gdańsk)—West Prussia a significant proportion of the Poles were considered suitable for 'Germanization'. The result of this was that a large number of the men were then conscripted into the army. Seen as a whole, the process of 'Germanization' was very broad in scope, though conducted in a variety of different ways in the individual territories. For the victims of expulsion and expropriation as well as of discrimination in the annexed territories, however, it was far-reaching and in some cases even fatal.

The second racially motivated project and undoubtedly the most radical was the persecution and murder of the Jews in the occupied territories. This is the subject of another essay in this volume (Chapter 7). I shall note here only that this systematic mass murder cannot be explained without the radical occupation policy in parts of eastern Europe. The 'Final Solution' would have been inconceivable without the general removal of the rights of eastern Europeans and the use of violence against them. On the other hand, this mass murder led to a general brutalization of large parts of the societies under occupation, and indeed it was seen as a warning that they would suffer the same fate. The murder of the Roma Gypsies was also carried out systematically. Although they were not considered enemies of the 'Aryan race', they were nevertheless regarded as racially inferior. It was above all the regional administrations and police headquarters that demanded the murder of the Roma because they viewed them as a 'social nuisance'. Even the murder of the mentally ill, which had its origins in a radicalized eugenic policy, was carried over from Germany to some of the occupied territories. In many places in Poland and the Soviet Union the SS and the police murdered the inmates of psychiatric institutions so that their buildings could be commandeered. And in Vichy France the health service administration starved large numbers of the mentally ill in their region to death.

From a National Socialist perspective persecution and murder were among the measures appropriate to increasing the security of the occupying power, and as anti-Semites they judged the Jewish minority to be a threat, being the seedbed of Bolshevism. Of course the German concept of 'security' in the occupied territories encompassed much more than anti-Semitism. Not only Bolshevism but also anything that boosted national identity could from a German perspective be designated a threat, in particular when found in nations known for their self-assertiveness such as Poland, Serbia and, to some extent, Greece. In 1939, immediately after the outbreak of war, the German security police began to murder members of the Polish elites as well as of anti-German organizations. The victims were members of the intelligentsia such as university graduates and priests and also activists from the German-Polish border clashes of 1919/21. According to

Polish estimates, in 1939/40 some 60,000 Poles were shot and others were put in concentration camps. From June 1941 German police and the army had been taking similarly radical measures against Soviet functionaries, tens of thousands of whom were shot, even if they were not Jewish.

Real resistance, however, was something the German forces of occupation encountered only from the summer of 1941 onwards. Remnants of the Yugoslav army banded together as Chetniks to resist the occupation and were soon followed by communist groups in the Soviet Union and in Yugoslavia. The occupiers then threatened to mount radical and deadly counter-measures against the population, with a hundred people to be shot in retaliation for the death of one German soldier at the hands of civilians. The German police and army preferred not to select victims from the majority groups in the population but in the first instance targeted Jews and in the Ukraine Russians also. In the autumn of 1941 these massacres reached genocidal proportions; by the beginning of 1942 some 60,000 people had been shot in the Soviet Union and in Serbia around 30,000. This policy of violence was unsuccessful, however; from the summer of 1942 armed resistance in the Soviet Union increased, while in Yugoslavia it moved to Croatia and Bosnia. In the occupied Soviet territories the SS, the police, and the army developed a system of large-scale 'band operations' in the war against partisans, each one causing thousands of deaths. The total number of deaths among the population came close to 500,000. As resistance grew from the end of 1942 onwards the German occupiers extended their use of violence too, at first to regions of Poland, then to Slovenia and Greece, and in the autumn of 1943 to occupied Italy as well. Finally, from mid-1944 some isolated massacres took place even in France. This violence reached its terrible climax during the Warsaw Uprising in August 1944. For several days German SS and police units attempted systematically to murder the residents of entire areas of the city, until they were reined in. Even so, some 160,000 inhabitants died in the uprising. In south east and western Europe such use of extreme violence aroused strong opposition within the bureaucratic hierarchy of the occupation, and indeed many regarded it as counterproductive, for it drove the population to join the resistance.

If one examines the essentials of occupation policy, and its implementation also, the differences between the individual territories seem less telling. Research, it is true, has repeatedly emphasized the complexity, indeed the chaotic nature of the bureaucracy of occupation, claiming that within the various administrations competition between various authorities and individuals was endemic, just as it was in the Reich. While it is true that conflicts of this kind—arguments about the scope of responsibilities and resources, even about personal vanities—were constantly arising, a broad consensus nevertheless prevailed concerning the crucial issues: securing the occupation; economic exploitation; the murder of the Jews, and 'Germanization'. There was even close cooperation across different departments.

A central point of reference for occupation policy, as for the entire National Socialist regime, was the 'Führer' Adolf Hitler. By contrast with Italy or Japan in the Second World War the German Reich did not possess a central authority controlling occupation; there were only the heads of the various occupying forces, who competed for access to Hitler. Though he kept himself up to date with the broad outline of developments in the occupied countries, he had only limited interest in these matters. The central Reich administration was largely excluded from this area and did not even have any real power to intervene in the *de facto* annexed territories in Poland, France, or Yugoslavia. Instead, NSDAP *Gauleiters* from the bordering regions were in charge in these places and often had a dual function in heading up the zones of occupation. The central authorities that emerged as determining occupation policy were rather Göring's economic administration, the Four Year Plan authority, and the SS and police organizations under Himmler. In addition, there were special commissioners such as the Plenipotentiary for Labour. Even the Foreign Ministry could influence occupation policy.

From a structural point of view the occupation administrations differed considerably. Military administrations were set up more or less in line with international law in Belgium and northern France as well as in Serbia and Central Greece (Saloniki-Ägäis). These were nominally the responsibility of the Wehrmacht high command, but they in fact developed autonomous occupation bureaucracies. In the eastern half of the occupied Soviet territories, where war was still being waged, the administration was under the command of the army.

The responsible Quartermaster-General of the army in this case did not develop an independent occupation policy. Although the military administrations were regarded as more conventional and less Nazified, they nevertheless pursued the policy of exploitation and suppression in a manner similar to that of their civilian counterparts. An important reason for this was that within military administrations it was civilian functionaries who in the main were responsible for occupation policy.

Civilian occupation administrations in Norway, the Netherlands, and in the western part of the occupied Soviet territories (including the Baltic States and parts of eastern Poland) were known as Reich commissariats. In central and southern Poland the equivalent was called the Generalgouvernement. High-ranking NSDAP cadres, who retained functions within the Reich, worked in them. These civilian administrations were set up in breach of international law, for it was only the territories bordering on the Reich that for cosmetic reasons were not blatantly annexed, though *de facto* they had been annexed.

Where politically expedient, even home governments could be left in place. Thus the Danish political system continued in existence to a great extent during the occupation, though a so-called Reich Plenipotentiary was set over it. France, on the other hand, was split into three areas for the purposes of occupation: the north and the Atlantic coast came under two separate military administrations; central and southern France were put under the control of an authoritarian French government with its official seat in the spa town of Vichy. Although the Vichy government had some freedom of action, it was subject to German instructions. In Hungary too the political system was largely retained after the army occupied the country in 1944. In other countries—the Netherlands, Belgium, Bohemia and Moravia, Serbia, and Greece—the native national administrations enjoyed significantly less autonomy.

It is surprising that Hitler and the German forces of occupation made so little use of indigenous fascist movements. Central administrations employing nationals were appointed from those belonging to conservative and right-wing nationalist circles. Their German superiors believed they could rely on such people to be more punctilious and efficient in carrying out policy. Only in occupied Norway did

Nasjonal Samling take over the reins early in 1942, just as the Hungarian Arrow Cross did for a few months from October 1944. In the police and regional administrations there were as a rule more fascists from the local population. In the main, all these administrations incorporating local people worked efficiently to carry what the Germans wanted and that meant being involved in most cases in the persecution of the Jews. They did attempt to mitigate the policy of exploitation. A number of representatives of these administrations made contact in secret with the western powers or with their governments in exile. Overall, however, German domination in Europe was inconceivable without the cooperation of functionaries from the occupied countries.

The German Reich was not the only occupying power in Hitler's Europe. South-eastern Europe was regarded as an Italian fiefdom and up to 1943 Italy controlled the territories on the Mediterranean coast from Nice to the Peloponnese. Hungary received from Hitler part of the territories it had lost under the Treaty of Trianon of 1920, not only in Yugoslavia, but also in the Romanian territory of northern Transylvania and in Carpatho-Ukraine, part of Czechoslovakia. Bulgaria established itself as an occupying power in Yugoslav west Macedonia and in Greek Macedonia as well as in western Thrace. As a reward for taking part in Hitler's war against the Soviet Union, Romania was given a zone of occupation in the Odessa area, and Finland one in Lapland. At a regional level too the 'Axis Powers' were able to pursue their own occupation policy even under German sovereignty, as in the case of the Hungarian military in eastern Ukraine. On the one hand, the other 'Axis Powers' profited from Hitler's Europe to pursue their own, in some cases brutal, policy of repression. On the other hand, as a result of latent tensions between the Axis partners, Hitler could take up a comfortable position as 'referee'.

The Social Structure of Occupation

The social groupings created by occupation were as diverse as the territories and varying organizational models themselves. It makes sense, however, to look at them as a whole because they underwent a fundamental change. The most important change was in the fact that a new elite was imposed on these countries in the form of the German occupying personnel. Several hundred thousand occupation functionaries were sent out into the occupied territories and they were supplemented by the military and police personnel charged with 'security'. The total probably came to well over a million. In the occupied Soviet territories in particular, but also in Yugoslavia, large numbers of troops were stationed in the hinterland. The occupation personnel were drawn from every corner of the Reich. Some 10 per cent of them, mainly employed in occupied south east Europe, came from Austria. Sudeten Germans, who had been taken into the Reich in 1938, worked almost exclusively in occupied Bohemia and Moravia, while other ethnic Germans had in the main only middle level or subordinate roles such as in local government or the police.

By far the majority of the occupying personnel were men. Women in the administrations were mainly secretaries, while a number had auxiliary roles in the army or were assigned to work in German infrastructure or to the 'Landdienst', where members of the Nazi girls' organization, the Bund Deutscher Mädel, helped in agriculture in the occupied territories. Some were used in the SS, in concentration camps with women's sections. Higher civilian functionaries were allowed to bring their families to their place of work. In time this practice gave rise to a regular German infrastructure with German shops, schools, and kindergartens. Although as a rule the occupation administration tried to keep the areas where Germans lived separate from those inhabited by the local population, the attempt was only partially successful.

The German occupation personnel were spread very unevenly. In the annexed territories a complete German administration was set up in which every post, down to the lowest level, and every specialist department was staffed by Germans, whereas in the Reich commissariats and in the Generalgouvernement this applied only at district and city level. The smallest proportion of German occupation personnel was found in the territories under military rule. There the work was done by relatively small local military administrations, though in the zones close to the front or in regions with many partisans there would often be tens of thousands of German soldiers as well.

The occupation officials were drawn in part from the Nazi Party apparatus and in part from the internal Reich administration. Below managerial level the personnel was a varied mixture, occasionally including men who had volunteered for service in the occupied territories. In the specialist departments, however, the majority of staff were professionally trained, for example in the fields of economics, labour administration, railways, postal services, and so forth. Among the latter category of staff, as well as in the case of occupation officers appointed from the army, there was a greater range of political attitudes, whereas the top ranks can be described as Nazified to a high degree.

Particularly in eastern Europe, the occupiers combined Nazi beliefs with a bearing commensurate with seeing themselves as the 'master race'; for them the inhabitants were inferior and were treated as such. They were extremely quick to use violence, whether against Jews or to put down resistance, though there was debate about the proper degree of large-scale violence directed against non-Jews, which should not go so far as to destabilize the rule of the occupying forces.

A position in the occupation bureaucracy generally guaranteed a comfortable life. The men in particular were relatively safe from being called up to fight at the front. On the other hand, in regions where many partisans were active occupation staff were their favourite targets. Even so, serving 'abroad' on the whole offered people the opportunity to gain considerable wealth, not least as a result of the extensive plundering of Jews and other eastern Europeans. Corruption was at least as extensive as in the Reich itself, as recent research has documented. All the same, not all occupation staff were satisfied with their jobs and in eastern Europe in particular they complained about the poor living standards and inadequate infrastructure. Many functionaries did not remain long in their posts but were transferred to other occupied territories, while some did a veritable 'administration tour' of Europe. This was a significant reason why the different occupation administrations shared such close links.

While the occupiers enjoyed an unchallenged position everywhere and in occupied eastern Europe could raise themselves to being arbiters of life and death, the native population had to resign themselves to a loss of national self-determination and of their personal freedom too in most cases. The degree of repression varied greatly from one country to another. Those societies Berlin regarded as Germanic were relatively speaking in the most favourable position.

The Flemish, Dutch, and Scandinavians were seen as Germanic and most likely to be treated with respect by the occupiers; the French and Walloons were viewed as 'civilized' and almost of equal status to Germans, though this did not apply to convinced democrats from the pre-war era, to anyone suspected of resistance, or to Communists, who were pursued by the occupying powers, condemned in politically motivated court actions or deported to concentration camps without any due process.

In particular in western and south eastern Europe the occupiers used propaganda to offer the population opportunities to integrate into the 'new order'. At first the country's defeat at the hands of the German army delivered a severe shock to people's sense of national identity and every government and every political system in the various countries lost legitimacy as a result. The symbols and practices underpinning national cohesion had been compromised or were forbidden by the occupying power. Denmark was the only country where the royal family and the government could remain during the German occupation. Even the political parties continued to exist and in March 1943 official parliamentary elections took place. The national leaders in other countries fled and as a rule established a government in exile in London. The fundamental change the elites experienced under occupation took a variety of forms. Whereas the elites in Poland and the Soviet Union were persecuted and murdered, in other countries there was a 'cleansing', in other words liberal and socialist personnel were dismissed. The heads of the military were in any case prisoners of war or sidelined. For the elites in the administration, business, and education, however, the situation was different; if they had not fled or been dismissed, the members of those elites, in particular in western and northern Europe, could continue in post. Even in the native police forces there was a relatively high degree of continuity. Recent studies show that as many as 10 per cent to 15 per cent of auxiliary policemen in the occupied Soviet Union had previously served at some point under Stalinism.

Whereas farming communities in most countries suffered through the recruitment of their young men to the military, skilled workers were less affected. Some received offers of considerable material benefit to them from the occupying power, particularly in industrial areas. Of course, any political activity tinged with socialism or communism was rigorously suppressed. In western and northern Europe in particular the occupying power permitted new organizations for entrepreneurs and employees as a means of promoting social harmony. These organizations amounted to nothing more than a rudimentary substitute for the banned trades unions, as the occupation administration wished to prevent any rise in wages in order to put a brake on inflation.

Under German occupation there were only very limited opportunities to maintain a national identity and it was possible only within the context of the 'New Order'. The countries with collaborating governments in particular developed a right-wing nationalist, authoritarian culture. The slogan of the Vichy government in France, *Travail, Famille, Patrie* (Work, Family, Fatherland) is typical of this socially conservative orientation and it was not without resonance, for many looked for 'national regeneration' after the disaster of military defeat. In this way fascist tendencies were integrated without dominating public discourse.

Within this environment a right-wing nationalist culture developed to which a fair number of well-known artists, intellectuals, and scholars contributed, most of whom had expressed favourable views about Germany before the war. Although the print media were controlled by the occupying powers and through censorship, they continued to be extensive and sophisticated. Most countries had their own cultural administrations. Belgium, for example, saw a veritable blossoming of Flemish culture, which before the war had felt somewhat disadvantaged. Native journalists definitively shaped the press and radio broadcasting during the occupation, with the exception of Poland and the Soviet Union, where radios were confiscated. This culture was of course strongly geared to the 'New Europe' and was deeply anti-Semitic.

At least up to 1942, societies had to adjust to the idea of permanent German rule and it was only after the turning point of the Battle of Stalingrad that a new perspective developed in anticipation of the return of sovereignty in the post-war era. At this stage the occupying powers looked for other strategies of integration and anti-Bolshevist propaganda was already in full swing.

After the German attack on the Soviet Union the whole of continental Europe had been called to join the fight against Bolshevism and was portrayed as being seriously threatened after the start of the Soviet advance in 1943. The mass graves near Katyn, where victims of the Soviet secret police had been discovered, played a particularly important role in the German propaganda campaign. It fell on especially fertile ground in the distinctly anti-Communist societies of eastern central and south-eastern Europe, which feared they were first in line to be invaded by the Red Army. At the same time the German Propaganda Ministry was pressing for more positive offers of cooperation to be made to the Slavs, even in Poland. Public discrimination was to be reduced.

It was in this context that individual groups began to cooperate (though it was usually referred to by the pejorative term 'collaborate') with the occupying powers. The occupiers made contact at an early stage with right-wing nationalist groups that would support German rule, though this support had to conform fully with German plans, so in other words it was not generally presented as a precursor to national autonomy. Thus nationalist underground groups in the Baltic States or in western Ukraine who had offered their services to the Germans in 1941 were rapidly disappointed. In Poland the occupying powers rejected offers of any kind of political cooperation. And yet in most countries collaborative regimes were established that could also count on support among the more conservative sections of society. Sufficient numbers of people from the native population were always available to work in the administration and the executive. It was even possible to set up militias, which were to be a substitute for military service. The Waffen-SS in particular was soon trying to recruit members of the home population for military action abroad. At first these were primarily western and northern Europeans from fascist groups but from the spring of 1943 eastern Europeans opposed to Communism were also recruited. In addition, Himmler, the SS chief, succeeded in recruiting many men from German minority populations outside Germany to the Waffen-SS.

Although by the end of 1942 the integration of societies under occupation into the 'New Order' was definitely advanced, large sections of the population wanted to have nothing to do with it and were hoping to be freed soon from German rule. There were, admittedly, few autonomous realms in these societies and establishing an alternative public sphere was impossible. The churches above all could act relatively autonomously under German occupation. In Poland the Catholic clergy was firmly suppressed because it was seen as the repository of Polish national assertiveness. Thousands of priests died in German concentration camps. By contrast, in the Soviet Union the churches experienced a renaissance under German rule after years of Communist persecution and thus were predominantly loyal to the occupying powers.

This was basically true also for the churches in the other occupied territories. Yet the churches not only offered a space to which German occupiers had only limited access, but they also symbolized the continuity of national identity. In particular after the war began to turn early in 1943, some of the churches distanced themselves from regimes collaborating with the occupation; the Vatican sought contact with the western Allies. The picture is mixed, however. Whereas, for example, western European churches or the Orthodox Church in Greece criticized the murder of the Jews, bishops in the Ukrainian and Romanian Orthodox Churches were still making frequent and blatant anti-Semitic statements in 1942/3.

Only underground movements enjoyed real autonomy under German occupation, though these were much more complex and had a more limited reach than has long been assumed. Up to the German invasion of the Soviet Union opposition groups were only small. The main political opponent of National Socialism, the Communists in Europe, was in waiting until the Molotov–Ribbentrop Pact was broken in June 1941. Then armed resistance developed relatively quickly in Byelorussia, Russia, and Yugoslavia. In the Soviet Union in particular the groups were most often organized by the Communist Party, the Red Army, or the secret police, and while most of these organizations had been smashed by the end of 1941 they were built up again in a systematic and centralized way in the course of 1942. In the other countries the underground developed only gradually. It grew to be most extensive in Poland, where the government in exile developed a veritable underground state, with an administration, armed cadres, and a counter-culture. By contrast with the Communist groups, the 'Home Army' (Armia Krajowa) did not at first provoke armed confrontation with the occupying powers, in order to avoid terrible reprisals in the form of massacres of civilians. After the war began to turn at the beginning of 1943 underground groups attracted more and more members and with the German army's large-scale retreats in the summer of 1944 liberation was within reach.

Resistance to the occupation came from a very broad political spectrum. Although from the middle of 1941 the Communists had led the way, at the same time the emergence of the Chetniks in Yugoslavia established a conservative Greater-Serbian movement. From 1943 onwards more and more right-wing groups joined in, some of whom were collaborating with the Germans in 1941. In the Baltic States and western Ukraine organizations were set up that, while fighting the Communists first and foremost, also fought against the German occupation. Even in France there was an extreme-right resistance to the German occupation.

These differences in political direction very soon led to a competition, and in some countries to civil war, to determine the post-war order. As early as the spring of 1941 the ultra-nationalist Ustasha movement in Croatia and Bosnia-Herzegovina had provoked a civil war through its massacres of the Serbian population. In the autumn of 1941 this spread to include large parts of Yugoslavia. When early in 1943 it became possible to glimpse a new post-war order this conflict became more intense. The anti-Communist underground in the Baltic States and in eastern Poland and western Ukraine was now fighting the Soviet partisans. The Ukraine resistance army went further. Anticipating an 'ethnically' homogeneous post-war Ukraine, individual groups massacred and expelled the Polish minority. Some 60,000 Poles died while the German occupation forces looked on. In occupied Greece conflict broke out between the national-conservative underground EDES and the Communist ELAS. These civil wars were continued in part up to 1947/9, long after the German occupying forces had withdrawn.

These were not the only territories in which the occupation was succeeded by other conflicts, however, for in almost every country that was liberated from German control scores were settled violently before the war ended, not only to punish collaboration but also in the political struggle to determine the direction these societies would take after the war.

Life Under Occupation

Closer examination of societies under occupation reveals that they differed from their pre-war state not only through changes to the elites and the new cultural emphases. First and foremost, the composition of societies changed. Basically, a paradox arose: culture became more 'masculine' as it was determined by war, conservative gender roles, and violence, while societies became more feminine. There were in any case more women than men living in the Soviet Union, a consequence of the civil war of 1918/20, but in the Second World War the ratio changed again significantly. Everywhere the men were being called up to serve and then becoming POWs or being killed. When the Germans invaded it was primarily the men who managed to escape or be evacuated. Finally, it was men who made up the majority of those deported as forced labourers or interned in camps and prisons. The result was that significantly more women than men lived under occupation, especially in the Soviet territories, where in a number of cities women made up two-thirds of the population.

Often the breadwinner of the family was gone and women flooded what at the beginning was in any case a very restricted labour market. It was not until a labour shortage emerged in 1942 that job prospects for women improved, though they were paid less well across the board than their male colleagues.

The same reasons led to a clear rise in the number of children in the labour market, in spite of the wartime fall in the birth rate. The same was true at first in the case of older people. They, however, suffered especially from the difficult living conditions and the death rate rose sharply. Thus it is hardly surprising that family life was drastically changed by the war and mothers assumed even more of a key role than previously.

In addition to the fear of German violence, daily life under occupation was determined by worries about getting something to eat. The war had partially destroyed the infrastructure and the refocusing of the economy produced shortages of many things. In principle, food was subject to rationing, and by comparison with the pre-war period it was inferior in quantity and quality, as many import markets were now inaccessible. The food situation can be put roughly into three categories. The best supplied countries in this respect were Belgium, the Netherlands, Norway, and Bohemia/Moravia. It was significantly worse in France, the Baltic States, Poland, and Yugoslavia. In the occupied Soviet territories the position was for the most part bad to catastrophic. Whereas in the eastern territories of the occupied Soviet

Union, in particular in the larger cities, the Germans applied what amounted to a starvation policy, in occupied Greece the food shortage crisis, which was especially acute in the Italian zone of occupation, arose from multiple factors. In the final months of the war, in the winter of 1944/5 the occupying power deliberately applied a hunger blockade in order to break strikes in northern Holland.

Food shortages did not affect every section of the population in equal measure. Rations for labourers in heavy industries were the most generous, while those for Jews were the most meagre. People who were in work were on the whole better provided for. Munitions workers had the biggest share. Another factor was that town and city dwellers were dependent on getting additional supplies, for example from relatives in the country. Older people on their own had only themselves to rely on and so were in a precarious position.

Everyday life was made more difficult as a result of German finance and labour policies. In most countries the value of the national currency was eroded in order to make it easier to finance the occupation in secret. Though the occupying authorities decreed that wages and prices would be frozen, an extensive black market soon developed with rapidly increasing prices. In Greece during the German occupation there was such hyper-inflation that the Germans were forced to stabilize the currency. Over all, the occupied countries saw a clear reduction in the real value of wages.

It is thus hardly surprising that in many regions the health of the population deteriorated. The problem was made worse by the shortage of medicines, the requisitioning of hospitals for use by the German army, and also by the murder of Jewish doctors. In Poland and France, for example, a considerable proportion of schoolchildren were suffering from deficiency diseases.

There were also considerable changes to working life in many regions. The destruction and closure of businesses, particularly in Poland and the Soviet Union, led in the first instance to a drastic rise in unemployment. In the west similar effects followed the loss of markets and the closure of businesses. As in Germany itself, the occupation administration soon took steps to regulate and control the labour markets. The German employment exchanges were among the most important institutions in any occupied territory. In Poland and the occupied Soviet territories a general obligation to work was decreed, which was essentially an obligation on everyone capable of work to register as such. Recruitment of workers for Germany began early on. At first this was to be voluntary, but from the end of 1941 onwards recruitment practice in Poland and the Soviet Union grew ever more oppressive, so that contract work became forced labour. In the autumn of 1942 at the latest, force was used to recruit in western and northern Europe also.

In 1942/3 the police and the German army were positively hunting recruits down. As by then hardly anyone was registered as unemployed, the occupying power targeted ever younger age groups. When the raids in the Ukraine were at their height in the summer of 1942 those caught up in them were primarily girls between 14 and 20, who were destined for work in German households or on farms. Finally, in 1943 the Germans deported whole families to Germany from territories where partisans were strong.

For the recruits the risks varied. Conditions for forced labourers from western Europe were better than those for the P workers (from Poland) or the 'Eastern Workers' (from the Soviet Union), who were placed in barracks, badly treated, and frequently categorized as criminals. Some 8.5 million people came to work in the Reich, of whom about 150,000 eastern European workers did not survive.

Whereas the forced labour carried out in Germany or Austria has been well researched, our knowledge about forced labour in the occupied territories is still fragmentary. This too was concentrated in Poland and the Soviet Union. Peasants and farmers were confined in the numerous work camps for not having adequately delivered their quotas, along with suspected partisans and others. It was not uncommon for women in the Soviet Union to be compelled to dig earthworks for the German army, and in Byelorussia the retreating army organized columns of forced labourers, who were made to accompany the troops. Overall it can be assumed that forced labour in the occupied territories became almost as extensive as it was in the German Reich.

On the whole it was impossible to avoid working for the Germans in one form or another. It was true of munitions workers just as it was for the peasants who had to deliver their quotas to the occupiers. Nor was there any way of avoiding cooperation in order to maintain public life: local administration, social and economic services and so on had to be preserved, as well as the guarantee of public order by the police.

In particular in those occupied territories where conditions were especially difficult such jobs were regarded as desirable. They ensured better rations and also provided protection from deportation as forced labour to the German Reich. For that reason quite a few local administrations in the occupied Soviet Union were positively bloated with staff. But in eastern Europe in particular working in the public services for the occupying power was an especially problematic enterprise. The local administrations were often involved in the persecution of the Jews, while the auxiliary police as a rule had a role in their deportation or directly in their murder.

The relationship of the population to those of their number who had joined the administration was also divided: quite a number of mayors or auxiliary police put on shows of being well-known fascists or made use of their good contacts with the Germans to enable them to gain power locally. In country areas in particular they were usually the only representatives of the occupying power.

Daily contact between the native population and the German occupiers was not in fact usual. Whereas tens of thousands of German soldiers were billeted in quite a number of Russian cities near the front and came in time to outnumber the local population, there were rural areas where after the invasion there was hardly a German to be seen. In cities, however, the occupiers were visible almost everywhere and their staff had always to be given preferential treatment. In the annexed Polish territories discrimination against the native population reached the point where they were forced to cross the road when a German came towards them. In the course of time, however, the population was able to distinguish very clearly between occupation functionaries to be judged as threatening and those to be judged as friendly. A report of the Polish underground noted that only about 1 per cent of the Germans there could be seen unreservedly in a positive light. Nevertheless, the native population adjusted to daily contact with the Germans, not least because it was often necessary to obtain official documents.

For their part, many of the German men took advantage of being in a foreign country and of the power relations of the occupation to engage in sexual adventures. It has been possible so far to piece together only a very fragmentary picture of the extent of sexual violence in the occupied territories, but in eastern Europe especially it seems to have been considerable. The German army itself set up brothels for the soldiers in the occupied territories. Intimate relationships with local women were, however, part of everyday life and were tolerated by the German authorities as long as Jewish women were not involved. The motives of the women in these relationships were various, from prostitution caused by poverty, to the search for protection, to actual love affairs. These women, however, such as the 'Moffenmeiden' in the Netherlands, were regarded by the majority of the native population as traitors. After the liberation they were frequently punished severely, and they and any children issuing from these liaisons suffered discrimination long after.

Violent interventions on the part of the occupiers were directed primarily against men, who were considered to be significantly more dangerous than women. In the case of crimes against Jews, Roma Gypsies, and the mentally ill, however, and also in the case of massacres in the war against partisans such distinctions were not observed.

There were huge differences in daily life under German occupation in the individual regions. Whereas in Denmark even public life continued almost without interruption, the cities in Poland saw mass death in the ghettos and barbaric deportations to the extermination camps. In the Netherlands the economy boomed, while in the territories in eastern Europe where partisans were active there was the constant threat of reprisal shootings by the German occupiers. It is therefore necessary to establish in more detail in what areas and at what times violence played a significant role and against whom it was directed. In occupied Poland, in the west of the Soviet Union, and in Serbia violence was virtually ubiquitous. This was where the large Jewish communities were based, and the extermination camps also. This was the place where soldiers of the Red Army died in their thousands in German prisoner of war camps, while in Byelorussia and Russia massacres were part of the war against the partisans. It was in this area that the mass deportations of non-Jews took place, also the brutal rounding up of people as forced labour. In these territories the German occupiers dispensed with efforts to keep their crimes particularly secret, as not only the groups being persecuted but the population as a whole was regarded as having no rights and no international protection. In addition, members of the local population were involved in various ways in the violence and not only as victims.

Above all, however, they were witnesses to the violence. Everyone in Poland and the Soviet Union knew about the mass killings and many had seen them with their own eyes. This experience demonstrated to people not only their own powerlessness but also the dissolution of the norms of civilized behaviour, as the violence of the Stalin era had done before. These were societies in crisis.

In the other occupied territories, on the other hand, violence was directed at relatively clearly defined groups, primarily Jews, Roma Gypsies, and members of the resistance. It was also not exercised in public but mainly through deportation or shooting behind prison walls. It was not until the autumn of 1943 that the open use of violence was extended beyond Poland, the Soviet Union, and Yugoslavia, but it was still restricted to particular regions and locations. The threat of violence, however, hung over the whole of occupied Europe and it was used if the Germans' rules were infringed or they were actively resisted. It is thus hardly surprising that, as in comparable situations throughout history, the general policy adopted by the population under occupation was to adapt and comply. Although the overwhelming majority of those living under occupation rejected German domination, this view was expressed only in private. Resistance movements had their origins in older organizations such as the dispersed fragments of former armies or Communist parties, or in the work of state organs of the Soviet Union. It was not until late 1942 / early 1943 that resistance attracted broader support. In eastern Europe young people attempted en masse to evade the squads sent out to press them into forced labour, while everywhere it was becoming clear that the Germans would lose the war. And it was only in 1944 that resistance movements grew to the size on which their post-war myth was based. They were certainly not widespread popular movements.

Going underground was extremely perilous. Not only did German agencies investigate any resistance group energetically, but the risk of denunciation was high. People were, after all, and particularly in eastern Europe, exposing those around them—family, neighbours, whole communities—to the danger of reprisals. Many neighbourhoods, even many families, were divided; one son would be in the auxiliary police, another son or a daughter with the partisans. In the end both collaboration and resistance were shifting categories and during the occupation quite a few people changed sides, sometimes more than once. Thus many auxiliary police who had once been involved in mass murder ended up among the partisans. In these exceptional circumstances no one's life trajectory was simple, and neither political loyalties before the war nor professional career determined what anyone's fate would be under the occupation.

Summary

Although Hitler had long planned his war to extend the German Reich and conquer 'living space' in the Soviet Union, the war took a course he did not expect. Thanks to a ruthless foreign policy that aimed only at expansion, though the lethargy of the western powers also played a part, he succeeded by April 1941 in bringing large swathes of the continent of Europe under his control. Early on, however, his central war, the conquest of the Soviet Union, was unsuccessful, but by mobilizing and exploiting the resources of Europe he was able to prolong the war for four years, until he had reduced half the continent to rubble.

If only for a short time, Hitler and the German elites created the most radical empire in history. It was radical in its aims: to bring about the world domination of the 'Aryan race' and the extermination of the Jews in Europe; in addition, to deport thirty-one million Slavs and to starve thirty million inhabitants of the Soviet Union to death or cause them to flee.

It was radical in practice too. The systematic murder of the Jews and Roma Gypsies is unique in history and although the use of massacres to put down resistance had parallels in Japanese, Italian and, to some extent, in the colonial practices of other nations, the case of Germany stands out clearly by virtue of its method. The Germans' policy of starvation in the Soviet Union was based on significantly more planning than Stalin's in 1931/3. Mass murder was accelerated by a radical policy of exploitation. The plundering, above all, of Soviet agriculture had devastating effects, not only for civilians in some regions but even more for Soviet prisoners of war, a considerable proportion of whom were starved to death. Finally, forced labour became the central method of exploitation, though it drove increasing numbers of people to join the resistance and from 1943 onwards was visibly linked to the murderous operations against partisans.

Eleven to twelve million Europeans lost their lives as a result of German crimes and millions more were jailed or deported, even though they survived the war. Untold millions were traumatized by the occupation, after being confronted with violence, injury, or losing those close to them. The experience of hunger also went on affecting people for the rest of their lives.

To sum up, the German occupation represented devastation on an immense scale of human lives, social structures, and social capital. Yet in spite of that, the majority of those living under German rule attempted, in difficult circumstances, to lead normal lives without compromising themselves. They managed to do so by adjusting in small and not so small ways to the occupiers. After liberation it was those who had the most political power who decided what would count as behaviour beyond the bounds of national loyalty. In the end far more members of the native populations were punished for their participation in German crimes or for various types of collaboration than were Germans. Most of the occupying Germans managed to escape and evade punishment for their deeds.

9

The Home Front

Julia S. Torrie

Introduction

As he waited for the Allies to land in France in early June 1944, the German soldier Kurt F. prepared a letter to his parents. A friend had told him that his home city, Hamm, had been bombed again, and as he watched planes flying overhead, he thought that maybe the Allies would never land, and would try to destroy the Third Reich entirely by air. 'The face of war has changed a great deal', he wrote, 'It's not like at the movies anymore, where the best places are in the rear.'

Typical narratives of war describe hardened men facing their enemies boldly while women hold families together in the relative peace of home. We tend to think about conflict in terms of opposed pairs: war and peace; front and home; male and female. Certainly, these pairs are convenient tools, but letters like Kurt F.'s remind us that such distinctions can be arbitrary. There are many connections between Home and War Fronts, for soldiers wrote letters constantly, describing experiences and feelings while their wives, families, and friends shared worries and hopes from day to day. Victories, and perhaps even more, setbacks in fighting affected civilians' mood, while morale at home touched soldiers at the front. Quite apart from shared preoccupations, 'home' and 'front' were part of the same conflict, and as Kurt F. noted, in World War Two, the rear was no longer as safe as it might have been in previous eras. Over the course of the war, violence bled from one zone to the other, as soldiers and civilians were acutely aware.

Within the broad context of the Third Reich at war, this chapter surveys life on the German Home Front through three main themes. The first is popular morale, and in particular the tension between the need to mobilize society for war, and the regime's fear that asking too much of people would undermine their support. Readers are encouraged to consider the interplay of Adolf Hitler and other key figures like Propaganda Minister Joseph Goebbels, Police and SS chief Heinrich Himmler, and Air Minister Hermann Göring with the *Volksgemeinschaft* ('community of the people'). To what extent did these men pay attention to popular morale, and what limits, if any, did this set on their pursuit of war?

A second theme explores how long-term fighting relied on the exploitation of Germany's occupied territories, which supplied labour, food, and raw materials for industry. To what extent were Germans conscious of their dependence on conquered resources? How did they interact with the many non-Germans on the Home Front, including forced labourers and prisoners of war? How much did they know about the inhumane treatment meted out to these individuals, and about discrimination toward, exclusion of, and then mass murder of Jews and others, a subject treated more fully elsewhere in this book?

Finally, this chapter emphasizes the interconnectedness of Home and War Fronts throughout the conflict. As war continued and initial successes gave way to stalemate and a reversal of Germany's fortunes, how did the population react? What was the situation of women, specifically, who made up the largest group on a Home Front that also included working men, resting and convalescing soldiers, the elderly, and children? Aerial bombing presented a growing threat, which, more than anything else, tended to elide differences between War and Home Fronts. Cowering in bunkers while airborne battles raged overhead, civilians saw little distinction between their own situation and that of soldiers. The impression deepened that Home and War Fronts, never fully separate, were blending together when last-ditch mobilization led to the conscription of young and old, women as well as men, while terror raged, order broke down, and the Third Reich slid toward collapse.

Morale at War's Outset

World War Two began without much popular enthusiasm even in Germany, where there was overall support for Hitler's expansionism.

Less than thirty years had passed since the end of the previous war, and Germans had little desire to engage in a new conflict. World War One had been marked by food and fuel shortages alongside an overall sense that resources had not been distributed fairly across the population. That war had ended in terrible losses and a peace treaty at Versailles that crippled Germany for years to come. Perhaps most significantly, many military and political leaders blamed the defeat on the Home Front, suggesting that if civilians' morale had been more robust, Germany would have won the war. This was patently false, but fears about civilians' ability to hold out through another conflict shaped planning for a new war.

Since the 1930s, the National Socialists had been preparing for war economically, politically, and with propaganda. Citizens were encouraged to see the Third Reich not as an expansionist aggressor, but as a beleaguered island, encircled by foes on all sides. When the war began, they perceived themselves as unwilling combatants duty-bound to defend their homeland.

Some of the earliest effects of war were felt on the western borders where, especially from 1938, construction of defences known as the Westwall brought thousands of young male workers into sleepy rural villages. Beginning in late August 1939, to clear German borderlands for troop movements and avoid having civilians fall into enemy hands, some half a million people were evacuated pre-emptively from the Saarland, the Palatinate, and Baden. Although most returned home after spending a few uncomfortable months billeted with strangers, this evacuation underlined the challenges that large-scale population transfers would pose throughout the war.

As the conflict got underway, the highest members of the party and state apparatus watched the popular mood for signs of weakness. Throughout the war, detailed reports from the Security Service (Sicherheitsdienst or SD) traced ordinary Germans' hopes, worries, and fears. Although some scholars argue that the SD reports tell us more about the views of those who compiled them than about popular morale *per se*, the authorities in Berlin asked for such reports because they wanted a clear reflection of the mood on the ground. For a dictatorship, Hitler's regime was remarkably sensitive to, and responsive toward, popular opinion. It needed the people's support in order to continue to fight, and this sensitivity sometimes gave civilians surprising power to influence policies on the Home Front.

At the same time, the authorities went out of their way to ensure obedience, notably by publicizing punishments meted out to those who listened to foreign radio, became intimate with a prisoner of war, plundered the house of an evacuee, or otherwise undermined the war effort. Although the police might have liked to control every aspect of life in the Reich, its totalitarian aspirations were limited by its means, and it relied heavily on the public's cooperation. Based on the denunciation of a neighbour, acquaintance, or even family member, the police might investigate wrong-doing and bring about a conviction. Speakers grew wary of giving away that they had been listening to foreign radio, or of having their neighbours suspect that they might have been doing so. It became difficult, if not impossible, to air an opinion critical of the regime, or to express concern about the war's outcome.

Although the party took people's willingness to denounce perceived crimes as a sign of support for its policies, this was far from being unambiguously clear. In fact, historian Robert Gellately has suggested that some three-quarters of all denunciations 'were provided for reasons that had little or nothing to do with obviously or expressly supporting the Nazis'. Rather, they were the result of petty jealousies, rivalries, and attention-seeking. Nonetheless, the ever-present danger of denunciation worked to intimidate the population, and furthered the regime's penetration of daily life.

Initial Successes

The sense of resignation with which Germans began the war soon gave way to relief as Hitler's forces easily defeated Poland. Through the winter, the population followed news of the war in Denmark and Norway eagerly, but everyone knew that the real contest lay in the west, against France and Britain. Anxiety mounted until it was released in the spring when the French, too, fell before German arms and British troops were driven off the continent. The victory over France had enormous symbolic significance, as Germans vanquished their 'arch-enemy', avenged the defeat of 1918, and redressed what they saw as an unjust peace at Versailles.

This was the war's most triumphant phase, symbolized by the enthusiasm with which soldiers soaked up the pleasures of western occupied areas. Young men wrote home about visiting France's historical monuments, swimming in the sea for the first time, and gorging themselves on Gallic delicacies. Just after Paris had been conquered, American journalist William Shirer saw occupiers, 'photographing Notre-Dame, the Arc de Triomphe, the Invalides', and noted that 'thousands of German soldiers congregate all day long at the Tomb of the Unknown Soldier, where the flame still burns under the Arc. They bare their blond heads and stand there gazing.'

Although their relatives at home understood soldiers to be doing their duty honourably, they behaved as conquerors with the run of the land. The war in the west in 1940 involved little of the brutality displayed on the Eastern Front just a year later, but it was not a fully 'clean' war either. Both fronts lay on a continuum of escalating violence, evidenced in 1940 by the murder of some 1,500 to 3,000 captured French colonial soldiers, as scholar Raffael Scheck has shown. Although this violence against a specific group was at first accompanied by generally benign treatment of French civilians, property was often plundered, and the exchange rate between the Reichsmark and the Franc set so low, at twenty to one, that even purchasing goods and services became a highly unequal arrangement.

Soldiers' wives were expected to be faithful to their absent husbands, but occupiers thought little of enjoying the sexual and other attractions available in conquered lands. Occupiers' behaviour threatened to undermine the positive image of themselves Germans were anxious to display in the west, but the army also recognized that relaxing in occupied areas was important compensation for the hardships of campaigning. Rather than forbidding pleasure, it channelled enjoyment by establishing official bordellos for occupiers and inviting them on bus tours of tourist sites. Carefully censored and managed pleasures had a positive effect on morale, for families enjoyed reading about the travel and consumption enabled by conquest.

On the strength of victory over France, and riding a wave of euphoria at home, Hitler now prepared to invade England. Major air raids across the Channel began, first targeting British shipping, then airfields, followed by London and other major cities. Germans' satisfaction that the war was being brought home to England was short-lived, however, because the Royal Air Force soon stepped up its own raids, and air war began to touch Germany directly.

Aerial defence had been encouraged since Hitler came to power, for it aligned with National Socialist preoccupations in several ways. Germans were fascinated by the technology of flight, and like their European neighbours, they firmly expected the next war to begin with a sudden air attack. Preparing for this eventuality enabled Hitler to mobilize society and put it on a war footing. As early as September 1933, the French newspaper *Le Matin* commented that, 'Aerial defence is pushed in Germany with a febrile activity that would make one believe the Reich is on the eve of incursions by enemy planes.' People's sense that Germany was under threat was reinforced by the Reich Air Defence League, which had 8.2 million members by 1936—one-sixth of all Berliners, and over 10 per cent of the population of Hesse, the Palatinate, and Baden, areas perceived to be vulnerable because they were easily accessible to French and Allied aircraft.

Although Göring had assured civilians that British planes would never reach even the Ruhr industrial area in the west, the first raid on the capital, Berlin, occurred in late August 1940. By the end of September, young people were being evacuated pre-emptively from Berlin and Hamburg. Children were viewed as the future of the nation, and remained the primary focus of the German evacuation programmes examined in greater detail below.

Adjusting to Prolonged and Brutal Conflict

Germany continued to bomb Britain through the winter of 1940–1, but partly this was intended to hide the fact that Hitler's attention had turned eastward. At daybreak on 22 June 1941, the army launched 3.5 million men in Operation Barbarossa, the invasion of the Soviet Union. Like the attack on Poland at the war's outset and the move westward the previous year, this new offensive was justified to the population on defensive grounds. Hitler argued that Germany needed to act pre-emptively to avoid encirclement by the British and Soviets who were working in concert to destroy the Reich.

Although they might not have expected war against the Soviet Union to begin so soon, people generally adjusted quickly. Some did, however, express concerns about the human costs of a long war, and voice doubts about how Soviet troops might treat men they took prisoner. Disquiet about the treatment of prisoners stemmed from long-held beliefs that Russia, and the Soviet Union more generally, was a land of bestial 'Asiatic' hordes. Already in World War One, German soldiers had fought what they saw as 'Russian barbarism', and this was now overlaid by a fear of Communist Russia's radical 'Bolshevism'. In the absence of real knowledge of Russians, propaganda substituted imagery of primitive and brutal fighters, backward peasants, and terrifying political commissars.

Some soldiers moved forward easily, thrusting deep into Soviet territory, while others struggled to make headway. Although atrocities had already been committed in the west and violence escalated there later in the war, fighting on the Eastern Front was on a larger scale and far more brutal from its outset. Soldiers tried to shield their families from news of the greatest atrocities, but occasionally, their letters contained information that surely marked their readers. On 7 August 1941, Bremen shopkeeper and reserve policeman Hermann Gieschen wrote to his wife from somewhere in Latvia. He told her that the previous night '150 Jews from this place were shot, men, women and children, all bumped off. The Jews are being completely exterminated . . . Please don't think about it, that's how it has to be. And don't tell [our son] R. about it, leave it for later!' Some men, like Gieschen, could not help themselves from sharing what they had witnessed, and occasionally letters slipped through postal censorship. These details represented mere hints of the violence that not only targeted Jews, but also local villagers when, for example, whole farming communities were burned to the ground in retaliation for supposed 'partisan' activity.

Equally disturbingly, there were rumours at home that mentally ill and disabled patients at German hospitals were being murdered systematically. Some Germans approved of these measures against individuals they saw as biologically 'unfit', but others were shocked that doctors and nurses who were supposedly caring for society's weakest members were actually killing them. Representatives of both Catholic and Protestant churches voiced the loudest objections to what became known as 'Aktion T4' after the Berlin address (Tiergartenstrasse 4) of the building from which it was directed.

In summer 1941, complaints about the treatment of psychiatric patients reached such a pitch that the authorities briefly halted the programme. Hitler ordered in late August that it should cease, but it was then quietly restarted, using lethal drug injections and starvation rather than the gas previously employed. Often, relatives heard about a family member's death only weeks after it had occurred, when they received an official certificate indicating a completely fabricated cause of death. Wartime conditions made it easier to carry out these murders, for relatives lost touch with psychiatric patients who, for example, were moved when their home hospital was converted into a trauma unit for the use of 'normal' civilian bomb victims. Throughout the conflict, individual Germans expressed concerns about the treatment of the mentally ill, but the systematic murder of psychiatric patients continued, justified by the authorities partly on racial grounds, partly on the grounds that individuals who could not work were taking valuable resources away from the rest of the population.

Drawing on the Resources of Occupied Europe: Food

By early 1942, the German failure to take Moscow suggested that the Soviet Union would not be vanquished soon. After the Japanese attack at Pearl Harbour, the United States had entered the war, and Germany faced an alliance whose resources outnumbered its own four to one. Morale took a further blow in the spring as Cologne was hit by an unprecedented '1,000–bomber' raid, a sign of Allied strength and a portent of aerial bombing's frightening future.

The Home Front began to experience shortages, notably of food. Rations had to be cut in April 1942, and the public mood remained sombre through the summer. The SD (Security Service) reported that the food situation had become 'one of the population's main subjects of conversation'. At harvest time in October 1942, Göring gave an important speech in the Berlin Sport Palace (*Sportpalast*) announcing an increase in bread and meat rations, from 8,000 to 9,000 grams and 1,200 to 1,620 grams respectively, for a 'normal consumer'. Although it did not make up for earlier cuts and had to be reversed the following spring, the public mood improved.

Food supplies could only be sustained by exploiting Germany's occupied territories, however, and plunder of these continued apace.

Germans were beginning to understand that this war, which they still conceived of as defensive, required maintaining a European empire upon which they could draw to pursue the fight. Four months before invading Poland in 1939, Hitler had informed his commanders that, 'it is a matter of expanding our living space in the east and making food supplies secure'. Food shortages had caused volatile tension between the population and government in World War One, and the authorities were determined to do things differently this time around.

Rationing was imposed at war's outset, with three categories for 'normal consumers', 'heavy workers', and 'very heavy workers'. By the end of the conflict, there were sixteen categories to cover individuals of varying ages and needs. Pregnant and nursing mothers as well as young children received greater allotments of milk, while labourers doing shift and night work were compensated with extra calories. Nutritional research suggested that a typical worker's family consumed about 2,750 calories per person each day, and the system worked to redistribute nourishment by providing as many as 4,200 calories to 'very heavy workers'. Since white-collar workers typically received 2,400 calories, heavy labourers' extra rations were also a sign of their political importance—because they made war industries turn, the regime could not afford to risk these men's dissent.

Although the regime hesitated to cut back on consumer goods early in the war, essentials like soap and clothing were increasingly closely rationed. The women's magazine *NS-Frauenwarte* ran regular articles explaining the rationing system and encouraging civilians to take care of clothes and shoes so that they would last as long as possible. As in other warring nations, there were scrap metal drives and campaigns to discourage wastage. Efforts to foster frugality included promoting the *Eintopf*, a low-cost one-pot meal that German households were supposed to consume once a month on Sundays from the early 1930s. Party representatives went door to door to collect the money saved, and the funds were donated to the National Socialist *Winterhilfswerk* (Winter Help Works), a charitable organization that provided assistance to needy members of the *Volksgemeinschaft*. The whole venture was designed to underline German solidarity and feelings of community as photographs circulated of Hitler and other Reich officials demonstrating their willingness to sacrifice alongside the people by enjoying a convivial one-pot meal.

The authorities were likewise at pains to connect military and civilian eating to avoid any sense that one or the other group might be privileged consumers. As of January 1942, all restaurants in Germany were required to serve a one-pot meal or other simple fare on Tuesdays and Thursdays. By sharing field kitchen style food, Germans could perform the unity of Home and War Fronts, and the unity of the *Volksgemeinschaft* more broadly.

Well before the war, Hitler had begun preparing for the possibility that, as in World War One, Germany might be blockaded. He aimed to exploit existing agricultural land fully and sought substitutes for foreign goods that might become difficult to obtain. One of the biggest challenges was the supply of fertilizer, in large part because making chemical fertilizers used many of the same raw materials as manufacturing explosives. Fat and protein were also concerns, leading to government-funded research into animal breeding, milk production, and the cultivation of plants not traditionally grown in Germany, such as soya.

The authorities tried to preserve food better to make healthy nourishment available year round. Canned foods had several drawbacks, including their overall quality, their weight, and the fact that can-making required imported tin-plate. Fast-freezing, developed in the United States in the 1920s, promised to preserve vitamins better and require less packaging. The National Socialists supported domestic research in this area and, to make large-scale freezing feasible quickly, in 1939 purchased the rights to the industrial process developed by American Charles Birdseye. As historian Ulrike Thoms points out, this surprising purchase for Hitler's nationalist regime suggests that Germans saw a sizeable role for freezing in ensuring proper food stocks for an upcoming war. By 1940, some 22,000 tons of frozen food were being made, of which fish represented 7,000–8,000 tons, fruits and vegetables 14,000 tons. Transporting and storing frozen goods required special equipment, however, and National Socialist dreams were soon limited by the material constraints of wartime. Freezing facilitated the exploitation of Norwegian fish, as well as French meat and vegetables mainly for military use, but new technology did not translate into mass consumption of frozen foods.

Although wartime innovations laid the groundwork for later expansion, it is difficult to tell how much cooking and eating practices actually changed for most Germans during the war. Certainly, dehydrated foods were introduced in greater numbers, soya beans and sprouts were employed to pad meat rations, and soya powder gave substance to instant soups. Traditional foods remained dominant, however, with quantities of meat and fats decreasing as consumption of root vegetables, including potatoes, rose.

Occupied countries made a significant contribution to the supply of food and consumer goods on the Home Front. In 1940, the sheer richness of France's resources had amazed soldiers, who began sending everything from soap and silk stockings to butter and even eggs home. From late September 1940, except in the case of rationed goods, the Wehrmacht decided that in France, 'the individual member of the military may purchase whatever he likes'. Complementing the many goods shipped by field post, the soldier headed home on leave with his rucksack bulging and parcels dangling around his neck became a familiar sight. His welcome arrival helped offset shortages, made the soldier feel like a magnanimous hero, and, historian Götz Aly has argued, reinforced popular support for Hitler's expansionist programme. When aerial attacks on Germany grew severe from 1943 onward, enlisted men scoured occupied areas urgently, looking for basic household goods to send home to their bombed-out families. Shopping became a substitute for, and a supplement to, more open forms of despoilment.

Although west European populations suffered many hardships and remember the war years as hunger years, the exploitation of occupied areas was taken furthest in the Soviet Union. The State Secretary at the Food and Agriculture Ministry, Herbert Backe, argued that mining eastern food resources was essential in order 'to ease the nutrition situation of Europe and to lighten the pressure on transportation links'. German soldiers were instructed to live off the land, regardless of civilian needs for, as the Wehrmacht's Quartermaster General explained with regard to the civilians of besieged Leningrad, 'Every train bringing provisions from the homeland cuts foodstuffs there. It is better that our relatives have something to eat and that the Russians starve.' As war dragged on, Germany could only continue to fight by draining its neighbours' resources completely.

Drawing on the Resources of Occupied Europe: Workers

In addition to food and industrial resources, the Reich also exploited people. Some individuals came willingly, drawn by incentives that, for example, promised to liberate one French prisoner of war for every three people who volunteered for work in Germany. But the vast majority were brought to the Reich against their will, either as prisoners of war, or as forced labourers. For both groups, working conditions grew poorer, rations shorter, and arbitrary violence more common as the war went on. Sickness and disease were regular visitors. Although everyone in Germany was vulnerable to Allied aerial bombing, foreigners were particularly endangered because their industrial workplaces were bombing targets, and they were not allowed the same opportunities to take shelter as their German co-workers.

Foreign workers were brought in to compensate for the fact that more and more German men were being called to active service. Scholar Ulrich Herbert shows that from a low of less than 1 per cent in 1940, the foreign population of Essen, home of armaments giant Krupp, expanded to over 10 per cent by early 1945. Workers were housed in camps, fed on rations that decreased markedly as the war went on, and subjected to arbitrary punishments. At least 170,000 Soviet and 130,000 Polish workers perished in Germany during the war, and because these numbers do not include those who died on their way to or from the Reich, the actual figures may be hundreds of thousands higher.

Initially, concerns about not having a large enough workforce led to relatively considerate treatment of foreign labourers. However, when 1.2 million soldiers were captured as France fell in 1940, Germany suddenly seemed to have an endless supply of labour, and moved toward a more ideologically-charged approach. Not waiting for orders from above, some local SS and Police representatives forbade Poles from using bicycles in case they tried to flee, and barred them from swimming pools and beaches. Across the Reich, their right to vacations and raises was revoked, and they were no longer allowed to attend local churches. From February 1942, all workers from the east were required to wear an identifying badge with the word 'Ost' (east) sewn onto their clothes.

Despite National Socialist racial doctrine that suggested workers from 'Aryan' nations would be more efficient than others, Germans found Polish workers to be just as effective, if not more so. At the same time, rather contradictorily, the SD concluded that most foreign workers were unsatisfactory labourers. They addressed the situation through repression, including opening special camps, called 'Work Education Camps' (Arbeitserziehungslager, or AEL) specifically intended to 're-educate' lazy workers. Although the first of these camps, Hunswickel near Lüdenscheid, was established as a measure to improve the performance of Polish labourers in particular, German citizens too were sent to the camp. It was run as a joint venture by the construction firm Hochtief, which provided work, and the Gestapo, which ensured prisoners' surveillance and punishment. Since no trial was required before a worker was sent to such a camp, Hunswickel and the approximately 200 other AELs that opened in Germany and the occupied territories during the war offered a quick and convenient way for factories and police to dispose of people perceived to be a problem. By the end of 1940, Hunswickel housed some 650 prisoners for six-week periods of 're-education'. Conditions in the camp were so poor that 25 per cent of the workers were routinely unable to work. In fact, Hochtief found the labourers who were still able to function so inefficient that it soon pulled out of the arrangement. According to Ulrich Herbert, other firms had come to rely on Hunswickel as a punishment and deterrent, and they quickly stepped in to support the Gestapo's venture. By the end of the war, there were enough spaces in AELs for some 40,000 people at a time, and they had become an essential part of the ever-widening repression apparatus, taking in not only workers but anyone at all whose behaviour was seen to be undermining the war effort.

In some cases, Germans and foreign co-workers laboured alongside one another fairly well. Sometimes, there was even a level of collusion and mutual aid, as workers understood that getting along with foreigners might help safeguard their own position in a factory, not a combat unit. For the most part, though, German workers do not seem to have shown any particular sympathy for foreign workers, nor paid attention to their lives outside of work, their overall treatment, or how they had come to be in Germany in the first place.

Of all foreigners in the Reich, Soviet prisoners of war probably faced the worst conditions. They were treated badly by their German supervisors and many were assigned to do hard labour in the mines of the Ruhr region. Here, a single local miner might both monitor the work and control the bread ration of five prisoners, and opportunities for arbitrary and capricious violence tempted many men.

More fortunate were the labourers and prisoners of war who worked in small businesses and especially on farms, where they provided much-needed replacements for men at the front. On a typical large farm in east Prussia, historian Nicholas Stargardt relates, just one soldier supervised twenty-five French POWs, while on smaller family farms one or two POWs might work during the day and return to shared sleeping quarters, or even stay on the farm unsupervised at night. The relatively relaxed oversight in these situations offered opportunities for fraternization between foreigners and local civilians. However, the regime viewed contact between foreigners and German women, especially, as opening the door to sexual intimacy and racial mixing. Fraternization was particularly dangerous for those seen to be 'racially inferior'. From June 1940 onward, Polish men accused of 'forbidden contact' with German women were hanged in public, the Nazi state and police apparatus stepping in to safeguard, as they saw it, the morality of Germany's women while their husbands were away. Women accused of being involved with 'racially inferior' foreigners were shamed in public, typically by being paraded through the streets with their heads shaved.

In some parts of Germany, this met with the approval of the local population, who believed that it set an example for others. In Thüringia, 800–1,000 people came out to see twenty Poles hanged, and the SD reported that the police turned away 600–700 others. However, in other areas, especially where Roman Catholicism dominated and there was fellow-feeling with Poles and French who were likewise Catholic, people disapproved of public shaming. Some Germans complained about the sexual double-standard being applied to women, but according to Robert Gellately, others thought that the women were as guilty as the men and should be hanged too.

In other countries, intimacy between prisoners of war, specifically, and civilians was forbidden, but the Third Reich treated it as military disobedience and punishments were severe. POWs were tried by military tribunal before being sent to an army prison for several years of brutal forced labour. Women were tried before a Special

Court (Sondergericht) on the grounds that they had 'undermined the national will to resist' (the newly-created crime of 'Wehrkraftzerset- zung'). They were usually punished with two years in the penitentiary (Zuchthaus), and the temporary loss of their civil rights, and they were required to pay the costs of their trial. According to Raffael Scheck, most cases of sexual fraternization with POWs involved Frenchmen, who could move around more freely and had more contact with the local population than other prisoners. The scale of the problem is indicated by the fact that records survive for some 15,000–20,000 trials of French POWs, and 80 per cent of these had to do with forbidden intimacy.

The police became aware of POW relationships through nebulous rumours or a denunciation by neighbours or co-workers. Sometimes, the Gestapo followed up if they found a woman's pregnancy suspi- cious. In close-knit rural environments, some women found it hard to resist the advances of a POW, and although clear-cut cases of rape seem to have been rare, the German judges also tended to believe that a woman should have resisted more vigorously if she did not agree to sexual activity.

Given their overall treatment, it is not surprising that neither foreign workers nor prisoners of war made efficient labourers. Occasionally, the authorities admitted this, and questioned specific measures on the basis of work performance. In spring 1942, Reinhard Heydrich's Reich Security Main Office, perhaps the most radical representative of National Socialist ideological and racial convictions, recognized the fact that food rations for Russian workers were too small to maintain working capacity. Rations could not be augmented, however, because they were being cut for Germans in the same period. The food supply for foreigners was not addressed until German rations rose in the autumn, and it remained shockingly low throughout the war. In this area, as in others, the regime chose to pursue discriminatory policies even when they undermined the war effort.

Public Knowledge of Measures Against the Jews

We can use the occasions when discrimination and inhumane treat- ment continued regardless of economic necessity and the pursuit of war to gauge the depth of National Socialist convictions. Perhaps the best example of this dynamic is the doggedness with which the Third Reich pursued its policies against the Jews. As war went on and anti-Jewish measures escalated, what did Germans on the Home Front know about the fate of Jews and others not considered members of the *Volksgemeinschaft?* Through the 1930s, many reports about the treatment of Jews, political opponents, and other prisoners appeared in major newspapers. Rather than hiding this information, the regime publicized it to reinforce the idea that National Socialism was 'tough on crime'. Repression was depicted as a way to rid the Reich of dangerous enemies, and newspaper readers were encouraged to see themselves as good citizens to which such measures did not apply. Hitler and the heads of police and propaganda both expected, and received, widespread popular support for measures against those defined as outsiders. At the same time, making information about vigorous policing tactics public helped ensure citizens' conformity with government policies.

After the beginning of the war, the media offered less information about repressive measures, but there were still occasional reports. Robert Gellately has pointed out that since the regime was deeply concerned about morale in wartime, press officials who allowed these reports 'must have felt that these stories were worth publishing and would be accepted and welcomed by good citizens'. From 1 September 1941 onward, all 'non-privileged' Jews from age five had to wear a yellow star of David sewn onto the left breast of their clothes. This measure singled Jews out and made them easy targets for popular contempt. The very visibility of the victims also made crimes against them more evident. For those who chose to look, it was clear that Jews were being shut out of public life, and that the total number of Jews in Germany was diminishing. Equally, there were opportunities to see Jews being herded onto trucks, pushed into trains, and carried off first to ghettos, then to death camps in the east.

Citizens also learned about what was happening to Germany's declared 'racial enemies' through letters from the front, such as the letter of Hermann Gieschen quoted above. The information they obtained was diffuse, but Germans knew what was occurring, and to varying degrees approved of it. The National Socialists were very adept at stirring up and reinforcing longer-standing prejudices as they coached people to see Jews as the ringmasters of a worldwide conspiracy to destroy the Reich. This conspiracy was painted as 'Anglo-American' or 'Bolshevik' by turns, but the key figures behind it were always the Jews.

The decrease in information about repression in the wartime media was counterbalanced by ever-growing permeation of German public space by various kinds of prison and concentration camps. Large and longer-standing camps like Sachsenhausen, Buchenwald, and Dachau were located near major cities (Berlin, Weimar, and Munich respectively), and had many satellites. Large new camps opened on the widening borders of the Reich, with inmates who were put to work in agriculture and industry. In easily-recognizable striped uniforms, they were also brought into major cities to clean up after air raids. Throughout the war, there was tension between the inhumane conditions in the camps and the desire to annihilate the Jews in particular, and the need for workers for the war effort. The fact that the National Socialists pursued mass murder even though it would have made sense to exploit camp labour for the war effort underlines the importance they gave to the project of ridding Germany and Europe of Jews.

At times, knowledge of the violence and killing in the east seems to have weighed on the popular mood. Soldiers confided their thoughts about the massive scale, brutality, and senseless violence of the war to their diaries, and shared their worries, and even a deep sense of guilt and shame with their families. Moreover, at least some people drew a connection between Germany's treatment of the Jews, and Allied aerial bombing, seeing the former as a cause of the latter. Popular opinion could be contradictory, however. In May 1943, for example, the SD in Halle reported that people accepted the regime's propagandistic claims that Jews had brought about the so-called 'dambusters' raids on German water reservoirs. Some people's response was to say, 'Kill all the Jews', but the same report cited other citizens' views that official measures against the Jews were irresponsible, for 'if the Jews had not been attacked by Germans, then peace would have come already'. Popular knowledge about what was being done to the Jews, then, was diffuse, often vague, and people responded in various ways. Some supported anti-Jewish measures whole-heartedly and believed that they should continue, while others expressed concern and linked their own fate to German treatment of Europe's Jews.

Carrying on after Stalingrad

With time, the optimistic mood of the war's early years gave way to a dogged sense of simple perseverance. At no point in the war was this change more evident than after the loss at Stalingrad. Through the fall of 1942, public mood had been buoyed by a temporary increase in rations, along with German troops' continued movement forward in the Caucasus. The army had set up an air-mail link to the Eastern Front, which meant that it took only two weeks for a letter to reach home, instead of four. With a short delay, therefore, families were able to follow their loved ones' forward trajectory as General Paulus's 6th Army moved toward Stalingrad. Controlling this industrial city was a key to protecting troops further south. Although Paulus's forces made initial progress in defeating Stalingrad, they were encircled and cut off by Red Army troops. Göring, head of the German Air Force, hastily declared that he could supply the closed-in troops by air, but the needs of some 300,000 men soon outstripped his means. By late fall, food, fuel, and ammunition were desperately short, and an attempt to counter-attack against Soviet forces in December failed. With orders from Hitler to hold Stalingrad at all costs, Paulus initially refused to break out of the encirclement, but by late January his position had become untenable. The remaining German forces surrendered, and in early February the battle was over, the pocket closed.

In the lead-up to this event, Hitler's propaganda had painted Stalingrad as a heroic sacrifice, the soldiers' deaths a tragedy that would be redeemed by victory. Such rhetoric had a longer history in Germany, where it was prevalent during World War One. Now, however, the 'heroic epic' backfired, since no victory was forthcoming and the German population, expecting success, was unprepared for failure. Perhaps most cruelly, the regime exploited the fact that the Soviet Union had not signed the Geneva Convention on the treatment of prisoners to claim that there was no verifiable information about the whereabouts of German prisoners. It did this in order to maintain the myth that the defenders of Stalingrad had died fighting, and to occlude the fact that 90,000 or more men, including many officers, had surrendered. For thousands of families, however, the lie meant months and years of uncertainty as they wondered whether their soldier relatives had died, had been taken prisoner and then died, or might someday return.

Wartime tragedies like this one often spurred Germans to turn at least temporarily to religious authorities, who tried to support and comfort them. Hitler's regime had an uncomfortable relationship with Protestant and even more with the Catholic Church, both of which it perceived as competitors for citizens' loyalty. Ultimately, Nazism was forced to accept the persistence of popular religious belief, however, allowing soldiers to attend church services in occupied areas, and many war victims to be laid to rest by religious, rather than party authorities.

Wanting to maintain popular support for the party in the wake of Stalingrad, Goebbels tried desperately to turn his propaganda around. The Propaganda Minister's well-known Sport Palace speech of 18 February 1943, which followed hard on the heels of the disaster at Stalingrad, spoke of the duty of the German people to fight on, and raised the spectre of defeat. Though films of the speech show the carefully-selected audience reaching a fever pitch of excitement in response to Goebbels' call for total war, in fact, the SD's inquiries suggested many people found the speech and audience response rather fake. Goebbels hoped to ride a wave of popular support toward greater powers to mobilize the Home Front, but for now, the system remained much as it had been.

Women and War

Women comprised the largest group of adults on the Home Front, and their attitudes to war were particularly important. National Socialist policies toward women were contradictory, and became more so as the war went on. On the one hand, the party espoused a traditional view of women as mothers and home-makers, essential care-givers who would both bear and raise future generations of soldiers. It created incentives for marriage and reproduction, and supported mothers' work through programmes like Mother and Child, an initiative of the National Socialist People's Welfare Organization (Nationalsozialistische Volkswohlfahrt or NSV). On the other hand, the regime also opened up opportunities for women outside the home through organizations such as the League of German Girls

(Bund Deutscher Mädel) and National Socialist Women's League (Nationalsozialististische Frauenschaft). It is important not to exaggerate this development, for women worked without pay and, while they were offered some leadership positions, their decision-making power was limited and they always reported to a male superior. Nonetheless, historian Nicole Kramer has pointed out, volunteer work in National Socialist organizations offered self-affirmation, and women used it to their advantage, for instance as a bridge to paying work or as a way to avoid compulsory war service.

The circumstances of war tended to push the regime toward widening women's roles. In the interwar period, opportunities to do clerical work, or take a job in the service sector had arisen alongside older forms of women's employment, for instance in a textile factory, as a maid, or on a family farm. After they came to power, the National Socialists had tried to address the overall problem of unemployment by discouraging women from working outside the home. Marriage loans were available to couples who met the regime's racial criteria, but only on condition that a woman leave her job. In 1937, however, this rule was quietly dropped, because preparing for war had created a labour shortage. The regime sought to exploit women's capacities more fully, though historians agree that it was less successful at doing so than Britain or the United States. Young women without family responsibilities were working already, and mothers with young children found factory work difficult to combine with their household responsibilities. Women's voluntary war work was significant, but industrial production relied far more on foreign workers than on women.

Along with voluntary work, some women took paid employment not only within Germany, but also in European areas occupied by the Reich. As educators and welfare workers, Elizabeth Harvey's research has shown, they spread German culture and National Socialist ideas abroad. As the demand for men in active combat roles increased, moreover, women took over military administrative and clerical roles. Most female military employees were aged between 19 and 35 and had no direct family responsibilities. Historian Karen Hagemann has pointed out that 'The scale of [German] women's deployment far outstripped that during the First World War'. By war's end, some 500,000 worked as military auxiliaries alone, while another 10,000 worked for the Security Service (SS), and 400,000 served as nurses under the German Red Cross. Like their male comrades, these women were away from home for months at a time, and their letters and visits became another conduit through which Germans at home heard about the war. On the Home Front itself, particularly from 1944, increasing numbers of women were deployed to operate radar equipment and spot enemy planes from Flak towers. These roles exposed them to enemy fire in conditions that were for brief periods comparable to those endured by soldiers. Their experiences underline that Home and War Fronts were permeable and interdependent spaces.

Responding to Aerial Bombing

This permeability became most apparent in the context of air war. The first Allied attacks on Germany were not especially destructive, but improved radar technology soon directed bombers more surely to their targets. Raids became increasingly devastating after February 1942, when the British passed a directive promoting area bombing. Spring and summer 1943 were marked by escalating raids on western Germany's Ruhr region, with its mines and industrial firms such as Krupp and Mannesmann. Cities elsewhere were also targeted, and in the last week of July 1943, British and American bombers took turns attacking Hamburg's downtown core. Helped by hot dry weather, incendiary bombs ignited a firestorm in an area the Hamburg Police President later estimated at 22 square kilometres. Within this zone, temperatures grew so hot that asphalt surfaces melted and fleeing civilians became mired in the pavement. The flames sucked oxygen right out of air-raid shelters, suffocating those within and incinerating them until only ashes remained. On the street, the Police President reported, 'Children were torn from the hands of their parents by the tornado and whirled into the flames.' Local organisms to help bomb victims became overwhelmed, and shocked survivors scattered to the countryside, bringing tales of horror that spread across the land. In all, somewhere between 34,000 and 40,000 people died and about 900,000 lost their homes.

Scholars disagree about the effects of aerial bombing on the German population. Soon after the war, the United States Strategic

Bombing Survey concluded that air raids had undermined civilian morale and made a decisive contribution to ending the war. More recently, it has been suggested that bombing gave rise to feelings of solidarity that helped counter its destructive effects on social cohesion. Perhaps the shared experience of trembling nightly in airless shelters as bombs crashed down overhead helped solidify the *Volksgemeinschaft* as everyone was made equal by the bombs.

The National Socialist preoccupation with air raid responses suggests, however, that it saw aerial bombing as a major threat to morale. Responding to raids with hot meals, clothing, and a train ticket to a safer region, the party and its welfare arm, the NSV, sought to demonstrate their concern while becoming involved in Germans' lives as never before. In mid-December 1943, Propaganda Minister Goebbels noted that, 'domestically, we are busy almost exclusively with air war'. Nearly a year earlier, to coordinate air raid responses, the government had established the Interministerial Air War Damages Committee (*Interministerielle Luftkriegsschädenausschuß*), which included representatives of the major ministries, as well as the military, NSV, Reich youth leadership, and other bodies. The director was Goebbels, whom Reich Chancellery head Hans Heinrich Lammers described as 'an energetic personality of high political standing and far-reaching influence on the Volk'. Placing the committee under Goebbels' control underlined the importance of air war to morale.

Bombs had been falling in Germany since 1940 and, as noted above, the Third Reich had engaged in an aerial defence programme with both real and psychological objectives well before that. As they cleared flammable junk out of their attics and blacked out their windows, citizens became Home Front warriors. They learned how to put out fires with water and sand, and volunteer representatives of the party (*Blockleiter* or *Blockwarte*) monitored compliance with air raid regulations. Major cities like Berlin and Hamburg, as well as industrial centres such as Hamm and Essen, built enormous concrete tower bunkers with platforms for anti-aircraft guns. With walls some four metres thick, Berlin's towers accommodated 10,000 people each—still just a tiny proportion of the city's population. Public shelters were also built in tunnels, and urbanites converted the basements of apartment houses so that when warning sirens sounded, they could seize their children and belongings and head below ground. Small-scale shelters offered little protection in the case of a direct hit, but nonetheless, their sleep interrupted night after night, citizens cowered in the dark and dust as explosives thudded to the ground. In addition to the explosives themselves, as in Hamburg, fires caused by incendiary bombs led to enormous loss of life. Overall figures are notoriously difficult to establish, but recent research estimates that between 350,000 and 380,000 people in Germany wcre lost to bombing by war's end.

In the face of this threat, it made sense to evacuate at least society's most vulnerable members from endangered zones. Limited population transfers had emptied the Reich's western border areas in 1939, but National Socialist authorities remained sceptical about the value of large-scale evacuations. They saw evacuations as a cowardly form of flight, and in August 1940, a Luftwaffe report still argued that 'these measures are out of the question for the German Reich territory'.

It came as a surprise, therefore, when a programme to evacuate children first from Hamburg and Berlin, then from other major cities, began in late September 1940. Responding to Germany's intensive attacks on British targets that summer, the Royal Air Force had stepped up its own raids. The increase in bombing, with its potential for causing civilian panic, was probably the most important reason the Germans began evacuating children. The children's programme broke with the pre-war anti-evacuation consensus and provided a model for measures to come. It was later joined by three other kinds of evacuations—voluntary evacuations of adults not considered essential to the economy of endangered areas; dispersals of factories and other installations to the countryside with their employees; and evacuations of civilians who had been bombed out of their homes.

The children's evacuation programme was called the *erweiterte Kinderlandverschickung* (extended programme to send children to the countryside) or simply Kinderlandverschickung (KLV). This term originally had referred to programmes run by the party to provide working-class urban children with a summer holiday in the country. Now, it was adopted for evacuation programmes that were meant to seem like extended summer camps. Advertising evacuations as a health measure might make them more acceptable to parents and it avoided implying that the government was unable to protect people from bombing. In late September 1940, Hitler put Baldur von Schirach, head of the Hitler Youth, in charge of evacuating

10- to 14-year-olds, while children aged 3 to 10 years, pregnant women, and infants were looked after by the NSV. Children from 3 to 10 years stayed with foster families or in a group facility with their mother if she was expecting a baby or had other young children. Older children were accommodated in youth hostels, hotels, and other requisitioned facilities. All children's evacuations were supposed to be free, although the authorities encouraged contributions from parents who could afford it. Throughout the war, parents could also arrange privately for children to live with relatives in safer areas and then apply for evacuees' allowances and benefits.

Children evacuated through the KLV typically travelled by train in groups of 500, or sometimes by river steamer up the Rhine or Elbe, to designated reception areas. Transports were accompanied by a doctor and two or three nurses, with additional NSV personnel as necessary. The camps for 10- to 14-year-olds were directed by staff approved by the National Socialist Teachers' Association (Nationalsozialistische Lehrerbund). There were separate camps for boys and girls, which followed roughly the same schedule of activities, from a wake-up call at 7:00 a.m. to bedtime at 9:00 p.m. Classes were held between 9:00 a.m. and 1:00 p.m., while the rest of the day was devoted to meals, sports, homework, light housework, and political education through radio programmes and films. Children's free time was limited, although certain evenings were set aside for reading or handicrafts. 'Somehow', former evacuee Ida-Luise Voigt remembered, 'we were always busy'. Keeping children busy furthered their education as good Nazis and helped address the serious problem of homesickness. Like other evacuees, 14-year-old Voigt missed her family terribly, though after a few weeks she came to see that, 'I couldn't change it, so I simply came to terms with the situation. Sometimes I wept. But that didn't help either, of course.'

Initially, evacuated children were sent as far away from British airfields as possible, to the southern and eastern parts of the Reich. Some travelled to occupied Poland, and later KLV evacuees went as far afield as Hungary. Anxious parents were reassured that, 'the children will not end up in the regions of our dear "Huns", but rather in purely German [*volksdeutsche*] centres'. By the end of 1942, entire schools were being evacuated together with mothers and younger siblings. This change meant that, from the summer of 1943, the

KLV increasingly blended with the rest of the German evacuation measures.

At the beginning of the KLV, the authorities estimated that about 13 to 15 per cent of Berlin and Hamburg's children probably could be evacuated voluntarily. By the end of the war, the actual numbers were much higher—according to historian Gerhard Kock, 850,000 children between the ages of 10 and 14 were sent to KLV camps, while the same number of 6- to 10-year-olds stayed with foster families, and a further approximately 500,000 were evacuated with their mothers. State-sponsored evacuations alone therefore affected over two million children.

Still, not everyone was invited to join the KLV. A medical examination was imposed to uncover infectious diseases (tuberculosis, polio) and conditions like lice. Children who could not be placed in a normal group setting, or with a family, were sent to specific camps. This included some children with special needs, like the deaf or blind, and children who suffered from minor behavioural problems and chronic bed-wetting. The rules further stated that, 'While registering the children, their worthiness and the appropriateness of their manner is to be verified as much as possible . . . children who are unsuitable due to their behaviour and manner are to be brought together in closed establishments [festen Einrichtungen].' Not only were good behaviour and a suitable manner KLV prerequisites, but Jewish children, children of families labelled 'asocial', and those with serious mental or physical disabilities were excluded. The children's evacuation programme was meant to save lives, but only those of certain children, and evacuations took place on the terms of policymakers, not of the families involved.

Just as evacuation provided an opportunity to bring children together under Hitler Youth leadership and indoctrinate them with the principles of the new state, party authorities exploited war relief to link vulnerable segments of the population to the regime. In responding to aerial bombardments, there was theoretically a division of labour between city authorities, who looked after immediate measures such as housing, and the party, whose responsibilities included 'leadership and care of the population'. The party typically preferred tasks where it could cast itself as benefactor (running soup kitchens, for instance, or distributing clothing), leaving less glamorous clean-up and billeting work to municipalities. Still, municipalities and the party worked together to establish jointly run centres of operations (*Einsatzstellen*) near badly-hit neighbourhoods. Bomb victims were given a hot drink, first-aid treatment, and other assistance by NSV or Nazi Women's Organization staff, supported by female nurses, teachers, and librarians. Personnel at the centres provided basic clothing and cash advances and helped bomb victims fill out damage declaration forms. Victims whose kitchens were unusable received a green identity card that entitled them to assistance and food from municipal, NSV, and army soup kitchens. An official in the Nuremberg area remarked in August 1942 that, 'it makes an excellent impression on the population that all party and state offices work tirelessly to bring swift and adequate relief to Volksgenossen who have suffered losses'.

Since it was impossible to build enough homes to compensate for the destruction, bomb victims tied to the city were billeted in temporary facilities until they could be accommodated elsewhere. Urban homeowners were required to fill out a questionnaire that became the basis for requisitions. The 1943 Order to Control Housing (*Verordnung zur Wohnraumlenkung*) was used to make room for bombed-out families, who in some cases moved into apartments vacated by deported Jews. On the whole, the housing shortage probably weighed more heavily on the working classes than on other groups, for workers' homes were closer to factories and thus more likely to be destroyed. Moreover, it was easier for better-off citizens and those who belonged to the party to find new homes quickly.

Anyone who did not work in an urban area was pressured to leave. Adult evacuees could go wherever they chose at first, but in April 1943, the Ministry of the Interior established a list of designated reception areas that partnered endangered zones with at least one safer southern or eastern area. This encouraged cross-regional coordination and make it easier to monitor evacuees. Residents of some industrial cities in western Germany, for instance, were sent to Baden in the southwest, while most Cologne evacuees ended up in Lower Silesia.

Throughout the war, there were problems with evacuees returning home without permission. The regime tried to prevent these so-called 'wild returns' that used precious space on trains and threatened the orderly pursuit of evacuation measures. By 1943, the flow of returning evacuees had reached alarming proportions, and the authorities responded by denying ration cards to people who came home without permission. Without ration cards civilians could not eat, and the intention was that they would be forced to return to their evacuation zones. However, on 11 October 1943, in the industrial city of Witten in the Ruhr area, 300 citizens demonstrated in response to this measure. Most of the demonstrators were women, though some were accompanied by their children and husbands, who were typically miners or essential war workers. The police refused to step in to break up the demonstration because, they pointed out, there was no legal basis for denying returned evacuees' ration cards, and they agreed fundamentally with the women's demands. Evacuation made no sense for these families, whose breadwinners were not soldiers, but lived at home where it was difficult to manage a household in addition to working long wartime shifts.

At first, the authorities tried to crack down further on 'wild returns'. On 2 November 1943, for example, Goebbels wrote in his diary that 'We must not bend to the will of the people on this point, for the people naturally does not have a clear view of the probable future development of air war.' Later that month, he reported that, 'the most difficult domestic policy issue we face is that of the flood of returning evacuees'. The free flow of people across the Reich overtaxed the transportation system and destabilized food supplies as the authorities struggled to make provisions available to evacuees and urbanites alike. In the end, however, Goebbels changed his mind about bending to the will of the people, and in late January, Hitler ordered that ration cards not be denied to evacuees who returned home without permission. Thus, very occasionally, when members of the German 'national community' objected to specific official measures, the National Socialist authorities changed course.

Growing Threats and Final Collapse

At the same time, when Hitler was faced with direct and openly political attempts to end his rule, he reacted swiftly and with great brutality. After printing anti-Nazi leaflets and writing slogans like 'Down with Hitler' on walls in Munich, the brother and sister student resisters Hans and Sophie Scholl were interrogated for three days and then executed in February 1943. Although these idealists had hoped that their deaths would cause mass rioting, the students at Munich University demonstrated to show their loyalty to the regime instead.

Later, a large-scale plot by members of the traditional military and political elite crystallized in an attempt on Hitler's life on 20 July 1944. Hoping to kill the Führer and then set up a non-authoritarian government that would allow Germany to sue for a favourable peace, the plotters came close to succeeding. However, the bomb that Colonel Claus Schenk, Count von Stauffenberg so carefully planted in Hitler's east Prussian headquarters wounded rather than killing the Führer. After initial disorder and contradictory reports, within hours, Hitler's survival had been confirmed and broadcast across Germany by radio. In the aftermath of the attack, not only the perpetrators themselves, but also members of their families were tracked down, killed, or imprisoned. Rather than weakening popular support for Hitler, the plot tended to augment it, as people expressed their relief that their leader had survived.

By summer 1944, Allied bombing intensified further and it became difficult to deny that Germany was losing the war. Once it no longer had domestic air supremacy, large swathes of land were vulnerable to terrifying raids. Daytime attacks became commonplace, and although these tended to be relatively precise, they were hardly less dangerous than the ongoing night-time area bombing raids. Planes targeted smaller centres as well as big cities, sometimes going after individual trains and streetcars. Implicitly if not explicitly, such raids targeted civilians, for they continued until almost the end of the war, beyond the point where they served any significant strategic purpose. Most notoriously, the city of Dresden was bombed from 13–15 February 1945, at a time when it was clear that the Germans' war was lost. According to Olaf Groehler, over half of the total Allied bomb tonnage fell in Germany during the last six months of the war, and half of the air raid casualties took place after August 1944.

Although propaganda about 'wonder weapons' such as the V-1 and V-2 rockets aimed at Britain sustained Germans' hopes for victory well into 1944, by early 1945, they began to understand the gravity of their situation. Some soldiers surely believed continuing propaganda that Hitler's Reich would yet be victorious, but most fought on because the alternative, total defeat, was unimaginable. As the military clung on desperately, authorities on the Home Front tried to marshal every resource for war. Boys as young as 16 and men over 50 were drafted, but since weapons production could not keep up with demand, these new soldiers were sent off with little equipment and less training. At home, the thousands of women who had already been managing anti-aircraft searchlights and radar equipment were joined by teenaged girls, enlisted so that their male counterparts could be sent into combat. Eating and sleeping where they worked, and trained to use pistols to protect their positions, these individuals took on roles little different from the men they replaced.

Under pressure from every side, the social order began to break down, and the authorities behaved in increasingly arbitrary ways. Although it had always been dangerous to express public doubts about Germany's ultimate victory, now an expression of mild scepticism about the war's outcome might lead to summary justice and death, or internment in one of the prisons and concentration camps that dotted German soil. Foreign workers, especially, drew the suspicions of the police, who often decided it was 'easier' simply to shoot them outright. According to Ulrich Herbert, thousands died in this way in the last days of the war, and records are so fragmentary that the real totals will probably never be known.

Terror also escalated when concentration camp inmates and other prisoners were driven on deadly marches toward the German heartland. The purpose of these marches was partly to safeguard prisoners' last working capacities for the Reich, partly to keep perceived 'enemies' from falling into Allied hands. In the case of the death camps in the east, the intention was also to hide the inhumane treatment and mass killings from foreign eyes. Records and killing facilities themselves were destroyed as the perpetrators realized that they might soon have to face post-war justice. At Auschwitz, prisoners too weak to move were murdered, or simply left to perish where they lay. In the freezing conditions of winter 1945, the rest were ordered to embark on brutal marches that, for the vast majority, ended in death.

Although some people on the Home Front came into contact with straggling groups of prisoners, the deplorable situation of the camp inmates did not touch most directly. They were more concerned about their own situation, which grew increasingly tense as the vice-grip of war tightened around Germany. Fleeing the Red Army in the east and the Anglo-Americans in the west, thousands of civilian refugees flocked toward the centre of the German Reich. In February 1945, the Reich Propaganda Ministry estimated that there were sixteen to seventeen million civilians on the move. Some families were able to get away early and in an orderly fashion, others took up their things hastily and fled in increasing chaos. Some rode trains and found relatives willing to take them in; others' journey involved many days' trekking across open country, often on foot, to find uncertain shelter with strangers.

Although western Germans also fled, the hardest hit were those in the east. By the summer of 1944, it was already becoming clear that military retreat would mean large-scale civilian displacements. Germans feared coming under Soviet control, for rape and cruelty by Red Army soldiers were common, and given Germans' own brutality on the Eastern Front, there was no reason to expect mercy from the enemy. Rather than making timely arrangements to evacuate civilians, policy makers waited until the very last moment to order people to leave, turning evacuations into chaotic and head-long flight.

In these difficult conditions, a bottle-neck arose at Danzig as civilians fled and retreating soldiers were transferred westward to shore up central Reich defences. The western-most stronghold of German east Prussia, Danzig, contained an estimated 1.5 million local residents, plus another 400,000 people in transit in February 1945. While 6,000 Germans left daily by boat and overland 'Trek', another 25,000 streamed into the city each day. On 30 January 1945, the Strength through Joy steamer *Wilhelm Gustloff*, overladen with soldiers and civilian refugees from the Danzig area, was torpedoed by a Soviet submarine off the Pomeranian coast. More than 9,000 of the approximately 10,000 aboard perished in the icy waters of the Baltic sea.

A month later, Anglo-American forces were closing in on the Rhine, and civilians grew disillusioned as they watched National Socialist Party bosses cruising to safety in requisitioned automobiles while other members of the supposed *Volksgemeinschaft* made the trip on foot. Replacing reliance on the party, a strong degree of popular self-reliance arose to compensate for the general administrative disorder of the last months of the war. People made do with what they had, lived where they could find shelter, and waited out the conflict. By the time peace came in early May, the postal service had not been running for several weeks, and many family members had been without news of one another for three or four months, or more. For families from the hardest-hit areas of the Reich, it was a challenge simply to determine the location of one's relatives, let alone to consider bringing them together, finding a way back to the home city, and starting anew. Germany, a modern nation at the heart of Europe, was in ruins.

Conclusion

If the preceding years had not already made clear the artificiality of distinctions between Home and War Fronts, in the final weeks of war, both areas were subject to unpredictable and deadly violence that affected civilians and soldiers alike. Women took on near-combat roles hitherto reserved for men, children and the elderly found themselves exposed to widespread aerial bombing. The Home and War Fronts that had been linked throughout the conflict now became virtually indistinguishable. Certainly, as Kurt F. had realized in 1944, the best places in this war were not in the rear.

Alongside the many connections between home and front, this chapter has also emphasized the extent to which Germany's continued pursuit of war relied on exploiting the European territories it controlled. Occupied areas provided labour as well as food and raw materials for industry. Although civilians did not necessarily acknowledge the change, the Home Front became an international space in which Germans worked and lived alongside Poles, Russians, French, Italians, and other Europeans. Interactions with these individuals ranged from open and sympathetic, in some cases even loving, to harsh and brutal, without recognition of shared humanity.

Controlling civilian interactions with foreign workers and prisoners of war was just one of the ways the authorities tried to direct Germans' behaviour and manipulate morale throughout the conflict. Notwithstanding official fears, civilians' morale did not break down and Germans continued to believe that they would win the war until near its close. Even when they no longer believed, they kept going, with social services and rehousing for evacuees carrying on in the last strongholds right through April 1945. On the whole, the Third Reich's leaders succeeded in their efforts to keep the Home Front satisfied. Hitler and his closest advisors tracked popular opinion, notably through the SD reports, and sometimes shifted policies to take civilians' wishes into account. Through jarring ups and downs and despite many sacrifices, there was no mass turn away from National Socialism. The Home Front's enduring support was a key ingredient in the effective pursuit of war.

10

Decline and Collapse

Robert Gellately

When did the Third Reich begin to decline? Certainly not in May and June 1940, when the Wehrmacht easily defeated France and pushed British forces off the continent. For with those victories Germany looked like a renewed and dominant military power, fully recovered from the disaster of the last war. Moreover, this triumph over old enemies fostered a sense among many Germans that their country had regained its 'rightful place' in Europe. The perceived change in the nation's fortunes was so overwhelming that, according to one official SD (Security Service) report, even 'organized resistance within communist and Marxist circles' had ceased to exist. While that opinion may have been an exaggeration, on the summer day in 1940 when Hitler returned to Berlin from France, the crowds lining the streets outdid the adulation they had showered on him before.

A year later on 22 June 1941, the Reich looked even stronger with the launch of Operation Barbarossa against the Soviet Union. If the German Home Front had been initially cautious, the popular mood soon picked up with the news, which began flooding back from the east about the success of the Wehrmacht. Its forces were sweeping from one victory to the next, while taking hundreds of thousands of prisoners. The Army Chief of Staff General Franz Halder was at first more guarded than many colleagues, at least until captured Red Army generals confirmed to him that on the other side of the Dvina and Dnieper Rivers, or beyond Minsk in Belorussia and Kiev in Ukraine, there were no Soviet armies 'strong enough to hinder German operational plans'. Thereupon, the once-sceptical Halder confided in his diary on 3 July 'It is probably no overstatement to say that the Russian campaign has been won in just two weeks.' Nor was he now alone in his confidence, because informed international opinion, and not just the National Socialist fanatics, regarded the Soviet Union as a 'Colossus with feet of clay'. The biggest question during that summer and early fall, was how long it would take Germany and its allies to vanquish the Red Army completely, and to root out the nest of communists in Moscow for good.

When did the War Become Unwinnable?

During the eastern campaign, the Führer often shared the optimism of those around him. Nonetheless, he also fell into bouts of pessimism and doubt, because in spite of taking vast tracts of territory, the securing of final victory kept taking longer than plans and preparations had anticipated. Then came the autumn rains that turned the dusty roads to mud, bogging down men and machines. At the front lines on 25 October, Infantry General Gotthard Heinrici scribbled in his diary the essence of the problem: His soldiers had the upper hand, could almost see Moscow, and finally had a 4:1 ratio in favour of German to Russian divisions. Yet because of the poor roads, 'We are stuck', he had to admit, with the motorway 'gridlocked for days', making travel incredibly difficult.

Hitler readily grasped the implications, and in a Munich speech on 8 November, he distanced himself from the *need* to win a 'lightning war', the Blitzkrieg, and said with repugnance that he had never used the 'completely nonsensical' term. Indeed, far from winning swiftly, General Friedrich Fromm, as director of the army's armaments effort, came with news on 24 November about the inadequate military production, and his candid advice to General Halder was that they should seek peace immediately. Nor was he the only one gently sounding the alarm, for at a meeting five days later arranged by Minister of Armaments and Munitions Fritz Todt, tank expert Walter Rohland warned of the superiority of Soviet tank production and winter preparations. Moreover, from his knowledge of America's military potential, he surmised that, if the United States entered the war, there would be no way Germany could win it. Then Minister Todt himself astonishingly told Hitler that the task of beating the Red Army was beyond Germany's capability. He added simply, 'This war can no longer be won militarily', to which the unflinching leader then calmly asked 'How, then, shall I end this war?' When Todt replied that the only option was to seek a political solution, the Führer meekly responded: 'I can scarcely still see a way of coming politically to an end.'

What could the popular Führer now say in a speech he had been planning to deliver on the great feats of his armies in their eastern crusade? Then, just prior to his talk, on 7 December and somewhat to his surprise, Germany's Japanese ally struck at Pearl Harbour. Propaganda Minister Dr Joseph Goebbels, who was with Hitler, said the news arrived 'like a gift that fell into our lap'. He noted in his diary two days later of the enormous effect within Germany of the outbreak of war with America in the Far east, 'The whole nation breathes a sigh of relief. The psychological fear of a possible outbreak of war between the USA and Germany has gone.'

Hitler believed that with the Americans in the war, they would be unable to continue aiding Britain and would have to reduce their naval presence in the North Atlantic. Now he could point to the resulting East Asian conflict, to assure his people that they were not taking on the world by themselves. When he finally spoke on 11 December, he confidently rattled off the staggering list of triumphs, the capture of 3.8 million Red Army soldiers, and a vast array of war materials. Even so, some Germans were taken aback to hear him report that their own forces had suffered around 162,314 deaths, 571,767 wounded, and 33,334 missing in action.

In this context, their leader presented the 'good news' of the Japanese attack on the United States, against whom he now needlessly declared war. With this step, Hitler put the final touches to creating what was now the Second *World* War. He claimed that America had been aiding and abetting Britain and the USSR, and so he insisted that Germany had to sink all vessels heading for either country. Then, and increasingly as he would at key moments during the war, he traced the enemy's behaviour back to the Jews. 'We know the power behind Roosevelt', he said, for 'it is the same eternal Jew that believes that his hour has come to impose the same fate on us that we have all seen and experienced with horror in Soviet Russia.'

The next day he met with his trusted Nazi Party *Gauleiter*, the regional bosses he would come to rely on in the latter stages of the war. Although we do not have a copy of that speech, we have Goebbels's substantial report of its contents. In it, Hitler declined to predict how long the war might now last, though he doubted that the entrance of the USA would prolong it. For the coming year he announced that he had 'firmly decided' to conquer Soviet Russia 'at least to the Ural Mountains', approximately 2,000 miles farther east of Moscow. He saw that area as Germany's 'future India', a 'colonial land that we will want to settle'. Did he still think that his merely setting such a goal would make it happen? The harsh reality was that already on 5 December the Red Army had begun pushing Hitler's army back from the gates of Moscow.

General Heinrici, who was on the spot, said in a note he hurriedly scribbled to his wife:

> I am writing with the greatest concern about the events here. The Russian penetrated the big gaps in our thin front at several places and forced us to retreat. We experience the same conditions as in 1812 [with Napoleon], deep snow, almost impassible roads, drifting snow, storms and freezing temperatures. I do not know what will become of it. One can only hope that we will eventually succeed in stopping the enemy. But none of us has the slightest idea how to do it.

Hitler's December speeches ignored any hint of such reversals and offered instead more comforting scenarios, as for example, when he told his Reich leaders, that given the progress of German anti-aircraft defence systems, there was little to fear from enemy bombing, which he wrongly predicted would decline in effectiveness. Inevitably, he touched on the Jewish question, and chillingly reminded his party comrades of his earlier 'prophesy' of what would happen to the Jews should they bring about another world war, as he alleged that they had done in 1914. Hitler had first uttered this threat on 30 January 1939, the anniversary of his appointment as German Chancellor. Now, as Goebbels recorded these remarks, he observed cryptically about the prophecy: 'This is no mere phrase. The world war is here, and the extermination of the Jews must be the necessary consequence. This question must be regarded without any sentimentality.' If the Germans had suffered so many casualties in the eastern campaign, then 'the authors of this bloody conflict must pay for it with their lives'.

In sum, at the end of 1941, with the Third Reich ostensibly still ascending, it was already facing a military crisis, on top of its serious underlying economic weaknesses compared to the combined strength of its enemies, namely the world's three great powers. Hitler responded, not by listening to informed advice, much less seeking a political way out and instead became more aggressive. He fatefully declared war on the United States, added still greater conquests to his imperial agenda, and doubled down on his determination to wipe out all the Jews. Indeed, since June 1941, SS task forces and their local collaborators had been executing hundreds of thousands of Jewish men, women, and children. In October 1941, construction began on the secretive first death camp at Chełmno in the Warthegau, and in November work started at Bełżec, the first of the Operation Reinhard sites whose staggering task was to murder the millions of Jews in the former Poland.

Hitler blamed the failure to knock the Soviets out of the war on his generals, and on 19 December, he dismissed the Commander-in-Chief of the German Army, Walther von Brauchitsch, and took on that role himself. The Wehrmacht lines did not collapse completely under the Red Army's counterattack, so that much to Hitler's relief, during the winter of 1941–2 his armies were not compelled to repeat Napoleon's ignominious retreat of 1812, and yet just establishing and holding defensible positions meant giving up some hard-fought gains, valuable weapons, and even food.

What the German military desperately needed was far more men, for whom it had to compete with the Fatherland's factories and farms. To make up for the shortage of workers, the Reich began recruiting, conscripting, or compelling foreigners all over Europe, especially from Poland, western Ukraine, and Belarus to work in Germany. Nazi racial theory defined these men, women, and adolescents, as 'racially foreign', with the authorities forcing them to wear either a 'P' (for Poland) or 'Ost' (for eastern workers) on their clothes. Nonetheless, even with the contribution of the millions who arrived, personnel shortages persisted in all branches of the economy and in the military.

The Wehrmacht faced tough slogging in spring 1942, though in early summer it began a major new operation on a brief positive note. In his 5 April directive for Case Blue (*Fall Blau*), Hitler boldly stated that its aim was to 'destroy once and for all, the enemy's still remaining military strength', while at the same time both eliminating the key resources of the Soviet war economy and capturing them for Germany. Launched on 28 June, the attack was weaker than the one the year before, and this time at his insistence, it drove not for Moscow, where Stalin had massed Red Army formations in wait. Instead, the Wehrmacht was to hold on in the north, possibly breaking Leningrad, while the main German thrust 'using all available forces' headed south to capture the oil fields of the Caucasus, and secondarily to capture the Soviet armament centre at Stalingrad. Once more, the Wehrmacht travelled exceptional distances, though by now the enemy had learned the prudence of retreat and so largely avoided mass encirclement and capture.

Hitler divided the attack into two wings, with a weaker northern one aiming for Stalingrad, as the stronger advance set out to break into the Caucasus region, initially grab the prize of the Maikop oilfields, and others all the way to distant Baku. Hitler already counted on an invasion in the west in 1942 or at the latest in 1943, so that he regarded Case Blue as absolutely essential for victory in the war. Of course as was to be expected, when on 8–9 August the Germans took Maikop, the Red Army already had rendered its refineries useless. We can gain a sense of the Wehrmacht's overreach at this point by recalling that the distance from Maikop to Leningrad (also a target of Case Blue) measures 1,134 air miles, almost as far as the entire eastern coast of the United States, from Boston to Miami.

The Third Reich Reaches its Peak

The Third Reich attained its greatest geographical reach in the summer of 1942, if we take the area to include Germany's broader sphere of influence, for it then stretched from the English Channel, to part of North Africa, and covered virtually all of present-day Europe. The Wehrmacht in Russia ranged north beyond Leningrad, then south to Moscow, on to Stalingrad, and farther still into the Caucasus Mountains, where on 21 August a few lonely troops made their way on the forbidding landscape and symbolically planted a flag on Mt Elbrus, the region's highest peak. Thereafter, the Third Reich began to contract.

As we now know from German documents recently uncovered in the Russian archives, by the time Hitler met with Head of High Commander of the Wehrmacht, Field Marshal Wilhelm Keitel on 18 September 1942, they knew that Case Blue had failed.

Additionally their meeting at Hitler's headquarters in Vinnytsia, Ukraine revealed a leadership crisis. Hitler was particularly upset by General Franz Halder, head of the Army's General Staff, whom he regarded, along with many of the older generals as 'used up'. They should be replaced by 'fresh' officers with a 'fanatical belief' in National Socialism. Although he sacked Halder on 24 September, that decision was not enough to improve the critical problems that the German forces faced. General Friedrich Fromm, in charge of the army's military supplies, reported to Hitler that the system was breaking down, and he repeated the dire warning he had given the year before, namely, that the only way of avoiding a complete disaster was to seek a negotiated peace. Halder was gone, and yet he had sensibly advised against tackling the forbidding Caucasus, and had spoken of the sheer impossibility of reaching the oilfields in Baku on the Caspian Sea. He had also concluded that Germany could not win the war in the east, and therefore, that it could no longer win the war as a whole. If he and Fromm now were silenced, getting rid of inconvenient military experts such as them did nothing to solve the structural problems facing the Wehrmacht, especially the utterly deficient transportation system, the impossible expanses to cover, and the shortage of well-trained troop replacements and adequate supplies.

Then news arrived at Hitler's headquarters of the deteriorating situation in North Africa, where on 23 October the British Eighth Army at El Alamein began forcing the retreat of the 'Desert Fox' Field Marshal Erwin Rommel. The Führer brushed aside advice from Foreign Minister Joachim von Ribbentrop to put out peace feelers to the Soviet Union. In fact, in his annual speech on 8 November to the party faithful, he explicitly and unequivocally ruled out any negotiated peace.

One of his mantras was that states should avoid negotiating at a time of weakness, a rational dictum in most circumstances, though in this case it ruled out ending the war either short of a military breakthrough or a crushing final defeat. It is also true that the western Allies and the Soviet Union had agreed among themselves that they would not consider any separate negotiations with Germany, and later at the Casablanca Conference in January 1943, Roosevelt and Churchill demanded nothing less than 'unconditional surrender'. Hitler paid no attention to such talk, until he and Goebbels came to the realization that they could capitalize on the Allies' slogan to make propaganda on their Home Front.

Facts on the ground were more difficult to brush aside, as we can see by the fate of the Sixth Army that had entered Stalingrad during the first two weeks of September 1942. When the Red Army counter-attacked on 19 November, in a matter of days it encircled the invaders. Yet Hitler unwaveringly refused the (newly promoted) Field Marshal Friedrich Paulus's requests to attempt a breakout. On 2 February 1943, the Battle of Stalingrad ended with heavy casualties, difficult to estimate and still disputed. Historians most commonly give 300,000 as the number of German soldiers surrounded (recently revised lower), with around 100,000 killed. The Red Army took 90,000 or more prisoners, of whom only 6,000 survived captivity. In this flurry of figures, we often forget that Germany's allies (Romania, Italy, and Hungary) also fought here and suffered grievous losses as well.

The disaster was not merely a question of the Axis powers' mis-judgements, for the tide turned both because of sacrifices of the Soviets and their having outperformed the German manufacture of military arms. Thus, already in 1942, and in spite of losing so many factories and having to relocate others east of the Ural Mountains, the USSR outdid German production of combat aircraft by a ratio of 2:1, small arms and artillery by 3:1, and tanks by 4:1.

As the fates of war inexorably turned against the Third Reich, there were still plenty of soldiers on the Eastern Front like Dr August Töpperwien, a veteran of the First World War, a teacher, a solid Christian, and never a Nazi Party member, who remained deter-mined to stay the course. In his diary for late January 1943, he noted, 'When it comes to people, the others have it over us, just as all together they produce more weapons than we can (USA!). Our confidence can only build on the *belief* in the National Socialist idea.' Therefore, the adversities, the first major defeats, and the poor pros-pects ahead made at least some of Hitler's army more determined to continue the fight and increasingly open to the allures of Nazism.

At his headquarters on 7 February, the German boss resorted to a kind of mythical explanation for what had just happened at Stalin-grad, when he spoke to his assembled Reich leaders, blaming first his allies—the Romanians, Italians, and Hungarians—and then targeting the Jews. The latter supposedly operated 'in all enemy states, as a driving force, and we have nothing comparable with which to counter it. This means that we must eliminate the Jews not only from Reich territory but from the whole of Europe.' As it was, by the time he now spoke of the Jews, it was just over a year since mid-March 1942, and some 75 to 80 per cent of the victims of the Holocaust had already perished in an extraordinary wave of mass murder.

None of this killing, any more than blaming other nations for the defeats, changed the inescapable military conclusions that began to dawn even on the Home Front, where the announcement of the Wehrmacht defeat at Stalingrad, at least according to Goebbels, 'had a kind of shock effect on the German people'. What made the news feel worse was that during the previous three months, the propagandists had led the nation to believe that victory was at hand. Now there was a sense of dismay, and the three days of official mourning intended to mythologize the fallen failed miserably. Goebbels realized too late that such a setback was 'unbearable' for people to face squarely, so that thereafter, news stories about even serious military reversals, took a low-key, matter-of-fact tone.

Partly to counteract the negative public response to Stalingrad, Goebbels finally obtained Hitler's permission to give a big speech on total war on 18 February 1943. In it the Propaganda Minister pointed to the 'immediate danger' that the Jews represented, and stated that 'Germany, in any case, does not intend to submit to this threat but instead to oppose it in a timely manner and if necessary with the most brutal measures'. Then he all but begged 'the Home Front to give evidence of its solidarity' with the troops and to 'take the same heavy burdens of war upon its shoulders'. Indeed, Goebbels had long believed that ordinary citizens would have been willing to sacrifice much more to win, though Hitler's reservations still prevailed.

While Goebbels spoke, more bad news was already in the making on another front, for the struggle in distant North Africa had been relentlessly grinding away, and by May 1943, it finally ended in utter defeat. The Allies took some 250,000 German and Italian prisoners, including what remained of the famed Africa-corps. This loss, in terms of captured and dead, was worse than Stalingrad. Also in May, for want of resources, Berlin had to cut back the submarine warfare in the North Atlantic.

In spite of these setbacks, Hitler said on 15 April 1943, that he 'had decided' on what would be a third strategic offensive against the USSR, which went ahead on 5 July as Operation Citadel. However, this time the enemy designed a defence to exhaust the attacker's resources, after which the Red Army followed up with counter-offensives in what became the Battle of Kursk that dragged on until 23 August. According to Russian sources, the Red Army suffered 863,303 casualties, including 254,470 dead and missing. German losses for the period 5 July to 23 August amounted to around 170,000, with 46,500 of them dead or missing. Although the Wehrmacht took fewer losses, it could only draw on a far smaller pool to find replacements.

Hitler had little choice but to halt Citadel after less than two weeks, which was ironic in that he said when he announced, before the battle began, that 'the victory at Kursk must work as a signal to the world', presumably showing that Germany was going to win against all odds. What should the world now conclude when the Wehrmacht lost? The aim had been to accelerate the breakup of the 'unnatural' political alliance of his enemies, by showing Stalin that the days of easy Soviet victories were over, and so force the Kremlin Boss to seek a separate peace. That effort failed completely, and worse still, according to General Walter Warlimont, present at the Führer's field headquarters, the painstakingly assembled German forces were 'the most important reserves' remaining, and now they 'were in most cases reduced to remnants'. This defeat was, he added, more than a lost battle: 'it handed the Russians the initiative and we never recovered it again right up to the end of the war'.

Afterwards, neither Hitler nor any of his generals came up with another grand strategy. Instead, he substituted a fanatical will to fight in defence of his 'continental fortress' against attacks from all sides. The ever-slimmer hope was that if the war continued, the obvious political differences among the Allies would inexorably lead to a breakup of their coalition, and Germany might be able to work with one side or the other.

War Comes to the Fatherland

The western Allies also moved closer to Germany, for on 10 July 1943, British and American troops landed in Sicily. Capping this development, on 24 July the Italian Fascist Grand Council dismissed Hitler's close ally Benito Mussolini from office. In early September, the Wehrmacht chose to invade Italy and encroached, as far down the peninsular as possible, though that strategy required troops already in short supply. Italy's soldiers had to choose between continuing the war in the ranks of the Axis, or face internment. Of the 600,000 or so who stubbornly refused to fight, and instead ended up slaving in Germany, 'not less than 40,000' and perhaps 50,000 of them lost their lives.

Taken together the significant crises on the battlefields during July 1943 marked another stage on the path to the Third Reich's collapse. On the Home Front, the Allied bombing campaign dominated ordinary people's immediate experience of the war, beginning especially in 1943 when the more than 200,000 tons dropped represented a dramatic increase over the first years. Contrary to the vague predictions of their leader, and in spite of advances in Germany's air defence, the raids became ever more intense and deadly. In 'Operation Gomorrah', for example, the attack on the North Sea port of Hamburg that started on 24 July 1943, and continued unremittingly until 3 August, the bombs created firestorms that incinerated whole areas of the city and killed an estimated 30,000 to 40,000 people.

Goebbels wrote that after the Hamburg attacks, a kind of panic swept the country's imagination, paralysing rather than strengthening the will to resist. Although the evacuees from Hamburg and other such cities drew the nation into the bombing war, they also spread rumours that magnified the horror and the death toll. In south Germany, for example, gossipers doubled and then tripled it, while in Silesia to the east, which until that point remained largely untouched by the bombing war, the exaggerated fatalities jumped to 350,000 in Hamburg. One official account stated that women from that city, traumatized and evacuated to distant Bayreuth in Bavaria, spread a sense of dread, when according to the report, they took their dead children's heads with them. Yet in Hamburg itself after the attack, far from crumpling under the weight of the catastrophe, Nazi Party officials, major industrialists, and the SS regrouped to pursue reconstruction and to increase armaments production.

In eastern Europe on the other hand, after Citadel in mid-1943, the Wehrmacht began retreating. On 12 August, Hitler ordered the creation of an 'Eastern Wall', to match the one along the Atlantic in the west, where the emphasis of the fighting would now shift. He believed that 'the danger in the East would remain', and that the size of the area made it possible to yield a great deal of territory without threatening the Fatherland itself. By contrast, in the west, any break-through would soon encroach on Germany.

As Hitler's army left parts of the east, and on his order of 14 February 1943, his soldiers used 'scorched earth' tactics: burning, destroying, killing, or driving people to the west. The young infantry-man Willy Peter Reese, once a reflective and thoughtful person, now wrote in the midst of this maelstrom, how he 'drifted into a spiritual vacuum. The last of my values collapsed; goodness, nobility, beauty perished; my high spirits left me.' As his unit headed toward the next town, he could see the smoke clouds on the horizon. 'Russia was turning into a depopulated, smoking, burning, wreckage-strewn des-ert, and the war behind the front bothered me still more, because those it affected were noncombatants.'

As if Hitler's troops lacked motivation, on 22 December 1943, their leader took steps to indoctrinate them with an even heavier dose of Nazi ideology. Hence, he established the National Socialist Leader-ship Staff at the headquarters of the Wehrmacht, where he employed experienced Officers (NSFO), modelled on the political commissars of the Red Army whom he once so despised and had earlier ordered liquidated. On 7 January in the New Year, he said that their job at the divisional staff level was to create 'complete unanimity between the leadership of state and the officer corps', for he wanted the entire Wehrmacht to accept the National Socialist body of ideas. Later that month he called numerous frontline commanders for a two-day 'educative course' at Posen and on 27 January, he spoke to them at his headquarters for two hours. The object was to bring them up to scratch on National Socialist ideology, and to prepare them for all eventualities, perhaps even some kind of arrangement with the Soviet Union.

After Stalingrad, Hitler avoided speaking before mass audiences, and throughout 1944, in keeping with the sombre times as well as his fading star power, the Führer did not appear in public even once, though he addressed one Nazi Party assembly, and he spoke twice on the radio. Instead, he buried himself in military matters deep in his underground headquarters, where his glance now shifted once again to the west. Indeed, as far back as 14 December 1941, in anticipation of an invasion along the Atlantic coast, he had already ordered the creation of a line of fortresses from France to Norway. In August the following year, he had expanded that into the Atlantic Wall, which by June 1944 eventually measured 2,685 kilometres along the coast. When Goebbels met with Hitler shortly before, the Führer assured him that whenever the invasion came, it would fail, and when that happened, it would 'accelerate' the supposed crisis in Britain, which in turn would create a scenario there, such as Germany had experienced in its 1918 revolution. Moreover, such a turn of events might make Stalin receptive to some kind of peace.

Hitler put his best man Rommel in charge of defending the western coastline, and they elected a sound strategy focused on the massively fortified and seemingly impenetrable Atlantic Wall. The plan counted on stopping the enemy on the beaches and stamping out the threat there and then, as had happened to the western Allies in 1915 at Gallipoli. However, on 6 June 1944, the western forces' point of attack came as a surprise, and the Atlantic Wall did not after all hold back the invaders for very long. They established a beachhead, and within one month General Dwight Eisenhower, the Supreme Commander Allied Expeditionary Force, had at his disposal one million men, including thirteen American and eleven British divisions, as well as one Canadian, and they soon fought their way through the coastal defences into the hinterland.

The German leaders, in failing to anticipate the possibility that their enemies might break through the 'Rommel belt' quite so rapidly, had no Plan B, nor sufficient reserves beyond the coast. Worse still, their strategic calculation did not take into account that by mid-1944, the Allied air forces dominated the skies, and that 'Fortress Europe', as President Franklin Roosevelt had observed already in an address to Congress back in 1943, 'did not have a roof'. Nevertheless, Hitler was far from simply yielding once the Allies secured a foothold in Normandy. He visited the downcast Rommel in France on 17 June to re-motivate him, succeeded easily in doing so, and then they drew up another defensive strategy that held back the Allies for weeks and then months.

The German military had long reckoned on the Allied landing, as had Hitler, who now visualized the scenario of a swift 'exterminatory battle', a new Dunkirk as in 1940, after which the Wehrmacht's entire armed might would deploy in a new Barbarossa in the east, repeating the successes of 1941. Should his schemes succeed, they would transform an impossible two-front war into two wars, each with a single front. At the very least, defeating the western Allies by pinning them to the beaches might open up options for negotiating a separate peace with Stalin. Consistent with this line of thinking, back on 8 March 1944 Hitler had ordered the creation of a line of 'fortress positions' (*Feste Plätze*) along the Eastern Front, running from Tallinn (Reval) near Leningrad, far south to the Black Sea west of Odessa. His directive stated that each was 'to allow itself to be surrounded, thereby holding down the largest possible number of enemy forces', as castles and fortresses had done in the distant past.

In the meantime, and coinciding with the Allied landing in Normandy, the Red Army had mobilized for a summer offensive named Operation Bagration. Even in its initial phase in Belarus, with at least 1.2 million Red Army troops (not counting partisans), Bagration outnumbered the Wehrmacht troops by a ratio of more than 3:1 and more seriously still, in tanks by 23:1. Finally launched on 22 June, the action coincided with the third anniversary of the German attack on the USSR. Having thus learned from the Wehrmacht, and to multiply their numerical advantage, Soviet forces focused on narrow segments of the enemy's lines. Moreover, with most of what remained of the diminished Luftwaffe tied down in the west, the Soviet air force dominated the eastern skies.

In that summer offensive, the Soviet attacks lasted into August and during that time the Red Army and the Wehrmacht reversed roles from three years before. Stalin's forces now conducted a war of movement as the Germans had done in 1941, while Hitler's army in 1944 had to copy the simple defensive stance of the Red Army from back then. Some Soviet generals in August 1944, and several military experts today, believe that the Red Army could have driven straight on to Berlin, thereby ending the war early. Instead, it stopped at the Vistula River just before Warsaw, where it waited for months, while German forces then mercilessly destroyed Polish resistance forces in the abortive Warsaw Uprising, in another of the many tragic and controversial episodes of the late war.

Historians still argue about the casualty figures in Operation Bagration, but counting its four fronts, and the Red Army's 2.5 million combatants, the Soviets suffered an astonishing 180,040 dead and missing, with another 590,848 wounded. Although the Wehrmacht's Army Group Centre had fewer casualties, it could not replace the 399,102 personnel losses (26,397 dead, 262,929 missing), and 109,776 wounded.

In the midst of this bloodbath, in July 1944 a group of German officers attempted to assassinate Hitler and end the war. The effort culminated when on 20 July Claus Schenk Graf von Stauffenberg planted a bomb at the Wolf's Lair, the leader's headquarters in East Prussia. The Führer survived the explosion, and to prove it, he went on national radio to report, for the first time in all of 1944 until then, that 'a tiny clique' of ambitious, unconscionable, and criminal officers had tried to kill him and his staff. Almost reflexively, he compared the plot to what had happened in Germany at the end of the war in 1918. Some of the conspirators committed suicide when they realized that Hitler had endured, for they knew that as long as he lived, the military elite would never disavow their oaths of loyalty to him. The Gestapo tracked down others and sent them to the People's Court for humiliating public show trials.

Studies of German public opinion generally agree that the attempt on Hitler's life was unpopular with 60 to 70 per cent of the nation, including members of the main churches. Even American surveys of German prisoners of war at the time turned up similar results. Of course, some former Communist and Social Democratic activists expressed disappointment that the coup failed, though on the other hand, there were citizens who said that Hitler had never been radical enough, had left untouched the 'reactionary' aristocracy and officer corps, and should have done more to create a real 'community of the people'.

Even with the Third Reich in obvious distress, it was still dangerous. Before dawn back on 13 June 1944, its flying bombs had targeted London for the first time. Goebbels persuaded Hitler to call them V-I (for *Vergeltung*, 'retaliation') rockets, thereby suggesting they were merely the first in a series of avenging missiles. A bigger V-2, although developed earlier, first exploded in London on 8 September 1944. Behind the bravado, however, Goebbels recognized the gravity of Germany's situation.

The Changing Dictatorship

Within days of the assassination attempt, Hitler decided to reinvigor-
ate his dictatorship by granting 'substantially more powers' to four
individual leaders, each of whom advocated a more radical course in
the conduct of the war. First, there was Minister of Propaganda and
Popular Enlightenment Goebbels, who on 23 July 1944 visited
Hitler's headquarters, and could not help noticing that the Führer
had 'gotten very old'. Still, the minister was pleased to obtain a
Hitler edict that two days later made him Reich Plenipotentiary
for Total War, though he still did not obtain the full social interven-
tionist powers he desired. With reluctance, Hitler soon acceded to
Goebbels's wish to close all theatres, orchestras, cabarets, and other
cultural institutions, and yet the Führer would not hear of stopping the
sale of candy and beer, supposedly because soldiers needed the former
on their way to the front, and Bavarians would be outraged if the state
cut off their beer.

Next among the top four leaders was Heinrich Himmler, Reichsführer SS and Chief of the German police, as well as Minister of the
Interior. Since Stalingrad, the Secret Police (Gestapo), also under
Himmler's command, had been tracking down more vigorously the
'chronic complainers', as well as anyone listening to forbidden
foreign radio broadcasts, and those suspected of 'subverting military
morale'. These police officials, many of whom rotated home from
murderous service in the east, were then less inclined than before to
give such suspects any benefit of the doubt. From mid-1944, in
bombed-out cities like Cologne or Düsseldorf, the Gestapo used
brutal interrogation methods against those deemed 'radical political
enemies', in a desperate attempt to avoid anything like the unrest of
November 1918.

Another in the top leadership was Hitler's deputy, the shadowy
Martin Bormann, who infused his own ideological radicalism into the
Nazi Party apparatus as needed, thereby stiffening the resistance of
activists across the country. Hitler regarded the regional Nazi Party
Gauleiter as his most loyal followers, and increasingly assigned them to
lead the struggle on their home turf. Under Bormann, they became as
of 1 September 1944 also Reich Defence Commissars (RVK), soon to
be responsible for mobilizing the *Volkssturm*.

This new civilian corps established by law on 25 September said that males between ages 16 and 60, who were capable of bearing arms, could be drafted to serve in a new *Volkssturm*, a kind of dad's army that eventually included boys from age 16, though mostly the men were between 55 and 60. This new formation embodied a concept dear to Hitler's heart of a nation in arms. Though based on his September law the regime announced it on 18 October, the anniversary of the 1813 Battle of the Nations at Leipzig, when several powers including Prussia combined to defeat Napoleon. However, in spite of the propaganda fanfare in launching the *Volkssturm*, its very existence was another sign of growing desperation. Although hundreds of thousands of men and boys enrolled, it was poorly armed and amounted to an insignificant military factor. No doubt, their mobilization made controlling these men easier in the last phase of the war, and yet there was more to it than that, because so many welcomed the chance to bear arms against the invaders and participated enthusiastically. Some of its units became involved in guarding concentration camp prisoners and foreign workers, as well as taking care of security after bombing attacks and other such duties that led them 'to make use of their weapons'.

Albert Speer was the last of the four chief power holders and the one usually credited with keeping the war machine going. He had been Hitler's architect since the mid-1930s, and he became Reich Minister of Armaments and War Production after Fritz Todt's accidental death in February 1942. In meetings with Hitler and Himmler from 20 to 22 September, they reached a fateful decision, because Speer and others argued in favour of moving concentration camp prisoners to the industrial sites, while Himmler had wanted to shift more factories to the camps.

Speer won the debate and soon armaments plants and other businesses all over Germany began preparing 'sub-camps' of the concentration camps on the facilities of existing industrial grounds, where engineers and specialists could capitalize on this cheap labour resource. The arrangement was for the SS to provide basic clothing, food, and sentry duty, while the companies supervised the prisoners at work and paid their daily 'wage'—a pittance—to the SS. In addition, the SS had businesses of its own, most notably rock quarries, such as at Flossenbürg and Mauthausen. The system was extensive and public, with for example, the Neuengamme camp near Hamburg, at its peak in December 1944 controlling 46,984 people distributed in eighty-six sub-camps, twenty-four of which were for women. At that moment, the main camp's population counted approximately 11,000.

In spite of ever-increasing Allied bombing, Speer managed an 'armaments miracle' of sorts, at least according to his own propaganda. However, Adam Tooze in a recent critical evaluation shows that while the production of all forms of weaponry increased between 1942 and 1944, the upsurge may not have been such a wonder, because it resulted from forces unleashed in the economy before Speer's appointment. Nonetheless, the considerably increased output happened on his watch, though by early 1945, Allied bombing shredded the 'miracle', for the attackers could operate at will and obliterate what remained of Germany's transportation and industrial systems.

At the national level, even when decision-making powers devolved to the group of four at the top—Speer, Himmler, Bormann, and Goebbels—Hitler retained ultimate authority over them all, including over the military. He kept to his plan for a knockout blow in the west, which finally went ahead on 16 December 1944, with a surprise counterattack through the Ardennes. If word of its early successes briefly raised hopes on the Home Front, the Allied forces on the ground, soon backed by overwhelming air superiority, held on in what became the Battle of the Bulge. Even before Christmas, the German advance began to falter, and within a week, it stalled or failed, though this brief venture bore shockingly high costs. While the western Allies suffered heavy casualties, Wehrmacht figures were only slightly lower, with the great difference being that Germany was unable to field replacements. The failure showed the impossibility of driving the western Allies from the continent, so that henceforth an ever-diminishing Wehrmacht would have to engage in a defensive struggle in the west as well as in the east.

In an effort to raise spirts, Hitler spoke in a national broadcast, in a much-anticipated New Year's address to the nation, only the second time in all of 1944 that he capitalized on using the weapon of the radio. He swore that there would be no capitulation, and no repeat of the mythologized 'betrayal' of November 1918. In his proclamation to the Wehrmacht on 1 January 1945, he said the troops knew they were in a 'struggle for life or death! Because the goal of the

Jewish-international world conspiracy opposing us is the extermination of our Volk.'

Hitler's air force adjutant Nicolaus von Below recalled that Luftwaffe boss Göring assembled 1,000 of his remaining aircraft for a major offensive on 1 January 1945 against various targets on the western border, seeking to open a 'successful' New Year with his own miracle. However, the planes ran into stiff resistance and worse still, on the journey home 'friendly fire' from German positions shot down many of these irreplaceable machines, a mistake that resulted from the 'top secret' nature of their mission. Then only a month from the end, the air force desperately created its own version of kamikaze airplanes *Rammjäger* (Ramming Fighters), which would attack either enemy power stations or key bridges to stop invading troops, with pilots bailing out at the end. Yet on 7 April, when used for the first time, the massive number of Allied fighter escorts accompanying the American bombers shot down most of the 180 German planes flown into battle. The irrepressible Dr Goebbels insisted that after a first trial of these ramming fighters 'the experiment need not yet be written off as a failure'. Remarkably, this endeavour had more volunteers (a reported 2,000) than machines, and in any event, the scheme like the Third Reich simply ran out of time.

Ordinary German citizens most feared the approaching Red Army, which on 12 January 1945 in another gigantic operation using 2.25 million men in nine army groups, began its Vistula–Oder attack along the entire front. While they bypassed Hitler's 'fortress positions', these still disrupted communications and slowed progress. Then, on 15 February, Soviet forces called a brief pause, partly because of a desperate German counterattack and the strain of fighting over long distances for such an extended period. The Red Army had fought its way nearly 300 miles across Poland and East Prussia and now stopped at the Oder River, in places less than 50 miles from Berlin.

In their memoirs, some of the Soviet generals said that when they returned to Moscow for consultations, Stalin told them of Germany's efforts to find a separate peace with the United States and Great Britain. For that reason, the Soviet aim to take Berlin could not afford to fail, or the western powers would capitalize and capture this ultimate prize. It is true that there were some regional negotiations in Italy with the western Allies, but they would never have agreed to a separate deal with Germany, though Stalin suspected the worst, particularly as regards capturing Berlin. As for Supreme Commander General Dwight Eisenhower, he estimated that they could not beat the Red Army to Berlin, it would be foolish to try, and the effort would have cost the lives of perhaps 100,000 of their men. It was not until early March that the Allied forces in strength had finally crossed the Rhine River, after a ferocious battle at the Remagen Bridge. By 1 April, they breached the Siegfried line, and by encircling the Rhine–Ruhr, captured 320,000 troops. Next Eisenhower and his strategic planners conceived of two advances, one north to isolate German forces in Norway and Denmark, and a second to head south of Berlin, to cut off escape routes where the Wehrmacht might make a last stand. This attack would stop at the Elbe River, 40 miles short of Berlin.

In keeping with established procedures, General Eisenhower sent Stalin a copy of this strategy on 28 March, a step needed to systematize communications and to determine how each side could recognize what the other was doing. This message went via the American military mission in Moscow, though by the time it reached Stalin on 31 March, the Red Army leaders he had recalled for consultations had arrived. They heard from Soviet intelligence of an alleged 'US–British Command under Montgomery' that was preparing to take Berlin in order to wrest the fruits of victory from them. There was no such plot, though Stalin used it to fire up Marshals Zhukov, Konev, and Rokossovsky, in order to get them to drive on their troops at any cost to get there first.

In Moscow on 31 March, Ambassador Averill Harriman and British ambassador Clark Kerr presented Eisenhower's plans to the Kremlin. 'Ike', they told Stalin, had said that Berlin 'was no longer a particularly important objective', and the Soviet boss agreed that the German capital 'had lost its former strategic importance'. Perhaps he thought that the Americans and British were merely spreading disinformation, though he lied when he then said the Red Army would be sending only 'secondary forces' to Berlin. In fact, the Soviets would mount a gargantuan operation. The mutual suspicions provided a foretaste of the political differences on which Hitler had long counted, though the east–west divide came to the surface only after he and his regime ceased to exist.

The Fatherland in Disarray

Albert Speer took a brief tour of western Germany and on 14 March 1945, he told Goebbels bluntly, 'Economically speaking, the war is lost.' He said that at most the economy could hold out for another four weeks, after which it would disintegrate. In response to the dire situation, Hitler issued a 'Nero Order' on 19 March to destroy everything of use to the enemy, including all 'military, transportation, communication, industrial, and supply facilities, as well as material resources within the territory of the Reich'. Speer would not follow this order and his disagreements with Hitler led to a break in their close relationship. Nevertheless, by the end of the month, Speer mended things and designed another plan to reorganize Germany's remaining weaponry.

Between January and April 1945, in conversations with Hitler recorded by Goebbels, the Führer continued to waver about whether it would be better to try opening talks with the east or the west. He inevitably concluded, as he had since late 1941, that for a political solution to be possible at all, his own forces had to strike a limited military success somewhere. Goebbels grew slightly alarmed by this dithering, while Anglo-Americans advanced on the capital with little opposition. Just as he continued trying to interest Hitler in putting out peace feelers, the Führer persisted in believing that the enemy coalition had to break up. The propaganda chief attempted for days to convince the man at least to speak on the radio to inspire the sagging morale of the army and the people. However, even the best propaganda has limits and cannot convince people they are winning the war when bombs rain down every night and enemy aircraft find next to no opposition. Perhaps recognizing that limitation, Hitler developed an aversion to the microphone that Goebbels found 'incomprehensible'.

The human face of the Fatherland had changed also because of the 7.7 to 7.9 million foreign workers (as of 1945) inside Germany. It might seem obvious that importing these men and women mainly from Poland and the western Soviet Union, all of them officially deemed 'racially inferior', contradicted the project of building a race-based 'community of the people'. On the other hand, the very presence and stigmatization of such outsiders labouring at menial tasks in factories, on farms, or in the home, provided daily reminders to the 'master race' of its own privileged status, and in any case the workers were desperately needed for their labour.

As the liberating armies grew closer, some of these foreign workers dared to show mild 'disrespect' for their employers. Alfred Rosenberg, Nazism's self-proclaimed ideologist-in-chief, who withdrew to a refuge outside Berlin in July 1944, was concerned that women from the east 'were walking around quite naturally, some gloomy and pinched looking, others broadly laughing'. 'To think', he wrote in his diary, 'that *these* kinds of humans might savage us if the Eastern Front were to collapse.' Such worries were widespread and culminated on 1 November, when the Berlin headquarters of the Gestapo delegated authority for 'special handling' (executions) to its regional centres. Soon hundreds of foreign workers were shot or hanged for the smallest crimes, like 'plundering' when they were found with a piece of soiled bread from a nearby train wreck. Various motives drove the local Gestapo's fanatical activities at war's end, though they took out their spite especially on the foreign workers, leaving (variously estimated) 10,000 to 30,000 victims in fresh mass graves that the Allied armies discovered sometimes only days later.

The police kept foreign workers—at least those not working on farms—'apart' in separate camps on factory grounds, subjugated in varying degrees of severity. The appearance of these places, ringed with barbed wire and guards, merged imperceptibly with the thousands of concentration camps that by war's end also invaded every corner of the Fatherland. We need to distinguish the latter from the death camps, which the SS dissolved back in 1943 and 1944, after perpetrating the single biggest murder of the war in the Operation Reinhard camps at Bełżec, Sobibór, and Treblinka. Those death mills killed 1.7 million Jews before the SS closed them down in October 1943. Only in January 1945 did they evacuate Auschwitz-Birkenau, the biggest single killer of all, where around one million people died.

In addition to the secretive death camps in Poland, networks of concentration camps and hundreds of their sub-camps, mostly with non-Jewish prisoners, spread like a cancer across Germany by war's end. Whereas in October 1934, the camps had all but disappeared, in 1936 Himmler and Hitler agreed to retain some of them and to give them new missions. However, it was in the war that this system really expanded. Even though the guards worked thousands to death each month, the total population of the camps increased dramatically, so that already in September 1942 their population reached into the six figures. The last census on 15 January 1945 counted 714,211 prisoners who now faced evacuations, processes that would turn into death marches, when the SS ordered weakened men and women to move out for unknown destinations (see Appendix).

Although some historians suggest that the SS intended to kill all the Jews on these marches (they made up between one-third and one-half of those involved), a more likely explanation is that the SS and Himmler wanted to retain the largest (if weakened) remaining pool of labour available, perhaps to continue the fight. In fact, in the first months of 1944, Hitler agreed to allow Jews once more to re-enter Germany, and in April, he authorized Speer to use 100,000 Hungarian Jews on various projects. More arrived from elsewhere in the east and in late summer 1944, around 40,000 of them ended up in sub-camps outside Munich, and still others came later to work elsewhere, including far to the north in Hamburg. These efforts strongly suggest that the motive behind evacuating places like Auschwitz was to exploit prisoner labour, though it was true that the guards persistently worked Jews to death.

The forced evacuations of the camps also occurred in the context of orders from Hitler to move out the entire population of areas of Germany directly threatened by the approaching enemy. Goebbels admitted in his diary that in some of the western areas civilians refused to move and that his leader's commands were 'academic exercises', for no one listened. Nevertheless, he added on 26 March 1945, 'the Führer is right since any human, material, or economic potential which we allow to fall into enemy hands will be turned against us in a very short time.' An additional worry, mentioned at the same time in conversation between Speer and Hitler, was that released or escaped prisoners might cause an uproar as enemy troops approached. Hitler said bluntly that if provisions failed, they should 'clear the camps' and if there was no transportation 'kill the prisoners and bury them'.

Local studies reveal that city officials and high-ranking industrialists had motives of their own, for example in Hamburg, where they took the initiative by starting negotiations with the SS to clear the city and factory premises of concentration camp prisoners in order to present a cleaner image to Allied troops when they arrived. Whatever the origin of the orders to move out the prisoners, the tragedy is that around 70,000 perished in this harrowing process. Often these unfortunates travelled through inhabited areas, so that their misery and often-horrific deaths became a public emblem of the apocalyptic end of the Third Reich.

'Community of the People' on the Way to Collapse

Since 1944, the Fatherland had long ceased being the idyllic Heimat of old. The bombing of Dresden on 13–14 February 1945 became a symbol for all that had been lost, a city considered by many as relatively safe because it was supposedly not a military target. The death toll ran up to an estimated 25,000, one of the few such events to provoke some discussion among the Allies, especially since on 18 February the American press carried stories of 'deliberate terror bombing' to hurt German morale. Goebbels jumped on the story and multiplied the Dresden death toll ten times, up to 250,000, a figure that then circulated in the Allied press as well. Ultimately, Winston Churchill issued a mild protest about what he called 'mere acts of terror and wanton destruction'. Though whatever the Prime Minister's reservations, which only came to light years afterwards, historian Richard Overy shows that British bombing of cities persisted in ways 'that were evidently punitive in nature and excessive in scale'.

In the midst of the chaos, what remained of Hitler's project of building a community of the people, the vaunted *Volksgemeinschaft?* He mentioned the topic often in his wartime speeches, and again in his speech of 30 January 1944, the anniversary of his appointment as chancellor, when he touched on the achievements that had made it possible to stand up to the enemy onslaught from all sides. He pointed with pride to what he and the German people had completed together and he applauded the inclusionary/exclusionary aspects of the German revolution, with its 'tremendous domestic cleansing and construction efforts'. That work on society had been necessary at the beginning of the regime, so he claimed, because Germany was 'itself so ill at the time, so weakened by the spreading Jewish infection that it could hardly think of overcoming the Bolshevik danger at home, not to mention abroad'.

Then Hitler put at the top of his achievements, the 'building of the German Volksgemeinschaft', this Germanic community, by 'the gentle as well as dogged conversion of the former state of classes into a new socialist organism'. That step, so he asserted, 'made it possible for the [new] German Reich to become immune to all attempts at Bolshevik infection. One decisive accomplishment of the National Socialist revolution is that, in this state today, every young German, irrespective of his birth, origin, wealth, the position of his parents, so-called education, and so on, can become whatever he likes, in accordance with his merits.'

He briefly returned to the topic in his last radio broadcast on 30 January 1945, when in spite of the obvious decline in the situation on the battlefront during the previous year, he persisted in seeking some kind of meaning in all that had happened since the distant days of his return from the First World War. Pronouncing the liberal social order and age of individualism as decayed and finished in 1918, he said that communities of the people were replacing the 'bourgeois states' that remained. Moreover, as he now saw things looking back, when he came to power in 1933, a fierce struggle against 'Jewish-Asiatic Bolshevism was already raging', like a fight against a disease, to which Germany would already have fallen prey, were it not that National Socialism had carried out a 'gigantic economic, social, and cultural reconstruction'. In his attempt to boost morale and to rationalize his own failure, his speech suggested that as horrid as were the misfortunes to befall the country in the current war, the misery and mayhem would be infinitely worse 'should the plutocratic-Bolshevik conspiracy win'.

Whereas many earlier historians commonly emphasized that terror was essential to keeping the Home Front from yielding to the Allied attacks, recently and in contrast Nicholas Stargardt rightly insists that terror was never the only or even the most important reason that people held on, because for the majority the war remained legitimate, perhaps more than Nazism itself. Of course, it is also true that these civilians and soldiers, in defending their country, helped to maintain and validate Hitler's National Socialist dictatorship and to keep it functioning.

One educated Wehrmacht officer, Dr August Töpperwien, a non-Nazi whose diary turned up not long ago, illustrated the will to carry on, for in late 1944 he welcomed the fact that his teenage son had been called up and he *wanted* his wife to serve in some way. 'There has never been a Christmas like this', he wrote on 22 December, 'Defensively, the entire Volk in arms, men and women, young boys and girls! The front everywhere, out there and at home! Merciless necessity!' Six days later, he noted that a military catastrophe was at hand and that Germany was bound to suffer terrible punishment. Nevertheless, he did not blame the Führer, because 'Nobody but he found the courage to act', presumably against Bolshevism, now moving ever closer from the east.

Although many historians insist that Hitler failed to build the new society, some of the German POWs secretly recorded by the Allies during the war, would seem to disagree. One captive officer in Britain put it this way: 'This principle of everyone working for the common cause, the idea of the industrialist is really the trustee for the capital represented by German labour and for the other capital, all sounds so easy, but no one managed it before.' Indeed, historian Norbert Frei has suggested that after the spring of 1933 and the violence used to eliminate parties and trade unions, the new regime began a serious and systematic effort to win over the 'German worker' and that 'before long these efforts had considerable success'. Recently German writer Maxim Leo, after speaking with his grandparents and looking at family diaries and letters, concluded his family history with the remark, 'Hitler made the little people big and the big people little.'

Social levelling never went quite that far, and the Third Reich could hardly have wiped the slate clean of all previous social classes, attitudes, and customs during its brief existence, any more than it could have established a utopian society. Nevertheless, it does seem that psychologically many in the nation felt the new dawn was on the way, at least during the years of triumph. It is true that during the war, corruption and favouritism became routine, especially in the occupied areas, though some of the fruits of that exploitation—such as goods stolen from the Jews—trickled down to ordinary people back home. We should note that the new society never aimed for complete equality, because the future idyll would be for heathy Germans only, while the infirm and a long list of social outsiders would face pitiless elimination.

Any explanation for how the Home Front coped with the massive destruction and death during the latter part of the war has to take into account the willingness of citizens to participate in numerous forms of self-help. While the Allies hoped to demoralize the population and alienate it from the regime, the bombing increased popular participation in self-protection organizations and institutions, regarded by the regime itself as needed to bind the new community together. In fact, German scholar Dietmar Süss recently hypothesized that the bomb shelters may have helped to transform the community of the people into a genuine *völkisch* community, for they included all 'racial comrades', young and old, though they notably refused entry to any Jews, stigmatized with the yellow star, who might still be in Germany.

We can follow these developments to some extent also in the diaries from those times, including the extensive one of Joseph Goebbels. He wrote of his disappointments in the morale of the troops and of the people especially after the Americans began crossing the Rhine at Remagen in March 1945. Reports streaming in to him spoke of war-weariness, which he fully understood, given the unremitting and now virtually unopposed air attacks. On 20 March when one of the party *Gauleiter* asked for fresh arguments to use in order to raise some hope in victory, Goebbels admitted, at least in his diary, that he had no satisfactory answer. Another regional leader explained to him a few days later, that people were 'so worn down by the months and years of enemy air raids that they prefer an end to this horror rather than an endless horror'. Some of these party bosses could not (or would not) follow Hitler's repeated orders to evacuate areas close to the fighting in the west, because citizens stubbornly refused to leave their homes. Party members or otherwise, they believed they could expect better treatment where they were rather than in the east which the Red Army already had under threat. Therefore, cracks inevitably appeared in the solidarity of the bond between the community and the dictatorship. Moreover, as enemy soldiers appeared before a city, town, or village, local residents, prominent citizens, and factory owners, some of them loyal Nazi officials or mayors, pleaded with the Wehrmacht to withdraw, in order to save their homes or businesses from destruction. When the SS, Gestapo, or the military encountered any such dissent, they usually crushed it mercilessly.

On the ground, events varied enormously by locality, with the Wehrmacht fighting to the death against hopeless odds in one place and elsewhere throwing away their weapons and surrendering without a struggle. During the last five months of the war, 1,540,000 Wehrmacht deaths occurred, which is to say that around 11,846 members of the Wehrmacht (including POWs) died every day during the final, hopeless struggle. Moreover, in the last seventeen months of the war, the Allies released three-quarters of all their wartime bombs, and caused approximately two-thirds of all bombing deaths, estimated most recently at between 350,000 and 380,000. Around 80 per cent of these fatalities were German civilians, meaning a significant number of the others were prisoners of war, foreign workers, or concentration camp prisoners.

The regime mobilized the ubiquitous Nazi Party block and cell leaders, and urged them to visit households regularly, not just to police them in the narrow sense, but also to assist the bombed-out, and to comfort widows, wounded soldiers, and so on. As the situation on the battlefront grew steadily worse, Berlin ordered more outright terror on the Home Front, signalled for example on 15 February 1945 when the Justice Ministry introduced new summary courts martial to dispense harsh lessons to anyone supposedly endangering morale, such as by 'plundering'. On 9 March, the regime created the new 'flying courts martial' to mete out executions even more expeditiously. One of these sentenced to death over fifty people, including hanging a well-respected local man in front of his home only days before American forces arrived in Zellingen am Main. Elsewhere, the victims included those daring to try surrendering their town in order to avoid needless loss of life or property. Another public symbol of defeat became the hanged soldier or Nazi Party leader for alleged dereliction of duty. In April, Himmler ordered even the Wehrmacht to shoot on the spot all men in the household of anyone showing a white flag or bedsheets, and to burn their home down.

We can reconstruct these everyday life and death stories at war's end, particularly the German on German terror, mainly by using the evidence collected for the many trials western and eastern Germany carried out after 1945. The Foundation for Research on National-Socialist Crimes, Amsterdam, had published innumerable such cases in its sixty-three volume series, *German Trial Judgments Concerning National Socialist Homicidal Crimes*. In my book, *Backing Hitler: Consent and Coercion in Nazi Germany*, I used some of this material to show how people experienced terror as increasingly capricious. If during the six years of peace, the police aimed primarily at the communist under-ground, social outsiders, and the Jews, in the last six months, no one was entirely safe and countless officials at the local level lashed out viciously.

Civilians reacted in many ways to feelings that the war was lost. In western Germany, for example in late March 1945, women in Sieg-burg demonstrated in front of the town hall and demanded that troops lay down arms, and there followed similar events in small towns like Ochsenfurt, and the next month in Windsheim and Gerolzhofen. In Trossingen, local Nazi leaders went further, refused to establish a *Volkssturm*, or implement Hitler's Nero order, which in effect would mean they would have to torch their own businesses. Instead, with others they negotiated with the German and French military for a peaceful handover of the town. On the other hand, not far away in Heidelberg, women and girls, young boys, old men, and hospital patients took up arms against even the western invaders.

In eastern Germany, the struggle was far more desperate and bitter, with the overriding motive to do everything possible to hold back the Red Army and its threatened rape, pillage, and plunder. Here mem-bers of the military, SS, Nazi Party, *Volkssturm*, or local administrators constituted themselves as judge, jury and executioners, and uncere-moniously shot or hanged not only obvious enemies, like escaped prisoners. They used the same means against their own people and on the slightest pretext. For example, in a village east of Dresden when overrun briefly by Polish troops in April 1945, a German had acted as translator. When the Poles withdrew, the people returned and set upon the man as an obvious 'traitor' that the SS then executed. At the same time in Berlin, civilians branded another translator as a likely 'spy' and took care of him.

Here are several examples drawn from the more recently published trials carried out in the German Democratic Republic (of East Germany) after the war. In the first of these, we read some details of how in late 1944 and early 1945, marches of concentration camp prisoners and POWs crisscrossed the country. Several of them passed through Frankenhain in the first days of April 1945. A post-war court heard that when any of the unfortunates tried to escape, the SS guards shot them, though some got away. One local man, a 33-year-old worker and proud SA man found five of them (males) in telltale camp garb. He got help from another SA member, and together put the five exhausted escapees on a wagon, brought them to a river, and shot them one at a time. Another illustrative case from this region occurred in Schwedt on the River Oder, when in February 1945 a 'flying court' led by the notorious SS-Obersturmbahnführer Otto Skorzeny met in town and sentenced at least ten members of the Wehrmacht to be shot or hanged, allegedly for refusing to fight. The 'court' also decided in the blink of an eye to execute the mayor of Königsberg (Neumark), who apparently had turned up in Schwedt without proper papers to leave his city. Skorzeny wanted local (and elderly) police to carry out the task and to provide a 'schooling', which meant a deliberately gruesome public hanging. A passing solider noted in his diary that, in addition to the mayor, they executed an air force general in charge of Königsberg airport, allegedly for not defending it. The same fate befell four soldiers, and all their bodies were to hang in place for several days. These scenarios developed in eastern Germany, though such cases occurred all over the country, as the bonds of civilization disintegrated. These post-war court cases reveal murder and mayhem in seemingly infinite variations, with many events that defy the imagination, as what remained of religious teachings and social mores collapsed.

A final case from the east involves suicide, common enough among prominent members of the party, and yet far out in the provinces, the rank-and-file took their own lives as well. Thus, in a small village in Schwerin directly south of Wismar, a family with four children in early May 1945, together with two grandparents, decided to commit suicide rather than fall into the hands of the approaching Red Army. The men led their dear ones to a nearby lake, and after drowning them—with some of the children resisting—the two decided against killing themselves after all and returned to the village, blaming the Soviet forces for what had happened to their missing families. Only years later did the police catch up with these culprits.

It is nearly impossible to calculate the rate of civilian suicides, though the most graphic scenes of mass suicide happened in the east, notably in Demmin, a small town in present-day Mecklenburg-Vorpommern, where as many as 900 or even more people, especially women, killed themselves just before or slightly after the marauding Red Army arrived on 30 April 1945. In fact, dozens of other places along the Soviet-German Front line recorded similar mass suicides, each taking the lives of hundreds, as if in a kind of mass epidemic, when in a 'frenzy of emotions', thousands of ordinary people took their own lives. Some simply despaired or guessed that Stalin's troops would soon have the run of their city or town; women in particular could no longer face the plague of rapes, while people such as Magda Goebbels in the Berlin bunker with her husband said she did not want to live in a world without Hitler and National Socialism. A handbook from 1949 on 'Berlin in Numbers' put the late-war suicides for the capital city at 7,057 a figure that some historians consider too low. Once the Soviets arrived, all civilians had to fend for themselves, because Red Army soldiers driven by revenge and all kinds of other motives, committed unspeakable outrages particularly against women. Anyone wishing to learn more should start with one of the most harrowing documents from that time, written by an anonymous person, *A Woman in Berlin*.

The Imponderables of War

Even in the midst of the seemingly irreversible tides of war, Hitler came to have faith in some sort of wonder, such as the death of one of his prominent enemies or the dissolution of an enemy's alliance, as happened in the time of Prussia's famous King, Friedrich the Great (1712–86), during the Seven Years War. On 12 April 1945, when President Roosevelt died suddenly, Albert Speer later reported Hitler's jubilation, with the ailing Führer showing him a newspaper clipping: 'Here, read it'! He continued: 'You never wanted to believe it. Here it is', he stammered, 'Here we have the miracle I have always prophesied. Who was right? The war is not lost. Read it! Roosevelt is dead!' Goebbels and even some hard-nosed generals believed that just as the passing of the Tsarina Elisabeth had saved Friedrich the Great, now fate would rescue their side after all.

A slightly more credible witness in the bunker seems to have remembered this event differently. Air force adjutant Nicolaus von Below recalled that Goebbels, while overjoyed at the news of FDR's demise, Hitler 'was more sober, without great optimism, though he still did not dismiss that the death could have political consequences for us'. Their joy, such as it was, about the fate of their old enemy did not last long, and yet even their fleeting hope suggests that Hitler did not want defeat, much less that he intended it to happen or that he had 'choreographed' it. Vienna soon fell, not long after that fighting collapsed in the Ruhr, and within the week, the Red Army started its final attack on Berlin where it continued to face bitter opposition.

Certainly not everyone had identified with the mission that Hitler and his movement had espoused, though by the latter 1930s, the great majority, with varying degrees of enthusiasm, had come to accept some or even much of it, and they continued doing so into the war years. To a similar extent, many shared the ambition of striving for a new National Socialist society, a racially based *Volksgemeinschaft*, and a great many were prepared to accept the exclusion of disliked or despised social outsiders. At a minimum, they went along with 'pushing out' the Jews, and some people rushed in to gather the spoils that remained when the Jews were gone. Christopher Browning may be right to suggest that the regime displayed 'unease about the extent of popular support for genocide', though Hitler and Goebbels said in public more than once, what they wanted to do, without spelling out the precise details. Of course, the Holocaust was not only about German behaviour, for the anti-Semitic crusade found an abundance of enthusiastic collaborators all over Europe, particularly in the east, where most of the murders occurred.

During those last months, Hitler occasionally ranted against his 'unworthy' nation, and he denounced them in Social Darwinist terms as deserving their fate. Yet for perspective, we need recall the leader's life-long valorization of all things German or glance at photos of the beaming Führer among the swooning crowds during festivals in the 1930s, which convey the overwhelming impression of a loving relationship that grew strained at the end. It would be an exaggeration to claim that Hitler was not a German nationalist, because from his youth the future leader passionately believed in Pan-Germanic unification and he kept that faith to his dying days.

Into April and May 1945, relatively few inside Germany took defeat as inevitable, for at every stage on the road to the end, there were many thousands in the military, the Nazi Party, the SS, or among the civilian volunteers who patched things together. Their mood (*Stimmung*) was no doubt dark, though their attitude (*Haltung*) was to carry on. They did so in spite of failures or hurried retreats, no matter how devastating the bombing raids and the destruction. Some civilians and soldiers kept going out of fear of retribution, worry about the Red Army's promised revenge, hatred of the Allied bombings, or because of the Nazi regime's outright reign of terror during the last months of the war. It is also true that some people surrendered, waved the white flag, and that there were troops who threw away their weapons, not unlike the situation in Hungary at the end, where whole SS panzer units gave in without a fight. Nevertheless, it would be a mistake to underestimate the abundant evidence of the persistence of the German spirit of self-sacrifice, whether in the name of the cause, for the nation, the home town, or for the sake of 'doing the right thing' with the enemy at hand.

On 16 April, the Soviets began a final assault on Berlin, throwing an estimated 1.5 million troops against a hopelessly outnumbered and outgunned defence. Even in his memoirs, Marshal Zhukov, the man who led the charge, persisted in repeating 'the need' to get to the capital as quickly as possible to subvert a suspected western Allies' plot with certain Wehrmacht units to rob the Red Army of its victory. Thus, once again, Soviet forces took unnecessarily high casualties, and the capture of Berlin, counting only from 16 April and using Russian sources, cost the lives of 78,291 out of 352,475 Red Army casualties.

Adolf Hitler, now prematurely aged, sickly, and reduced to hiding in his Berlin bunker, assured his last military conferences that if they could just hold on, the British and Americans might see that only with Germany's help could they head off the Soviet menace. On 25 April in conversation with Goebbels, Hitler insisted that alternatively, if Stalin saw how the western states reacted to the bitter defence of Berlin, he might realize he was not going to get the Europe he wanted and so might try to reach a deal with the Germans. Did the two men still believe that either side might really agree to talk? Heinrich Himmler had tried since February 1945 to initiate negotiations with the western Allies, until he finally offered to guarantee surrender. On 29 April, when Hitler heard that the BBC had broadcast news of these efforts, he immediately expelled the once 'loyal Heinrich' from the party and all offices of state. The Führer had done the same thing to Göring a few days before when he heard the man's attempt to assume the role of German leader, from a distant mountain perch in Berchtesgaden.

Indeed, many Nazi bigwigs attempted to flee, and sometimes were caught, as happened to Himmler and Göring, who later committed suicide. Other top officials anticipated or copied Hitler's suicide, as did eight of the forty-one party *Gauleiter*, seven of the forty-seven Higher SS and Police Leaders, and about one in ten of the army's generals.

What had remained of the top Nazis' faith in their cause evaporated during April, when soldiers of the United States First Army on the banks of the Elbe River near Torgau met members of the Red Army's First Ukrainian Army. Far from fighting each other as Hitler and others had hoped, the troops celebrated like comrades in a common cause. Four days later, trying to find significance in the last desperate struggle, he dictated a note to Bormann.

> Out of the sacrifice of our soldiers and out of my own close ties with them unto death, the seed will one day germinate in German history, one way or another, and give rise to a glorious rebirth of the National Socialist movement, and thus to the realization of a true Volksgemeinschaft.

Such words meant little to most German soldiers by then, and nothing to the Red Army, as it approached Hitler's Berlin headquarters on 30 April. That day, between 15:20 and 15:25, he and his new wife, the former Eva Braun, withdrew to his office, and committed suicide. Twenty-four hours later, Goebbels and his wife Magda poisoned their six children and then took their own lives.

In Hitler's brief 'political testament', signed on 29 April 1945 at 4:00 a.m., he repeated, twice, that he had not wanted war in 1939 with Britain and France, nor in 1941 with the United States. He had proposed a deal three days after the conflict's outbreak in 1939 over Poland, and he alleged that had failed because of 'leading circles in English politics', and partly also because of the 'propaganda organized by international Jewry'. The testament then recounted yet again his notorious 'prophesy' of what would happen to the Jews, should 'they' start another world war. Unlike in the aftermath of the war of 1914–18, he said, this time 'the real criminal' will have 'to atone for this guilt'. The last two lines of the testament said, 'above all I charge the leaders of the nation and those under them to scrupulous observance of the laws of race and to merciless opposition' to the Jews.

Even after Hitler's death, making peace with Germany turned into a complicated business. The clashing interests and ambitions of west and east coloured the grand finale in Europe and led to two signing ceremonies. At the first, Colonel General Jodl, Chief of the Operations Staff of the Armed Forces High Command, signed an Act of Military Surrender at 2:41 a.m. on 7 May in Reims, France, with representatives of the four Allied powers. The ceasefire was to come into effect the next day at 23:01 hours. When unauthorized press leaks broke this news, leaders in the United States, Britain, and France opted to announce victory on 8 May, so that crowds celebrated wildly around the globe, though not in the USSR.

Stalin was incensed that this procedure involved relatively secondary players in a small French town, and he claimed additionally that the document was only a 'preliminary protocol of surrender'. Indeed, the Soviet representative was General Ivan Alexeyevich Susloparov, only a Red Army liaison officer at the Supreme Headquarters Allied Expeditionary Forces, while the US General Walter Bedell Smith signed on behalf of General Eisenhower, with the French witness Major-General François Sevez.

The Soviet Boss demanded a proper ceremony in Germany's capital, Berlin, with the defeated nation's top military figures and his own commander in attendance. It would be an event to mark the occasion indelibly in history and demonstrate the Soviet Union's rightful place as the dominant force behind the German defeat. Therefore, on 8 May, three representatives of the western Allies led by Air Marshal Sir Arthur Tedder, Eisenhower's deputy, gathered at Marshal Zhukov's headquarters in Berlin-Karlshorst. Soon joining them were three leaders of Germany's armed forces, led by Field Marshal Keitel, Chief of the Supreme High Command of the Wehrmacht, who flew in from Flensburg, far to the north, the seat of what remained of the German government under Grand Admiral Dönitz. That paper regime sputtered on until 23 May when it ingloriously surrendered to Allied troops.

The west was unsure of how to report these important events in Berlin. Nonetheless, the *New York Times*, as well as Zhukov's account and those of others present (such as American general John R. Deane), agree that after some delays caused by Russian scrupulousness over the text, the procedure finally commenced shortly after midnight on 9 May, when the three German officers entered the hall.

Witnesses and participants give various times for 'the signing', which began with Keitel's first signature (between 00:15 and 00:28). There were nine copies of the document, three each in Russian, English, and German. Besides Keitel, the other German signatories were Colonel-General Stumpff from the Air Force, and Admiral-General von Friedeburg of the Navy; they signed on behalf of the High Command of the German Wehrmacht. Then Marshal Zhukov did so for the Supreme High Command of the Red Army and Air Marshal Tedder on behalf of the Supreme Commander Allied Expeditionary Forces. Finally, General Carl Andrew Spaatz of the United States and General Jean de Lattre de Tassigny of France added their signatures as witnesses.

The French general kept a precise record of the proceedings, and when they ended, he noted crisply, 'Keitel got up, saluted with his baton'—a formality not acknowledged by the victors—'and left with his suite. It was 00:45' on 9 May. Marshal Zhukov's account puts the end of this ceremony at 00:43, and, whatever Stalin's intentions, 9 May became the 'Victory Day' celebrated annually in Russia to this day.

A number of historians have insisted that the Third Reich had 'self-destructed', and the distinguished German military expert Bernt Wegner even goes so far as to suggest that Hitler 'choreographed' the defeat that he knew was coming since 1942, if not before. That argument will continue, though here it is worth noting that after the Soviets and the Americans celebrated their victory, when they met at Torgau in late April 1945, there were still untold thousands of Germans who struggled on. In fact just down the road, members of the Wehrmacht, SS, Nazi Party, local administration, as well as civilians acting on their own volition, were still killing escaped prisoners, foreign workers, 'stragglers' from the Wehrmacht, or their own people in order to continue the fight or to stop any sign of dissolution. The end came not so much by Germany's 'self-destruction' as through the determination and concerted efforts of the world's remaining great powers, who together resolutely waged war, at enormous cost in blood and treasure, in order to terminate the Third Reich and to discredit the ideas of which it was a product.

Appendix: Daily Inmate Numbers in the SS Concentration Camps, 1934–45

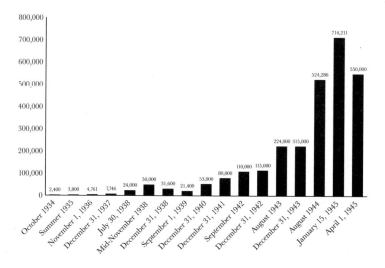

Source: Nikolaus Wachsmann, KL: A History of the Nazi Concentration Camps (London, 2015). By permission of Nikolaus Wachsmann.

Further Reading

Introduction

Abel, Theodore, *Why Hitler Came into Power*, orig. ed. 1938 (Cambridge, MA, 1986).

Arad, Yitzhak, *The Pictorial History of the Holocaust* (London and Jerusalem, 1990).

Arad, Yitzhak, *The Holocaust in the Soviet Union* (Lincoln, Nebraska, and Jerusalem, 2009).

Berghoff, Hartmut, 'Enticement and Deprivation: The Regulation of Consumption in Pre-War Germany', in Martin Daunton and Matthew Hilton, eds, *The Politics of Consumption: Material Culture and Citizenship in Europe and America* (Oxford, 2001), 165–84.

Browning, Christopher R., *The Origins of the Final Solution: The Evolution of Nazi Jewish Policy, September 1939–March 1942* (Lincoln, NE, 2004).

Buggeln, Marc, *Slave Labor in Nazi Concentration Camps* (Oxford, 2014).

Burleigh, Michael, *The Third Reich: A New History* (London, 2000).

Cesarani, David, *Eichmann: His Life and Crimes* (London, 2004).

Ehrenburg, Ilya, and Vasily Grossman, eds, *The Complete Black Book of Russian Jewry* (London, 2002).

Evans, Richard J., *The Coming of the Third Reich* (London, 2003).

Friedländer, Saul, *Nazi Germany and the Jews: Vol. 1, The Years of Persecution, 1933–1939* (New York, 1997).

Gellately, Robert, *Backing Hitler: Consent and Coercion in Nazi Germany* (Oxford, 2001).

Hamann, Brigitte, *Hitler's Vienna: A Dictator's Apprenticeship* (Oxford, 1999).

Herbert, Ulrich, 'National Socialist and Stalinist Rule: Possibilities and Limits of Comparison', in Manfred Hildemeier, ed., *Historical Concepts between Eastern and Western Europe* (Oxford and New York, 2007), 5–22.

Kershaw, Ian, *Hitler, 1889–1936: Hubris* (London, 1998).

Krausnick, Helmut, ed., *Anatomy of the SS-State* (New York, 1968).

Longerich, Peter, *Goebbels: A Biography* (London, 2015).

Matthäus Jürgen, and Frank Bajohr, eds, *The Political Diary of Alfred Rosenberg and the Onset of the Holocaust* (Lanham, MD, 2015).

Römer, Felix, *Kameraden. Die Wehrmacht von innen* (Munich, 2012).

Rubenstein, Joshua, and Ilya Altman, eds, *The Unknown Black Book: The Holocaust in the German-Occupied Soviet Territories* (Bloomington, IN, 2008).

Ullrich, Volker, *Adolf Hitler, Volume 1: Ascent, 1889–1939* (London, 2016).

Wachsmann, Nikolaus, *KL: A History of the Nazi Concentration Camps* (New York, 2015).

Weber, Thomas, *Hitler's First World War: Adolf Hitler, the Men of the List Regiment, and the First World War* (Oxford, 2010).

Weber, Thomas, *Becoming Hitler: The Making of a Nazi* (New York, 2017).

Chapter 1: The Weimar Republic and the Rise of National Socialism

Bessel, Richard, *Political Violence and the Rise of Nazism: The Stormtroopers in Eastern Germany, 1925–1934* (New Haven and London, 1984).

Boak, Helen, 'Mobilising Women for Hitler: The Female Nazi Voter', in Anthony McElligott and Tim Kirk, eds, *Working Towards the Führer: Essays in Honour of Sir Ian Kershaw* (Manchester, 2003), 68–92.

Carsten, F. L., *The Reichswehr and Politics, 1918–1933* (Oxford, 1966).

Evans, Richard J., *The Coming of the Third Reich* (London, 2003).

Falter, Jürgen W., 'The Social Bases of Political Cleavages in the Weimar Republic, 1919–1933', in Larry Eugene Jones and James Retallack, eds, *Elections, Mass Politics, and Social Change in Modern Germany: New Perspectives* (Cambridge, 1992), 371–97.

Fischer, Conan, *The Rise of the Nazis* (2nd edn, Manchester, 2002).

Goltz, Anna von der, *Hindenburg: Power, Myth, and the Rise of the Nazis* (Oxford, 2009).

Hastings, Derek, *Catholicism and the Roots of Nazism: Religious Identity and National Socialism* (Oxford, 2010).

Jackisch, Barry A., *The Pan-German League and Radical Nationalist Politics in Interwar Germany, 1918–39* (Farnham, 2012).

Kellogg, Michael, *The Russian Roots of Nazism: White Émigrés and the Making of National Socialism, 1917–1945* (Cambridge, 2005).

Kershaw, Ian, *Hitler, 1889–1936: Hubris* (London, 1998).

Large, David Clay, *Where Ghosts Walked: Munich's Road to the Third Reich* (London, 1997).

Longerich, Peter, *Goebbels: A Biography* (London, 2015).

Mason, Tim, 'National Socialism and the Working Class, 1925 to May 1933', in Mason, *Social Policy in the Third Reich: The Working Class and the 'National Community'* (Oxford, 1993), 41–87.

McDermott, Kevin, and Jeremy Agnew, *The Comintern: A History of International Communism from Lenin to Stalin* (Basingstoke, 1996).

Nicholls, A. J., *Weimar and the Rise of Hitler* (4th edn, New York, 2000).

Peukert, Detlev J. K., *The Weimar Republic: The Crisis of Classical Modernity* (London, 1993).

Phelps, Reginald, 'Before Hitler Came: Thule Society and *Germanenorden*', *Journal of Modern History*, 35/3 (1963), 245–61.

Stibbe, Matthew, *Germany, 1914–1933: Politics, Society and Culture* (Harlow, 2010).

Taylor, Frederick, *The Downfall of Money: Germany's Hyperinflation and the Destruction of the Middle Class* (London, 2013).

Turner, Henry Ashby Jr, *Hitler's Thirty Days to Power: January 1933* (London, 1996).

Urbach, Karina, *Go-Betweens for Hitler* (Oxford, 2015).

Wildt, Michael, *An Uncompromising Generation: The Nazi Leadership of the Reich Security Main Office* (Madison, 2009).

Winkler, Heinrich August, 'Choosing the Lesser Evil: The German Social Democrats and the Fall of the Weimar Republic', *Journal of Contemporary History*, 25/2 (1990), 205–27.

Ziemann, Benjamin, *Contested Commemorations: Republican War Veterans and Weimar Political Culture* (Cambridge, 2012).

Chapter 2: The Nazi 'Seizure of Power'

Abel, Theodore, *Why Hitler Came into Power* (Cambridge, MA, first published in 1938).

Allen, William S., *The Nazi Seizure of Power: The Experience of a Single German Town 1922–1935*, 2nd edn (Chicago, 1984).

Beck, Hermann, *The Fateful Alliance: German Conservatives and Nazis in 1933* (Oxford, 2010).

Beck, Hermann, 'The Anti-Bourgeois Character of National-Socialism', *Journal of Modern History*, 88/3 (2016), 572–610.

Bessel, Richard, 'The Nazi Capture of Power', *Journal of Contemporary History*, 39 (2004), 169–88.

Broszat, Martin, *The Hitler State: The Foundation and Development of the Internal Structure of the Third Reich* (London, 1981).

Diels, Rudolf, *Lucifer ante Portas. Es spricht der erste Chef der Gestapo* (Stuttgart, 1950).

Evans, Richard J., *The Coming of the Third Reich* (London, 2003).

Feuchtwanger, Lion, *The Oppermanns* (New York, 1934).

Haffner, Sebastian, *Defying Hitler: A Memoir* (New York, 2000).

Isherwood, Christopher, *The Berlin Stories* (first published 1935, New York, 1954).

Jones, Larry Eugene, 'Nazis, Conservatives, and the Establishment of the Third Reich', *Tel Aviver Jahrbuch für deutsche Geschichte*, 23 (1994), 41–64.

Larson, Erik, *In the Garden of Beasts* (New York, 2011).

Nagorski, Andrew, *Hitlerland: American Eyewitnesses to the Nazi Rise to Power* (New York, 2012).

Noakes, Jeremy, and Geoff Pridham, *Nazism*, Vol. 1: *The Rise to Power 1919–1934* (Exeter, 1998).

Ryback, Timothy W., *Hitler's First Victims: The Quest for Justice* (New York, 2014).

Turner, Henry Ashby Jr, *Hitler's Thirty Days to Power: January 1933* (Reading, MA, 1996).

Wildt, Michael, *Hitler's Volksgemeinschaft and the Dynamics of Racial Exclusion: Violence against Jews in Provincial Germany, 1919–1939* (New York, 2012).

Chapter 3: Elections, Plebiscites, and Festivals

Benz, Wolfgang, 'The Ritual and Stage Management of National Socialism: Techniques of Domination and the Public Sphere', in John Milfull, ed., *The Attractions of Fascism: Social Psychology and Aesthetics of the 'Triumph of the Right* (New York, 1990), 273–88.

Bertrand, Romain, Jean-Lousi Briquet, and Peter Pels, eds, *Cultures of Voting: The Hidden History of the Secret Ballot* (London, 2007).

Boak, Helen, 'Mobilising women for Hitler: The Female Nazi voter', in Anthony McElligott and Tim Kirk, eds, *Working Towards the Führer: Essays in Honour of Sir Ian Kershaw* (Manchester, 2003), 68–92.

Burström, Mats, and Bernhard Gelderblom, 'Dealing with Difficult Heritage: The Case of Bückeberg, Site of the Third Reich Harvest Festival', *Journal of Social Archaeology*, 11/3 (2011), 266–82.

Childers, Thomas, *The Nazi Voters: The Social Foundations of Fascism in Germany, 1919–1933* (Chapel Hill, 1983).

Chrystal, William G., 'Nazi Party Election Films, 1927–1938', *Cinema Journal*, 15/1 (1975), 29–47.

Corner, Paul, ed., *Popular Opinion in Totalitarian Regimes: Fascism, Nazism, Communism* (Oxford, 2009).

Deutschmann, Linda, *Triumph of the Will: The Image of the Third Reich* (Wakefield, NH, 1991).

Friedrich, Karin, ed., *Festive Culture in Germany and Europe from the Sixteenth to the Twentieth Century* (Lewiston, NY, 2000).

Gellately, Robert, *Backing Hitler: Consent and Coercion in Nazi Germany* (Oxford, 2010).

Herf, Jeffrey, *Reactionary Modernism: Technology, Culture, and Politics in Weimar and the Third Reich* (Cambridge, 1984).

Hermet, Guy, Richard Rose, and Alain Rouquié, eds, *Elections without Choice* (London, 1978).

Hilton, Christopher, *Hitler's Olympics: The 1936 Berlin Olympic Games* (Sutton, 2006).

Jessen, Ralph, and Hedwig Richter, eds, *Voting for Hitler and Stalin: Elections Under 20th Century Dictatorships* (Frankfurt, 2011).

Milfull, John, ed., *The Attraction of Fascism: Social Psychology and Aesthetics of the 'Triumph of the Right'* (New York, 1990).

Mosse, George L., 'Fascist Aesthetics and Society: Some Considerations', *Journal of Contemporary History*, 31 (1996), 245–52.

Sontag, Susan, 'Fascinating Fascism', in Susan Sontag, *Under the Sign of Saturn* (New York, 1980), 71–105.

Welch, David, 'Manufacturing a Consensus: Nazi Propaganda and the Building of a "National Community" (Volksgemeinschaft)', *Contemporary European History*, 2/1 (1993), 1–15.

Welch, David, 'Nazi Propaganda and the Volksgemeinschaft: Constructing a People's Community', *Journal of Contemporary History*, 39 (2004), 213–38.

Wilson, William John, 'Festivals and the Third Reich', Diss. Thesis, Hamilton, ON, UMI Dissertation Services, Ann Arbor, MI, 1994.

Chapter 4: Architecture and the Arts

General

Hermand, Jost, *Culture in Dark Times: Nazi Fascism, Inner Emigration, and Exile* (New York, 2013 [2010]).

Mosse, George L., *Nazi Culture: Intellectual, Cultural and Social Life in the Third Reich* (New York, 1981 [1966]).

Potter, Pamela, *Art of Suppression: Confronting the Nazi Past in Histories of the Visual and Performing Arts* (Berkeley, 2016).

Rabinbach, Anson, and Sander Gilman, eds, *The Third Reich Sourcebook* (Berkeley, 2013).

Steiner, George, *In Bluebeard's Castle: Some Notes Towards the Redefinition of Culture* (New Haven, 1971).

Steinweis, Alan, *Art, Ideology, and Economics in Nazi Germany: The Reich Chambers of Music, Theater and the Visual Arts* (Chapel Hill, 1993).

Architecture and Design

Hochman, Elaine, *Architects of Fortune. Mies van der Rohe and the Third Reich* (New York, 1989).

Jaskot, Paul, *The Architecture of Oppression: The SS, Forced Labor and the Nazi Monumental Building Economy* (New York, 1999).

Lane, Barbara Miller, *Architecture and Politics in Germany, 1918–1945* (Cambridge, MA, 1968).

Stratigakos, Despina, *Hitler at Home* (New Haven, 2015). See also Albert Speer, *Inside the Third Reich* (New York, 1970).

Taylor, Robert, *The Word in Stone: The Role of Architecture in the National Socialist Ideology* (Berkeley, 1974).

Visual Arts (including plundering)

Adam, Peter, *Art of the Third Reich* (New York, 1992).

Barron, Stephanie, ed., *'Degenerate Art': The Fate of the Avant-Garde in Nazi Germany* (Los Angeles, 1991).

Dean, Martin, *Robbing the Jews: The Confiscation of Jewish Property in the Holocaust, 1933–1945* (Cambridge, 2008).

Hinz, Berthold, *Art in the Third Reich* (New York, 1979).

Jaskot, Paul, *The Nazi Perpetrator: Postwar German Art and the Politics of the Right* (Minneapolis, 2012).

Nicholas, Lynn, *The Rape of Europa: The Fate of Europe's Treasures in the Third Reich and Second World War* (New York, 1994).

Peters, Olaf, ed., *Degenerate Art: The Attack on Modern Art in Nazi Germany 1937* (Munich, 2014).

Petropoulos, Jonathan, *Art as Politics in the Third Reich* (Chapel Hill, 1996).

Petropoulos, Jonathan, *The Faustian Bargain: The Art World in Nazi Germany* (New York, 2000).

Petropoulos, Jonathan, *Artists Under Hitler: Collaboration and Survival in Nazi Germany* (New Haven, 2014).

Spotts, Frederick, *Hitler and the Power of Aesthetics* (London, 2003).

Music

Hamann, Brigitte, *Winifred Wagner: A Life at the Heart of Hitler's Bayreuth* (London, 2005 [2002]).

Kater, Michael H., *Different Drummers: Jazz in the Culture of Nazi Germany* (New York, 1992).

Kater, Michael H., *The Twisted Muse: Musicians and Their Music in the Third Reich* (New York, 1997).

Kater, Michael H., *Composers of the Nazi Era: Eight Portraits* (New York, 2000).

Levi, Erik, *Music in the Third Reich* (New York, 1994).

Monod, David, *Settling Scores: German Music, Denazification, and the Americans, 1945–1953* (Chapel Hill, 2005).

Prieberg, Fred, *Trial of Strength: Wilhelm Furtwängler and the Third Reich* (London, 1991).

Literature

Baird, Jay, *Hitler's War Poets: Literature and Politics in the Third Reich* (Cambridge, 2008).

Barbian, Jan Pieter, *The Politics of Literature in Nazi Germany: Books in the Media Dictatorship* (New York, 2010).

Krispyn, Egbert, *Anti-Nazi Writers in Exile* (Athens, GA, 1978).

Mitchell, Allan, *The Devil's Captain: Ernst Jünger in Nazi Paris, 1941–1944* (Cambridge, 2011).

Ritchie, J. M., *German Literature under National Socialism* (London, 1983).

Ryback, Timothy, *Hitler's Private Library: The Books that Shaped His Life* (New York, 2009).

Theatre and Dance

Gadberry, Glen, *Theatre in the Third Reich: The Prewar Years* (Westport, CT, 1995).

Jelavich, Peter, *Berlin Cabaret* (Cambridge, MA: 1993).

Lilian, Karina, and Marion Kant, *Hitler's Dancers: German Modern Dance and the Third Reich* (New York, 2004).

London, John, ed., *Theatre under the Nazis* (Manchester, 2000).

Chapter 5: Photography and Cinema

Arani, Miriam Y., *Fotografische Selbst- und Fremdbilder von Deutschen und Polen im Reichsgau Wartheland 1939–45. Unter besonderer Berücksichtigung der Region Wielkopolska* (Hamburg, 2008).

Conze, Linda, Ulrich Prehn, and Michael Wildt, 'Sitzen, baden, durch die Straßen laufen. Überlegungen zu fotografischen Repräsentationen von "Alltäglichem" und "Unalltäglichem" im Nationalsozialismus', in Annelie Ramsbrock, Annette Vowinckel, and Malte Zierenberg, eds, *Fotografien im 20. Jahrhundert. Verbreitung und Vermittlung* (Göttingen, 2013), 270–98.

Crew, David F., 'Normal Pictures in Abnormal Times: Photographs of Jewish Weddings during the Holocaust', *Not Even Past*, 2011. http://www.notevenpast.org/discover/normal-pictures-abnormal-times.

Fremde im Visier, Fotoalben aus dem Zweiten Weltkrieg: http://www.fremde-im-visier.de.

Führer, Karl Christian, 'Pleasure, Practicality and Propaganda: Popular Magazines in Nazi Germany, 1933–1939', in Pamela E. Swett, Corey Ross, and Fabrice d'Almeida, eds, *Pleasure and Power in Nazi Germany* (Basingstoke, 2011), 132–53.

Rentschler, Eric, *The Ministry of Illusion: Nazi Cinema and its Afterlife* (Cambridge, MA, 1996).

Ross, Corey, *Media and the Making of Modern Germany: Mass Communications: Society and Politics from the Empire to the Third Reich* (Oxford, 2008).

Stargardt, Nicholas, *The German War: A Nation under Arms, 1939–1945* (New York, 2015).

Struk, Janina, *Photographing the Holocaust: Interpretations of the Evidence* (London and New York, 2004).

Umbach, Maiken, 'Selfhood, Place and Ideology in German Photo Albums, 1933–1945', in *Central European History*, 48 (2015), 335–65.

Chapter 6: The Economy

Aly, Götz, *Hitler's Beneficiaries: Plunder, Racial War, and the Nazi Welfare State* (New York, 2006).

Bajohr, Frank, *'Aryanization' in Hamburg: The Economic Exclusion of Jews and the Confiscation of Their Property in Nazi Germany* (New York, 2002).

Dean, Martin, *Robbing the Jews: The Confiscation of Jewish Property in the Holocaust, 1933–1945* (New York, 2008).

Gregor, Neil, *Daimler-Benz in the Third Reich* (New Haven, 1998).

Gruner, Wolf, *Jewish Forced Labor Under the Nazis* (New York, 2006).

Harrison, Mark, ed., *The Economics of World War II: Six Great Powers in International Comparison* (New York, 1998).

Hayes, Peter, *Industry and Ideology: IG Farben in the Nazi Era* (New York, 2001).

Hayes, Peter, *From Cooperation to Complicity: Degussa in the Third Reich* (New York, 2004).

Herbert, Ulrich, *Hitler's Foreign Workers* (New York, 1997).

Klemann, Hein, and Sergei Kudryashov, *Occupied Economies: An Economic History of Nazi-Occupied Europe, 1939–1945* (London, 2012).

Overy, Richard, *War and Economy in the Third Reich* (New York, 1994).

Tooze, Adam, *The Wages of Destruction: The Making and Breaking of the Nazi Economy* (New York, 2006).

Chapter 7: The Holocaust

Aly, Götz, *'Final Solution': Nazi Population Policy and the Murder of the European Jews*, trans. Belinda Cooper and Allison Brown (London, 1999).

Bartov, Omer, *Hitler's Army: Soldiers, Nazis, and War in the Third Reich* (New York, 1991).

Bartov, Omer, *Anatomy of a Genocide: The Life and Death of a Town Called Buczacz* (New York, 2017).

Bloxham, Donald, *The Final Solution: A Genocide* (Oxford, 2009).

Browning, Christopher R., *Ordinary Men: Reserve Police Battalion 101 and the Final Solution in Poland* (New York, 1993).

Browning, Christopher R., *Remembering Survival: Inside a Nazi Slave-Labor Camp* (New York, 2010).

Browning, Christopher R. et al., *The Origins of the Final Solution: The Evolution of Nazi Jewish Policy, September 1939–March 1942* (Lincoln, NE, 2004).

Friedländer, Saul, *Nazi Germany and the Jews*, I: *The Years of Persecution, 1933–1939* (New York, 1997). II: *The Years of Extermination, 1939–1945* (New York, 2007).

Garbarini, Alexandra, *Numbered Days: Diaries and the Holocaust* (New Haven, 2006).

Gellately, Robert et al., eds, *Social Outsiders in Nazi Germany* (Princeton, NJ, 2001).

Gerlach, Christian, 'The Wannsee Conference, the Fate of German Jews, and Hitler's Decision in Principle to Exterminate All European Jews', in Omer Bartov, ed., *The Holocaust: Origins, Implementation, Aftermath* (London, 2000).

Goldhagen, Daniel Jonah, *Hitler's Willing Executioners: Ordinary Germans and the Holocaust* (New York, 1996).

Grabowski, Jan, *Hunt for the Jews: Betrayal and Murder in German-Occupied Poland* (Bloomington, IN, 2013).

Greif, Gideon, *We Wept Without Tears: Testimonies of the Jewish Sonderkommando From Auschwitz* (New Haven, CT, 2005).

Gross, Jan Tomasz, *Neighbors: The Destruction of the Jewish Community in Jedwabne, Poland* (Princeton, NJ, 2001).

Gross, Jan Tomasz, *Fear: Anti-Semitism in Poland after Auschwitz: An Essay in Historical Interpretation* (New York, 2006).

Heer, Hannes, ed., *War of Extermination: The German Military in World War II, 1941–1944* (New York, 2000).

Hilberg, Raul, *The Destruction of the European Jews*, 3rd edn (New Haven, CT, 2003), published originally in 1961.

Horwitz, Gordon J., *Ghettostadt: Łódź and the Making of a Nazi City* (Cambridge, MA, 2008).

Jäckel, Eberhard, *Hitler's World View: A Blueprint for Power*, trans. Herbert Arnold (Cambridge, MA, 1981).

Levi, Primo, *The Drowned and the Saved*, trans. Raymond Rosenthal (New York, 1989).

Longerich, Peter, *Holocaust: The Nazi Persecution and Murder of the Jews* (New York, 2010).

Longerich, Peter, *Heinrich Himmler* (Oxford, 2012).

Lower, Wendy, *Nazi Empire-Building and the Holocaust in Ukraine* (Chapel Hill, 2005).

Snyder, Timothy, *Bloodlands: Europe between Hitler and Stalin* (New York, 2010).

Stangneth, Bettina, *Eichmann Before Jerusalem: The Unexamined Life of a Mass Murderer*, trans. Ruth Martin (New York, 2014).

Stone, Dan, *The Liberation of the Camps: The End of the Holocaust and its Aftermath* (New Haven, CT, 2015).

Chapter 8: War and Empire

Bank, Jan, and Lieve Gevers, *Churches and Religion in the Second World War* (London, 2016).

Bennett, Rab, *Under the Shadow of the Swastika: The Moral Dilemmas of Resistance and Collaboration in Hitler's Europe* (Basingstoke, 1999).

Collingham, Lizzie, *The Taste of War: World War II and the Battle for Food* (New York, 2012).

Conway, Martin, and Peter Romijn, eds, *The War on Legitimacy in Politics and Culture 1936–1946* (New York, 2006).

Cooke, Philip, and Ben H. Shepherd, eds, *European Resistance in the Second World War* (Barnsley, 2013).

Deák, István, *Europe on Trial: The Story of Collaboration, Resistance, and Retribution During World War II* (Boulder, CO, 2015).

Dear, I. C. B., and M. R. D. Foot, *The Oxford Companion to World War II* (Oxford, 1995).

Germany and the Second World War Vol. 5: Organization and Mobilization in the German Sphere of Power: Wartime Administration, Economy, and Manpower Resources. 2 vols. (Oxford, 2000/2003).

Gildea, Robert, Olivier Wieviorka, and Anette Warring, *Surviving Hitler and Mussolini* (New York, 2006).

Kennedy, David M. et al., ed., *The Library of Congress World War II Companion* (New York, 2007).

Klemann, Hein A. M., and Sergei Kudryashov, *Occupied Economies: An Economic History of Nazi-Occupied Europe, 1939–1945* (London, 2012).

Levene, Mark, *The Crisis of Genocide. Vol. 2. Annihilation: The European Rimlands, 1939–1953* (Oxford, 2013).

Madajczyk, Czesław, ed., *Inter arma non silent musae: The War and the Culture 1939–1945* (Warsaw, 1977).

Maren, Röger, and Ruth Leiserowitz, eds, *Women and Men at War: A Gender Perspective on World War II and its Aftermath in Central and Eastern Europe* (Osnabrück, 2012).

Mawdsley, Evan, ed., *The Cambridge History of the Second World War*. 3 vols. (Cambridge, 2015).

Mazower, Mark, *Hitler's Empire: Nazi Rule in Occupied Europe* (London, 2008).

Overy, Richard, ed., *Oxford Illustrated History of World War II* (Oxford, 2015).

Rich, Norman, *Hitler's War Aims*, 2 vols. (New York, 1973/4).

Scherner, Jonas, and Eugene White, eds, *Paying for Hitler's War: The Consequences of Nazi Economic Hegemony for Europe* (New York, 2016).

Stargardt, Nicholas, *Witnesses of War: Children's Lives Under the Nazis* (New York, 2006).

Weinberg, Gerhard, *A World at Arms: A Global History of World War II* (Cambridge, 1994).

Wever, Bruno Der, Herman van Goethem, and Nico Wouters, eds, *Local Government in Occupied Europe (1939–1945)* (Gent, 2006).

Zeiler, Thomas W., and Daniel M. DuBois, eds, *A Companion to World War II*, 2 vols. (London, 2012).

Chapter 9: The Home Front

Collingham, Lizzie, *The Taste of War: World War II and the Battle for Food* (London, 2012).

Corni, Gustavo, and Horst Gies, *Brot, Butter, Kanonen. Die Ernährungswirtschaft in Deutschland Unter Der Diktatur Hitlers* (Berlin, 1997).

Echternkamp, Jörg, *German Wartime Society 1939–1945: Exploitation, Interpretations, Exclusion*. Vol. IX/II. *Germany and the Second World War* (Oxford, 2014).

Gellately, Robert, *The Gestapo and German Society: Enforcing Racial Policy, 1933–1945* (Oxford, 1990).

Gellately, Robert, *Backing Hitler: Consent and Coercion in Nazi Germany* (Oxford, 2001).

Gerhard, Gesine, *Nazi Hunger Politics: A History of Food in the Third Reich* (Lanham, 2015).

Hagemann, Karen, 'Mobilizing Women for War: The History, Historiography, and Memory of German Women's War Service in the Two World Wars', *Journal of Military History*, 75/4 (October 2011): 1055–94.

Harvey, Elizabeth, *Women and the Nazi East: Agents and Witnesses of Germanization* (New Haven, 2003).

Herbert, Ulrich, *Hitler's Foreign Workers: Enforced Foreign Labor in Germany under the Third Reich* (Cambridge, 1997).

Kock, Gerhard, '*Der Führer Sorgt Für Unser Kinder...*': *Die Kinderlandverschickung Im Zweiten Weltkrieg* (Paderborn, 1997).

Kramer, Nicole, *Volksgenossinnen an der Heimatfront Mobilisierung, Verhalten, Erinnerung* (Göttingen, 2011).

Kundrus, Birthe, *Kriegerfrauen: Familienpolitik und Geschlechterverhältnisse im Ersten und Zweiten Weltkrieg* (Hamburg, 1995).

Noakes, Jeremy, ed., *Nazism 1919–1945, vol. 4: The German Home Front in World War II* (Exeter, 1998).

Scheck, Raffael, *Hitler's African Victims: The German Army Massacres of Black French Soldiers in 1940* (Cambridge, 2006).

Shirer, William, '*This Is Berlin*': *Radio Broadcasts from Nazi Germany, 1938–40* (Woodstock, NY, 1999).

Stargardt, Nicolas, *Witnesses of War: Children's Lives under the Nazis* (London, 2005).

Stargardt, Nicolas, *The German War: A Nation under Arms, 1939–45* (London, 2015).

Steber, Martina, and Bernhard Gotto, eds., *Visions of Community in Nazi Germany: Social Engineering and Private Lives* (Oxford, 2014).

Thoms, Ulrike, 'The Innovative Power of War: The Army, Food Sciences and the Food Industry in Germany in the Twentieth Century', in Ina Zweiniger-Bargielowska, Rachel Duffett, and Alain Drouard, eds, *Food and War in Twentieth Century Europe* (Burlington, VT, 2011), 247–62.

Torrie, Julia S., *For Their Own Good: Civilian Evacuations in Germany and France, 1939–1945* (New York, 2010).

Chapter 10: Decline and Collapse

Anon., *A Woman in Berlin: Eight Weeks in the Conquered City. A Diary* (New York, 2006).

Berghoff, Hartmut, and Cornelia Rauh, *The Respectable Career of Fritz K.: The Making and Remaking of a Provincial Nazi Leader* (New York, 2015).

Browning, Christopher R., *The Origins of the Final Solution: The Evolution of Nazi Jewish Policy, September 1939–March 1942* (Lincoln, NE, 2004).

Echternkamp, Jörg, *German Wartime Society 1939–1945: Exploitation, Interpretations, Exclusion*. Vol. IX/II. *Germany and the Second World War* (Oxford, 2014).

Frei, Norbert, 'People's Community and War: Hitler's Popular Support', in Hans Mommsen, ed., *The Third Reich between Vision and Reality: New Perspectives on German History 1918–1945* (New York and Oxford, 2001), 51–77.

Gellately, Robert, *Backing Hitler: Consent and Coercion in Nazi Germany* (Oxford, 2001).

Gellately, Robert, *Lenin, Stalin and Hitler: The Age of Social Catastrophe* (New York and London, 2007).

Gellately, Robert, *Stalin's Curse: Battling for Communism in War and Cold War* (New York and Oxford, 2013).

Herbert, Ulrich, *Hitler's Foreign Workers: Enforced Foreign Labor in Germany under the Third Reich* (Cambridge, 1997).

Hürter, Johannes, ed., *A German General on the Eastern Front: The Letters and Diaries of Gotthard Heinrici, 1941–1942* (Barnsley, 2014).

Hürter, Johannes, and Matthias Uhl, eds, 'Hitler in Vinnica. Ein neues Dokument zur Krise im September 1942', *Vierteljahrshefte für Zeitgeschichte*, 63 (2015), 581–638.

Kershaw, Ian, *The 'Hitler Myth': Image and Reality in the Third Reich* (Oxford, 1987).

Kershaw, Ian, *Hitler 1936–45: Nemesis* (New York, 2000).

Kershaw, Ian, *The End: The Defiance and Destruction of Hitler's Germany, 1944–1945* (London, 2011).

Leo, Maxim, *Red Love: The Story of an East German Family* (London, 2013).

Longerich, Peter, *Heinrich Himmler* (Oxford, 2012).

Longerich, Peter, *Goebbels: A Biography* (London, 2015).

Matthäus, Jürgen, and Frank Bajohr, eds, *The Political Diary of Alfred Rosenberg and the Onset of the Holocaust* (Lanham, MD, 2015).

Neitzel, Sönke, ed., *Tapping Hitler's Generals: Transcripts of Secret Conversations, 1942–45* (Barnsley, 2007).

Noakes, Jeremy, ed., *Nazism 1919–1945, vol. 4: The German Home Front in World War II* (Exeter, 1998).

Overy, Richard, *The Bombing War: Europe 1939–1945* (London, 2013).

Reese, Willy Peter, *A Stranger to Myself: The Inhumanity of War: Russia, 1941–1944* (New York, 2005).

Stargardt, Nicholas, *The German War: A Nation under Arms, 1939–45* (London, 2015).

Steber, Martina, and Berhard Gotto, eds, *Visions of Community in Nazi Germany: Social Engineering and Private Lives* (Oxford, 2014).

Steinert, Marlis G., *Hitler's War and the Germans: Public Mood and Attitude during the Second World War* (Athens, OH, 1977).

Süss, Dietmar, *Death From the Skies: How the British and Germans Survived Bombing in World War II* (Oxford, 2014).

Tooze, Adam, *The Wages of Destruction: The Making and Breaking of the Nazi Economy* (London, 2006).

Trevor-Roper, Hugh, ed., *Hitler's Table Talk: His Private Conversations, 1941–44* (London, 1973).

Wachsmann, Nikolaus, *KL: The History of the Nazi Concentration Camps* (New York, 2015).

Wegner, Bernd, 'Hitler, der Zweite Weltkrieg und die Choreographie des Untergangs', *Geschichte und Gesellschaft*, 26 (2000), 493–518.

Wegner, Bernd, 'The Ideology of Self-Destruction: Hitler and the Choreography of Defeat', *German Historical Institute London Bulletin*, xxvi/2 (Nov. 2004), 18–33.

Weinberg, Gerhard L. ed., *Hitler and His Generals: Military Conferences 1942–1945* (New York, 2002).

Index